THE CONGLOMERATE CORPORATION

The Conglomerate Corporation

An Antitrust Law and Economics Symposium

edited by
Roger D. Blair
Robert F. Lanzillotti
Graduate School of Business
University of Florida

 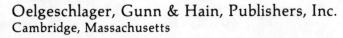 Oelgeschlager, Gunn & Hain, Publishers, Inc.
Cambridge, Massachusetts

Copyright © 1981 by Oelgeschlager, Gunn & Hain, Publishers, Inc. All rights reserved. No part of this publication may be reproduced, stored in a retrieval system, or transmitted in any form or by any means, electronic mechanical photocopy, recording or otherwise, without the prior written consent of the publisher.

International Standard Book Number: 0-89946-051-8

Library of Congress Catalog Card Number: 80-22093

Printed in West Germany

Library of Congress Cataloging in Publication Date
Main entry under title:

The Conglomerate corporation.

 Papers presented at a symposium, in spring 1980, sponsored by the Public Policy Research Center and the College of Law, University of Florida.
 Includes index.
 1. Conglomerate corporations—United States—Congresses. 2. Industry and state—United States—Congresses. I. Lanzillotti, Robert Franklin, 1921-II. Blair, Roger D. III. Florida. University, Gainesville. Public Policy Research Center. IV. Florida. University, Gainesville. College of Law. HD2756.2.U5C65 338.8'042 80-22093 ISBN 0-89946-051-8

Contents

v

PART I

Introduction

Chapter 1

The Conglomerate Corporation—A Public Policy Problem?

Robert F. Lanzillotti

Since the end of World War II, a large body of economic and legal literature has emerged on the subject of economic concentration, the structure of the American economy, and the phenomenon of the "conglomerate" corporation, i.e., a company with a highly diversified line of products, related and unrelated as to production processes. In the early 1950s, concern was directed to a perceived trend toward the formation of conglomerate companies through mergers and acquisitions. Some scholars and members of Congress believed that this trend was leading to a fundamental transformation of the American economy away from firms specializing in particular products and meeting "traditional" economic standards for efficiency. It was argued that this new breed of corporation would make it difficult, if not impossible, for analysts to trace and evaluate the flow of economic resources through the economy. An additional concern was that the increase in the absolute size of certain businesses might result in the dominance of the American economy by giant enterprises, with possible industry-government interlocks along the lines of the Japanese Zaibatzu.

The analytical arguments against conglomerates raise such questions as the following:

1. Does a conglomerate firm derive some special economic power from diversification over a range of products and markets?

2. Does a highly diversified firm with a large absolute size and a large treasury have special abilities to "outbid, outsize, outspend, and outlose" smaller competitors and thus insure its survival almost irrespective of its own management expertise and productive efficiency?
3. Does the large conglomerate firm have unique access to political power and the opportunity to transform governmental processes into an instrument of privilege and protection?
4. In consequence, does the conglomerate form of business organization pose a unique threat to the free enterprise market system and a threat to democratic government?

In recent congressional debates and public testimony about the level of economic concentration in American industry and the rise of the conglomerate form of business, one is apt to run across phrases like "the only alternative to capitalism is some form of statism." The injection of such political concerns into the analysis of economic issues may be appropriate, but it does not help answer the question whether political influence is appropriately controlled by amending or extending antitrust statutes to impose special limits on corporate size or growth patterns. We all can pay due respect to the Jeffersonian ideal of a society of "smalls," but this does not constitute evidence that competitive practices (or political abuses) and corporate size (or type of corporate organization) are correlated, with respect either to *incidence* or *magnitude*.

Analysis of the available empirical evidence on the growth of large companies over the past thirty years by well-respected scholars discloses sharply different conclusions about the importance of large corporations in the economic life of the nation. Essentially, the findings on conglomerate growth patterns can be boiled down to the following: (1) large companies clearly play a major role in American industry today; (2) not all companies, whether large or small, grow at the same rate, with the result that new and rapidly growing companies both challenge the position of the 200 largest enterprises and displace other large companies that have grown less rapidly or disappeared from the market; and (3) while mergers and acquisitions have accounted for part of the growth of many large corporations, on the average they have played a *less* significant role than *internal* growth.

Despite these findings, fears and myths still persist about the growth and influence of large, multiproduct, multi-industry, multimarket, and multinational corporations. In a society whose heritage is rich with the tradition of the invisible hand of Adam Smith, such concerns about size per se should not be surprising. But today's fears are an eerie echo of concerns expressed in the early twentieth century about competitive "fairness," "communities" of business interest, and the political "influence" of "big" business, which led to the hasty enactment of legislation with questionable if not negative competitive effects.

The history of the 1930s should be instructive, with its rash of congressional actions against certain types of business firms that resulted from a fear that irreversible damage might occur if something were not done quickly. In consequence, some states imposed graduated taxes on "chain" stores because the chain form of business enterprise purportedly represented a threat to "small business." The fact that the self-service chain store was a more efficient form of retail distribution was lost in the economic hysteria. The 1930s was also the decade that produced the Robinson–Patman Act, a statute ostensibly designed to protect small companies from certain proscribed competitive practices, but which over time has been transformed so that it legalizes forms of protection from competition itself. In all of this wave of government intrusion into the marketplace, the *form* of business organization was mistakenly identified as the problem, rather than the particular excesses and abuses of certain companies and managements.

As the chapters in this volume demonstrate, the nature of conglomerates does not in and of itself trigger any of the traditional economic criteria to qualify as a special antitrust problem. The fundamental question is whether the present arsenal of antitrust weapons is adequate to cope with the conglomerate phenomenon. Also, an uneasiness prevails today among some economists and lawyers who wish that the great clarity characterizing the case law on horizontal and vertical mergers and acquisitions were true for conglomerate mergers and acquisitions. This is partly because economic theory, empirical findings, and legal opinions remain in a state of flux regarding the short-run and long-run economic effects of conglomerate mergers and acquisitions.

Despite this situation, or perhaps *because* of it, new klaxons have been sounded for Congress to limit corporate size and to prohibit in some *per se* manner the growth of conglomerate companies via the merger and acquisition route. As a result, several legislative proposals have surfaced. Currently, the bill sponsored by Senator Edward Kennedy (S. 600) is receiving almost all the attention. This bill would add severe presumptions of illegality to the present array of antitrust tools. Specifically, the bill forbids a merger when either firm is large in an absolute sense or when one is large absolutely and the other is relatively large in its market. Passage of this type of legislation would introduce the use of presumptions, which is not characteristic of present antitrust enforcement.

The papers included in this volume examine in depth both theoretical propositions and empirical evidence regarding public policy issues associated with conglomerate firms. The papers were commissioned for presentation at a symposium in the Spring of 1980, sponsored jointly by the Public Policy Research Center of the Graduate School of Business and the College of Law, University of Florida.

In the first section, which deals with public policy aspects of conglomerate firms, William Comanor says that "a policy directed against conglomerate mergers comes not from actual proven harms as much as from basic ideological concerns that such harms do exist." He concludes that attempts to revise public policy to restrict the growth of conglomerates, such as proposed by S. 600 (the "Kennedy bill"), clearly involve sacrificing efficiency for other objectives.

John Siegfried's paper surveys the research literature regarding various hypotheses that conglomeration threatens the continued vigor of American political democracy. His review of eleven empirical studies leads him to conclude that the evidence to date does not provide any empirical support for the proposition that economic changes precipitated by conglomerate mergers will have important implications for the operations of the American political system, at either the state or federal levels.

Steven Wiggins examines various theories advanced to explain conglomerate mergers, including maximization of the growth rate of a firm, stockholder wealth maximization, manager utility maximization, and pure market power motives. He concludes that there is a wide variety of explanations for conglomerate mergers, which imply quite different appropriate responses from a public policy standpoint.

Dennis Mueller presents the "case against conglomerate mergers" essentially in terms of the proposition that "there is no strong case for them." He develops a theory of why mergers occur without promise of market power or efficiency increases, and examines some empirical evidence regarding the efficiency effects of mergers. He finds that although the evidence on the effects of mergers does not constitute a case for them, it also is probably not sufficient for a case against them. Nonetheless, Mueller concludes that those who favor decentralized, market, and democratic solutions to the fundamental allocation and distribution questions society faces should favor rules that constrain the growth of both private and public bureaucracy.

The second section of the volume examines various economic aspects of conglomerates. Roger Blair and Yoram Peles develop some theoretical propositions concerning efficiencies of conglomerates beyond those customarily associated with economies of scale. They find that diversified production can provide a firm with advantages based on efficiencies; specifically, when scale economies in non-production activities exceed the scale economies in production, diversified output can reduce average total costs of the firm. In addition, they identify other potential efficiencies that lead to an expansion of final output. This they regard as an unambiguous, proconsumer result that may not be possible with specialized production.

Margaret Monroe presents some empirical evidence regarding alternative financial theories and hypotheses of conglomerate mergers. After examining investment, diversification of earnings, "co-insurance" theories, and empirical studies, she concludes that "shareholders may expect gains from pure conglomerate mergers— even if acquisitions provide no earnings synergy—by avoiding some bankruptcy costs and reducing taxes in a way that only such mergers can provide."

Ira Horowitz discusses the relevant market criterion in a Section 7 Clayton Act analysis of conglomerate mergers. He indicates that the multidimensional aspects of relevant market definitions (product, market, and time span) makes it extremely difficult to draw sharp distinctions on any one dimension; hence, relevant market delineation is likely to remain arbitrary. He concludes that all mergers—conglomerate or other types—should be evaluated within the same general framework, with particular attention given to the presence of conditions conducive to collusion. Finally, although determination of relevant market will continue to remain somewhat arbitrary, he stresses the importance of requiring *some* definition as a frame of reference within which demand and cost elasticities and number of sellers can be determined.

George Hay and Charles Untiet discuss questions associated with statistical measurement of the conglomerate problem. They develop and compare various measures of aggregate concentration: sales, assets, value-added, profits, and employment. And they also examine Federal Trade Commission data on the role mergers have played in aggregate concentration in the U.S. economy. They indicate that for policy purposes it would be presumptuous to conclude that if acquisitions by the largest firms had been prohibited since 1948, the level of aggregate concentration would be less than it is today.

Howard Lurie reviews the decisions of the Burger court on conglomerate mergers, and concludes that the court will not view challenges to conglomerate mergers with much sympathy. He observes that since, by definition, a conglomerate merger does not combine rivals, it does not eliminate actual competition in a market. Moreover, the alleged primary vice of a pure conglomerate is a "feared concentration" of economic and political power in a few hands, but this vice is *not* one against which Section 7 of the Clayton Act extends protection in the absence of an injury to competition. Thus, Lurie concludes that given the Burger court's reluctance to engage in *presumptions* as to anticompetitive effects, it is extremely unlikely that the Court will conclude that a conglomerate merger is unlawful under Section 7.

Stephen Rubin examines the judicial development of rules of presumptive illegality, particularly the premises of presumption, current antitrust rulemaking, and the future of presumptions. Rubin observes that by defining various categories of violations in terms of easily identified operative facts, rules impart a high degree of structure and predictability to antitrust analysis. Moreover, he notes that nonrules do more than decide cases; they decide cases in a particular way. He concludes that proposed legislative amendments to antitrust statutes combine the historic advantage of legal presumptions with the flexibility of limited defenses based on current economic thinking.

Joseph Brodley's paper offers a defense for presumptive rules as an approach to legal rulemaking for conglomerate mergers. He suggests that the simple dichotomy between per se and rule-of-reason rules be rejected in favor of a more discriminating classification system for rule feasibility, which should be based on the tractability of legal proof and the confidence level of legal advice. He concludes that (1) an effective merger policy is the only means by which to give substance to the antitrust ideal that private, as well as public, powers should be limited in a democratic society; and (2) a strengthened antitrust policy for conglomerate mergers, utilizing presumptive rules, provides a cost-effective approach to this goal.

Edward Cooper presents the case against a new presumptive approach to conglomerate mergers. He notes that paradoxically, the arguments against controlling conglomerate mergers by presumptions are also arguments in favor of adhering to rules of legal presumption. His thesis is that creating new presumptions of illegality would narrow the range of permissible conglomeration. Moreover, the balance of uncertainty between arguments for and against greater control is too close to warrant any change from the present course of judicial decision. He concludes that (1) presumptions drawn in economic terms but justified in noneconomic terms are likely to produce the most confused and least satisfactory of all possible situations, and (2) the case has not yet been made for venturing beyond economic theory to condemn very large acquisitions solely on grounds of size.

Betty Bock, Richard Schmalensee, Theodore Craver, and Peter Steiner offer a critique and synthesis of the various papers. Bock suggests that those concerned with developing or implementing public policy on competition really have better things to do than to focus on "conglomerate" corporations since it is difficult, if not impossible, to recognize a conglomerate in any categorical sense. She tests some of the fears of corporate bigness in terms of statistical data on changes over time among the largest corporations and the growth and acquisitions of conglomerates, as well as the need for (a) a long-range view of "markets" for going companies and parts of companies, and (b) the need to rethink the conditions under which policy should sanction the freedom to restructure enterprises through open markets. She concludes that the policy choice is whether competition is viewed as an unending, simplified series of transactions among small firms, or in terms that are appropriate for large, flexible, multicategory firms operating in a changing world order.

Theodore Craver comments that the available evidence on alleged adverse effects of conglomerates is not adequate to answer the questions posed by various authors, and unconvincing even with respect to certain narrowly-defined issues. Moreover, he finds the proposal for using presumptive rules for judging conglomerate mergers appalling, woefully premature, and unfounded. He concludes that the problem is even more serious because the authors of chapters, both pro and con, do not fully understand the phenomenon of conglomerate acquisitions.

Schmalensee discusses the need to improve our measures of the real effects of mergers, because without that all we can do is "tell stories," and the anticompetitive stories are not very strong. In short, he believes it is difficult to make a case for overall restriction against mergers, since there is no strong theoretical or empirical basis for restricting conglomerate mergers generally in the interests of efficiency. He states that the appropriate task is to figure out what, if anything, is a legitimate problem. The consensus among the papers appears to be that competitive impact is the issue, but it is difficult to figure out what to do about it.

Finally, Steiner advances several propositions that he believes all the authors could agree upon (concerning reasons for mergers *viz* the presence of real economies, tax advantages, speculative motives, managerial and insider considerations, and the quest for political influence). He indicates that the real policy challenge is to recognize that mergers are heterogeneous, which requires some sensible "partitioning" either in terms of judicial roles, or legislative role, or ways of thinking about the problem. He observes that there is no logical, theoretical way to choose between the "ideological partition" that emerges from the chapters, since the two polar positions are simply different responses to uncertainty surrounding the effects of a particular merger. Beyond the ideological partitions, Steiner concludes that partitioning the problem in terms of size is not a very useful or helpful notion, since firm size is positively related to the size of potential benefits as well as to the size of potential costs. Hence, proposals to limit firm size (e.g., S. 600) amount to "solutions in search of a problem."

PART II

Public Policy Aspects
of Conglomerates

Chapter 2

Conglomerate Mergers: Considerations for Public Policy

William S. Comanor

THE FACTUAL BACKGROUND

Current policy toward anticompetitive corporate mergers is one of the towering peaks of antitrust. In only a few areas can one point to a clear and overwhelming impact of policy measures, but this is surely one of them. What has been affected, however, is the composition rather than the extent of merger activity. Whatever the impact on the type of mergers entered into, available data do not suggest that the extent of merger activity has been substantially altered.

The major effect of current policy has been a considerable decline in the number of substantial horizontal mergers. While there may be debate about the desirability of this policy, there can be little doubt about its impact. Horizontal mergers currently account for only a

I am grateful to Alan Fisher, Dennis Mueller, and John Peterman for helpful comments on this chapter. Table 2.1 and the notes to that table were prepared by Richard Duke. An earlier version of this chapter appears as testimony on S. 600 before the Committee on the Judiciary of the United States Senate given March 8, 1979. The views expressed here and in the earlier testimony are the author's and do not necessarily represent those of the Federal Trade Commission or of any individual commissioner.

small share of total merger activity as contrasted with the shares accounted for both in the past and in other Western developed countries.[1]

In accord with the objective of promoting competition, the antitrust laws have been successful largely in preventing horizontal acquisitions that might lessen competition. These laws, however, have not restrained the pace of conglomerate mergers, since most have seemed unlikely to produce substantial anticompetitive effects in particular markets. As a result, conglomerate mergers have become more frequent.

Because of the altered character of corporate mergers, we would not expect to find much effect on concentration in individual industries. On the other hand, we would expect to see the effect of recent mergers reflected in levels of aggregate concentration, which measure the share of total assets or employment accounted for by the largest firms in the economy.

There have been some systematic investigations of the relationships between conglomerate mergers and aggregate concentration. The most complete of these studies, which covered mining and manufacturing assets between 1950 and 1960, concluded that mergers accounted for nearly two-thirds of the increase in the share of these assets held by the 500 largest firms, and almost three-fourths of the increase in the share held by the hundred largest firms.[2] Another study reported that between 1960 and 1968, mergers were responsible for increasing the share of assets held by the 200 largest manufacturing firms from 51 percent to 61 percent.[3]

Despite the substantial number of conglomerate mergers that have taken place, with their apparent impact on the manufacturing and mining sectors, it is striking that no increase in aggregate concentration throughout the economy has taken place. Available data suggest indeed that aggregate concentration levels have remained stable even though quite high. Relevant data are presented in Table 2.1. In 1958, the fifty largest nonfinancial corporations controlled approximately 24 percent of all nonfinancial corporate assets; this figure declined slightly to approximately 23 percent in 1972, and remained at about the same level through 1975, the last year for which complete data are available. Similar results appear for aggregate concentration ratios that apply to the 200 largest nonfinancial firms. These percentages declined from 41 percent in 1958 to approximately 40 percent in both 1972 and 1975.

Although aggregate concentration appears to have increased in the manufacturing and mining sectors, a different picture is obtained by focusing on a broader range of the economy.[4] For all nonfinancial corporations, aggregate concentration has been relatively stable and has perhaps even declined slightly. The different pictures obtained can be explained by the declining share of total output accounted for by the manufacturing and mining sectors of the economy.

A MATTER OF JEFFERSONIAN IDEALS

While we could investigate further the effects of conglomerate merger activity on aggregate concentration, a more interesting issue for public policy is what difference it makes. Why should we be concerned with aggregate concentration as a matter of public policy? The courts have not subjected conglomerate acquisitions to severe restrictions despite the proscription against anticompetitive mergers under the antitrust laws. If this pattern of judicial decisions is correct, and conglomerate mergers do not impact on the degree of competition, what other considerations might warrant a public policy concern?

Some discussions of this question have emphasized the possible social and political effects which may flow from high aggregate concentration and large firm size. It has been suggested that even in the absence of anticompetitive effects, undesirable social or political implications may flow from these acquisitions. Whether these effects in fact exist is a matter of some debate. However these issues are resolved, they do not focus, in my judgment, on the fundamental concerns for public policy.

The relevant issue for conglomerate merger policy springs from the popular support that persists in the United States for policy actions of this type. This support is derived not from evidence of actual harms, however defined, but rather from a *fundamental ideological concern* with giant aggregations of privately held assets and the political power that is presumed to flow from them. Support for a policy directed against conglomerate mergers comes not from actual proven harms as much as from basic ideological concerns that such harms do exist.

Ideology always refers to a fundamental perception of reality and provides an overall vehicle for explaining that reality. Its precepts are not readily subject to empirical verification. Ideological propositions are more strongly contested by a competing ideological statement than by factual refutation. Although some might argue that their own policy recommendations rest entirely on empirical

Table 2.1.   Assets of the 450 Largest Nonfinancial Corporations Relative to All Nonfinancial Corporate Assets

Asset Group	1958	1963	1967	1972	1975
Top 50	24.4%	24.4%	24.5%	23.4%	23.3%
Top 100	32.1	31.7	32.0	30.7	30.6
Top 150	37.4	36.7	37.3	35.9	35.6
Top 200	41.1	40.5	41.2	39.9	39.5
Top 250	43.9	43.4	44.1	43.0	42.6
Top 300	46.1	45.5	46.4	45.3	45.0
Top 350	47.9	47.3	48.3	47.2	47.0
Top 400	49.5	48.9	50.0	48.8	48.6
Top 450	50.8	50.2	51.4	50.1	50.0

Sources: Fortune, The Fortune Directory, Moody's Industrial, Public Utility, and Transportation Manuals. For all nonfinancial corporate assets, Internal Revenue Service, Statistics of Income, Corporation Income Tax Returns (various years). (See note on methodology.)

Note on Methodology: The method used to select the 450 largest nonfinancial corporations (in terms of assets) was based on four of Fortune's lists of the largest corporations, the lists Fortune calls industrials, retailing, transportation, and utilities. These lists were supplemented by various Moody's manuals as follows: (1) A search of Moody's Public Utility Manual and Moody's Transportation Manual for each of the years involved. (2) An examination of all corporations listed in Moody's Industrial Manual as conducting grocery, mail order, or retail operations. (3) An examination of the twenty largest corporations (in terms of assets) on Fortune's second 500 industrial list. (Since Fortune first published this list in 1969, the twenty largest corporations in 1969 were examined for 1958, 1963, and 1967 and were included if large enough.) (4) An examination of sixty-six corporations named by Fortune in 1968 and 1969 as omitted from its lists because, even though large enough, they did not fit into the categories for which Fortune compiled its lists. (Since then Fortune has broadened its industrial category, and several of these companies are listed regularly.)

Data compiled by the Internal Revenue Service were used to measure the assets of all nonfinancial corporations. The latest data available from IRS are for 1975, and, therefore, measures for 1977 could not be included in Table 1. In general, IRS data do not include overseas assets of U.S. corporations; however, the assets of corporations as reported in Fortune and Moody's do include such assets. Thus, the figures in Table 1 are biased toward overstating the share of all nonfinancial corporate assets held by the 450 largest nonfinancial corporations. (A Commerce Department survey of U.S. direct investment abroad found that the assets of majority-owned foreign affiliates of U.S. corporations amounted to $89 billion for all nonfinancial corporations in 1966. In comparison, IRS reported assets for all nonfinancial corporations in 1966 were $837 billion. The Commerce Department is currently conducting another survey of foreign assets of U.S. corporations.)

observation, in fact their views typically rely on an underlying ideological premise which has been implicitly accepted. The current debate over public policy toward conglomerate mergers cannot be understood without paying explicit attention to the ideological premises on which it rests.

I refer of course to the Jeffersonian creed, which occupies a peculiar position on the American scene. This element of the

American psyche is quite different from ideologies found in other Western countries; it is specifically American. In its simplest form, it represents an instinctive fear of large aggregations of private power.

Jeffersonian, or populist, ideology was defined in the crucible of debate between Hamilton and Jefferson. These early debates set the tone for much discussion of economic policy, which has continued to this day. Jefferson argued that we should be concerned with the concentration of economic power and recommended that measures be adopted to disperse this power as widely as possible throughout the society. He believed that the yeoman farmer was a primary source of democratic values to be fostered and supported. Hamilton, on the other hand, cautioned the new nation of moving too far in this direction. He believed that such action might dampen the performance of the economy, on which living standards must ultimately depend. He argued essentially that we should be concerned with economic efficiency.

Throughout the next two centuries, this debate has reappeared at various times in various forms. There have been times when Jeffersonian ideals were ascendant, but others when Hamiltonian practicality was dominant. Throughout, the underlying issues have been fundamentally unchanged. The current discussion and debate over proposals to limit large conglomerate mergers is a recent manifestation of this classic American debate.

Neither side has been fully dominant because neither extreme has seemed fully appropriate. While we as a nation have eagerly sought Jeffersonian ideals, we have been concerned with the economic costs of taking steps in this direction. We have sought with equal fervor an efficient and productive economic system, while continuing to worry about the concentration of economic power that has accompanied our economic gains. Our goal has been to balance the achievement of Jeffersonian ideals with that of promoting an efficient economy.

For the most part, policy measures dealing with American industry have been adopted whenever there is a confluence of opinion which flows from these competing ideological strains. While there are surely exceptions, major policy measures have not been adopted and fully accepted without some degree of concurrence from both schools of thought.

A case in point is the antitrust laws, which serve as a fundamental charter for American industry. These laws evade the essence of this debate for they are generally in accord with both competing ideological currents. They support Jeffersonian ideals regarding the dispersion of economic power and promote competition leading to a more efficient economy. To be sure, there has been some controversy over the latter assertion, but informed opinion supports this position, especially as it applies to horizontal merger policy.

To the extent that merger activity restricts the degree of competition, it should of course be subject to existing antitrust statutes. But what of merger activity that has no such anticompetitive effects but is suspect only because it is inconsistent with Jeffersonian ideals? What actions are appropriate in this realm? To an extent, one's view depends on where one stands in the classic division between Hamilton and Jefferson.

Since the early days of the Republic, Jeffersonians have feared an assault on democratic values from the increasing power and position of the industrial sector. This concern is vividly stated by de Tocqueville in his classic statement on *Democracy in America:*

> I am of opinion, upon the whole, that the manufacturing aristocracy which is growing up under our eyes is one of the harshest which ever existed in the world; but, at the same time, it is one of the most confined and least dangerous. Nevertheless, the friends of democracy should keep their eyes anxiously fixed in this direction; for if ever a permanent inequality of conditions and aristocracy again penetrate into the world, it may be predicted that this is the gate by which they will enter.[5]

Recent proposals to limit conglomerate mergers arise, in large measure, from these same concerns.

The Jeffersonian objective of the widest possible dispersion of economic power concerns the distribution of decision-making authority across economic agents. That substantial authority lies in the hands of government is unquestioned, but this authority has the legitimacy derived from frequent accountability to the popular will.

The issue of "legitimacy" relates to the ultimate question of why one particular person or group should exercise authority, and not others. Legitimacy may be defined as "the rightful possession of power."[6] Within the United States, legitimacy follows in large measure from the exercise of authority to achieve a public purpose within accepted constraints. Among these constraints are competitive processes. But these constraints are often quite weak, sometimes for good economic reasons, and therefore the question of legitimacy is raised.

Even with limited competition in product markets, however, managerial discretionary authority may be constrained by stockholders, financial markets, or takeover threats. Unfortunately, transaction costs and limited information reduce the effectiveness of these forms of control.[7] The managers of giant corporations remain unaccountable to a significant degree. They appear to many as private governments, subject to few external constraints and able to bring considerable resources to bear on any issue they choose. Particularly in their dealings with local governments, they respond with equal standing rather than as a citizen subject to the law, so that matters of local taxation, for example, become subject to negotiation.[8] Inevitably, local control is diminished. Although market forces exert substantial control on much corporate behavior, considerable discretionary authority remains, even in our generally competitive economy.

For this and other reasons, giant firm size conflicts with Jeffersonian ideals. These firms appear as enormous aggregations of economic resources, but with few of the legitimizing attributes associated with public purpose or competitive markets. Management is largely self-perpetuating, and control passes from one person to another with few of the cleansing attributes of public accountability. With our Jeffersonian heritage, it is hardly surprising that so many in our society have a deep-seated and fundamental distrust of giant firms, whether conglomerate or not: they oppose this exercise of substantial discretionary authority by a single hierarchical unit.[9]

HAMILTONIAN CONCERNS

Prohibiting large conglomerate mergers might promote Jeffersonian ideals regarding the concentration of decision-making power, but what of Hamiltonian concerns about the possible effects on economic efficiency?

There are two primary routes through which conglomerate mergers may lead to a more efficient economy.[10] First, these mergers provide a realistic threat to displace inefficient management. If one group of managers believes it can manage a particular firm more profitably than is currently being done, a merger may be proposed so long as the expected increase in profits exceeds the costs of making the acquisition. It has been suggested that the threat of a takeover is one of the more effective forces leading to managerial efficiency. By this account, actions which limit or retard this threat solidify the position of existing management, make it more immune to replacement, and therefore retard a movement toward more efficient management.

A second efficiency gain from conglomerate mergers is related to the operation of the capital markets. An important aspect of conglomerate firm organization is the use of internal or administrative processes to reallocate capital within the firm rather than through the capital markets. For some large reallocations, capital markets which can allocate funds across firms may be superior, but for other more limited purposes, the transaction costs involved may exceed the corresponding costs of internal financing. An economic system that makes use of both types of procedures is therefore likely to be the most efficient.

Despite the possible gains from the conglomerate form of organization, it is striking that economic studies have not found that profitability is higher, on average, for conglomerate firms. While some studies have suggested that conglomerate firms earn lower profit rates than their rivals, others have found no substantial differences. In any event, no indication exists that conglomerate firms earn higher profit rates, even though greater efficiency might be indicated by increased profitability.[11]

To be sure, the stockholders of the acquired firm generally gain from mergers, in that they receive prices for their shares which generally lie above, and often substantially above, the prices at which the shares had previously sold. These premiums in part reflect differences between marginal and average valuations of the shares of acquired firms. The former are defined by the lowest value attributed to a firm's shares by investors who still wish to own the shares. Marginal valuations determine market values. On the other hand, average valuations are simply the average value attributed to these shares across all current investors, but it is this value which sets the price which must be paid for the entire firm. Since average valuations typically exceed marginal valuations, higher prices must be paid to purchase the entire firm than to purchase one or a small number of shares.

Without more than their mere existence, however, these premiums have no implications for the presence or absence of economic efficiencies which might result from an acquisition. The amortized cost of the premium paid is an appropriate deduction from earnings, so that net profits may be no higher despite the presence of synergistic gains. The benefits from these acquisitions may therefore be realized by the stockholders of the acquired firm and not necessarily appear as increased profits of the composite firm.

Whether efficiencies do or do not result from an acquisition, the payment of a premium indicates that the acquiring firm anticipates some benefit from the merger. Otherwise, it presumably could invest the same amount in the shares of various firms, pay the market price as determined by appropriate marginal valuations, and reap its returns. Willingness to pay this premium therefore suggests that the acquiring firm foresees additional gains from the acquisition, or at least the absence of further costs.

Yet, while the payment of a premium indicates that the acquiring firm anticipates a benefit from the merger, this benefit need not reflect economic efficiencies. What the managers of the acquiring firm clearly gain is control over the assets of the acquired firm. Some or all of this premium may represent payment for this control, which is desired by corporate managers even though profits may not be enhanced.

While conglomerate acquisitions may not be made for economic gain, the fact that substantial premiums are paid, together with the frequent observation that firms making these acquisitions earn no lower profits than those which do not, both have implications for whether economic efficiencies result from these mergers. Indeed, Professor Baxter argues that "these two facts, taken alone, have only one possible interpretation. These mergers are generating efficiencies roughly commensurate in their magnitude with the premiums paid to the acquired firms."[12] He concludes that the premiums paid reflect the additional value which results from combining disparate assets into a single firm.

What this argument does not explain, however, is why all of the gains from the acquisition generally go to the prior owners of the acquired firm and none to the acquiring firm. One could of course argue that this division results from substantial competition among prospective acquirers for the assets acquired. But this explanation seems unlikely given the high costs of gathering information on the value of the assets of the acquired firms. Moreover, we do not typically observe multiple suitors for the same company.

Other explanations have been offered. To the extent that the shareholders of acquiring firms experience losses of wealth that are approximately equal to the gains received by the owners of acquired firms, there is no net premium to be explained. But this explanation requires that firms making conglomerate acquisitions earn lower profit rates than their counterparts who have made no such acquisitions. While this result has been found by some researchers, there is no general agreement.

More important, it has been suggested that mergers generally occur when acquired firms are temporarily undervalued in the stock market.[13] In other words, the original market valuation of the acquired firm understates the true value of the assets so that the acquisition takes place in a disequilibrium context. This argument requires, however, that financial markets undervalue some firms for substantial periods of time, about which there is considerable debate.

Note also that if financial markets undervalue some shares, an efficient allocation of resources is promoted if these prices are increased to reflect their true values. Market values can then serve as an appropriate signal for further investment. As a result, there may be gains from such mergers in the form of improved market processes. At the same time, acquisitions by the largest firms in the economy are not necessary elements in this process; the required increases in stock prices can occur through other routes.

SOME POLICY CONCLUSIONS

At the outset of this chapter, I placed this discussion in the context of the issues raised originally in the debates between Hamilton and Jefferson. It remains there. Appropriate public policy should be designed to support Jeffersonian ideals in terms of limiting increases in aggregate concentration achieved through conglomerate acquisitions so long as no significant economic costs result.

While many proposals have been advanced to deal with conglomerate mergers, the one that I would support, and that has been supported by the staff of the Federal Trade Commission, deals explicitly with both sets of concerns. This proposal would restrain external growth by the very largest firms in our economy but would not prohibit acquisitions. Indeed, under this proposal, mergers among the largest firms are specifically permitted so long as the acquiring firm creates or "spins off" another viable firm of approximately the same size as the one acquired within a reasonable period of time either prior to or after the acquisition. A cap on external growth would be established without the inhibiting effects of a ban on all mergers.[14]

Various questions remain. One has to do with the size limitations which should apply. For this purpose, it is useful to examine the overall size distribution of firms, which reveals that the largest firms in this distribution are very much larger than those that mark the fiftieth largest firm, the one-hundredth largest, and beyond. A closer examination indicates that beyond some point in the size distribution the percentage differences in size among firms becomes constant. Before this point, however, which might include the seventy-five largest, firms are substantially larger. Consequently, the seventy-five largest firms occupy a distinct position in the overall size distribution, and therefore policy-makers might wish to focus their attention on them.

There are further questions as well. One concern is how a permitted spin-off may proceed, and what is meant by a viable firm in this context. It should be noted, however, that the tax-free treatment of a spin-off to shareholders requires that a "separate trade or business" be created. This should contribute to the viability of the new business entity.

Furthermore, existing security laws prohibit fraud in the sale of securities, and the requirement of detailed registration statements would further assist major stockholders in appraising the true value of a spun-off entity. The threat of stockholder suits should also given an acquiring firm the incentive to insure that what they spin off is viable.

While further questions regarding this proposal need to be answered, there is much to recommend it. Policy measures that prohibit all large conglomerate mergers may promote Jeffersonian ideals but without sufficiently allowing for Hamiltonian concerns for an efficient economy. The existing policy, which essentially permits all such acquisitions to proceed, largely ignores the ideals for which Jefferson argued. This proposal answers both sets of concerns and is worthy of serious consideration.

NOTES

1. Scherer reports that 40 percent of all assets acquired between 1951 and 1954 represented direct horizontal mergers, while only 8 percent of such assets were accounted for by horizontal mergers between 1967 and 1968. The relevant percentages for vertical mergers were 9 percent in the early period and 7 percent in the later one. All other mergers—which include product extension mergers, market extension mergers, and pure conglomerates—increased their share of all acquired assets from 52 percent between 1951 and 1954 to 85 percent between 1967 and 1968 (F. M. Scherer, *Industrial Market Structure and Economic Performance* [1970], p. 489). In a sample of large mergers undertaken in the Netherlands, fully seventeen out of twenty-five represented horizontal mergers. Similarly, for large mergers in the United Kingdom, nearly half, or 109 out of 225, were horizontal mergers (D. C. Mueller, ed., *The Determinants and Effects of Mergers: An International Comparison* [1980]).
2. J. J. McGowan, "The Effect of Alternate Anti-Merger Policies on the Size Distribution of Firms," 5 *Yale Economic Essays* 455 (1965).
3. Federal Trade Commission, *Economic Report on Corporate Mergers* 189–93 (1969).
4. Some further data are illustrative. In 1955, the 200 largest industrial corporations, ranked on the basis of sales, counted for 53.1 percent to total assets held by

manufacturing and mining corporations. By 1975, this figure had increased to 61.7 percent. These data are obtained from *Fortune* (May 8, 1978) and from various editions of the *Statistical Abstract of the U.S.*
5. A. de Tocqueville, *Democracy in America*, Richard D. Heffner, ed. (1956), p. 220.
6. A. A. Berle, Jr., *Power without Property* (1959), p. 99.
7. Smiley estimates that the transaction costs associated with tender offers have approached 14 percent of the value of the acquired firms (R. H. Smiley, "Tender Offers, Transaction Costs and the Theory of the Firm," 58 *Review of Economics and Statistics* 22 (1976).
8. N. E. Long, "The Corporation, Its Satellites, and the Local Community," in *The Corporation in Modern Society*, E. S. Mason, ed. (1959), pp. 202-17. See also R. N. Stern and H. Aldrich, "The Effect of Absentee Firm Control on Local Community Welfare: A Survey." Paper Presented at FTC Conference on firm size, market structure, and social performance, Washington, January 17-18, 1980.
9. For a modern statement of this concern, see C. Kaysen, "The Corporation: How Much Power? What Scope?" in *The Corporation in Modern Society*, E. S. Mason, ed. (1959), pp. 85-105.
10. See O. S. Williamson, *Markets and Hierarchies: Analysis and Antitrust Implications* (1975), pp. 158-62.
11. The most complete review of the available empirical evidence is contained in D.C. Mueller, "The Effects of Conglomerate Mergers," 1 *Journal of Banking and Finance* 315 (1977).
12. W. F. Baxter, "Statement," *Mergers and Economic Concentration*, Hearings before the Subcommittee on Antitrust and Monopoly of the Committee on the Judiciary, United States Senate, 96th Cong., First Sess., on S. 600, The Small and Independent Business Protection Act of 1979, Part II (1979), p. 28.
13. F. M. Scherer, "Statement," *Mergers and Economic Concentration*, Hearings before the Subcommittee on Antitrust and Monopoly of the Committee on the Judiciary, United States Senate, 96th Cong., First Sess., on S. 600, The Small and Independent Business Protection Act of 1979, Part II (1979), p. 142. See also M. Gort, "An Economic Disturbance Theory of Mergers," *Quarterly Journal of Economics* 624 (November 1969).
14. A similar proposal has been made by Williamson, note 10 *supra*, pp. 170-71.

Chapter 3

The Effects of Conglomerate Mergers on Political Democracy: A Survey

John J. Siegfried

INTRODUCTION

Although the link between conglomerate enterprise and business political power has long been recognized, the recent hearings on the Small and Independent Business Protection Act of 1979 (S. 600, 96th Congress, 1st Session) have emphasized the policy implications of that connection. After a long history of debate on the economic efficiency consequences of conglomerate firms, advocates of strict controls on conglomerate mergers have finally predicated their position on what seemed all along to be the real basis of their fears—namely, the consequences of conglomerate growth for American political democracy. Senator Edward M. Kennedy introduced S.600 by urging Congress to consider "the impact of corporate power not only upon the character and responsiveness of individual economic markets, but upon the very social and political fabric of a nation committed to diversity and individual freedom of choice."[1] Federal Trade Commission Chairman Michael Pertschuk likewise urged the Congress to control conglomerates as a means of

Malcolm Getz, Katherine Maddox, and George Sweeney provided helpful comments on an earlier draft.

ensuring "the bedrock political principle enunciated by Jefferson...
[of] . . . dispersed [political] power."²

Social goals such as dispersed political decision making and
individual freedom are at least as important to the American people
as maximizing the net value of produced goods and services. If these
social goals are affected by the economic structure of corporate
America, then that structure is a legitimate concern of Congress.
Unfortunately, there is considerable disagreement over whether
economic structure affects the dispersion of political power or
individual freedom.

The fears expressed by Senator Kennedy and Chairman
Pertschuk are based primarily on a belief that conglomeration
threatens the continued vigor of American political democracy.
This chain of reasoning has several links. Certainly the acquisition
of additional companies without corresponding spinoffs or divestitures increases firm size. Whether mergers increase *relative* size
depends on the size of the acquiring firms, as well as on the internal
growth rates of firms of different sizes. The effect of either absolute
or relative firm size on political power is the final link.

That private economic power may influence policy decisions
made by governments has not escaped twentieth-century leaders.
Woodrow Wilson's frank assessment of the matter reflected a
popular view of government: "The masters of the government of the
United States are the combined capitalists and manufacturers of
the United States. . . . The government of the United States at
present is a foster child of the special interests."³ Herbert Hoover
perceived a philosophic dichotomy, namely, that "the basic foundations of autocracy, whether it be class government or capitalism in
the sense that few men through unrestrained control of property
determine the welfare of great numbers, is [sic] as far apart from the
rightful expression of American individualism as the two poles."⁴
Expressing his fear of big business, Franklin D. Roosevelt added, "I
am against private socialism of concentrated economic power as
thoroughly as I am against government socialism."⁵

Such sentiments have gained acceptance in recent times.
President Johnson's Cabinet Committee on Price Stability
concluded that "further merger-achieved centralization of economic
power and decision-making may seriously impair the proper functioning of our competitive, free enterprise economy, as well as
threaten the social and political values associated with a decentralized economic system."⁶ In 1969 President Nixon's Attorney
General, John Mitchell, after observing trends in the control of
industrial assets by the nation's leading firms, warned of "[T]he

danger that this super-concentration poses to our economic, political, and social structure. . . ."[7]

Academics have also articulated concern over the noneconomic effects of economic structure. Corwin Edwards argued in 1955 that the financial resources of the large firms often enable them to gain an advantage in nonmarket uses of power: "The campaign contributions of large companies and the occasional use of direct or indirect bribery are probably the least significant sources of the large company's political power. More important, the large company spends whatever money is needed to argue effectively on behalf of its interest where a political issue affects it."[8] Carl Kaysen expressed similar sentiments: "The market power which large absolute and relative size gives the giant corporation is the basis not only of economic power but also of considerable political and social power of a broader sort."[9]

Harlan Blake has described a more explicit tie between conglomerate mergers and political influence:

> One of the most potent economies of scale of large conglomerate firms is surely the effective presentation of their case for favorable treatment by government. A single-product firm, operating directly or through a trade association, has relatively few possible payoffs over which to amortize large investments in lobbying or political goodwill. A conglomerate's many divisions, however, deal with every important agency of government, and the number of possible payoffs is much greater. Furthermore, conglomerate firms can mobilize special interest support from a much wider range of sources: they are likely to deal with more unions, more categories of suppliers and customers, and more mass media than single-product firms; and they are likely to be, or deal with, important constituents in more states and electoral districts.[10]

There is no shortage of proclamations regarding the importance of the connection between economic structure and business political influence. Unfortunately, what is in short supply are careful theoretical analyses of the intertwined relationships between business and politics and systematic objective empirical evaluations of those relationships. The greatest confusion probably arises from the failure to distinguish among the multiplicity of attributes possessed by conglomerate firms, each of which may affect differently their intensity of effort and effectiveness at influencing policy.

The sweeping assertions illustrated by the litany of charges documented above create a confusion that has hindered the development of intelligent thought on the relationship between conglomerates and political power. Conglomerates may be associated with larger firm size, increased market concentration, greater product diversification, and more widespread geographic dispersion. The independent effects of these different characteristics are usually mixed together in expressions opposing the social and political consequences of conglomerate mergers. This is unfortunate, since the separate effects of these various aspects of economic structure may differ markedly, and specific conglomerate merger legislation might be designed to handle each differently.

For business to influence political outcomes successfully, there must be sufficient incentives to make such efforts, adequate resources to mount them, enough knowledge of the political process to apply the resources effectively, and, finally, a response from the political decision-makers that achieves the desired goals. I believe that much of the ignorance surrounding the debate on political influence of conglomerate firms emanates from the failure to recognize that individual market structure elements (e.g., market concentration) principally determine the incentives to influence government policy, while characteristics of firm size primarily dictate the efficiency with which such efforts are transformed into results. That is, the theoretical reasons to expect firms in more *concentrated industries* to have a greater effect on political decisions arise from the larger *effort* firms in concentrated industries are likely to muster. The reasons to expect *large firms* to have more effect on political outcomes are based on the greater *efficiency* with which they apply their resources to achieving the objectives, holding constant the intensity of their effort.[11]

If this characterization of the political influence process is accurate, measures of market concentration should be more successful in explaining the intensity of efforts to influence policy, for example lobbying efforts and campaign contributions. Absolute firm size should be more successful in explaining differences in political outcomes, holding the effort variables constant. Unfortunately, both conceptual and practical difficulties hinder progress toward carefully specifying and separating the components of the process—effort and efficiency. Since most of the empirical analyses relate both market structure and firm size to political outcomes, it is not possible to segment the process, and the whole issue continues to be surrounded by conflicting interpretations of the results.

OVERVIEW OF THE RESEARCH
METHODOLOGY

The research on political influence has relied heavily on case studies, mainly because of the absence of an integrated theory from which testable hypotheses can be derived. Perhaps the important questions of political influence are, as Charles Lindblom argues, inherently untestable.[12] Lindblom contends that the really important impacts of business on public policy are through slow-moving changes that cannot be detected using standard statistical techniques. His view is that the major effect business has on public policy is through its successful propagation of the attitude within government that business must be protected and aided for the viability and success of the government and economy in general. The visible efforts of business to influence policy are usually aimed at repelling opposition to this attitude, but these efforts are minor skirmishes compared to the major war. Since most of the research in this area has focused on the minor skirmishes, the popular view of business political influence is distorted. If Lindblom is correct, most of the research literature reported on here is, indeed, irrelevant. Unfortunately, if Lindblom is correct in his claim that the important effects of business on politics are so gradual as to be undetectable by available techniques, any resolution of the debate on conglomerate mergers is unlikely. The battles will continue to be fought on the basis of subjective assertions. Although such debates provide amusing entertainment, they rarely lead to logical resolution of disagreement.

Even if Lindblom is correct, the statistical research on political power can provide valuable lessons so long as its limitations are recognized and it is not used as the basis for drawing inappropriate generalizations.

Unfortunately, the case study literature is subjective and open to the charge of either explicit or implicit bias. Scott and Hunt, for example, note that the reliance on case studies has led to an image of business influence success stories, probably because researchers know how to recognize political influence when they see it. Sightings, rather than lonely nights of unrewarded searching, sell books and newspapers.[13]

Case studies do have value, however. They can provide the foundation for an integrated rigorous model of the effect of business on political outcomes. If such a theory were imminently forthcoming, the incremental value of additional case studies would be limited. The state of the research art, however, leaves us far from a systematic theoretical framework for analyzing the impact of business on politics. The theories are ad hoc, contradictory, and disjointed. Although kernels of good ideas are among them, we remain a long way from simply having to test an accepted theoretical framework with sophisticated empirical methods and data. Consequently, additional case studies may prove worthwhile. They should no longer be studies of single firms or single incidents, however, but rather should try to identify sets of firms or industries with many common characteristics so that the independent effect of remaining differences among them can be observed. A realistic yet rigorous model of the process will necessarily be based on such insights.

Various possibilities might form the basis for a theory of business political influence. The work of Randall Bartlett uses the literature on information and uncertainty to analyze political influence.[14] Jonathan Pincus has formalized and adapted Mancur Olson's work on the theory of collective action in the context of political exchange.[15] In addition, the work of public choice economists on log-rolling and voting models and research on strategic responses of businesses to government constraints might aid in the development of an integrated theory.

THE RESEARCH LITERATURE

What is known about business political influence today is contained in several disparate bodies of literature. Perhaps the least familiar of these is the research of economists (some might say imperialistic economists) who have recognized the general applicability of economic principles and methodology to matters extending beyond traditional income and employment questions. This literature, reviewed below, is soundly based on theories that, although admittedly ad hoc, contain promise of developing an integrated explanation of business political influence. This literature begins to go beyond the selected case study, to examine whether the hypotheses developed from case studies can be derived from a formal model, and to evaluate those hypotheses empirically.

Although these studies may be an offshoot of the main literature on the political influence of business, focusing attention on them is justified on several grounds. First, they exhibit a theoretical basis for future insights and empirical results that might contribute more light than heat to the debate. Second, the other literatures, created by political scientists, lawyers, and other observers of the American political process, have been exhaustively reviewed elsewhere.[16]

This survey examines the more substantial models of the political influence process that have been created by economists; identifies and organizes the various ad hoc hypotheses that have been offered to explain the relationships of firm size, market structure, product diversification, and geographic dispersion with political outcomes; and, finally, reviews, summarizes, and presents a critique of the empirical studies.

THE ECONOMIC APPROACH TO POLITICAL INFLUENCE

The general approach of all the economic studies has been to postulate that individuals are self-interest-seeking and act either individually or through groups (here, firms) to further their interests. They invest in specific efforts to create political influence if the expected benefits to them exceed the expected costs. Two important economic concepts in this benefit-cost calculus are the divergence between individual and group incentives and scale economies.

The divergence between firm and industry incentives to contribute to group efforts to influence public policy is based on the "public good" nature of most policy outcomes. In particular, it is usually difficult to exclude noncontributors from obtaining benefits. This feature arises from the advantages of broadening the scope of affected parties, for example, from an individual firm to an industry. Broadening the impact of advocated policies helps to diffuse opposition, conceals the self-serving nature of the attempted influence, and creates additional constituencies and potential support. But it also invites individual firms to refrain from contributing to the effort in anticipation of obtaining a free ride and enjoying the benefits anyway. If this reasoning permeates the entire industry, sufficient funds for successful lobbying will be absent, and political influence will not arise.

Scale economies arise from large elements of fixed costs in the production function. Many observers believe that the important ingredients in "influence production" have this character (e.g., access, contacts, prestige, expertise, persistence, continuity). Consequently, larger scale efforts achieve lower average total costs of political influence production and if benefits are proportional to size, are more likely to generate expected costs that are less than the expected benefits. The average cost of creating influence is less for the larger firm, thus creating a production efficiency advantage.

The only treatise-length effort to create an integrated theory of political influence is Bartlett's theory of government, which incorporates the interaction of elected officials, bureaucrats, voters, and producers.[17] Bartlett assumes that all individuals are self-interest maximizers making decisions under uncertainty. The mechanism of influence is information subsidization. Individuals can be expected to acquire information that reduces uncertainty so long as the expected benefits from fewer mistaken decisions exceed the acquisition costs of information. Therefore, reducing marginal costs of acquiring information can influence elected officials or bureaucrats (or voters or producers) to consume selective information, thereby influencing decisions.

Producers can affect political outcomes in several ways. First, they may selectively subsidize the conveying of information to elected officials or bureaucrats in order to alter decisions in favor of the producers. Lobbying is the obvious illustration. Second, they may provide resources to bureaucrats which in turn enable the bureaucrats to subsidize the conveying of information selectively to elected officials, thereby generating favorable outcomes for both the bureaucrats and the producers. An example of this type of subsidization would be an industry-financed research effort to provide "facts" to an administrative agency seeking to increase its budget for the purpose of purchasing certain goods and services. Third, producers may provide resources that enable elected officials to subsidize the conveying of information selectively to voters (e.g., through newsletters, campaign advertisements, etc.) in order to generate grassroots support for positions favored by the producers. Campaign contributions serve this purpose.

MARKET CONCENTRATION, FIRM SIZE, GEOGRAPHIC CONCENTRATION, AND PRODUCT DIVERSIFICATION

We now turn to a systematic inventory of the various hypotheses relating the characteristics of conglomerate firms to political influence.

Market Concentration

It has been argued that conglomerate mergers cause an increase in market concentration.[18] Reasons include the impact of conglomerate mergers on limiting potential competition, the increased possibility of reciprocal dealings involving highly diversified firms, and the increased potential of conglomerates to finance predatory activities. If these arguments are valid it is necessary to inquire into the relationship between market concentration and political influence as an indicator of the effect of conglomerate mergers on political democracy.

Market concentration affects the incentives of individual firms to contribute to group efforts to influence political decisions. The nature of the product creates a divergence between firm and industry incentives to invest in these activities. In a competitive industry each individual firm is likely to calculate—correctly—that it will reap some of the benefits of any successful efforts to influence policy regardless of whether it assumes part of the costs, because the costs of excluding noncontributors from the benefits are prohibitive. Indeed, in order to collect sufficiently broad support for a policy initiative or position, proponents will likely find it in their interest to broaden their appeal beyond a single firm, to an industry or sector of the economy, which increases the opportunity for free riders.

The standard theory of collective action yields the prediction that, as a public good, influence will be supplied at less than the efficient level.[19] Olson identified the number and size distribution of individuals (here, firms) constituting a group (here, industry) as the primary factor determining the effectiveness of group efforts to produce public goods.[20] There are several reasons for this logic. First, the fewer the firms in an industry, the better the chance that their values and objectives will coincide, thus reducing the bargaining and organizational costs of forming a collective-action group. Second, the fewer the firms in an industry, the greater will be the relative share of benefits accruing to each individual firm (other things, such as size distribution, held constant), in which case the expected dollar value of benefits from participation rises relative to expected costs. This increases the possibility that one firm will undertake the investment on its own. Third, the fewer the firms in an industry, the easier it is for the collective-action group to enforce any voluntary agreements that it may enter. For example, three firms, each of which has pledged $10,000 to a certain lobbying effort, can evaluate compliance with the pledge more easily than each of 100 firms pledging $300 each can determine the level of compliance with their agreement because the impact of noncompliance on the remaining firms increases inversely with the number of firms. Fourth, as the size distribution of firms becomes more unequal, the chance of any one firm finding it in its interest to pursue the public policy alone increases because the share of benefits that would accrue to the largest firm usually rises with its relative share of the market. For these reasons, which together minimize the possibility that any one firm will attempt to be a free rider if the market is more concentrated, we expect efforts at political influence to increase with market concentration. If results are related to efforts, we should observe more concentrated industries achieving their political goals more frequently than competitive industries.

A different reason to expect greater political efforts from concentrated industries arises from the commonly accepted positive association between industry profits and market concentration.[21] Regardless of the reason for the relationship—higher prices or lower costs of firms in concentrated industries—if economic rents do accrue to firms with market power, they may be used to further political objectives. On the other hand, if investments in political influence were better than alternative investment opportunities of a firm, why would they have to be financed out of economic rents?[22] In any case, this argument is a common one and is therefore included in the catalog.

The impact of market concentration on political influence might be negative if the visibility that usually accompanies high levels of market concentration tends to attract adverse public attention and to increase opposition to political efforts by firms in highly concentrated industries. If opposing efforts are encouraged, the projected marginal product of investments in political influence would fall, thus reducing the optimal level of such efforts.

Another reason to expect a negative effect of market concentration on political influence is the problem of interpreting the relationship. Caves notes that market concentration might be an inverse representation of the dispersion of an industry's activity among enterprises.[23] If dispersion of production among various enterprises and in different geographic regions increases the pressure points at which Congress and the rest of the political structure might be vulnerable, then we would expect more competitive industries to be more effective at influencing policy. Used in this way, market concentration represents geographic dispersion. Many of the studies have independently controlled for dispersion, in which case this confusion is reduced. Pincus, for example, used both a measure of market concentration and a measure of the number of different firms in an industry to explain political success.[24] He interpreted the concentration variable as representing the divergence between firm and industry incentives, and the number of firms variable as an indicator of political contact points. Both variables obtained the expected positive association with political influence.

In recognition of the conflicting hypotheses, those who conduct studies of political influence have approached the effect of market concentration with open minds, applying two-tailed statistical tests to determine the dominating effect. Most, however, either explicitly or implicitly, seem to favor the free-rider argument as recommending a positive relationship between market concentration and political outcomes.

Most studies of the importance of competition use concentration ratios defined for economically meaningful markets. This usually means that the Census concentration ratios need to be adjusted for exports and imports, for regional submarkets, and for noncompeting subproducts and interindustry competition.[25] In the case of political influence, however, the local market adjustment is unnecessary. The relevant group for the purposes of political influence is that which is identified by the policy makers and public as "the industry." It is likely that firms in industries with local markets will be treated similarly by public policy in spite of the absence of competition among them. Thus, the concentration ratios available directly from the Census may be used without adjustment for regional markets.

A final problem with the interpretation of statistical results correlating political outcomes to market concentration is that causation may be reversed. It may be that certain political outcomes themselves effect concentration. For example, tariffs and tax reductions increase the after-tax profitability of domestic producers, thereby tending to increase the number of firms and decrease the level of concentration. For this reason a negative correlation might be observed even though concentration is causing more political influence.

Firm Size

The relationship between absolute firm size and political power seems to be the basis for much of America's concern about conglomerates and rising aggregate concentration. Presumably the hypothesis is that one large firm would have more political influence than ten firms, each one-tenth the size of the larger firm. Thus, aggregations of economic power yield proportionately greater quantities of political power.

Even when mergers have little or no effect on individual market concentration because they are between firms that do not compete, they will increase firm size and thus will be identified as targets of those who fear increasing concentration of political power.

There are three main reasons for expecting absolute firm size to create disproportionate amounts of political power. First, large firms have a greater incentive to participate in politics because large firms generally (although certainly not always) have greater market shares and thus would be more likely to enjoy benefits from their efforts that exceed the expected costs even if other firms in their industry ride free. The theory of collective choice provides an identical argument as to why one should expect more concentrated industries to participate more intensively in political influence. Here it is hypothesized that the important dimension of the size distribution of firms is the relative share of the leading firm (in contrast to the four leading firms' share), which is likely to be correlated with the absolute size of firms.

Second, larger firms may have greater access to the critical resources for producing political influence because they are more likely to have acquired these resources already for their production of nonpolitical goods and services. There may be important elements of joint cost in performing economic and political activities. Carl Kaysen and Corwin Edwards both suggested that economic power is an important source of political power, either directly, through campaign finance, or indirectly, through the purchase of expertise to generate information important to the policy process.[26] The larger firms already have the public relations experts, attorneys, Washington law firms, and executives with personal contacts throughout the political system. This network makes a political influence effort possible at reasonable marginal cost.

Third, what makes the absolute size of available resources, and hence firm size, so important politically is the fact that political involvement has certain fixed costs attached to it. The larger firms will be better able to reach the minimum initial resource constraint necessary to attain a profitable level of influence production. The heavy fixed-cost nature of the inputs to political influence means that the average cost of influencing policy by large firms will be lower than for small firms. Since small firms can rarely reach the minimum size to participate efficiently in the political process, they must rely on group participation, with all of the intraorganizational differences, lack of control, and consequent weakening of influence that go with it.

The influence of larger firms (as well as firms in more concentrated industries) might be mitigated, however, by their visibility and the concomitant likelihood they face of attracting an aroused and vocal opposition, thereby raising the costs to the large firm of successfully influencing policy. If large firm size discourages efforts to influence political outcomes, the effect of firm size on political outcomes would be negative.

Legal constraints might also disadvantage larger firms. For example, firms may establish as many political action committees as they wish, but they are limited by law (the Federal Election Campaign Act Amendments of 1976) to a single $5,000 contribution per candidate for each election. By merging, two firms will effectively reduce their combined contribution limit from $10,000 to $5,000.

Geographic Concentration

If each member of Congress has many constituent groups competing for his attention, and if he allocates his time to their requests in proportion to their likely impact on his reelection, then it follows that an industry must be sufficiently large in each congressional district to gain recognition. Consequently, for a given industry size, industries with firms located in fewer different geographic areas will be more likely to capture the attention of their representatives and to achieve their political influence goals. In other words, there are economies of scale in obtaining a hearing for one's views and therefore, a larger single presence in congressional districts produces advantages.

In addition, conflicts of interest between potential group members are less likely to occur within specific regions than if the firms have diverse locations. For example, Sun Belt v. Snow Belt issues may cloud the formation of an interest group that would otherwise be successful. Therefore, geographic concentration may increase the prospect for successful collective action and subsequent political influence.

While geographic concentration may improve the chances for obtaining the attention and support of a sponsor for certain legislation, industries that are highly concentrated geographically may lack the broad-based political support necessary to pass the legislation, and to have it implemented. The optimal geographic dispersion may be a few areas in which the industry is highly concentrated and clearly significant to the political representatives, with the rest of the industry spread over at least one-half of the districts, so that a majority voting for special legislation favoring the industry can claim a victory for some constituency.

Dispersion might also be expected to be inversely related to political efforts and successful outcomes, because it may increase the communications and organizational costs of forming an effective political action group.

Product Diversification

Diversification is another attribute of conglomerates that may create greater incentives or efficiency in influencing public policies through the political apparatus. First, just as it is true that diversified firms are likely to reap larger rewards from research and development because of the multiplicity of uses for their discoveries, it is also true that diversified firms might find the cultivation of political gardens for one purpose profitable for their other interests. When special problems arise, a diversified firm is more likely to have dealt with them at one time or another in some part of its total operation. Furthermore, as Blake argues, diversified firms can mobilize support for their efforts to influence policy from a wider range of sources and will be more likely to find support from some important constituencies.[27]

Highly diversified firms tend to have varied interests which may be affected in contrary ways by a specific policy. For example, if a firm is both an exporter and an importer, which position should it take on tariffs? The importance of this fact for political influence is ambiguous. A conglomerate merger between two firms which previously had produced political influence in opposition to each other might lead to a resolution of the conflict within the new firm and a single focused effort at influencing policy. Consequently, conglomerate mergers may increase political power. On the other hand, the internal organizational characteristics of some firms might inhibit a strict profit-maximizing approach in favor of negotiated settlements among disputants within a firm. Such settlements might take the form of agnosticism toward controversial issues, thereby eliminating any net effect the competing efforts might have made and consequently reducing political influence.

Finally, it has also been argued that diversified firms cannot press as hard on any one issue as a single-purpose organization can, because they are more likely to jeopardize their success in another area. Therefore, diversified firms might be less successful in influencing policy on any one issue.

Other Variables

Although not directly related to conglomeration, the impact of industry size deserves attention. Depending on which other variables are included in the analysis, the absolute size of the industry may be a proxy for certain dimensions of the size distribution of firms, or the absolute size of firms. Industry size is also likely to be a proxy for employment and, if "labor has the votes," should have an impact on political effectiveness.

Whether there is organized opposition to an effort to influence public policy is also important. Hayes makes the useful distinction between distributive and redistributive policies.[28] Distributive policies are those that allocate benefits to a concentrated group of individuals but disperse the costs among a large group, so that no one individual expresses great opposition. Redistributive policies are those in which both the benefits and the costs are highly concentrated among a few individuals. To predict the success of policies aimed at redistribution, the economic characteristics of opponents may be just as important as the characteristics of proponents. For distributive policies, opposition is likely to be weak or absent, in which case the economic incentives and efficiency of the proponents alone will be determinant.

EMPIRICAL STUDIES OF BUSINESS POLITICAL POWER

The systematic empirical studies of business political influence fall into two categories: investigations of the effect of economic variables on political instruments such as campaign contributions or lobbying efforts, and studies that relate economic variables directly to political outcomes. Studies of political instruments should be most useful in assessing the validity of the free-rider theory, which predicts greater political involvement by firms in more concentrated industries. The political outcome studies are more difficult to interpret since a correlation between economic variables and political results could be the consequence either of greater efforts by firms to influence policy or of greater effectiveness in using a given amount of resources to achieve their goals. Since conflicting hypotheses exist regarding each of the economic variables, two-tailed statistical tests are appropriate for weighing their relative importance.

Four studies of political instruments are reported here. Pittman and Marx examine the determinants of campaign contributions and Mann and McCormick investigate the relationship between firm attributes and lobbying efforts in California.[29] Eight studies relate the economic environment directly to policy results from three policy areas: regulation, tariff protection, and tax burdens. The studies are reported chronologically.

Stigler

In an attempt to explain the supply of regulation, George Stigler theorized that every industry or occupation with sufficient power to utilize the government will seek to do so, primarily by limiting entry.[30] He identified several factors that would increase the chances of success: industry size, potential benefits, costs of organization (geographic dispersion), and opposition to the policy.

Stigler conducted a rough test of his theory by comparing the dates at which various occupations became licensed in different states. He found that occupations with higher incomes, local markets, more stable membership, and those less often employed by business (which could raise substantial opposition) were licensed sooner. Occupations in local markets have higher market concentration and lower organization costs, thus supporting the free-rider theory.

Siegfried

John Siegfried attempted to correlate firm size, industry size, market concentration, geographic concentration, and profit rates with the success realized by various industries in obtaining special-interest legislation designed to reduce their federal corporation income tax liabilities.[31] He compared the success of various IRS mining and manufacturing "minor industries" in reducing their tax burdens in 1963 and found that industries with larger typical firm size, fewer employees, less concentration, and lower profits were more likely to enjoy the advantages of favorable tax legislation. The effect of geographic dispersion was ambiguous. Firm size was measured as the capital size of the firm that accounted for the midpoint asset dollar of the industry. Because the dependent variable is a tax *rate,* any correlation with firm size indicates a disproportionate effect of larger firms on political outcomes. In studies that measure political outcomes in absolute dollars, a disproportionate impact of firm size is revealed only by an elasticity of the outcomes with respect to size that exceeds one (see Mann and McCormick survey below).

Siegfried's results lend support to the theory relating large firm size to political influence but are contrary to the usual expectations regarding industry size, market concentration, and profits. Although explanations exist for each of the surprising results, the main reason for them is probably the strong interrelationship among the variables. For example, holding firm size constant and increasing industry size means that the market concentration of firms will be reduced. Consequently, the negative coefficient on industry size can be interpreted as support for the free-rider hypothesis. In addition, by factoring out the effects of number of firms (by including firm size and industry size simultaneously) and profit rates, the only hypothesis left for the market concentration variable to capture is the higher visibility of firms in concentrated industries. Thus, it is not too surprising that the effect of market concentration on tax avoidance is negative. The absence of any impact of the geographic concentration variable does not necessarily mean that the hypotheses about it are invalid. It could mean that both positive and negative factors are at work, but that their approximately equivalent effects cancel out in the empirical test.

McPherson

Charles McPherson uses number of firms, concentration ratio, industry size (employment), geographic concentration, labor intensity, and a consumer-producer good binary variable (as a measure of organized opposition) to explain variations in nominal and effective tariff rates across approximately 100 United States industries in 1954 and 1963.[32] His results are very disappointing. Only the consumer good binary variable is consistently significant; industries facing buyer concentration had less tariff protection. None of the other variables reveals a consistent relationship with tariff rates. Hayes has developed an explanation for these disappointing findings, namely that tariff policy in the United States in the 1950s and 1960s was redistributive, with important and powerful interest groups opposing trade barriers.[33] The failure to identify and characterize the opposition consequently omits an important set of explanatory variables from the analysis.

Pittman I

Using public data on the campaign contributions to three Midwestern Senate races in 1972, Russell Pittman postulated a model that explained variances in contributions on the basis of the stakes that various industries had in political influence, market concentration, and industry size.[34] He keyed individuals' contributions to corporate affiliations. His results supported the idea that people associated with larger and more concentrated industries contributed more to campaigns, but people associated with regulated industries, which he had hypothesized to have greater stakes in political influence, surprisingly contributed less.

Pittman II

In a second study Pittman used data on what were thought at the time to be secret campaign contributions to the 1972 Committee to Reelect the President to extend his test of the relationship between economic structure and political influence.[35] These data were later made available to the public as the result of litigation. Pittman argued that data on contributions considered secret by their donors were better than data on contributions known to be public at the time of donation because the former were free of distortions created by the desire of some firms to avoid publicity.

Pittman examines the effect of government involvement through regulation, procurement, or antitrust investigation on the propensity of firms in concentrated and unconcentrated industries to contribute to Nixon's reelection campaign. The results revealed that "[f]or the unconcentrated industries none of the . . . government influence variables has a significant effect, leaving only industry size as a significant determinant of contributions. For the concentrated industries, on the other hand, all [of the] government influence variables are significant at the .05 level or better, [with the predicted signs]."[36] Thus, a strong difference between firm and industry incentives is observed on the basis of the effect of market concentration. In the presence of high concentration, a "dependence" on government generates campaign contributions, whereas in unconcentrated industries the "dependence" on government does not manifest itself in greater contributions, probably because the free-rider problem creates a barrier to effective group action.

Pincus

Jonathan Pincus attempted to explain 1824 tariff rates in the United States with measures of market concentration, industry size, and geographic dispersion.[37] He found higher tariffs for industries with greater market concentration, more geographic concentration, and representation in a large number of different states. He concluded that "although pressure came mainly from the relatively few, larger establishments, the mere existence of numbers of smaller, dispersed firms helped lend weight in Congress, so industries with many establishments and with sales spread more evenly across states or with establishments in many states obtained higher duties."[38] These results on the tariff issue are certainly more encouraging for the free-rider theory than McPherson's.

Caves

Richard Caves attempted to explain differences in tariff rates among Canadian industries in the 1960s.[39] He postulated three competing models in which vote maximization, interest group incentives, and national policy were the leading themes. His empirical tests revealed that both nominal and effective tariff rates were higher in less concentrated industries. Two measures of geographic dispersion yielded conflicting results, and a measure of product diversification had no impact on tariffs at all.

Salamon and Siegfried

Lester Salamon and John Siegfried examined the effect on state-by-state variations in the motor fuel excise tax rate caused by overall size of the petroleum industry in a state and the extent to which large firms populate the industry within the state.[40] They found that tax rates were lower where the petroleum refining industry is large and where it is dominated by large firms, which is consistent with the free-rider theory.

Coolidge and Tullock

Cathleen Coolidge and Gordon Tullock performed several simple correlations aimed at the firm size–political influence hypothesis.[41]

They found no correlation between the number of *Fortune* 500 firms with headquarters in a state and state corporation income tax rates, no correlation between the number of large commercial banks in a state and the state corporation income tax rate, no correlation between the fraction of GNP attributable to the largest corporations and corporation income tax rates in fourteen states and no correlation between the number of "special tax favors" to lure business into states and the number of major corporate headquarters in each state. They explain these findings on the basis that economies of scale typically found in lower ranges of productive activities are likely to be exhausted long before the size of most American businesses. On these grounds they questioned the Siegfried findings of a positive impact of firm size on political influence. Siegfried, however, also found no relationship between firm size and lower corporation income tax rates in a simple correlation between the two. It was only when other factors, such as market concentration, geographic dispersion, industry size, and profits were controlled, that the positive correlation between firm size and political influence surfaced.

Coolidge and Tullock also reanalyzed the Siegfried data. By removing selected industries from the set of observations, they are able to make the positive correlation between firm size and tax favors disappear.[42] Finally, they challenged the interpretation that Salamon and Siegfried place on the regression results explaining corporation income tax avoidance, because of the complicated and intimate relationship among firm size, market concentration, and industry size. Because any two of these variables formally define the third (although in the Siegfried and also in the Salamon and Siegfried studies the correlation is far from perfect due to different measurement bases, different data sources, and discontinuities in the data), they argue that the relationship is confounded. This problem, however, should not bias the estimates of the relationship, but rather simply reduce our confidence in them. Because the firm size variable was statistically significant in spite of this multicolinearity, the relationship should probably be regarded as a real one, at least for the particular situation analyzed.

Mann and McCormick

H. Michael Mann and Karen McCormick used data on corporate lobbying expenditures from the state of California to examine the relationship between economic characteristics and attempts to influence public policy.[43] These lobbying data are much better than those required on reports to the federal government. Mann and McCormick consider each of the major four elements of conglomeration. They find that larger firms spend more on lobbying efforts, but not proportionately more than smaller firms. Increased firm market share (market concentration) yields higher levels of expenditures, as do higher profit rates for the firms. On the other hand, geographic concentration and product diversification seem to have little effect on lobbying effort, although in one model the more geographically concentrated firms (having plants in fewer different ZIP codes) spent less.

The Mann and McCormick study is based on individual firm data, and therefore firm size can be defined and measured directly. Market concentration for an individual firm was defined as the weighted average of the firm's market share across the four-digit industries in which it operates.

Marx

Thomas Marx has examined the effect of conglomerates on political influence directly.[44] He uses a sample of seventy-five conglomerates and seventy-five matched nonconglomerates of similar size to assess the hypotheses. He finds no correlation between a binary variable that identifies conglomerates and federal corporation income taxes as a percent of net income before taxes. In contrast to Siegfried, Marx presumes that those tax breaks related to capital intensity are part of a legitimate corporation income tax and not "special provisions." He does not examine the effect of firm size on tax rates but rather holds firm size constant by matching the two sets of firms on that basis.

Expanding the Coolidge-Tullock analysis, Marx uses his data to test the hypothesis that state corporation income taxes will be lower and special business tax incentives will be greater where conglomeration is more prevalent. The relationship between diversification and state tax rates or tax incentives appears to be nil.

Marx also looked at the effect of diversification on the voting patterns of congressmen. He found no correlation between conglomeration and voting indexes of liberalism (Americans for Democratic Action and AFL-CIO's Committee on Political Education) or probusiness voting (U.S. Chamber of Commerce).

Finally, Marx also examined the correlation between conglomeration and the intermediate variable, political contributions. He found that conglomerates tended to form Political Action Committees more frequently than nonconglomerates, but the difference in average contributions per PAC was not significant. This suggests a greater effort on the part of conglomerates to influence legislation, but the earlier tests reveal no difference in the results. Together his findings suggest that conglomerates are handicapped in converting political resources into results, but they do not help to distinguish between inefficiency and more potent opposition as explanations for this phenomenon.

Other Studies

Coolidge and Tullock report the results from an unpublished paper by Charles Cox, which states that more concentrated industries had their prices pushed down farther by price controls than did firms in unconcentrated industries.[45]

Epstein reports the results of an unpublished study by John Rose that assessed political influence on the basis of Senate voting in 1975 on the controversial bill to postpone the starting date for nationwide NOW (Negotiable Order of Withdrawal) accounts.[46] He found no correlation between market concentration in commercial banking and respective senators' voting patterns, but the percentage of banks with deposits exceeding $250 million had an expected negative effect on the postponement, larger banks being less opposed to expanding the use of NOW accounts. Thus, Rose found no effect of concentration and a positive effect of firm size on political influence.

SUMMARY

The eleven empirical studies that are reviewed here report varied and conflicting results. They are summarized in Table 3.1. The studies of political instruments (campaign contributions and lobbying expenditures) agree on the positive effect of market concentration on efforts to influence policy. These results are consistent with the theory of private versus group incentives, from which we derive the proposition that effort to influence policy should be determined by the divergence of individual and group interests.

On the other hand, the studies of political outcomes reveal quite diverse results. The three studies of tariff protection report a negative, neutral, and positive effect, respectively, of market concentration on rates of protection. Siegfried's study of corporation income tax rates finds a negative effect of concentration on political influence, but Stigler finds that industries with local markets, wherein market concentration is higher, obtained entry regulation sooner than other industries. The tests of the free-rider hypothesis seem, overall, to favor it, but there are some bothersome exceptions.

A likely explanation for McPherson's negative effect of market concentration on political success is his failure to consider explicitly the strong opposition and its economic characteristics to higher tariff rates in the 1950s and 1960s in the United States. Siegfried's negative effect of market concentration might be explained by the inclusion of industry and firm size in his model, so that together the control variables captured the incentive to free-ride, leaving only the higher visibility effect to the market concentration variable. Such ex post rationalization, however, does not invalidate the surprising empirical facts.

The evidence on firm size is also mixed. Mann and McCormick find that larger firms spend more on lobbying, but not as much more as one would expect on the basis of their size. Siegfried and Salamon attribute greater success in obtaining special tax favors to larger firms, but Coolidge and Tullock and Marx find no evidence to support such a conclusion. If larger firms actually devote proportionately less to political lobbying, as Mann and McCormick find, and yet are more successful in achieving their goals, as Salamon and Siegfried find, their relative efficiency advantage in producing political influence (the economies of scale argument) can be inferred to be quite large.

Geographic concentration does not appear to matter. Pincus finds geographically concentrated industries more effective in obtaining protective tariffs in 1824; this is consistent with dependence at that time of communications costs on physical proximity. But studies have failed to find any systematic relationship between the effect of geographic concentration on contemporary policy and political influence. The three studies that looked explicitly at product diversification, the most apparent characteristic of conglomerates, found no net impact on political influence, with the exception of Marx's positive relationship between conglomeration and campaign contributions.

What is the appropriate interpretation of this research? For one thing, unanswered and controversial questions remain. Also, a solid integrated theory is in high demand. Improvements in the modeling of the political influence of business will have to deal successfully with major weaknesses in the current approach. First, the direction of causation between the "dependent" and "independent" variables in the empirical specifications is not clear. For example, the effect of higher tariff rates or lower tax rates on market concentration or firm size might be the source of any statistical relationships between the

Table 3.1. Summary of Statistical Studies of Business Political Influence

Author	Dependent Variable	Time Period	Impact on Successful Political Influence			
			Market Concentration	Firm Size	Geographic Concentration	Product Diversification
Stigler	State occupational licensing	—	+			
Siegfried	Effective corporation income tax rate	1963	—	+	0	
McPherson	U.S. tariff rates	1954, 1963	0		0	
Pittman I	Senate campaign contributions	1972	+			
Pittman II	Presidential campaign contributions	1972	+			
Pincus	U.S. tariff rates	1824	+		+	
Caves	Canadian tariff rates	1960s	—		+1	0

Table 3.1 *(continued)*

Author	Dependent Variable	Time Period	Impact on Successful Political Influence			
			Market Concentration	Firm Size	Geographic Concentration	Product Diversification
Salamon and Siegfried	Motor fuel excise tax rates	1967		+		
Coolidge and Tullock	Tax rates	1970s		0		0
Mann and McCormick	Lobbying expenditures	1975–1976	+	−[a]	0	0
Marx	Federal corp. income tax rates	circa 1977				
	State taxes	1978		0		0
	Probusiness voting	1978		0		0
	Campaign contributions	1978				+

[a]Effect of firm size on absolute expenditures was positive, but less than proportionate.

latter two. Second, individual issues do not stand alone. Sophisticated modeling of the political process will have to incorporate logrolling. Perhaps the individual issues examined in the empirical papers cannot be well explained by economic environment characteristics because they are part of political exchanges, and the tribute for votes is not observed. Third, what to "hold constant" in the empirical specifications is unclear. If more variables are included individually in the model, then the chances of statistical problems rise. But confusions in interpretation may emerge if more than one variable serves to measure a single idea. On the other hand, if each of the separate theories of political influence is not accounted for by an individual measure in the models, one variable may capture (in an unknown manner) the combined effect of several ideas and be impossible to interpret. Fourth, each of the analyses that has been examined is a partial analysis. For example, there may be reasons why large firms do not exert their political clout on tax issues but choose instead to invest in political capital on tariff issues. Without a broad spectrum of issues to examine, findings from one area of political influence will fail to inspire much confidence. Fifth, future modeling should also try to account for the potential asymmetry between intensity of feelings generated by gains and losses. That is, it may be more difficult to muster the political effort to generate favorable redistributions than to oppose unfavorable ones of equal size, even though their net impact would be identical. People may not view a foregone benefit as equivalent to a direct loss. Sixth, future modeling should attempt to segregate the effort devoted to political influence from the efficiency with which that effort is transformed into results. And finally, Charles Lindblom's critique of this entire literature, namely that it is misdirected because the important influence of business on politics is through the slow-changing effect on attitudes, should receive more attention. Perhaps there are ways to evaluate that hypothesis as well.

The evidence to date does not give any empirical credence to the proposition that economic changes precipitated by conglomerate mergers will have important implications for the operations of the American political system at either the state or federal levels. On the other hand, it does not support contrary ideas either.

Because of the importance of understanding the relationship between economic and political power, much more comprehensive empirical research, based on carefully specified theoretical models of the interaction between business and political institutions, is required. Such a call for more research, in addition to fulfilling the usual obligatory ending to a survey paper, sounds like a self-serving lobbying effort to improve the economic welfare of economists and political scientists. Because of the height of the pedestal on which most Americans place the goal of decentralized decision-making (especially in contrast to the goal of economic efficiency), however, calls for more energetic efforts to improve our knowledge of the role of business in politics will likely create group as well as individual benefits.

NOTES

1. Edward M. Kennedy, *Opening Statement,* Hearings on the Small and Independent Business Protection Act of 1979, before the Senate Committee on the Judiciary, March 8, 1979, p. 1.
2. M. Pertschuk, *Testimony* before the Senate Committee on the Judiciary on the Small and Independent Business Protection Act of 1979, March 8, 1979, p. 5.
3. W. Wilson, *The New Freedom* (1913), pp. 57–58.
4. H. Hoover, *American Individualism* (1922), p. 18.
5. Special message to Congress endorsing what became the Public Utility Holding Company Act of 1935.
6. *Studies by the Staff of the Cabinet Committee on Price Stability,* (Washington, D.C.: U.S. Government Printing Office, 1969).
7. Speech before the Georgia Bar Association, June 6, 1969, Savannah.
8. C. D. Edwards, "Conglomerate Bigness as a Source of Power," in *Business Concentration and Price Policy* (1955), p. 346.
9. C. Kaysen, "The Corporation: How Much Power? What Scope?" in *The Corporation in Modern Society,* E. S. Mason, ed. (1959), p. 99.
10. H. Blake, "Conglomerate Business and the Antitrust Laws," 73 *Columbia Law Review* 591–92 (1973).
11. Large firm size should also effect the incentives to influence policy, since larger firms stand to gain a greater share of whatever benefits are produced, but this role of firm size, namely its impact on the size distribution of firms, is included in the market concentration argument. Firm size here is considered with other things, in particular the size distribution of firms, held constant.
12. See C. E. Lindblom, *Politics and Markets* (1977) and "Comments of Firm Size, Market Structure and Political Influence," in *The Economics of Firm Size, Market Structure and Social Performance,* John J. Siegfried, ed. (1980).
13. A. M. Scott and M. A. Hunt, *Congress and the Lobbies* (1960), p. 6.
14. R. Bartlett, *Economic Foundations of Political Power* (1973).
15. J. J. Pincus, *Pressure Groups and Politics in Antebellum Tariffs* (1977); M. Olson, *The Logic of Collective Action* (1965).
16. See E. M. Epstein, *The Corporation in American Politics,* (1969) and "Firm Size and Structure, Market Power and Business Political Influence: A Review of the Literature," in Siegfried, note 12 *supra.*
17. See Bartlett, note 14 *supra,* and also "An Economic Theory of Political Behavior: Firm Size and Political Power," in Siegfried, note 12 *supra.* For a brief synopsis see J. J. Siegfried, "Book Review," 5 *Public Finance Quarterly* 397 (1977).
18. For a strong advocacy of this position, see *Economic Report on Corporate Mergers,* Staff Report to the Federal Trade Commission (1969).
19. See, for example, J. M. Buchanan, *The Demand and Supply of Public Goods* (1968), ch. V; A. Downs, *The Economics of Democracy* (1957); and Olson, note 15 *supra.*

20. Olson, note 5 supra.
21. For a review of the enormous literature on the concentration-profits relationship see L. W. Weiss, "The Concentration-Profits Relationship and Antitrust," in Industrial Concentration: The New Learning, H. J. Goldschmid, H. M. Mann and J. F. Weston, eds. (1974).
22. Perhaps because it is difficult, if not impossible, to obtain a bank loan to engage in political activities.
23. R. E. Caves, "Economic Models of Political Choice: Canada's Tariff Structure," 9 Canadian Journal of Economics 278 (1976).
24. Pincus, note 15 supra.
25. See, for example, L. W. Weiss, "Average Concentration Ratios and Industrial Performance," 11 Journal of Industrial Economics 233 (1963).
26. Kaysen, note 9 supra; Edwards, note 8 supra.
27. Blake, note 10 supra.
28. M. T. Hayes, "Exchange Theories of Corporate Power: A Transactional Critique," unpublished manuscript, Rutgers University (1979).
29. R. Pittman, "The Effects of Industry Concentration and Regulation on Contributions in Three 1972 U.S. Senate Campaigns," 27 Public Choice 71 (1976) and "Market Structure and Campaign Contributions," 31 Public Choice 37 (1977). T. G. Marx, "Political Consequences of Conglomerate Mergers," 8 Atlantic Economic Journal 62 (1980). For more details see T. G. Marx, "Political Consequences of Conglomerate Mergers," unpublished paper, General Motors Corp. (1980). H. M. Mann and K. McCormick, "Firm Attributes and the Propensity to Influence the Political System," in Siegfried, note 12 supra.
30. G. J. Stigler, "The Theory of Economic Regulation," 2 The Bell Journal of Economics and Management Science 3 (1971).
31. J. J. Siegfried, "The Relationship Between Economic Structure and the Effect of Political Influence: Empirical Evidence from the Federal Corporation Income Tax Program," Ph.D. dissertation, University of Wisconsin (1972).
32. C. P. McPherson, "Tariff Structures and Political Exchange," Ph.D. dissertation, University of Chicago (1972).
33. Hayes, note 28 supra.
34. Pittman (1976), note 29 supra.
35. Pittman (1977), note 29 supra.
36. Pittman (1977), note 29 supra, p. 47.
37. Pincus, note 15 supra.
38. Pincus, note 15 supra, p. 163.
39. Caves, note 23 supra.
40. L. M. Salamon and J. J. Siegfried, "Economic Power and Political Influence: The Impact of Industry Structure on Public Policy," 71 The American Political Science Review 1026 (1977).
41. C. Coolidge and G. Tullock, "Firm Size and Political Power," in Siegfried, note 12 supra.
42. Of course such selective inclusion of data generates dangers of undermining the entire hypothesis-testing methodology.
43. Mann and McCormick, note 29 supra.
44. Marx, note 29 supra.
45. C. C. Cox, "The Enforcement of Public Price Controls," unpublished paper cited in Coolidge and Tullock, note 41 supra.
46. J. T. Rose, "Aggregate Concentration in Banking and Political Leverage: A Suggested Methodology," unpublished paper (1976), cited in Epstein, note 16 supra.

Chapter 4

A Theoretical Analysis of Conglomerate Mergers

Steven N. Wiggins

INTRODUCTION

The essence of any merger, as opposed to a simple transaction in the stock of the acquired firm, is the change in the corporate control of the acquired firm. This is a costly transaction, as viewed from the eyes of the stockholders of the acquiring firm, since estimates indicate that a premium of at least 10 to 15 percent of the stock market valuation of the acquired firm must be paid to its stockholders.[1] Any valid theory of conglomerate mergers must explain why the acquiring firm is willing to pay this premium in order to gain control of the acquired firm.[2] The purpose of this chapter is to set forth in a systematic fashion the possible reasons why firms are willing to pay the observed premium. This discussion can be conveniently divided into two parts, the first viewing managers of conglomerates as not representing the interests of their stockholders.[3] The second group of theories views managers as maximizing the value of their firm to their own stockholders. Later sections of the chapter contain an analysis of the former and discussions of the latter. Let us now turn to the first group of theories of conglomerate mergers.

The author would like to thank Thomas R. Saving for helpful comments.

THEORIES WHEREIN MANAGERS DIVERGE FROM SHAREHOLDER INTERESTS

Any theory of conglomerate mergers that does not posit a means by which the value of the combined firms is higher than the value of the two firms separately owned implies that the management of the acquiring firm is diverging from the interests of its shareholders. This result follows from the premium that the shareholders of the acquired firm must be paid in order to gain control. In other words, an acquisition is a costly transaction that lowers the wealth of the shareholders of the acquiring firm by the amount of the premium paid; if there is not an offsetting benefit, the shareholders are unambiguously worse off. We will now discuss three such "theories" of conglomerate mergers that leave the shareholders of the acquiring firm worse off.

The first of these theories was proposed by Gort, who assumes that the stock market price of a firm represents the marginal portfolio valuation of the firm by owners and nonowners.[4] In other words, nonowners value the firm at less than its market price or else they would buy it at that price; the reverse is true for owners. Gort further assumes that there is an entire distribution of the owners' average valuations of the shares of the firm that stretches from the current market price to the right along the real line. A similar distribution stretches to the left of the current market price for nonowners. This distribution of valuations implies that owners' average valuations will be higher than nonowners'. Gort also assumes that investors use past information about prices, earnings, and other factors in determining the value of the firm. Finally, economic disturbances supposedly decrease the reliability with which future income streams can be predicted, increasing the variance in valuations by all parties, which implies a random change in the ordering of valuations between owners and nonowners. This increases the probability that some current owners (after the disturbance) assign less value to the firm than some nonowners, which implies a sale of the stock.

Gort's theory implies that during periods of economic disturbances there will be a higher rate of stock turnover than in other periods. As such, the theory is valid and interesting; however, it does not explain why the increase in stock transactions takes the form of a merger. In other words, he gives no reason why the acquiring firm is willing to pay a premium for control of the acquired. Thus Gort's theory, while contributing significant insight into the turnover of stock and its relation to economic disturbances, does not explain why the acquiring firm is willing to pay the premiums that are observed; therefore it is *not* a theory of conglomerate mergers.[5]

Another so-called theory of conglomerate mergers, the "bargains theory," leaves the motive for mergers unexplained.[6] According to this theory, the stock market undervalues certain firms, and the essence of a merger is that the acquiring firm buys out these "bargains." The theory resolves the payment of the premium for the acquired firm as bidding up the price to the true market value of the acquired firm. However, if a number of bargains are available, as would be suggested by the presence of merger waves, there is no reason for a firm's managers to concentrate their buying in the stock of a single firm, thereby bidding up its price. Thus this theory can explain why one firm might wish to buy the stock of another firm, acting as an investment advisor to its stockholders, but it does not explain mergers.

The final theory of mergers to be discussed here was developed by Mueller.[7] Of the theories that we have discussed to this point, it is the only legitimate one. What distinguishes it from the two theories just discussed is that it posits why the acquiring firm wishes to change the corporate identity and control of the acquired. Mueller suggests that the acquiring firm's managers have some discretionary latitude in decision making and attempt to maximize the growth of the firm subject to a minimum profit constraint.[8] One means to increase their growth rate is to acquire other firms, a strategy that can be continued as long as the premiums paid for the acquired firms are not so high as to drive the firm's profits below the minimum profit constraint. Thus conglomerate acquisitions can be viewed as a form of discretionary behavior on the part of managers.

The common thread that runs through the preceding three theories of conglomerate mergers is that the managers of the acquiring firm are engaging in behavior that is not in the best interests of their shareholders. For the first two of the three theories, no explanation of why the managers would engage in such behavior is offered. Therefore these two cannot be properly considered theories of mergers. On the other hand, Mueller's theory suggests that the managers are maximizing their own utility by engaging in this particular form of discretionary behavior.

All three of these theories imply that the value of the combined firm is unaltered by the merger. This fact, when combined with the fact that a significant premium is paid for the acquired firm, implies that the value of the acquiring firm should fall on the day that news of the merger becomes available on the stock market.[9] A significant amount of empirical evidence addresses this issue.[10] All the studies agree that the market value of the acquired firm increases significantly more than that of other comparable firms in the period during which news of the merger becomes known to the stock market.[11] Most of these studies report a roughly constant valuation for the acquiring firm during this same period.[12] This implies that investors believe a net increase in the value of the combined firms results from the merger. If one assumes that financial markets quickly assimilate information about the effect of a merger on the value of the acquiring firm and that the Mandelker and Halpern results are correct, this evidence rules out the three theories of mergers that have been discussed in this section.[13] This is particularly important for Mueller's theory since the other two have already been eliminated on theoretical grounds. Furthermore, it seems unlikely that the stock market would persist in an inefficiency of this kind, repeatedly revaluing the acquiring firm upward at the time of a merger when the revaluation should be downward. Thus, if this efficient market assumption for the stock market is justified, we must turn elsewhere for an explanation of conglomerate mergers.

STOCKHOLDER-WEALTH-MAXIMIZING THEORIES OF CONGLOMERATE MERGERS

One class of theories of conglomerate mergers assumes that the managers of the acquiring firm are acting in the best interests of their stockholders by maximizing the market value of the firm. If this is so, the combined firms must somehow be more valuable to shareholders than when the firms were operated as separate entities, given that in most mergers a significant premium is paid for the acquired firm. There are several ways in which such an increase in valuation could take place and, for ease of discussion, a number of different ways of classifying these various changes. However, since a primary concern in any discussion of mergers is policy implications, this discussion will be subdivided into those reasons for conglomerate mergers that entail a social gain and a private gain, those that result in a private gain with neither a social gain nor loss, and those that entail a private gain and a social loss.[14]

Socially Desirable Reasons for Conglomerate Mergers

If a conglomerate merger results in the net creation of wealth to society, it is said to have socially desirable consequences. This can happen in several ways, all of which revolve around taking certain transactions out of markets and placing them in a hierarchical setting. This discussion is similar in spirit to a great deal of recent work on the theory of the firm. According to this modern literature on the emergence of firms, many transactions can be handled more efficiently in a hierarchical (or organizational) setting than they can be handled by markets.[15] As a result, firms emerge that bring both of the parties to the transaction into one hierarchical setting in order to reduce the transactions costs of exchange. This theory has been used to explain vertical mergers and, as will be seen below, it also offers potential for explaining some conglomerate mergers.[16] However, it must also be noted that these potentialities are, as yet, in the formative stage and the discussion will reflect that fact. The primary reason that transactions costs may explain conglomerate mergers is that markets may be quite inefficient, relative to hierarchies, in handling certain economic transactions. These inefficiencies arise from a variety of sources that vary with the type of transaction under consideration, as will be well illustrated in the examples below.

A primary way in which net social wealth can be improved by a merger is if it results in the transfer of superior technology from the acquiring firm to the acquired firm. However, since there can be (and are in some cases) markets for technological innovations, the question is whether a hierarchical arrangement would be more efficient than a market for handling certain of these transactions. A simple example will illustrate the inefficiencies of the market in at least some such cases.

To begin, assume that the acquiring firm is the monopolistic possessor of a cost-reducing technological advance. For simplicity, also assume that the developer has no market power other than the cost advantage conferred by the innovation. In this case the obvious fair rental rate for the innovation is the cost saving that results from the innovation. In order for this innovation to be transferred through the use of markets, the two parties must agree on the value of the innovation and enter into a binding contract that results in the innovator being paid the dollar amount of the cost saving obtained by the licensee through the use of the innovation. Such a contract can be written at two times: *ex ante*—before the licensee has used the innovation and *ex post*—after the licensee has observed the cost savings.

Ex ante, the only information on cost saving is the experience of the innovator, which, in the case at hand, will have been in a separate, though presumably related, field. Since the rental fee is contingent upon these cost savings, the innovator has an incentive to overstate them. By so doing the innovator can capture a portion of the returns to the licensee's *existing* fixed capital.[17] Such possibilities make an *ex ante* agreement undesirable for the licensee.

Ex post, the renter has had an opportunity to observe the actual cost saving; this removes the problem discussed in the previous paragraph. However, in the *ex post* negotiations the licensee has an incentive to understate the cost saving and thereby reduce the rental fee. In addition, it will be very costly, if not impossible, for the innovator to observe the actual cost saving enjoyed. The possibility also exists that, *ex post,* the licensee will be able to circumvent the patent of the innovator (this is especially likely if, as assumed, he has a working knowledge of the innovation) and make no payment for the innovation.

This is a classic problem of information impactedness. For either of the times during which the contract can be written, only one of the parties to the contract has available information that is crucial to the agreement. This makes a contract a very unwieldy instrument subject to large "haggling" costs. In this case, the natural solution to the problem is for the innovator to buy out the potential licensee and adopt the innovation in the newly acquired firm.

However, in the case of a conglomerate merger, is it likely that there will be the potential for significant efficiency gains from the transfer of technology? The answer appears to be yes. While it is true that by definition conglomerate mergers will not involve firms that produce the same products, at least not for sale in the same markets, many cost-saving innovations developed in a particular area would probably have applications well beyond a narrow economic market. One potential overlap in technology across industries would be in the marketing area, which is well illustrated by the Phillip Morris–Miller Brewing merger. Phillip Morris transferred its cigarette marketing technology to the beer industry with spectacular success. In addition, since many closely related but noncompeting markets enjoy similarities in production techniques, there are many instances in which a production innovation can be successfully transferred across industries. Finally, superior decision-making capabilities in one economic area are often applicable in related but noncompeting fields. For example, a particular manager (or management team) may be particularly efficient and fully capable of handling a firm much larger than the largest firm in a given industry (i.e., unexploited economies of scale are associated with a given manager). These efficiencies can be further exploited by an expansion of the firm through a merger.

In back of these theoretical arguments and possibilities lie some interesting, though preliminary, empirical observations. Gorecki presents empirical evidence showing that conglomerate firms tend to diversify within their own two-digit and three-digit industry area.[18] Presumably this empirical finding is in some way related to the theoretical arguments that have been discussed here. In addition, Kahn, in his classic study of the chemical industry, shows that successful chemical firms are well diversified across various chemical submarkets. He attributes this diversification to advantages in exploiting the product of research in a wide variety of areas.[19] It must be emphasized that, while clearly suggesting that technology transfer may be an important element in certain conglomerate mergers, these empirical results are only suggestive. More work needs to be done in this area to determine accurately the role of this factor in the broad sweep of conglomerate mergers and waves.

A second efficiency gain that could result from a conglomerate merger is the replacement of inefficient management. Such inefficiencies could result from poor planning, outdated decision techniques, or managerial pursuit of goals that are inconsistent with stockholder wealth maximization. Such inefficiencies can persist in a widely held corporation because stockholders face a significant public goods problem in monitoring the activities of their management and staying informed about the best current practices in the industry. However, a raider can avoid this public goods problem (or at least reduce it) by buying the entire corporation.

If the existing management deviates sufficiently far from stockholder wealth maximization to cover the raider's transactions costs, one would expect a raid to occur, the result being an increase in net social wealth through an increase in the efficiency of the operation of the firm. In many respects this theory resembles the management transfer argument discussed above, except that in the present case it is assumed that the superior management and production strategies are widely known and practiced and the takeover target has failed to adopt these practices.

A third efficiency gain that can be associated with conglomerate mergers is an increase in the real allocational efficiency of resource use. Assume that there is a firm experiencing high net positive cash flows.[20] Assume also that there is a low expected return to current investment in the given industry, but that in other industries the expected returns to investment are high while current earnings and production are low. In this case shareholders of the firm in question may receive significant returns if the managers transfer the current high cash flows across fields to areas where investment opportunities are greatest.

There are two basic issues regarding the transfer of these resources through a hierarchical arrangement as opposed to the use of capital markets. The first is whether the firm can internally generate the signals concerning the efficient use of capital more cheaply than capital markets can. The second is whether there are private incentives to use internal resource control rather than capital markets. As regards the former, opinion is mixed. Many economists believe that capital markets are efficient at providing capital to worthwhile new ventures and some empirical evidence exists to support this position. On the other hand, there is persistent evidence that small equity and debt issues are consistently sold by investment banks at a large premium over the underwriting price which the firm receives from the sale of the issue. This suggests a large transactions cost in the generation of capital for the affected firms. Thus, there are two sets of results that are at odds with each other and the only way to resolve the issue is for more research to be carried out in the area.

However, regardless of true efficiency gains to the internal reallocation of resources within the firm, there are clear-cut private incentives due to the differential tax treatment of capital gains and straight income.[21] Since capital gains are taxed at a lower rate, there is a private incentive for firms to invest their shareholders' money internally. This will persist as long as internal capital investment decisions are not sufficiently less efficient than the market to outweigh the tax savings.

Another efficiency issue of a similar nature would be if the current high production area were expected to experience a decline in production in the future. If such a decline came about, it would be necessary to transfer factors of production out of the declining area and into other areas. If it is costly to use the market for such a transaction in secondhand factors, then it may well be more efficient to carry out these transactions within the firm. Furthermore, inefficiencies in the secondhand market could easily arise since there will be asymmetric information in such a market. In other words, there will be certain pieces of equipment of high quality and others of low quality, and it will be difficult for the market to function in this situation. This is the standard Akerlof "lemons" market problem.[22]

This problem may be particularly important in the case of management and other personnel in an industry that is expected to decline. If a decline is widely expected and there are transactions costs associated with finding a new job after being laid off, then potential employees will require sufficient additional compensation to offset these costs. One would expect such costs to be substantial, since it is very difficult for an outsider to evaluate the true reason for the termination of any individual employee in such a situation. In other words, it will be almost impossible for a potential new employer to distinguish between employees fired as a result of unsatisfactory work and those who had to be laid off because of declining production. However, if a firm owns a subsidiary in a rapidly expanding area, then it will be possible to transfer employees horizontally through the hierarchy. Furthermore, since this will reduce the expected transactions costs to employees, the firm can reduce current compensation and capture the efficiency gain.

It is difficult to determine how widespread such reasons for conglomerate mergers are, but there are a few examples worth mentioning. The first is the current spate of oil company mergers with coal and other energy-related companies. The transfer of resources as a possible reason for these mergers is strengthened when it is noted that expected future declines in oil companies' production may be matched very closely by expansion of activity in these other energy fields. Further, one would expect the factors of production, especially human capital, to be relatively easily transferred across these areas. Another potential example of this motive for merger is Swift and Company (Esmark), which diversified out of a fairly narrow line that is declining as its newer lines are prospering. These examples are only suggestive and further empirical research seems warranted.

Another efficiency reason for conglomerate mergers is due to diversification. If two firms have less than perfectly correlated income streams, then shareholders' risk can be lessened if the income streams are combined in a portfolio. However, this result is not, per se, a reason for mergers because shareholders can accomplish this by buying the shares of the two firms themselves; this also avoids payment of a large premium with the merger. In order for diversification to be a valid reason for mergers, one must introduce either debt or the potential for financial distress. The potential for savings through an increase in the debt equity ratio centers around taxation and the redistribution of income resulting from tax savings; this will be discussed in the next section.

Turning to financial distress, assume that there is a nonzero probability that the firm will go into reorganization in a particular period.[23] Further, define reorganization as a state of the world in which there are insufficient liquid assets to pay off current obligations, but distinguish reorganization from bankruptcy in that there is an excess of assets to liabilities. Finally, assume that reorganization entails a significant fixed cost. In this case, the stockholders of the firm will experience an increase in wealth as a result of a merger that diversifies their income stream, since the reduction in variance will reduce the probability of incurring the fixed cost of reorganization.[24]

The mechanism of operation for this social benefit is that it may be difficult for financial markets to distinguish between failing firms and those suffering from a liquidity crisis. Further, it may be more efficient to convey such information through hierarchies than through markets. This would be true, for example, if employees in a failing branch hope or desire to continue working for the overall firm independent of the health of the individual operating unit.[25] Finally, to the degree that financial markets are unable to distinguish between firms suffering a liquidity crisis and failing firms, the former group will effectively subsidize the latter in the amounts paid for short-term funds, and this will generate inefficiencies.

The final efficiency reason for conglomerate mergers is possible economies of scale in advertising, research and development, or both. This argument is distinguished from the transfer of superior marketing or production technology previously discussed in that the current argument implies *economies of scale* in the development or use of particular techniques. Relatively little evidence exists supporting scale economies either in the effectiveness of advertisements or pecuniary economies in their purchase.[26] As to potential of scale economies in R & D, it is difficult to determine the exact importance of this factor. Scherer presents evidence that these are not important.[27] Both of these issues bear closer examination.

Socially Neutral Reasons for Conglomerate Mergers

In this section we discuss several potential reasons for conglomerate mergers that have socially neutral (at least to a first approximation) consequences. The common motive that underlies these reasons for merger is a redistributive one. The first group to which we will turn involves tax reasons for merger or a redistribution of income from society as a whole to the owners of the firm. This can be considered socially neutral as long as the real resources of society are not used in the pursuit of these tax savings. Throughout this subsection we will assume that the distribution of earnings of the individual firms is unchanged by the merger. This is not to say that such changes will not occur contemporaneously. Rather the assumption permits us to focus attention on the changes that occur because the earnings streams of the two firms are combined and on the private advantages that might accrue to such a combination.

The first form of tax savings that can occur from a merger becomes possible because of two peculiarities in the tax laws.[28] First, dividend payments are not subject to the same tax treatment as capital gains and, second, debt payments are not subject to the corporate income tax. The former condition encourages firms to reinvest profits rather than pay them out as dividends, while the latter encourages the firm to increase its debt equity ratio. Let us examine how the firm could pursue both tax-saving goals simultaneously. Let us assume that there exist a series of investment projects of equal variance and expected return and that these make up the investment opportunities set for the firm. In this case the firm should invest in those projects that are the least correlated with its current portfolio of projects, since this will mean that they will contribute as little as possible to the overall variance of the firm's earnings stream. Further, the lesser the variance in the firm's earnings stream (for a given expected value), the higher the firm's debt-equity ratio can be with a constant default risk for leaders. Since default risk is thought to be the primary factor limiting firms' attempts to increase the debt-equity ratio, this strategy will maximize the firm's debt and thereby its tax saving. Finally, the natural choice from the investment opportunities set may well be a conglomerate merger since one would expect the earnings of a conglomerate acquisition to be less correlated with a given firm's earnings than many (if not most) other investments that are available. This is especially true if these alternative investments are in the same, rather than different, lines of business.

A second tax-related reason for mergers is a tax-loss carry-forward for income tax purposes. If a firm is in a failing industry (or if its fixed costs force losses but average revenue is greater than average variable cost), then losses become an asset that can be sold with the firm as a whole. Alternatively, the firm can buy other firms that make positive profits and pay lower taxes on their earnings because of its own losses.

The final example of conglomerate mergers for motives that are socially neutral is the Mueller theory of mergers discussed earlier. Since Mueller suggests that mergers take place because managers prefer to manage larger, faster growing corporations, and since they are willing to pay a larger premium for these firms, there is a redistribution of wealth from the shareholders of the acquiring firm to the shareholders of the acquired firm. However, this must be considered a socially neutral reason for merger, since there is no net change in social wealth as a result of the merger.[29]

Socially Undesirable Reasons for Conglomerate Mergers

We now turn to the potentially undesirable motives for conglomerate mergers. These reasons for merger involve a change in the competitive structure of the market as a result of the introduction of the conglomerate firm into the market. Such changes could happen in a variety of ways, and we will examine several of the more obvious possibilities.

To begin, a conglomerate merger might change the competitive structure of the individual market if the conglomerate firm engaged in any of a number of anticompetitive activities. The list of such activities includes reciprocal dealing, exclusive dealing, tie-in-sales, and predatory pricing (cross-subsidization). It is obvious that a conglomerate merger would increase the potential for such activities in a market. What is not so obvious is whether these activities will result in adverse consequences. The best available discussion of these issues is found in Lorie and Halpern.[30]

To begin, Lorie and Halpern establish that a necessary condition for reciprocal dealing to have adverse effects on the competitive structure of the market is that at least one of the firms involved possess unexploited market power. In this case the possessor of the power can force the purchase of goods from a newly acquired subsidiary at more than the competitive price. An example of this would be a monopolist forbidden to price discriminate by Robinson-Patman prohibitions. In this case, it could extract additional surplus from the purchaser through the use of a reciprocal dealing agreement.

Another form of anticompetitive behavior that may result from a conglomerate merger is an exclusive dealing arrangement or a tie-in sale. And, once again, Lorie and Halpern argue that for these weapons to be useful, one of the involved firms must possess some unexploited monopoly power. The most commonly cited (potential) example of exclusive dealing comes from the Procter and Gamble-

Clorox merger case in which it was argued that Procter and Gamble could use its monopoly power with grocery stores to force them to abandon other kinds of bleach. For tie-in sales, if purchases of the tied item vary systematically with consumer surplus for the monopolistically supplied item, it is obviously possible to extract consumer surplus by noncompetitive pricing of the tied item. However, for both of these cases it is obvious that the monopolist (or equivalently for a monopsonist) must be prohibited from full exercise of his extant monopoly power, and that tying or exclusive dealing agreement permits a fuller exercise of that power. In neither of these cases has it been empirically established that such agreements can be effective at more than redistributing sales in a competitive market.

Another potentially anticompetitive effect of conglomerate mergers is predatory pricing. Predatory pricing may be defined as pricing below rivals' costs (and perhaps below one's own as well), in order to drive competitors out of the market and subsequently raise price. Gaskins has shown this to be an optimal strategy under certain conditions.[31] However, a necessary condition is the existence of barriers to new entry in the period of high prices. And while the theoretical case for such behavior has been clearly established, remarkably few instances of it have been reported.[32] In fact, a significant number of supposed cases of predatory pricing have been clearly refuted by careful economic analysis.[33] Thus, while we must conclude that predatory pricing is an interesting theoretical possibility, there is insufficient evidence for major policy actions based upon such potentialities.

The common denominator of the above methods of the above list of anticompetitive effects of conglomerate mergers is that they should all result in an increase in market concentration.[34] Fortunately, there is some recent empirical evidence examining the effect of mergers on market concentration.[35] Goldberg analyzes the effects of conglomerate mergers on both four- and eight-firm concentration ratios in the industry of the acquired. His results indicate that there is no positive relationship.[36] To the extent that these results are reliable, one would have to question the empirical importance of the above anti-competitive effects of conglomerate mergers since they imply increases in market concentration.

The above theories of conglomerate mergers hypothesize specific overt action on the part of the conglomerate firm. Another class of theories can be developed by focusing attention on the responses of the other firms in the market to actions of the conglomerate firm. The motivation of these theories comes from basic oligopoly theory, the only universal result of which is that the pricing structure of the market (and the degree to which it diverges from competitive pricing) depends crucially on how firms in the market *believe* other market participants will respond to their actions. These so-called "reaction functions" form the heart of the differences of the various oligopoly theories and their results. As a consequence, if the reaction functions of firms are changed in a market wherein sellers have some discretion over price (in other words, *any* market other than the literal perfectly competitive market), the pricing and output behavior of the firm in the market would also change. Furthermore, the assumption that a large conglomerate enterprise could buy out a firm in a market and not change the way in which competitors believe the firm would react to various competitive strategies seems an exceedingly strong one to me. However, without such an assumption, it follows directly that the entrance of a conglomerate firm into a market will change the competitive behavior of the market. Following are a few brief speculations about how such behavior might change.

To begin, the conglomerate firm becomes a natural price leader in the market. Other firms, *ceteris paribus*, should see a conglomerate as more able, and possibly more willing, to enforce oligopolistic discipline. In addition, one would expect other firms to be less inclined to use overt means, such as a major advertising campaign, to erode the leader's market share, although secret price-cutting and other such activities might become more prevalent. Finally, if the conglomerate was viewed as a likely entrant into the marketplace before its purchase of an existing firm, this should also change the competitive structure of the market.

The final possibility for anticompetitive behavior resulting from conglomerate mergers is the "mutual forebearance" or "spheres of influence" hypothesis. The basis for this theory is that the concentration of sellers within individual markets is only one aspect of economic concentration. In particular, if large firms come into frequent contact with one another across markets this can affect the conduct and performance of the individual markets independent of the concentration levels in any particular market. For example, assume that firm A has significant power in market X and that firm B is a potentially significant factor in the market but is currently earning low profits. Further, assume that firms C and D correspond respectively to A and B in market Y. Finally, if there is a merger between C and B as well as one between D and A, one could easily imagine that the competitive aggressiveness of both "fringe firms" would be less than if the mergers had never occurred. This is because both "conglomerates" realize that potential gains in one market could be offset by losses in another. Furthermore, such possibilities seem to be no less theoretically valid than traditional oligopoly theory as applied to the individual market.

Thus the issue is not theoretical validity but empirical importance. However, there is only sketchy empirical evidence on this issue. Heggestad and Rhoades show that there is greater relative stability in market share in banking markets when leading firms have multiple contacts across markets.[37] And, while the theoretical implications of their empirical results are not clear-cut, their work clearly suggests this as a fruitful area for further research. In addition, Gorecki indicates that conglomerates specialize in certain areas, suggesting a concern for these intermarket linkages.[38]

SUMMARY AND CONCLUSIONS

In the preceding sections we have put forth a number of potential theories of conglomerate mergers. Some, particularly those in section 2, seem inconsistent with economic or financial theory, or both. In that vein, Gort's theory and the "bargains theory" are not true economic theories of mergers since they fail to explain the economic return—either public or private—that accrues to those engaging in a costly acquisition. Therefore they cannot be considered legitimate theories of conglomerate mergers. However, it was also pointed out that Gort's theory is a potentially valuable aid in the explanation of the timing of the consummation of mergers that are undertaken for another reason, and this is a significant contribution.

The first legitimate theory of conglomerate mergers reviewed was that of Mueller. He indicates that managers undertake mergers for reasons that diverge from stockholder wealth maximization. In particular he suggests that managers are maximizing the growth rate of the firm and that one way in which they can accomplish this is to engage in mergers. The crucial distinction between the above theories and Mueller's theory is that Mueller provides a reason for firms to engage in the economically costly merger transaction.

Theories that explain mergers as resulting in an increase in private wealth were then discussed. These were divided into reasons that resulted in a net creation of social wealth from the merger, those that left net social wealth unchanged but redistributed it (primarily through tax savings), and those wherein private pursuit of a greater share of social wealth reduced the total wealth available. In all three cases, a number of theoretically valid theories of mergers were examined.

Given the current wave of these mergers, the implications of these results for public policy are quite important. A wide variety of potential explanations for conglomerate mergers has been discussed. And the reasons discussed imply quite different appropriate responses to the conglomerates "problem" by the antitrust authorities and Congress. Conglomerates should not be discouraged on economoic grounds if they emerge primarily to reduce market transactions costs. However, if these mergers are primarily intended to generate and/or exploit market power, the opposite policy response is appropriate. Further work is warranted to distinguish empirically among these possibilities.

NOTES

1. A number of empirical studies have reported a premium of approximately this size. These include R. Smiley, "Tender Offers, Transactions Costs, and the Theory of the Firm," *The Review of Economics and Statistics* (1976); G. Mandelker, "Risk and Return: The Case of Merging Firms," *Journal of Financial Economics* 303 (1974); P. J. Halpern, "Empirical Estimates of the Amount and Distribution of Gains to Companies in Mergers," *Journal of Business* (October 1973); and M. Frith, "The Profitability of Takeovers and Mergers," *The Economic Journal* 316 (June 1979). More recent estimates indicate that this premium may be closer to 30 percent.
2. The central role of the change in control of the acquired firm cannot be overemphasized since it is at the very heart of the phenomenon to be explained.
3. A necessary condition for such behavior is not only the existence of significant stockholder monitoring costs (and/or a public goods problem in monitoring) but also transactions costs associated with a takeover raid.
4. M. Gort, "An Economic Disturbance Theory of Mergers," *Quarterly Journal of Economics* (November 1969).
5. It appears that Gort's theory may also offer insight into the *timing* of mergers, but the explanation of *why* the change in ownership takes the form of a merger must come from another source.
6. The bargains theory of mergers is distinct (at least in this paper) from theories wherein the acquired firm is not valued at its full potential because of mismanagement. The bargains theory simply states that firms are undervalued because of imperfect investor information.
7. D. C. Mueller, "A Theory of Conglomerate Mergers," *Quarterly Journal of Economics* (1969).
8. The minimum profit must be high enough so that the present value of the difference between minimum and maximum profits is less than the transactions costs of a takeover.
9. This result is obvious for Mueller's theory. For the Gort theory and the "bargains theory" the result also follows unless the stock market as a whole revalues the acquired firm upward on the day of purchase by exactly the amount of the premium paid. However, this result implies that the other actors in the market effectively

suspend their own judgment of the value of the acquired firm on the date of purchase and accept whatever value the acquiring firm places upon it. This would be very peculiar.

10. See Mandelker, Smiley, Halpern, and Firth, note 1 *supra.*

11. In general this period should stretch backward in time from the announcement date of the merger to the point when news of the possible merger began to become available to the market (often, approximately 6 months) and forward in time to the date on which the market views the probability of the merger going through as one.

12. For example, see Mandelker and Halpern, note 1 *supra;* Firth, note 1*supra,* using 1U.K. data, finds a decrease in the value of the acquiring firm. However, there are errors in his estimation of the acquiring firm's B's which bias downward his estimation of the change in their value, which may be the source of his results. (Compare Firth, note 1 *supra,* p. 319, with Mandelker, note 1 *supra,* pp. 309-10, 321-24).

13. Mueller presents some evidence that bears on this issue in his paper in this volume. It should be noted that his results show an increase in the value of the acquiring firm *in the 6 months either side of the announcement date.* This suggests that stock market participants believe that the merger will lead to an increase in the value of the firm. Thus, we are back to the condition described above: if the market is efficient at assimilating this kind of information, there is a net creation of private wealth by the merger.

14. Another natural way to divide the discussion would be to discuss those reasons for mergers that shift the distribution of the earnings of the combined companies so as to make them more valuable and those that result in the combined earnings stream being more valuable simply because the two firms are combined. The latter group of reasons center on financial gains to mergers.

15. See O. Williamson, "Markets and Hierarchies: Some Elementary Considerations," *American Economic Review* (1973) and *Markets and Hierarchies: Analysis and Antitrust Implications* (1975) and A. Alchian and H. Demsetz, "Production, Information Costs, and Economic Organization," *American Economic Review* (December 1972) for recent developments in this area. Much of this literature can be traced back to the seminal work by R. H. Coase ("The Nature of the Firm," *Economics* (November 1937)) and is surveyed in parts of Marris and Mueller (R. Marris and D. Mueller, "The Corporation and Competition," *Journal of Economic Literature* (March 1980)).

16. See O. Williamson ("The Vertical Integration of Production: Market Failure Considerations," *American Economic Review* (May 1971)) for an analysis of vertical integration that emphasizes transactions costs of using markets for exchange.

17. Such overpricing will cause the licensee to observe a capital loss which can be no greater than the combined value of capital already committed to the industry (or the transactions costs of transferring it to another industry) and any rents and/or quasi-rents that he expects to earn in the future.

18. P. Gorecki, "An Inter-Industry Analysis of Diversification in the U.K. Manufacturing Sector," *Journal of Industrial Economics* (December 1975).

19. A. E. Kahn, "The Chemical Industry," in *The Structure of American Industry,* W. Adams, ed. (1961).

20. These cash flows are assumed to result from a normal return to capital previously invested and/or windfall gains associated with shifts in market factors.

21. It should be noted that the mention of differential tax treatments in this section dealing with efficiency gains to mergers does not imply that there are gains to this form of tax avoidance. These incentives for merger are properly classified as

socially neutral reasons, as will be discussed in the next section. They are briefly discussed here solely for expositional convenience.

22. See G. A. Akerlof, "The Market for 'Lemons': Quality Uncertainty and the Market Mechanism," *Quarterly Journal of Economics* (August 1970).

23. The reader is encouraged to consult the paper by Monroe in this volume. The conclusions reached there and those described here are different because she does not consider the case of reorganization but concentrates on the case of bankruptcy.

24. If one introduces the possibility of bankruptcy (defined as a state in which assets of one of the firm's assets are less than its liabilities) into the above model, the story is greatly complicated. This is because in the case of bankruptcy the benefit of the reduction in variance goes to the bondholder as is discussed in the paper by Monroe. If both possibilities are introduced into the same model it would appear that both stockholders and bondholders will share the benefits of diversification.

25. It should be noted that managers should be quite averse to reorganization since being forced out as the manager of a reorganized firm often eliminates jobs, thereby, presumably, reducing one's human capital and forcing one to incur the search costs associated with finding a new job.

26. The interested reader should consult R. Schmalensee, *The Economics of Advertising* (1972), pp. 228ff, on this issue.

27. F. M. Scherer, "Firm Size, Market Structure, Opportunity, and the Output of Patented Inventions," *American Economic Review* (1965).

28. This is a summary of the discussion of these issues found in R. Sherman, "How Tax Policy Induces Conglomerate Mergers," *National Tax Journal* (1972).

29. There are two conditions under which such mergers do not lead to socially neutral results. The first occurs if the purchasing firm is less efficient in the management of the acquired firm than the previous management. The second occurs if the growth-maximizing management of the acquiring firm invests the resources of the acquired firm in new capital spending projects that have an expected return that is less than the competitive return.

30. J. H. Lorie and P. Halpern, "Conglomerates: The Rhetoric and the Evidence," *Journal of Law and Economics* (April 1970).

31. D. Gaskins, "Optimal Pricing by Dominant Firms," PH.D. dissertation. Univ. of Michigan (1970).

32. For some examples of predatory pricing see B. S. Yamey, "Predatory Price Cutting: Notes and Comments," *Journal of Law and Economics* (1972).

33. See M. A. Adelman, *A & P: A Study in Price-Cost Behavior and Public Policy* (1959); J. McGee, "Predatory Price Cutting: The Standard Oil (N.J.) Case," *Journal of Law and Economics* (1958); and K. Elzinga, "Predatory Pricing: The Case of the Gunpowder Trust," *Journal of Law and Economics* (1970).

34. Other potentially anticompetitive effects of conglomerate mergers that do not result in an increase in concentration will be discussed below.

35. See Lawrence G. Goldberg, "Conglomerate Mergers and Concentration Ratios," *Review of Economics and Statistics* (1974), pp. 303–309.

36. It should be noted that Goldberg uses a short time frame for his analysis and it would be desirable to use a longer period since increases in concentration would not occur quickly. In addition, because his regression equations are very simply specified, they are difficult to interpret.

37. A. Heggestad and S. Rhoades, "Multi-Market Interdependence and Local Market Competition in Banking," *Review of Economics and Statistics* (1978), pp. 523–532.

38. Gorecki, "Inter-Industry Analysis."

Chapter 5

The Case Against Conglomerate Mergers

Dennis C. Mueller

The case against conglomerate mergers is that there is no strong case for them. Many mergers do not appear to be consummated with the intent to achieve efficiency gains. True, there are many hypotheses regarding the kinds of efficiencies mergers might achieve, but for the most part they are subject to logical counter-arguments or second-best strategies for improving aggregate economic efficiency, or they are inconsistent with the available empirical evidence. Moreover, whatever the motivation behind mergers, they usually do not have the effect of improving economic efficiency. It is impossible to prove from the available empirical evidence that the performance of either the individual merging firms or the economy at large is significantly better as a result of all the mergers that have occurred in this country.

In this chapter I first present a theory of why mergers occur without promise of market power or efficiency increases, and then indicate the advantages of this theory over some of its more popular alternatives. Next I examine some empirical evidence regarding the efficiency effects of mergers. Finally, I comment on how all of this amounts to a "case against conglomerate mergers."

MERGERS AND THE LIFE CYCLE
OF FIRMS

Most firms come into existence to exploit some innovative idea, to fill some market interstice. If the innovation is a good one, the company thrives and grows until the gap in the market has been filled. As this product market matures, new markets will have to be entered to sustain growth. As Schumpeter depicted it, the corporation can grow (survive) indefinitely only by continually innovating.[1] The successful, mature corporation is one whose managers can "manage" innovation and thereby sustain a continual flow of new products and processes.[2]

Alternatively, the mature corporation may choose to acquire its "new" products and processes from outside, that is, to engage in mergers. When additional products are acquired through the purchase of established firms, however, assets are acquired whose value is already established in the markets for corporate debt and equity. If these markets are efficient, these prices should fully anticipate all future profit streams. If the acquiring firm's profits are not to suffer, it must do something with the acquired firm's assets that improve its profitability—for example, enhance its market power or internal efficiency.

I shall not review all the hypotheses concerning mergers and efficiency or market power, since this has been done elsewhere.[3] One hypothesis, which is quite close to the life-cycle theory, must be mentioned, however. Several writers, most notably J. Fred Weston and Oliver Williamson, have argued that mergers may be the most efficient way to redeploy capital from mature corporations with low internal investment opportunities to young(er) companies with high(er) internal rates of return.[4] Since the higher expected returns of the younger firm are already reflected in its market price, this argument still relies on some extra profits being generated after the merger. One possibility is that the mature firm's management team is highly efficient, and that a loss would be suffered if it had to be disbanded.

But managers have incentives to preserve their team, to maintain and expand their organization, even when its internal efficiency is not superior and is perhaps even inferior to that of other organizations.[5] Managers can be expected to resist a slow-growth, gradual decline trajectory for their company even when following this path would be in the best interests of their stockholders and society. Thus evidence that mature firms engage most frequently in mergers is consistent with both a managerial, life-cycle view and a neoclassical, redeployment-of-capital hypothesis.[6] To distinguish between the two, additional predictions and observations are needed.

The managerial-growth hypothesis is one of a family sharing the following assumptions: (1) managers have discretion to pursue goals in conflict with their stockholders; (2) this pursuit is constrained by the threat of takeover should the firm's share price fall too far; and (3) the means to pursue these goals are the company's internal cash flows. The various theories differ according to the assumed use to which these funds are put, for example, expansion of sales, staff and emoluments, security. The life-cycle, growth hypothesis assumes that these funds are invested to achieve growth (avoid decline) even when some of the funds could have been more profitably redeployed by stockholders elsewhere. The acquisition of companies at prices substantially above their current market value is an obvious potential form of this growth-oriented investment.

Several additional points must be made. First, the theory assumes managerial discretion, not the separation of ownership and control. Widespread stock ownership does in general provide managers freedom from owner control to pursue managerial goals. But the converse does not necessarily follow. Concentration of share ownership need not result in the maximization of stockholder welfare. If a large fraction of shares is held by management, its discretionary power is increased, for the probability of a successful takeover is reduced. While the managers' pecuniary interests are more closely tied to the stockholders' interests in this situation, the costs of an extra dollar of on-the-job consumption are still shared, and the benefits accrue entirely to management. If managers with large shareholdings favor their goals qua-managers to their interests as stockholders, their companies may exhibit the most extreme form of managerial behavior of all.[7] Thus, one cannot simply dismiss the hypothesis that the managers of acquisition-oriented conglomerates with poor performance records were pursuing growth at the expense of share price, simply by pointing to the large shareholdings of their managers, as some are wont to do.[8]

In the absence of full information on the part of stockholders, any exogenous event that raises a company's share price should reduce the threat of takeover and increase management's discretion to pursue its own goals. A general rise in stock prices may make managers more willing to undertake mergers, because the rise in prices may offset any negative impact a merger's announcement has on the acquiring company's shares, and/or because in the bullish environment of a stock market upswing, news of the merger might be treated more favorably than in a normal or bear market situation. Thus, the danger to the acquiring firm that an adverse price reaction in the announcement of a merger will result in a significant increase in the threat of takeover is likely to be smaller in a rising stock market.

Several researchers have observed an increase in the returns earned on acquiring company shares prior to a merger.[9] While these unexplained increases in returns are too far in advance of the mergers to be explained by them, perhaps the increases explain the mergers. An unanticipated improvement in the performance of a company's common shares should reduce the threat of takeover and free a management to engage in acquisitions it otherwise could not engage in. Note that there is no reason under the neoclassical theory why an improvement in the acquiring firm's position should precipitate a merger. An acquiring company's shareholders will benefit from a merger only if the performance of the acquiring company or the acquired company is improved *through the merger*. Thus, any neoclassical explanation for mergers must depend on the characteristics of the acquired company or the combination of the two firms. Changes in the acquiring firm's position alone or the market's view of its position cannot make an otherwise unprofitable merger profitable.

The important role cash flow plays in the managerial theory is not generally appreciated and is a possible source of empirical validation of the two theories. As Dale Jorgenson has repeatedly emphasized, a cash flow model of investment is inconsistent with the neoclassical theory.[10] The neoclassical cost of capital is the rate of return the shareholders can earn on investments (e.g., stocks in other firms) of comparable risk.[11] The cost of using internal and fund flows to finance investment is the same as for new debt or equity. Internal fund flows are not relatively "cheap" in the seventies any more than new debt or equity was relatively "cheap" in the sixties. Thus, the level of merger activity in the seventies, and the heavy reliance on internal cash flows to finance acquisitions, at least relative to the sixties, cannot be easily explained as some shift in the neoclassical cost of capital.

Nor can one sustain the argument that mergers are taking place today because the assets of many firms are undervalued. The capital asset pricing literature teaches us that the capital market is efficient in using the available information about a firm's prospects to price its securities.[12] If market values are low today relative to book values, that is because the market does not expect firms to do well in the future, a prediction not without some justification. Assets are not undervalued today, any more than they were overvalued in the sixties when market values were way above book values.[13] Managers can increase the value of their company's shares through an acquisition only if they know something the market—and the other firm's managers and their own stockholders—do not, or if they can do something with these assets that the incumbent managers cannot. But these explanations for mergers are valid at any time. Superior talent or omniscience on the part of acquiring firms' managers can always justify a merger.

A related argument one sometimes hears is that mergers are occurring today because it is cheaper to buy a given bundle of assets as an ongoing firm than as new capital equipment. As a statement about relative prices of capital this may be true, but as an explanation of mergers it begs the question. If a company is selling for less than the replacement value of its assets, then the market does not think that the purchase of these assets at book value would provide a normal return on investment. The company's managers paid too much for them. Why, given this evaluation by the market, is the acquiring firm's management committed to acquiring assets in this industry? Do they know something the market does not know, or are they perhaps pursuing another goal?

In contrast to the neoclassical theory, the managerial-growth hypothesis is quite compatible with the evidence of the seventies. A growth-oriented management with excess cash will purchase additional assets, even at expected returns below its stockholders' opportunity costs, whereas a neoclassical management will not. Evidence supporting a cash flow theory of investment is evidence consistent with the managerial theory of the firm.[14]

The expected returns on internal investment in new capital, R&D, and advertising appear to have fallen during the seventies. The most vivid evidence of this is the value the market places on existing tangible and intangible capital stocks. Cash flows have not fallen so dramatically, however; thus, they are large relative to internal investment opportunities. Under neoclassical theory this should lead to greater dividends or stock repurchases if taxes are to be minimized,[15] but neither of these contributes to growth. The return to be earned on acquiring another firm has not fallen relatively, however; it is what it always has been—the normal return being earned in the market less the cost of transacting a merger. Thus, mergers have increased in attractiveness relative to internal investment, and those managerial firms that are fortunate enough to have ample cash flows will use them to acquire other companies.

Let me close this section with a prediction that follows directly from the discussion. Petroleum firms now dominate the 10-, 50-, and 100-largest lists. Known reserves and likely new finds will not allow these companies to maintain these relative size positions. Petroleum companies must diversify or decline. Currently, however, they are blessed with substantial cash flows. Thus, we have companies in the very mature stages of their product life cycle, with large internal fund flows. The managerial theory predicts heavy merger activity by these companies. I do not see, however, why the combination of mature product cycle and large cash flows should make petroleum managers particularly expert at spotting "undervalued" firms or *managing* companies outside the petroleum area. Thus, I would not expect to see heavy merger activity in this industry on the basis of neoclassical motives.

THE EFFICIENCY EFFECTS
OF MERGERS

There are so many hypothesized causes of mergers that some must successfully explain some mergers. Moreover, the life-cycle, managerial theory has many features in common with some of the neoclassical theories. Thus, an evaluation of competing theories cannot be made from arguments and evidence regarding determinants alone. We must examine their effects. If mergers have improved efficiency substantially, then all theories making this prediction receive support, and the case against mergers is weakened. If mergers have not led to efficiency increases, then the managerial theory is supported, and so, too, is the case against mergers.[16]

Evidence from Outside the United States

I would like to begin by summarizing results from an international comparison of mergers soon to be published.[17] These results are of interest because they come from an additional, unexplored data source and because they deal predominantly with horizontal mergers. Since the neoclassical hypotheses presume a market-power or efficiency-increasing objective, which is easiest to accomplish by horizontal acquisition, the results from other countries should confirm the neoclassical theory, if any do. Indeed, we were so certain that these predominantly horizontal mergers would produce profit increases that we intended to focus on their effects on sales. If a merger increases market power, price will rise, and if the firm was

Table 5.1. Comparison of Profit Rate Changes Following Mergers for Merging and Nonmerging Firms

Country	Profit/Assets Difference	t	Profit/Equity Difference	t	Profit/Sales Difference	t
MAGMAD[a]	.012	.02*	.015	0.11*		
Belgium						
Projected[b]	.003	0.81*	.011	0.39*		
MAGMAD[a]	-.002	-0.41	-.018	-0.79	-.006	-0.82
France						
Projected[b]			-.028	-1.28	-.016	-1.27
MAGMAD[a]		-3.30		-3.42		-0.85
Holland						
Projected[b]		-2.59		-3.24		-0.91
MAGMAD[a]	-.008	-0.77	-.010	-1.24	-.002	-0.70
Sweden						
Projected[b]			-.007	-0.28	-.001	-0.15
MAGMAD[a]	.003	0.18	.035	0.35	.027	0.79
West Germany						
Projected[b]	.007	0.65	.066	0.68	.004	0.55
MAGMAD[a]	.009	2.36	.009	2.86	.006	1.88
United Kingdom						
MAGMAD[a]	-.038	-0.92	-.084	-0.83	-.029	-0.89
United States						
Projected[b]	-.045	-1.15	-.065	-2.37	-.038	-1.17

*Level of significance based on t-test.
[a]MAGMAD: Difference from sample mean for a weighted average of nonmerging firms matched by size and industry.
[b]Projected: Difference from mean of sample of projected values based on merging companies' industry trends.

maximizing profit it will be in the elastic portion of its demand schedule, so sales will fall. If efficiency increases, price should fall, and sales rise. Thus, at the outset we thought that the interesting part of our study would be the differentiation of profitable, horizontal mergers into market-power-increasing or efficiency-increasing.

But on average the mergers did not prove to be profitable. The effects of mergers on profits for the seven countries in our study are summarized in Table 5.1.[18] For each pair of merging companies we computed the combined profit rate for the two companies over the 5 years preceding the merger. This was subtracted from the profit rate for the merged companies for the 3 to 5 years (depending on data availability) after the merger. This difference was the change in profit rate attributed to the merger. To adjust for cyclical and other time-dependent factors, an analogous statistic was computed for a pair of nonmerging companies matched by size and industry (MAGMAD) with the two merging companies over the same time period. The statistics in Table 5.1 are the differences in sample means for these two samples, and the *t* statistic from a comparison of their means. Thus, the entry for France for the profit/equity ratio of -.018 indicates that, for the same time interval, the change in profit/equity ratio for a pair of merging firms was on average 1.8 percentage points *below* that of a matched nonmerging pair of firms. The *t* value of -0.79 indicates that the differences in sample means is not statistically significant. For Belgium the *levels* of statistical significance are reported, rather than *t,* values. In addition, the actual changes in profit rates of the merging firms were compared to changes in their profits projected (PROJECTED) on the basis of the changes in average profit rates of their base industries.

If we confine our attention to the six European countries, we find that for three (France, Holland, and Sweden) the entries are all negative, and for the other three (Belgium, West Germany, and the United Kingdom) they are all positive. Thus, there is an even split between profit declines and increases following mergers. The same holds true if we confine our attention to statistically significant differences. For the United Kingdom, all three comparisons of means were statistically significant, but the merging firms exhibited an improvement of less than 1 percentage point in each of the three profit rate measures compared to the nonmerging control group. Here one must note the differences in sample sizes across countries. In the United Kingdom and the United States we had over 200 observations, enough to make most differences significant if there was any systematic tendency at all. In France and West Germany we had closer to fifty or sixty observations, in the smaller countries only twenty-five or thirty.

Mergers do not appear to have had much of an impact, positive or negative, on profits in the six European countries. Given the dominance of horizontal mergers in the sample, the fourteen authors of these studies were surprised by these results. They made the tests separating mergers into market-power-increasing and efficiency-increasing somewhat anticlimatic. Nevertheless, these results are surprisingly consistent and quite revealing. In *none* of the seven countries did the sales of the merging companies expand faster than they did for the control groups. In Holland and the

United States, the sales of the merging firms showed a significant relative decline. In the other five countries there was no statistical difference in sample means.

Since we had but 3 to 5 years after the mergers to test for their effects, it is possible that not enough time was allowed for improvements in profitability. Therefore, we tested for the impact of the mergers on the returns of the shares of the acquiring companies. If the mergers promise future profit increases, these should be reflected in the prices of the acquiring company's shares and yield increases in the returns on these shares. We again used before and after matched-sample comparisons. The time period after the merger was defined variously as (1) the year of the merger, r_t, (2) the year of the merger and the following year, r_t+1, (3) the 3-year period including the year of the merger and the following two years, r_t+2, and (4) the year of the merger and the following 3 years, r_t+3. Thus, we allowed for a range of possible time periods over which the market could evaluate the consequences of the merger.

Column 1 of Table 5.2 (column 2 for Holland) indicates that the market's initial reaction to the mergers was generally favorable. Eight of the ten comparisons are positive, six are positive and statistically significant. As more time elapses, however, the picture changes. In France, Holland, the United Kingdom, and the United States (for the control group firms matched by size and industry, MAG), there is a clear deterioration in the performance of the acquiring companies' common shares relative to either the size-industry-matched nonmerging control groups or the returns for the acquiring firms projected from industry changes. In Belgium and Sweden the relative deterioration in performance is not as steady or significant, but the indication that the shareholders of acquiring firms were better off, which appears in the year of the merger, has disappeared 3 years after the merger.

Thus, if one allows the market a full 3 years to evaluate the consequences of the mergers, none of the comparisons with the different control groups indicates that the stockholders of the acquiring companies are better off. In the United Kingdom and the United States they would appear to be significantly worse off. The last result is somewhat intriguing, since the United Kingdom and the United States have the most sophisticated stock markets. In all six countries the performance of the acquiring companies was worse 3 years after the merger than it was at the time of the merger. In four of the six countries, as time elapsed, the data suggested a continual relative decline in the market's evaluation of the mergers.

To our knowledge, our study is the only one to have examined the

Table 5.2. Comparisons of Rates of Return on Common Shares Following Mergers for Merging and Nonmerging Firms

Country	r_t		r_{t+1}		r_{t+2}		r_{t+3}	
	Difference	t	Difference	t	Difference	t	Difference	t
MAG[a]	0.047	.08*	-.032	.32*	-.034	-0.31*	-.055	-0.16*
Belgium								
Projected[b]	0.083	0.04*	.068	.27*	.067	0.14*		
MAG[a]	.116	3.69	.086	1.99	.058	1.29	.021	0.27
France								
MAG[a]				2.03		1.79		0.92
Holland								
Projected[b]				0.14		0.68		-0.17
MAG[a]	-.040	-0.34	.014	0.17	-.044	-0.70	-.029	-0.57
Sweden								
Projected[b]	.083	1.08	.025	0.44	-.040	-0.73	-.022	-0.27
MAG[a]	.119	1.99	-.002	-0.05	-.056	-2.00	-.050	-1.78
United Kingdom								
MAG[a]	.088	2.61	.039	1.43	.017	0.69	.004	0.19
United States								
Projected[b]	-.048	-2.22	-.048	-2.57	-.046	-2.56	-.040	-2.43

*Level of significance based on t-test.
[a]MAG: Difference from sample mean for average of a control group sample of nonacquiring firms matched by size and industry to acquiring firm.
[b]Projected: Difference from mean of sample values based on projections of rate of return performance of average company in acquiring firms' base industry.

effects of mergers on profits and returns on common shares for the continental countries and Sweden. Other work has been done on the United Kingdom, however. Using a sample of more than one thousand mergers, Geoffrey Meeks examined the impact of mergers on the merging companies' assets.[19] He concluded that the mergers had, if anything, worsened the operating performance of the merging companies. In our study, Meeks' findings with respect to operating performance are thus more negative than those of Cosh, Hughes, and Singh. Michael Firth studied the impact of the announcement of mergers on share prices. He found that shareholders of the acquired companies were significantly better off and those of the acquiring firms were significantly worse off.[20] Moreover, the losses to the shareholders of the acquiring companies more than offset the gains of the acquired companies' shareholders, a result Firth suggested may reflect the transaction costs of undertaking the mergers. Last of all, with respect to the United Kingdom, mention must be made of the massive study by Keith Cowling and his associates.[21] They examined in detail the impact of mergers on nine companies. As might be expected of the case study approach, no single pattern of results emerged for all mergers. Some increases in market power were observed, some improvements in efficiency, some worsening of efficiency. Their overall conclusion, however, was that the negative effects of mergers at a minimum balanced out the positive effects. On net, society did not appear to be better off.

Donald Thompson reached a similar conclusion for Canada.[22] An investigation of the postmerger profitability of twenty-four conglomerate mergers revealed thirteen with improved performance, eleven with worsened performance.

Thus, the evidence from Canada, the United Kingdom, France, West Germany, Belgium, the Netherlands, and Sweden consistently points to the conclusion that, on net, mergers do not improve economic efficiency. These results place one in a bit of a conundrum, if one reaches the conclusion that mergers in the United States *have* led to improvements in efficiency. Canada and the European countries have had considerably more permissive policies toward mergers than the United States has; and so managers in these countries have had more freedom to choose a merger partner they preferred. Not surprisingly, in Europe at least, they favored partners in their own industry. Nevertheless, on average these mergers have not been successful. Can we expect mergers in the United States to have been more profitable? Are the synergies of conglomerate expansion greater than the economies and market power advantages from horizontal mergers? Should we conclude that Congress spared U.S. firms from engaging in this apparently unprofitable form of merger by amending Section 7 in 1950 and diverting companies to more profitable conglomerate mergers? As they persisted in pursuing horizontal mergers, have managers in Europe been obtuse in not recognizing the superior efficiency gains from conglomerate acquisitions?

The Evidence from the United States

Fortunately, the results for the U.S. are sufficiently close to those just cited to allow us to avoid these conundrums. At least this was the conclusion I reached in a survey of the literature published in 1977. Although a couple of additional studies have appeared since then, they do not seem to alter the picture.

First of all, returning to Tables 5.1 and 5.2, we see from our international comparison study of the United States that the effects of mergers appear to be neutral, if not negative. Profit rate change comparisons yielded negative but insignificant results. The relative decline in sales was negative and significant (not shown). Rates of return on stockholder common shares fell continuously following the mergers when compared to the size-and-industry-matched–nonmerging companies. The returns on the shares of acquiring companies were significantly below the average returns earned on shares in their base industry.

The relative decline in common share performance we observed in one of our U.S. comparisons and in several European countries has been observed by others for the United States. Weston, Smith, and Shrieves found that conglomerates outperformed a sample of mutual funds through the peak of the late 1960s stock market boom.[23] Melicher and Rush confirmed this superior performance by conglomerates through the stock market's peak, but found that their relative advantage was completely wiped out during the first two years of the stock market's decline in the early seventies.[24] As with our results for the international comparison study, one had the impression that the decline in the conglomerates' relative performance would have continued had Melicher and Rush extended their data series.

Mandelker also observed a gradual decline in the performance of the acquiring companies' shares over the 40 months following the mergers.[25] Perhaps more interesting, Mandelker found that the acquiring companies' shares experienced a gradual and continual improvement in performance commencing some 2 years before the mergers.

The same pattern has been observed by Langetieg and Dodd and Ruback.[26] Langetieg's study is a direct follow-up to Mandelker's, using a similar sample. He attempts to control for other factors that might affect share performance, however, by introducing an industry factor and a control group sample. Over the period from 6 years prior to the merger to 7 months prior, the acquiring companies earn significantly higher returns. The biggest increase in returns comes over the period from 18 months to 7 months preceding the merger, a rise of 7.72 percentage points. Starting 7 months before the merger the acquiring companies' shares begin to decline in performance. Their cumulative fall is 1.61 percent. During this 7 months the acquired companies shares rise dramatically. Thus, this 7-month premerger period appears to correspond to the period when news of the merger reaches the market. This news drives up the price of the acquired companies' shares and drives down the price of the acquiring companies' shares. Following the merger the performance of the acquiring companies' shares continues to deteriorate, but the differences from the control group samples are not statistically significant. Langetieg concludes that some motive other than maximizing stockholder welfare must govern merger activity.

Although Dodd and Ruback's results for tender offers seem similar to Langetieg's results for mergers, they reach the conclusion that tender offers have a *positive impact* on the shares of *both* the successful bidding and target firms. If one takes the residuals from regressions of the returns of the bidding firms on the returns to the market portfolio and plots the *cumulative* residuals for the successful bidding firms against time, normally they should hover around zero.[27] Significant movements away from zero indicate market reactions to new information about the firm.

There are two noticeable turning points. Some 43 months prior to the tender offer's announcement the cumulative residuals begin to rise. It is difficult to believe that the capital market can anticipate the nature of a successful tender offer 3½ years before it is made. Thus, it does not seem legitimate to count this long improvement in the performance of the bidding firms' shares as part of the positive impact of the acquisition. The managerial theory argues that reverse causality is involved. Substantial improvements in the profit and share performance of companies can reduce the threat of takeover and increase management's resources sufficiently to permit management to undertake an acquisition and make an otherwise unattractive merger attractive.

The second change occurs some 6 months after the tender offer is made. The results of Mandelker and Langetieg indicate that information about a merger hits the market about 7 months before the merger takes place. In the case of a merger following a successful tender offer, the announcement of the tender offer itself probably is the single most important piece of news to reach the market. Thus, 6 months after the tender offer is made probably corresponds roughly to the point in time when the market realizes that the tender offer will in fact be a success. After that point, the cumulative residuals experience a steady decline.

Thus, the general pattern of return performance of firms making successful tender offers is one of a long and substantial improvement starting some 3½ years before the offer and concluding 6 months after it, followed by a continual and gradual decline in performance commencing roughly when the merger actually takes place. One might wonder from these results how Dodd and Ruback reach the conclusion that the tender offers had a significant positive impact on the shares of the successful bidding firms.

Dodd and Ruback break the 10 years surrounding a tender offer into 5 time periods: (1) from 60 to 13 months prior to the offer, (2) the 12 months prior to the offer, (3) the month of the offer, (4) the 12 months after the offer, and (5) the period from 13 to 60 months after the offer. But a glance at their data indicates that there is no reason for dividing the time around the merger in this way. Nothing different appears to be happening 12 months prior to the merger than was happening 6 months prior, or 24 months prior. Dodd and Ruback's conclusion that the tender offer has had a positive impact appears to rest on three deductions: (1) bidding firms' shares experienced positive and significant improvement in performance over the 12 months preceding the announcement; (2) they also exhibited a significant increase of 2.82 percentage points in the month of the announcement; and (3) the cumulative residuals over the two time periods following the announcement of the tender offer, although negative, were not statistically different from zero. But it does not seem legitimate to attribute the improvement in the bidding firms' share performance over the prior 12 months to the tender offer, since this improvement appears to be an extension of a trend starting 3½ years ahead of the offer. Indeed, the positive residuals earned in the announcement month itself, and over the subsequent 6 months, do not appear to be a significant deviation from this long-run trend. I doubt if most observers would want to argue from this residual pattern that important news reached the market 7 months prior to B (but not at B), and that the residual pattern over these 7 months represents a significant upward deviation from the long-run trend between A and B. Yet such an inference would seem to be required if one is to conclude that the announcement of the tender offer has brought important, positive news to the market.

It is, of course, noteworthy that the shares of the successful bidding firms experienced a statistically significant improvement in performance of 2.83 percentage points. Thus, a shareholder who bought into a firm at the beginning of the month it made a tender offer and sold out at the end of the month would be almost 3 percent ahead. But, it is also noteworthy that if he did not sell out at the end of the month, but held the shares over the next 5 years, he would be nearly 3 percentage points *worse off* than if he never bought in at all. Moreover, if he made the mistake of buying in 6 months after the offer's announcement and held until the end of the period, he would be 8.6 percentage points worse off. I do not have the data to determine whether these declines are statistically significant. But even if they are not, that fact alone would suffice to reject the hypothesis that the mergers have had a positive impact. The only way one can conclude that the tender offers had a positive impact on the shares of the bidding firms is to add in a large fraction of the increase occurring over the 3½ years preceding the offer and ignore all of the decline occurring after it.

Further indication that these preannouncement gains are not part of the impact of the mergers is obtained by examining the cumulative residual pattern for the unsuccessful bidding firms. They, too, experienced a sustained improvement in performance prior to making their tender offers. The only difference in their preoffer performance is that the improvement is not as long or dramatic. This pattern again suggests that it is the improvement in performance that precipitates the offer, rather than the reverse. Nielsen and Melicher found that the premiums paid by acquiring companies in mergers were positively related to their own P/Es and cash flows.[28] Perhaps the unsuccessful bidders did not experience a sufficient improvement in performance to make them willing to undertake the transactions costs and offer the premium required to make the tender offer a success.

The postoffer performance of the unsuccessful bidders' shares was also interesting. Unlike what occurred for the successful bidders, no gradual decline in cumulative residuals was observed: they meandered around zero as might be expected under normal conditions. Thus, while some negative news appears to reach the market some 6 months after a successful tender offer is made, no news—negative or positive—is implied by an unsuccessful bid.

Kummer and Hoffmeister have also published results suggesting that the shareholders of both the target and bidding firms are better off as a result of the tender offer.[29] As in the Mandelker and Dodd and Ruback studies, they find a significant improvement in share performance for the bidding firms over the 2 years preceding takeover, implying that the bid was precipitated by this share-return performance. They also find a significant improvement in share performances over the 3 months preceding and 1 month following the takeover. They do not extend their analysis beyond a month past the takeover; thus, one cannot determine whether additional time would have eroded these gains, as occurred in Mandelker and Dodd and Ruback studies.

The studies by Dodd and Ruback and Kummer and Hoffmeister focus on tender offers. Tender offers are a small fraction of all mergers in the United States. Presumably, the acquiring firms resort to this "hostile" form of acquisition only after considering and rejecting a "friendly" acquisition on the grounds that the target company's managers would not be receptive. Thus, takeovers are likely to involve the displacement of bad managers if any acquisitions do. Therefore, the probability that they increase efficiency is greater than for other mergers. Whatever conclusions one draws from these two studies of tender offers, one should be cautious in generalizing them to all forms of mergers in the United States. Given the alternative interpretation of these results presented above, I do not believe one can conclude that they overturn all the evidence from the rest of the literature, which indicates that the stockholders of acquiring firms are no better off and are perhaps worse off as a result of mergers.

It is again worth emphasizing that the managerial theory does not hypothesize that *all* mergers are unprofitable, only *some*. Although I expect that the fraction of mergers that are unprofitable is large, it is possible that some studies will draw samples from the population of all mergers containing a predominant number of profitable mergers, particularly if the sample selection criteria favor such a selection. In judging the need for additional antimerger legislation, however, the key questions are: what are the net effects of *all* mergers, or what were the effects of those mergers that would be prohibited by new legislation? The overwhelming answer that emerges from the literature on acquiring firms is that a substantial fraction of all mergers could be prohibited without any loss in economic efficiency.

If shareholders of acquiring companies have not fared very well, the same cannot be said of the shareholders of the acquisition targets. To transact an acquisition, a substantial premium is usually paid for the target firm's shares, resulting in a handsome return to the shareholders. Many observers seem willing to conclude that the existence of these gains alone suffices to demonstrate that mergers improve economic efficiency. The argument runs as follows. Acquirers compete in a market for corporate control. The maximum price they are willing to pay for another firm is predicated on the expected gains from managing those assets. The market for corporate control is perfect, and all firms anticipate the same gains from acquiring a given firm. Bidding ensues. The price of the acquired firm rises to reflect the full gains expected from acquiring it. Perfect competition in the market for corporate control leads to all of the gains from merger accruing to the acquired companies' stockholders. If the shareholders of acquiring companies at least break even, society is better off by the full amount of gains to the shareholders of acquired companies.

Two things are wrong with this argument. First, the notion that competitive bidding for acquisition targets takes place does not fit the facts. Thompson's case study research on mergers in Canada revealed that two-thirds of all transactions were initiated by the selling firm.[30] Once negotiation was underway, an "institutional ethic" against bringing in other buyers prevented any bidding from taking place. The same merger environment seems to exist in the United States. Seldom is more than one buyer involved, and very rarely more than two. Thus, the appropriate market analogy is not the competitive, Walrasian auction market, but a bilateral monopoly. Why then does the larger, economically more powerful firm always give up all of the gains from trade? How does the smaller seller always force the buyer back to its corner of the contract curve? Even if the fiction of competitive bidding is maintained, the assumption that the acquiring companies earn zero returns is inconsistent with the neoclassical assumption that their managers are maximizing stockholder welfare. The variance in the returns to acquiring firms from mergers appears to be quite large.[31] Why do the managers of acquiring companies continue to make large investments for their risk-averse shareholders that have zero expected returns and a high variance?

The second thing wrong with the argument that gains to shareholders of acquired companies constitute net gains to society is the assumption made in the existing literature that acquiring-firm shareholders break even. Several studies already cited in this paper or in my earlier survey concluded that the acquiring companies or their shareholders are worse off following the mergers.[32] This conclusion can be reached for our international comparison study, for example, with respect to either profit rate changes or returns on common shares for Sweden, Holland, the United Kingdom, and the United States.[33]

The variance on the returns to acquiring companies from mergers are so large, however, that most studies have concluded that their effects, plus or minus, statistically are not significantly different from zero. These variances are probably large enough in most cases to wash out the gains to the acquired firms too. In our U.S. sample, the acquired companies averaged 10 percent of the size of their acquirers, a fraction that is certainly larger than the average of all mergers. The median premium for the six studies Halpern cites was 21%.[34] Thus, the gains to acquired-company shareholders are around 2 percent of the market value of the acquiring firms. It is more than likely that the large variances in returns that led to the conclusion that the mean returns to shareholders of acquiring firms are not statistically different from zero would also have sustained the conclusion that they were not statistically different from -0.02.

For example, in the Dodd and Ruback study the decline in the cumulative residuals for the acquiring firm between the month before the tender offer was made and 60 months after it, was 3.1 percent.[35] The increase in cumulative residuals for the target firms over the same period was 27.6 percent. If the target firms averaged 10 percent of the size of their acquirers, the decline in value of the acquiring companies would fully offset the gains to the target firms. In Langetieg's study the acquiring-firm shareholders experienced a loss of 1.61 percent during the 6 months preceding the consummation of the merger; the acquired-company shareholders, a 12.9 percent gain.[36] Again adjusting for relative size differences, the losses to the former are more than enough to offset the gains to the latter. Halpern's is the only study for the United States with which I am familiar that actually combines the results for the acquiring and acquired firms.[37] He concludes that the mergers are a success on the basis of a nonparametric test of the fraction of mergers yielding positive combined returns. While it is noteworthy that the combined returns to acquiring-company and acquired-company shareholders are positive more often than not, it is also interesting to note that the mean of these returns is but one-sixth of their standard deviation. Certainly such a large dispersion of results should lead one to be cautious about evaluating the economic significance of the returns from mergers, whatever their statistical significance. Caution is further warranted because Halpern bases his conclusions on the returns earned up to the date of the mergers and especially because several studies have reported declines in the returns on acquiring-company shares over the postmerger period. Thus I do not think it is possible at this time to conclude that the premiums paid for acquired-company shares constitute a net gain to shareholders as a group, and a fortiori that society is better off by this amount.

Although the literature focuses on the effects of mergers on individual companies, the key issue is, of course, their net aggregate effect on corporate efficiency and the performance of the economy. Many claims have been put forward regarding the social gains from mergers. They are supposed to improve the allocation of capital, resulting in higher returns on and consequently more investment in new capital. This argument can be extended to investment in R&D. In addition, since conglomerate diversification reduces the riskiness of a company's asset portfolio, greater expenditures on risky investments like R&D should be encouraged. All companies should exhibit greater internal efficiency because bad managers are eliminated by the corporate takeover process. All managers should work harder to further their stockholders' interests and avoid becoming takeover targets.

Figure 5.1 depicts the intensity of merger activity, capital investment, and R&D since 1960. It is difficult to discern any upward shift in the latter two series in response to the first. If any relationship exists at all, it appears that the three investments move together, perhaps in response to a common stimulus such as cash flow or business conditions.[38] In particular, no upward movement in investment and R&D in response either to the wave of the late sixties or the cumulation of mergers over the last two decades is visible. Increases in productivity have been erratic but since 1973 have followed a downward trend. Currently, the economy exhibits no improvement in productivity whatsoever.

Defenders of mergers will quickly respond that many additional factors affect investment and productivity, and, I suppose, that the economy's performance would have been still worse had it not been for the beneficial effects of mergers. The government, we now all know, is run by power-hungry politicians and budget-maximizing bureaucrats, who together have expanded its size and influence on the private economy to the point where the latter can scarcely survive. If we would only break up unions, place constitutional constraints on bureaucrats bent on expanding their budgets, and then allow corporations to merge and grow without bound, all would turn out for the best in this best of all Pareto-optimal worlds. Perhaps. But I think a skeptic is justified in demanding some more tangible evidence of the beneficial social effects of the more than 22,000 mergers that have occurred over the last two decades.

MERGERS AND PUBLIC POLICY

Although the evidence on the effects of mergers does not constitute a case for them, it also is probably not sufficient for a case against them. The latter rests in part at least on their sociopolitical effects. The case against mergers is based on the evidence that they contribute significantly to corporate size, and that corporate size and (undesirable) political power are positively related.

I shall not attempt to establish a relationship between mergers and overall concentration here. I am familiar with only two studies that systematically attempt to determine what the level of overall

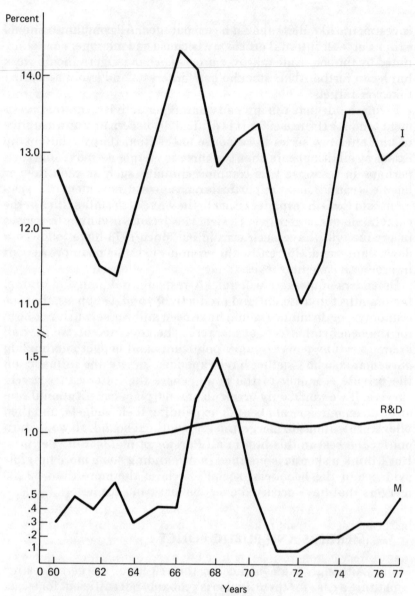

Figure 5.1. Investment, R&D, and merger intensity.

I   stands for investment in manufacturing as a percent of GNP accounted for by manufacturing. Data are from the *Economic Report of the President*, 1979, Tables B4, B5, B45.

R&D stands for Industry R&D expenditures as a percent of GNP. Data are from *National Science Indicators*, 1979 (National Science Foundation, 1979), Tables 2–2, 2–3, pp. 170–171.

M   stands for assets acquired in manufacturing as a percent of Total Manufacturing Assets. Data are from the FTC merger series and the Statistical Abstract.

concentration would have been without any mergers; they compare that level with the level actually realized. Let me simply emphasize that these studies conclude that much, if not all, of the increases that have occurred are attributable to mergers.[39] It is also noteworthy that the only period in this century in which aggregate concentration appears to have fallen substantially is from the bottom of the Depression to the end of World War II. This period also "happens" to be the only one of sustained economic expansion in the United States that has not coincided with heavy merger activity. One must assume that a substantial curtailment of mergers would also produce a secular decline in overall concentration.

Economists are probably not the best social scientists to answer the question of whether corporate size leads to political power. A recent book by noted political scientist Charles Lindblom argues the point quite forcefully.[40] One might now ask defenders of corporate mergers to demonstrate that large corporations do not exercise political influence.

In addition to curtailing the growth of large corporations, new antimerger legislation could actually curtail the growth of government and its influence on the private sector of the economy. The existence of large and powerful corporations fosters the growth of government and the kind of government-business partnership John Kenneth Galbraith described so well over a decade ago.[41] The recent Chrysler bailout illustrates the point. Here was a company in need of a takeover if ever one was. Why were there no corporate bidders? Why did the market for corporate control not prevent Chrysler's management from leading the company as far down the road to bankruptcy as it did? The answer is obvious, I think. Chrysler is just too big to be taken over by almost any other company. One of the advantages of size is the freedom from takeover. Singh has shown that growth through merger, even at some sacrifice in profits, can be better protection from takeover than maximizing the present value of assets.[42] Once a company reaches the size of Chrysler, government intervention may be required to avert bankruptcy, whereas it would not if the company were much smaller.

The mergers that produced the Chrysler Corporation occurred some time ago. Any legislation curbing mergers today would leave existing size and other avenues to growth untouched. Is this fair or desirable? The issue of fairness does not arise here. The right to merge is not one of those inalienable rights we inherited from the Enlightenment. The corporation is a creature of the state, and the state can place any restrictions it chooses on the privilege to operate under this legal form. The state can deny corporations the privilege of merging in the same way it can deny them the privilege of contributing to political campaigns, without necessarily being open to a charge of unfairness.

There are three reasons for singling out growth through merger for special treatment.

1. It is administratively the easiest form of growth to control. Thus, this constraint on corporate growth is the most compatible—of all other policies one might consider—with the goal of curbing the growth of government size and intervention.
2. Controlling corporate growth through merger is probably sufficient to produce significant reductions in overall concentration in the long run.
3. This policy seems unlikely to have an adverse effect on the performance of the economy.

If policies attacking size and other forms of growth directly have these three characteristics, then they, too, should be seriously considered. But in the absence of such policy proposals, there is no reason to set aside consideration of an effective antimerger policy.

This point can be illustrated by again looking at the petroleum industry. Here is an industry dominated by large corporations that possess and exercise political power.[43] Proposals to curtail this power and break up these firms have appeared from time to time, but have never survived the counterattacks of the target firms. An antimerger law would have no effect on the power the petroleum companies now have. But to maintain their size and influence into the twenty-first century, they must and undoubtedly will undertake a substantial volume of mergers. This form of perpetuation of size and power would be prevented by a tough antimerger law, and it would prevent other firms from using mergers to expand and fill the places left by the decline of the petroleum firms.

From the numerous descriptions of the capital market's failures necessitating mergers, the crucial role of mergers in disciplining and replacing bad managers, and the like, I sometimes get the impression that capitalism might be incapable of surviving were it not for this form of corporate transaction. Ironically, it seems that the capital market, except when it comes to evaluating the future consequences of mergers, is among capitalism's least efficient markets. Apparently our business schools retain the best of their students to teach on their faculties and send the rest out to work in business. Despite their incompetence, these graduates rise to the top of their companies and cling on so that their unfortunate stockholders can be rescued only through an outside acquisition. To weed out these incompetents and keep capital flowing to its most productive uses in the economy, we need some 1000 mergers per year.

Perhaps I am only a naive optimist, but I think our market economy is resilient enough to survive and even prosper without the corporate merger to aid it in achieving its allocational tasks. We should remember that the corporate manager is a bureaucrat acting in an institutional environment quite similar to that of his public counterpart. Just as the public bureaucrat will exceed the mandate given him to correct traditional market failures, the corporate bureaucrat can be expected to exceed whatever mandate he senses he has to correct the failures of the capital market and his fellow managers. The growth of the public and private bureaucracies over the course of this century are parallel manifestations of the same individual motivation functioning in an environment with similar institutional constraints. Those who, like myself, favor democratic, decentralized, market solutions to the fundamental allocation and distribution questions faced by society, should favor rules that constrain the growth of both private and public bureaucracy. An effective antimerger policy would be one such rule.

NOTES

1. J. A. Schumpeter, *The Theory of Economic Development* (1934).
2. J. A. Schumpeter, *Capitalism, Socialism and Democracy* (1950).
3. G. J. Benston, "Conglomerate Mergers: Causes, Consequences and Remedies," in *Mergers and Concentration, Part 2,* Hearings before the Subcommittee on Antitrust Monopoly and Business Rights (1979); D. C. Mueller, "A Theory of Conglomerate Mergers," 83 *Quarterly Journal of Economics* 6-43 (1969), "The Effects of Conglomerate Mergers: A Survey of the Empirical Evidence," 1 *Journal of Banking and Finance* 315 (1977), and "Do We Want a New Tough Antimerger Law?" 24 *Antitrust Bulletin* 807 (1979); P. O. Steiner, *Mergers* (1975), chs. 2, 4, and 5.
4. J. F. Weston, "The Nature and Significance of Conglomerate Firms," 44 *St. John's Law Review* 66 (1970); O. E. Williamson, *Corporate Control and Business Behavior* (1970) and *Markets and Hierarchies* (1975).
5. See R. Marris, *The Economic Theory of Managerial Capitalism* (1964), ch. 2.
6. Weston and Mansinghka place the latter interpretation on their findings that the firms that grew by merger during the sixties to become "conglomerates" started out as relatively low profit companies. (J. S. Weston and S. K. Mansinghka, "Tests of the Efficiency Performance in Conglomerate Firms," 26 *Journal of Finance* 919 (1971)).
7. The argument can go either way however. See W. A. McEachern, *Managerial Control and Performance* (1975).
8. See, e.g., Benston, note 3 *supra*, sections 3, 4.

9. See, e.g., P. Asquith, "Mergers and the Market for Acquisitions," mimeo., U. of Chicago (1979); P. Dodd and R. Ruback, "Tender Offers and Stockholder Returns," 5 *Journal of Financial Economics* 351 (1977); P. Halpern, "Empirical Estimates of the Amount and Distribution of Gains to Companies," 46 *Journal of Business* 554 (1973); D. R. Kummer and J. R. Hoffmeister, "Valuation Consequences of Cash Tender Offers," 33 *Journal of Finance* 505 (1978); T. C. Langetieg, "An Application of a Three-Factor Performance Index to Measure Stockholder Gains from Merger," 6 *Journal of Financial Economics* 365 (1978); and G. Mandelker, "Risk and Return: The Case of Merging Firms," 1 *Journal of Financial Economics* 303 (1974).

10. See D. Jorgenson, "Econometric Studies of Investment Behavior: A Survey," 9 *Journal of Economic Literature* III (1971) and D. Jorgenson and C. Siebert, "A Comparison of Alternate Theories of Corporate Investment," 58 *American Economic Review* 681 (1968).

11. M. H. Miller and F. Modigliani, "The Cost of Capital, Corporate Finance and the Theory of Investment," 48 *American Economic Review* 261 (1958).

12. This literature is huge. For a survey see E. F. Fama, "Efficient Capital Markets: A Review of Theory and Empirical Work," 25 *Journal of Finance* 383 (1970).

13. If the mergers of today can be explained by the underevaluation of company assets by the market, what explains the mergers of the sixties?

14. J. W. Elliot, "Theories of Corporate Investment Behavior Revisited," 63 *American Economic Review* 195 (1973); H. G. Grabowski and D. C. Mueller, "Managerial and Stockholder Welfare Models of Firm Expenditures," 54 *Review of Economics and Statistics* 9 (1972).

15. Proponents of neoclassical explanations of mergers make a great deal out of the role the higher tax on dividends plays in explaining mergers. It should be recognized, however, that no loss in social efficiency will come from legislation banning mergers that have tax avoidance as their justification. Such mergers have purely redistributive effects. Personally I doubt that merger activity would come to a grinding halt if capital gains were taxed upon accrual at the same rate as dividends.

16. Here one must point out that the managerial thesis is not that *all* mergers are unprofitable, only that some are—those on the margin. Thus, it is somewhat ambivalent as to what the average effect will be. But, if the average improvement is zero or negative the managerial theory is certainly supported.

17. D. C. Mueller, ed., *The Determinants and Effects of Mergers: An International Comparison* (1980).

18. Each country's results were obtained by scholars from the respective country. They are Belgium (A. M. Kumps and R. Wtterwulghe), France (F. Jenny and A. P. Weber), Holland (H. Peer), Sweden (J.-O. Edberg and B. Rydén), W. Germany (J. Cable, J. Palfrey, and J. Runge), U.K. (A . Cosh, A. Hughes, and A. Singh), and U.S. (D. C. Mueller). For details see Mueller, note 17 *supra.*

19. G. Meeks, *Disappointing Marriage: A Study of the Gains from Merger* (1977).

20. M. Firth, "The Profitability of Takeovers and Mergers," 89 *Economic Journal* 316 (1979).

21. K. Cowling, P. Stoneman, J. Cubbin, J. Cable, G. Hall, S. Dornberger, and P. Dutton, *Mergers and Economic Performance* (1979).

22. D. N. Thompson, "Mergers, Effects, and Competition Policy: Some Empirical Evidence," mimeo. York University, Toronto (1979).

23. J. F. Weston, K. V. Smith, and R. E. Shrieves, "Conglomerate Performance Using the Capital Asset Pricing Model," 54 *Review of Economics and Statistics* 357 (1972).

24. R. W. Melicher and D. F. Rush, "The Performance of Conglomerate Firms: Recent Risk and Return Experience," 28 *Journal of Finance* 381 (1973).
25. Mandelker, note 9 *supra*.
26. Langetieg, note 9 *supra*; Dodd and Ruback, note 9 *supra*.
27. Dodd and Ruback did this by simply summing the figures for each month that they presented in their Table 2 (pp. 364-366).
28. J. F. Nielsen and R. W. Melicher, "A Financial Analysis of Acquisition and Merger Premiums," 8 *Journal of Financial and Quantitative Analysis* 139 (1973).
29. Kummer and Hoffmeister, note 9 *supra*.
30. Thompson, note 22 *supra*.
31. M. Gort and J. T. Hogarty, "New Evidence on Mergers," 13 *Journal of Law and Economics* 167 (1970); Halpern, note 9 *supra*.
32. Mueller (1977), note 3 *supra*.
33. See also Meeks, note 19 *supra*, and Firth, note 20 *supra*, for the United Kingdom; T. F. Hogarty ("The Profitability of Corporate Mergers," 43 *Journal of Business* 317 (1970)), R. A. Haugen and T. C. Langetieg ("An Empirical Test for Synergism in Merger," 30 *Journal of Finance* 1003 (1975)), and R. H. Mason and M. B. Goudzwaard ("Performance of Conglomerate Firms: A Portfolio Approach," 31 *Journal of Finance* 39 (1976)) for the United States.
34. Halpern, note 9 *supra*, p. 556.
35. Dodd and Ruback, note 9 *supra*.
36. Langetieg, note 9 *supra*.
37. Halpern, note 9 *supra*. Firth's study, note 20 *supra*, does the same thing for the United Kingdom and reaches the opposite conclusion.
38. To discriminate between factors that move the three expenditures in the same direction and substitute and complement relationships, one needs to set up a simultaneous equation model.
39. See J. J. McGowan ("The Effect of Alternative Antimerger Policies on the Size Distribution of Firms," 5 *Yale Economic Essays* 423 (1965)) and the paper by Hay and Untiet in this volume for the United States and L. Hannah and J. A. Kay (*Concentration in Modern Industry* (1977)) for Great Britain. My views on this are presented in Mueller (1977, 1979), note 3 *supra*.
40. C. E. Lindblom, *Politics and Markets* (1977).
41. J. K. Galbraith, *The New Industrial State* (1967).
42. A. Singh, *Takeovers: Their Relevance to the Stock Market and the Theory of the Firm* (1971).
43. See, e.g., J. M. Blair, *The Control of Oil* (1976).

PART III

Economic Aspects of Conglomerates

Chapter 6

Conglomerate Mergers: Efficiency Considerations

Roger D. Blair and Yoram C. Peles

INTRODUCTION

The promulgation of the Justice Department's Merger Guidelines provided notice that certain mergers would be challenged automatically.[1] This had a profound effect on horizontal and vertical merger activity because of the fairly settled status of the law in these areas. To the extent that the guidelines have been successful, firms have turned increasingly to conglomerate mergers. These have been somewhat safer from successful challenge under Section 7 of the Clayton Act, which requires showing an adverse effect on competition for illegality.[2] The traditional avenues for attacking conglomerate mergers have depended on the doctrines of (1) potential competition, (2) entrenchment, and (3) reciprocity. Recent court decisions indicate that these antitrust weapons are being viewed with some disfavor.[3]

One response to the difficulties of successfully challenging conglomerate mergers under Section 7 has been to propose legislation.[4]

The authors appreciate the financial support provided by the Public Policy Research Center. Jerome Stein's helpful comments on an early draft of this paper are gratefully acknowledged. Ira Horowitz and Lawrence Kenny also provided useful suggestions. We retain responsibility for the final product.

The most prominent example is the Kennedy Bill, which forbids mergers between large firms.[5] The proposed prohibitions, however, are not absolute. There are two affirmative defenses: (1) if the merger "will have the preponderant effect of substantially enhancing competition" or (2) if the merger "will result in substantial efficiencies," presumably it will not be unlawful.[6] Interestingly, such defenses are good only every two years.[7] Nonetheless, an efficiency defense can be offered every other year.

In this chapter, we shall examine the efficiencies attendant upon diversified production. Most analysts who are skeptical of conglomerate efficiencies focus on scale economies in production. But a conglomerate firm does more than produce output: it buys physical inputs, it frequents the capital market, it promotes and distributes its products, and so on. All these activities can produce efficiencies or inefficiencies that are as real as those stemming from scale economies in production. In addition, the firm deals with uncertainty in part by diversifying production. This can also lead to efficiencies.

DIVERSIFIED PRODUCTION AND
THE NATURE OF THE FIRM

The perfect substitutability between firms diversifying production and individuals diversifying their investment portfolios is often justified on the assumption of identical options being available to both. Proponents of this view claim, for example, that in a perfect capital market, portfolio diversification by investors is precisely equivalent to diversified production by firms through conglomerate mergers. Thus, the combined value of two separate firms should equal the value of both firms merged.[8] There are conditions, however, under which this argument does not hold. Consequently, inferences based on that argument are misleading. Diversifying output not only lowers the risk run by individual investors, but it also provides an opportunity for reallocating factors of production among different industries. This activity may save resources and thereby permit greater total output. When resources are saved, society benefits from *real*, as opposed to pecuniary, economies.

In a well-known article, Coase explains the existence of firms (and vertical integration) by economies in coordinating production by entrepreneurs, rather than by market forces.[9] Accordingly, firms can be viewed as groups of vertically-related activities that are coordinated more efficiently by entrepreneurs than by market forces. This analysis explains the firm's function in linking consecutive production activities. But firms may serve an additional social function. In a world where the demands for various goods and services fluctuate randomly, society must reallocate factors of production from industries whose demand has declined to industries whose demand has increased.[10] This reallocation can be accomplished through the free market or by entrepreneurs. For example, a firm with falling demand will release workers into the labor market, thereby making them available to firms in other industries. Since there are costs in using the market, this process is expensive in terms of time and money. In contrast, in the case of an entrepreneur who runs a firm with diversified output, resource reallocation can be performed by the person in charge of the firm.[11] The administrative reallocation of inputs is not free: it requires time and managerial effort. Given conditions of changing demand, the profit motive will lead the firm to employ the most profitable method or combination of methods. This will result in the outcome that is socially most efficient. Administrative allocation of resources will be extended until the marginal cost of administrative coordination is just equal to the marginal cost of coordinating through market forces. Consequently, in a broader context, we must view the firm as a system that organizes not only vertical production activities but also the production activities of diversified products.

MERGER DECISIONS OF THE FIRM

For the individual firms, a decision to merge will depend on the anticipated effect on profits. They have to compare the expected profit that can be achieved by the merged firm with diversified production against the sum of the expected profits available to the separate firms with specialized production. A merger would appear to be justified economically whenever the expected profits of diversified output exceed the sum of the expected profit of the separate firms. By focusing on expected profits, we are assuming that the firms are risk-neutral. This assumption will be relaxed later.

Assuming a competitive market structure, a firm's revenue from the production of good i is the price of i times the quantity of good i: P_iQ_i.[12] A firm that produces $n-1$ commodities will elect to merge with a firm that produces commodity n if

$$E\left[\sum_{i=1}^{m-1} P_i Q_i - C(Q_1, \ldots, Q_n)\right] >$$

$$E\left[\sum_{i=1}^{n-1} P_i Q_i - C(Q_1, \ldots, Q_{n-1})\right] + E[P_n Q_n - C(Q_n)] \qquad (1)$$

where E is the expectations operator and $C(\cdot)$ is the cost function. This follows because the profit of the more diversified firm exceeds the sum of the profits of the less diversified firm. It should be noted that all of the firm's costs are being included in $C(\cdot)$: administrative costs, distribution costs, production costs, and so on.

Suppose there are two firms specializing in a single product. In that case a merger makes sense provided that

$$E[P_1 Q_1 + P_2 Q_2 - C(Q_1, Q_2)] >$$

$$E[P_1 Q_1 - C(Q_1)] + E[P_2 Q_2 - C(Q_2)] \qquad (2)$$

There are three possible cases that we can analyze. First, suppose that the cost of producing Q_1 is unaffected by whether the producer of Q_1 also produces Q_2. If this is the case, then the cost function is separable:

$$C(Q_1, Q_2) = C(Q_1) + C(Q_2) \qquad (3)$$

With a separable cost function, the left-hand side of Eq. (2) can be written as

$$E[P_1 Q_1 + P_2 Q_2 - C(Q_1) - C(Q_1)] = E[P_1 Q_1 - C(Q_1)]$$

$$+ E[P_2 Q_2 - C(Q_2)]$$

due to standard properties of mathematical expectation.[13] In this case, the maximum profit for the merged firm equals the sum of the maximum profits of the two specialized firms. Under either organizational alternative, the same quantities of the commodities will be produced. Thus, there is no advantage or disadvantage in merged production.

Second, suppose the cost of producing Q_1 is an increasing function of Q_2 produced by the same firm. When this substitution in production occurs, we know that:

$$\partial^2 C(Q_1, Q_2) / \partial Q_1 \partial Q_2 > 0$$

This kind of cost function might exist if there is a common factor of production subject to diseconomies of scale, e.g., management. In this case, for any given positive quantities $Q_1{}^\circ$ and $Q_2{}^\circ$, it follows that:

$$C(Q_1^0, Q_2^0) > C(Q_1^0) - C(Q_2^0)$$

As a result, specialization in production is cheaper for any given output levels. Moreover, the first-order conditions for maximum expected profit of the diversified firm will require smaller quantities than the optimal quantities of the specialized firms. Under these conditions, we should not expect to see a merger. In fact, we may even observe divestitures.

Finally, there may be complementarity in production. This will cause the cost of producing Q_1 to be a decreasing function of Q_2:

$$\partial^2 C(Q_1, Q_2)/\partial Q_1 \partial Q_2 < 0$$

For any given positive quantities of $Q_1{}^\circ$ and $Q_2{}^\circ$, it will be true that:

$$C(Q_1^0, Q_2^0) < C(Q_1^0) + C(Q_2^0)$$

Consequently, diversified output costs less, and a merger of the two specialized firms is socially beneficial. The merged firm will produce more of both products than would the two specialized firms.

The effect of producing Q_2 is to lower the marginal cost of producing Q_1. This may be caused by the existence of scale economies in one or more of the firm's activities: management, purchasing inputs, frequenting the capital market, promoting the products, distributing the products, and so on. The question is whether these economies can be exploited most efficiently by adding a second output or by increasing the production of the first commodity. For example, suppose there are economies of scale in financial activity—the average cost of raising funds declines as the quantity of capital raised increases. Such economies exist whether the funds are used to increase the production of existing goods or to add a new product. If the scale economies in financial activity exceed those in production, the optimal policy may be to employ the financial activity to support production of several product lines.

One question remains, however. Specifically, why is a multi-product firm preferable to a multiplant firm in which each plant produces the same product? One answer is that firms operating in certain industries may be precluded from horizontal expansion by the antitrust laws.[14] In such instances, the law could lead to a serious efficiency loss if conglomerate expansion were not possible.

Consider another alternative. Suppose that concentration within any single market is not a problem. If each firm supplies only a small share of any market, what is the point of product diversification? The answer is that some advantages exist only with diversified production. For example, the cost of capital may decline with diversification of production due to the reduced probability of bankruptcy. This would be a return to diversification per se and would exist even if the total dollars raised remained constant. But there are other benefits to diversification, and we shall examine two of them in the following sections. First, we will show that when the demands for output are subject to random fluctuations, negatively correlated demands will provide incentives for diversification. Second, when demands fluctuate, a diversified firm can reallocate factors of production and reduce the transactions costs of varying its output mix. Each benefit is independent of the other. The first lowers risk and confers a benefit upon a risk-averse firm. The second reduces the costs of reallocating inputs and therefore confers a benefit that is independent of the firm's attitude toward risk.

THE CASE OF AN EXPONENTIAL UTILITY FUNCTION

In this section, we shall obtain some concrete results by assuming that the firm's von Neumann-Morgenstern utility function is exponential:

$$U(\Pi) = -e^{-\alpha \Pi}, \alpha > 0 \tag{4}$$

where α is the well-known Pratt-Arrow index of absolute risk aversion. In an exponential utility function, α is a constant. This means, of course, that the scale of profit does not affect the firm's willingness to bear a risk of a given size. As Lintner has argued, constant absolute risk aversion may be a useful approximation for intermediate decisions of the firm.[15]

Under certain conditions, it can be shown that maximizing the expected utility of profit is equivalent to maximizing

$$M = \bar{P}_1 Q_1 + \bar{P}_2 Q_2 - \sum_{j=1}^{n} w_j x_j + \lambda F(Q_1, Q_2; x_j)$$

$$- (\alpha/2)\{Q_1^2 \sigma_1^2 + Q_1 Q_2 \rho_{12} \sigma_1 \sigma_2 + Q_2 \sigma_2^2\} \tag{5}$$

where P_i denotes the expected price of the ith good, ρ_{12} is the correlation coefficient between P_1 and P_2, λ is a Lagrange multiplier, $F(\cdot)$ is the firm's transformation function, and, finally, w_j and x_j are the price and quantity of the jth input.[16]

The first-order conditions for a maximum require that the first partial derivatives of M vanish:

$$\frac{\partial M}{\partial Q_1} = E[MR_1] + \lambda \partial F / \partial Q_1 - \alpha(Q_1 \sigma_1^2 + Q_2 \rho_{12} \sigma_1 \sigma_2) = 0 \qquad (6)$$

$$\frac{\partial M}{\partial x_j} = MFC_j + \lambda \partial F / \partial x_j = 0 \qquad (7)$$

$$\frac{\partial M}{\partial \lambda} = F(Q_1, Q_2; x_j) = 0 \qquad (8)$$

where MR_i is marginal revenue in the ith market and MFC_j represents the marginal factor cost of input j.

If we rearrange Eq. (7) and divide by Eq. (6), we obtain the following relationship:

$$MFC_j = \partial Q_1 / \partial x_j \{ E[MR_1] - \alpha(Q_1 \sigma_1^2 + Q_2 \rho_{12} \sigma_1 \sigma_2) \} \qquad (9)$$

If the firm is risk neutral, α is zero and condition (9) is the stochastic analog of the familiar condition that a firm should hire each input until its marginal factor cost equals the marginal revenue product. In this case, the right-hand side would be the expected marginal revenue product of input j in producing output 1. For risk-averse firms, α is positive and the term in braces is the certainty equivalent marginal revenue. Thus, risk-averse firms employ inputs until the marginal factor cost is equal to the certainty equivalent marginal revenue product.

For a single product firm, the condition that corresponds to (9) is

$$MFC_j = \partial Q_1 / \partial X_j \{ E[MR_1] - \alpha \sigma_1^2 Q_1 \} \qquad (10)$$

Risk aversion causes an employment distortion because expected marginal revenue product is not equal to the marginal factor cost. We can compare the distortion for the single product and multiproduct firm by comparing the differences between MFC_1 and $(\partial Q_1 / \partial X_j) E[MR_1]$:

$$\alpha \sigma_1^2 Q_1 - (\alpha \sigma_1^2 Q_1 - \alpha Q_2 \rho_{12} \sigma_1 \sigma_2) = - \alpha Q_2 \rho_{12} \sigma_1 \sigma_2 \qquad (11)$$

If $\rho_{12} < 0$, then the right-hand side of Eq. (11) will be positive. This means that the multiproduct firm will have a smaller distortion. Consequently, the output of Q_1 in the diversified firm is larger than in the specialized firm. The output expansion will be larger—the greater the degree of risk aversion, the larger the output of commodity 2, and the larger the variance in the price distribution of either commodity. This example demonstrates the benefits of a multiproduct organization: the disutility of bearing risk is reduced. In addition, the firm may experience cost saving from resource reallocation.

REALLOCATION OF INPUTS

Among other things, Dhrymes recognized that a diversified firm could reduce its costs by reallocating its inputs.[17] We shall examine several characteristics of the products involved that affect the benefits of such reallocations. First, the more volatile the demands for Q_1 and for Q_2, the greater will be the flows of inputs into and out of these productive activities. Consequently, the greater will be the benefits from coordinating these flows. Thus, this characteristic influences the amounts of factors to be transferred. Not surprisingly, it has been claimed that conglomerate merger activity has been high in industries suffering from fluctuating demand. Among these industries are aerospace, industrial machinery, auto parts, and textiles.[18]

Second, the lower the correlation between the demands for Q_1 and Q_2, the greater the opportunity for shifting resources from one productive activity to another. The more stable the "combined" demand for Q_1 and Q_2, the more stable will be the firm's demands for inputs. Thus, the firm will be able to reduce meaningful transaction costs associated with hiring factors of production. A simple example can be found in the garment industry where a single firm usually produces both winter and summer clothing. The peak demand for winter clothes coincides with a trough in demand for summer clothes, and vice versa. Since the firm produces both types of clothing, the workers and other factors of production do not have to move between firms specializing in either product. This lowering of costs through diversified output corresponds to the risk reduction achieved through portfolio diversification.

Third, the greater the similarity between the input mix in the production of Q_1 and Q_2, the higher the probability that a significant number of the factors of production are transferable between these two productive activities. When the similarity of the productive factors is high, two products may be remote substitutes in consumption, but close substitutes in production. This characteristic determines the complexity of the route to the final position, which, in turn, influences the cost of the adjustment process. In the previous example of the garment industry, both workers and equipment can be transferred quite easily from one product to another.

The input reallocation route, however, may be more tortuous. A decrease in demand for product Q_1 and a contemporaneous increase in demand for Q_n may cause a series of transfers—input X_1 goes from producing Q_1 to Q_2 thereby releasing factor X_2 which moves to Q_3 and so on to Q_n. Similarly, a shift in demand may release several factors of production, each going into the production of other commodities. In these cases, an efficient internal coordination facility should control the production of all the products involved in the reallocation.

In the case of labor, the costs of using the marketplace include job seeking, transferring accumulated benefits (e.g., pension fund benefits) from old to new firms, loss of seniority, and so on. Other costs arise from negotiating new contracts, getting acquainted with a new organization and its personnel, losing firm-specific human capital, and, of course, all the costs involved in changing dwellings. These may also arise when a worker moves from one plant to another one belonging to the same firm. Similarly, using the market for transferring equipment and other fixed assets also entails costs, some of which are of the same type mentioned earlier in connection with transferring labor.

Factors of production have different degrees of uniqueness in use. It is quite conceivable that physical factors of production are more likely to be product-specific; marketing factors can serve larger varieties of products; and management and finance activities might cover a very broad span of different production possibilities. A conglomerate firm is, by definition, a case in which diversification of production is very high. Consequently, a change in demand may require reallocation of activities such as marketing, management, or finance, rather than of mechanical production.

Marketability refers to the ease of transferring an asset into a sum of money that is close to the factor's or asset's last quoted sale price. The identification of market reallocation costs is most easily seen in extreme cases where the costs amount to the total value of the productive factor.[19] For example, it is often cheaper to scrap machinery than to try to sell it, although identical pieces of equipment are being traded in the marketplace by firms that have lower search costs. There are, however, other more important factors of production whose costs of reallocation via the market are prohibitive while the intrafirm reallocation costs are quite reasonable. Some of what accountants call the firm's intangible assets— goodwill, for example—fall into this category. The market for these intangibles is imperfect and they can be reallocated only within the firm. Consequently, the firm can reap the value of such intangible assets only when the firm as a whole is sold in the marketplace.[20] Examples of such productive factors are the image or good name of the firm (e.g., Coca Cola or Rolls Royce), a good managerial team, a good R&D department, and the like.[21] Other factors of production could be traded in the market, but legal restrictions prevent such trades, e.g., the accumulated or expected losses for corporate tax purposes. In many countries a firm cannot sell a tax deduction right to its losses. But, with certain restrictions, the same firm can lower its tax bill with such losses. Therefore, the common method of transferring this type of "factor of production" or asset is for the firm with negative earnings to acquire a profitable firm, and then, within the combined firm, to employ this factor of production.[22] Thus, firms whose market value is largely composed of intangible factors of production are more likely to be transferred in the marketplace in their entirety, i.e., merged. As stated before, the "need" for a reallocation of factors exists especially between firms producing products that simultaneously face declining and rising demand. Therefore, once the merger occurs and the factors of production can be reallocated, we may expect the combined firm to invest and expand production of the increasing demand product.[23] To the extent that antitrust enforcement prevents these mergers, the law is preventing the correction of a serious market imperfection or failure.

To some extent, the previous analysis can explain some empirical results on the profitability of mergers.[24] The motivation for merger may simply be that it provides a cheaper way of transferring factors of production between firms. If this method of transfer is widely known to all firms, and taken into account by security investors in valuing shares, then one should not expect to observe a higher market value for the merged firms than the sum of market values of the firms prior to the merger. Consider again the previous tax-loss example. The value of this asset is determined when the losses are realized and the merger allows only the transfer of factor without significantly changing its value.

Since diversified output is, among other things, a means to reallocate productive factors, it is not merely a substitute for investors diversifying their portfolios. The latter only lowers the variance of returns (or some other measure of risk). But by diversifying output, a firm achieves two purposes. First, it lowers the variance of return, assuming that the expected return from each output is the same whether produced by one entrepreneur or by two distinct firms. This is a pure substitute for investors' diversifying their own portfolios. It saves the transactions costs that an investor would have to bear if he had diversified this portfolio at his own expense. Second, diversification facilitates the reallocation of productive services. By performing this service a firm can avoid the cost of reallocation through market forces. Note the similarity between these two functions of the firm. The need for both arises out of fluctuations in the demand for the firm's product. The solution for both is achieved by holding units between which there are low correlations. But diversification by firms, rather than by individual investors, arises only when there is an imperfection in the capital market such that the cost of diversification by the firm is lower than the cost that the individual investor would have had to bear if he had diversified by himself. The second function of the firm—diversifying output to avoid the cost of transferring productive services—stems from a friction in the market for factors of production, in the sense that using this market entails a cost. This friction creates a need for the firm's second function, which cannot be achieved by a diversified portfolio.

As was mentioned earlier, pursuing the above purpose is not free. Consequently, the firms will continue to diversify output up to the usual necessary optimum condition. By that is meant equality on the margin between these costs and the combined benefit from diversified output, i.e., the benefit from efficient resource reallocation and from lowering the variance of return.

CONCLUDING REMARKS

We have considered the phenomenon of diversified production. At least a few explanations for its existence do not depend on anticompetitive motive. We have seen that diversified production provides the firm with advantages based on efficiencies. Specifically, when scale economies in nonproduction activities exceed the scale economies in production, diversified output can reduce average total costs for the firm. In addition, random demand fluctuations offer two further possibilities for efficiencies: (1) by reducing risk and (2) by reducing the costs of reallocating factors of production. To the extent that these potential efficiencies materialize, the effect will be an expansion of final output. This is an unambiguous proconsumer result that may not be possible with specialized production.

Proposed legislation, such as the Kennedy Bill, results from the notion that conglomerate mergers pose a public policy problem due

110 / Economic Aspects of Conglomerates

to the ineffectiveness of the current antitrust arsenal. Since many view conglomerates as conferring no benefits on society, while posing some vaguely articulated risks, legislative proposals rely on presumptions. Passage of such legislation may impose significant costs on society by preventing the exploitation of the advantages discussed in this chapter. This is hardly in the public interest.

NOTES

1. See the Merger Guidelines, Antitrust Division, Department of Justice. Department of Justice Release, May 30, 1968. Reprinted at 360 ATRR pp. X-1 f(June 4, 1968).
2. Section 7 of the Clayton Act reads in relevant part "That no corporation engaged in commerce shall acquire, directly or indirectly, the whole or any part of the stock or other share capital and no corporation subject to the jurisdiction of the Federal Trade Commission shall acquire the whole or any part of the assets of another corporation engaged also in commerce, where in any line of commerce in any section of the country, the effect of such acquisition may be substantially to lessen competition, or to tend to create a monopoly."
3. For an excellent analysis of recent conglomerate merger cases and the trends thereby suggested, see J. P. Bauer, "Challenging Conglomerate Mergers Under Section 7 of The Clayton Act: Today's Law and Tomorrow's Legislation," 58 *Boston University Law Review* 199 (1978).
4. Bauer, note 3 *supra,* suggested the need for new legislation to deal with conglomerate mergers.
5. In early 1979, Senator Edward Kennedy introduced S. 600, a bill to preserve the diversity and independence of American business, which is referred to as S. 600 in this paper.
6. These defenses are found in Section 3. (a) (1) and . . . . . . 3. (a) (2) of S. 600.
7. Section 3. (b) states that the affirmative defenses are unavailable "if one of the parties . . . has within one year previous to the transaction been a party to a prior transaction coming within the provisions of section 2(b) or 2(c)."
8. For example, see J. Lintner, "Expectations, Mergers and Equilibrium in Purely Competitive Securities Markets," 61 *American Economic Review (Papers and Proceedings)* 108 (1971). Another interesting view is provided by H. Levy and M. Sarnat, "Diversification, Portfolio Analysis and the Uneasy Case for Conglomerate Mergers," 25 *Journal of Finance* 795 (1970).
9. R. Coase, "The Nature of the Firm," 4 *Economica* 386 (1937).
10. In this paper, joint products are considered to be a single good. For example, a firm producing both hides and meat is not defined as a conglomerate.
11. An early effort to deal with this problem is provided by P. J. Dhrymes, "On the Theory of the Monopolistic Multiproduct Firm under Uncertainty," 5 *International Economic Review* 239 (1964).
12. For an analysis of conglomerate mergers under a variety of market structures, see P. Areeda and D. Turner, "Conglomerate Mergers: Extended Interdependence and Effects on Interindustry Competition as Grounds for Condemnation," 127 *University of Pennsylvania Law Review* 1082 (1979).

13. Specifically, if X and Y are random variables, the expectation of the sum equals the sum of the expectations:
$$E[X + Y] = E[X] + E[Y].$$
14. This is most likely to occur where the first market is highly concentrated.
15. J. Lintner, "The Impact of Uncertainty on the 'Traditional' Theory of the Firm: Price-Setting and Tax Shifting," in *Industrial Organization and Economic Development*, J. Markham and G. Papanek, eds. (1970).
16. A more general treatment of this problem and more detailed derivations are contained in R. D. Blair and A. Heggestad, "The Impact of Uncertainty upon the Multiproduct Firm," 44 *Southern Economic Journal* 136 (1977).
17. Dhrymes, note 11 *supra*.
18. See, for example, J. F. Weston and S. K. Mansinghka, "Tests of the Efficiency Performance of Conglomerate Firms," 26 *Journal of Finance* 919 (1971).
19. The difference between the borrowing and lending rates on capital funds is an example of the costs of transferring a productive factor. In this case, the loss in value is easily identified albeit quite small. In the case of physical equipment, some of these costs exist due to asymmetric information. For a development of this argument, see G. Akerlof, "The Market for 'Lemons': Qualitative Uncertainty and the Market Mechanism," 84 *Quarterly Journal of Economics* 488 (1970).
20. "Opinions of the Accounting Principles Board" (of the AICPA) No. 17, Aug. 1970, p. 332 states: "Other types of intangible assets lack specific identifiability . . . unidentifiable assets cannot be acquired singly. The excess of the cost of an acquired company over the sum of identifiable net assets, usually called goodwill, is the most common unidentifiable intangible asset."
21. The same is also true for reallocating monopoly power. For example, one way to sell the rights to operate an airline route is to sell the whole firm—a merger.
22. In such cases of nonmarketable, intangible productive factors, the costs of reallocation through the market amount to almost their total value. Thus, in the case of a bankrupt firm where no merger occurs, its tax-offset potential will be lost and cannot be captured in the market by sale as can the firm's other assets. Therefore, the value of this intangible asset is the minimal cost of using the marketplace for reallocation. Empirically, many mergers, conglomerate as well as others, purportedly result because of the transference of tax loss offset rights between firms.
23. Empirically, Berry found positive correlation between growth and diversification, mainly between firms that produce similar products and thus use similar factors of production. See C. H. Berry, "Corporate Growth and Diversification," 14 *Journal of Law and Economics* 371 (1971), especially p. 379.
24. See J. Segall, "Merging for Fun and Profit," 9 *Industrial Management Review* 17 (1968). This is one example of evidence on the nonprofitability of mergers.

Chapter 7

Conglomerate Mergers: Financial Theory and Evidence

Margaret Monroe

Corporate mergers occur for many reasons, some more obvious than others. Vertical mergers may occur to reduce the costs of inputs or costs associated with search and negotiation for contracts, for example; horizontal mergers may occur in an effort to achieve monopoly or oligopoly power, or to realize economies of scale in such areas as production, distribution, or promotion. If these effects are expected to make the merged firm's profits greater than the sum of the original firms' profits, the value of the merged firm should become greater than the sum of the values of the two firms before merger. This result is commonly termed "synergy." There should then be an increase in shareholder wealth—an obvious incentive for shareholders to seek such mergers.

The benefits to shareholders become less clear when we move to conglomerate mergers. Even the word "conglomerate" seems to have several meanings. It is often used as a spillover category to include all mergers that are not strictly classified as horizontal or vertical. For example, even if firms are in different businesses, a conglomerate merger joining them might combine products with cross elasticities of demand, or might make use of a common technology, promotion, or distribution channel. Such conglomerate mergers might result in the same expected benefits as those from the horizontal and vertical mergers mentioned above: enhancement of market power or cost savings from increased efficiency. Benefits of this type are outlined in Lintner and will not be discussed further here.[1]

The "pure" form of conglomerate merger—described by Lintner as one in which "expected net operating profits (before interest and taxes) of the merged firm be identically equal to the sum of the expected net operating profits of the separate firms being merged"—elicits the most difficult questions.[2] We shall call the situation in which the merged expected net operating profits are greater than the sum of the expected net operating profits of the separate firms "earnings synergy" (not to be confused with the standard synergy relating to firm values already mentioned).

How are such pure conglomerate mergers explained? In the absence of any expected earnings synergy, why would such a merger occur? Is the acquisition of a company in an unrelated field often just one more investment, earning a competitive rate of return for the acquiring firm? Or are there other benefits resulting in synergy that accrue to the pure conglomerate and that cannot be duplicated by the separate firms? Does the merger result in synergy for reasons other than cost savings or increased market power and, if so, who benefits—the shareholders or the bondholders? Finally, are such benefits from conglomerate mergers possible only because of imperfections in the market?[3]

The purpose of this paper is to address the questions outlined above, first by tracing through the theory pertaining to the pure conglomerate in recent literature, and then by examining relevant studies.

THEORY

Investments

One possible reason for a firm to acquire a company in an unrelated business is for investment purposes: the acquisition may be viewed as an investment like any other, providing a high enough expected rate of return for its risk, such that the equity value of the firm increases.[4] Suppose that a company is considering a choice between paying a dividend or using that money to acquire a firm that will provide the same rate of return and risk as its current investments.[5] Miller and Modigliani have shown that, under certain assumptions, such an acquisition will leave the firm's shareholders with no more wealth than if they had received the money as a dividend: the acquisition would produce a capital gain exactly equal to the dividend foregone to make the investment, and the investor would be indifferent between the two.[6] The two assumptions used were rational behavior (investors prefer more wealth to less, regardless of the method of payment) and perfect capital markets.

If the above assumptions hold, the firm's owners would have no incentive to invest in the firm we have just described. The dividend would be as attractive as the capital gain from the merger. This statement can be extended to apply to any acquisition that would provide a competitive rate of return. It can be shown that any investment by the firm that earns a competitive rate of return—an expected rate of return that exactly compensates the investor for the risk of the investment—will not increase the value of the firm's shares above the amount of the investment.[7] For such investments, shareholders will be indifferent between retention of earnings for the acquisition and payment of the earnings as dividends. The shareholder will receive a capital gain from the retention that would exactly equal the foregone dividend. Therefore, in perfect capital markets, the owners of a firm should be indifferent between investing in a company that promises a competitive rate of return and paying out the money as a dividend.

Later, we shall discuss evidence indicating that acquiring firms do not earn more than a competitive rate of return on conglomerate mergers. The next question follows naturally: would shareholders be in favor of such an acquisition if the assumption of perfect capital markets did not hold, and does this explain the conglomerate merger movement? One evident deviation from perfect capital markets is the differential tax treatment on dividends and capital gains.[8] Since the tax on capital gains is lower than that on dividends, the investor ends up with more wealth from the capital gain due to the acquisition than from the offsetting dividend. Faced with the choice between a capital gain and a dividend, the shareholder will now prefer the acquisition of the firm to the payment of a dividend which is hit harder by taxes.

This market imperfection is not an incentive for mergers, as some seem to believe. It is merely an incentive for the firm to reinvest in any projects with competitive rates of return rather than to pay out the money as dividends. We are still left with this question: why would shareholders of a firm choose a conglomerate merger rather than an investment in its current line of business? The most likely answers lie not in the level of profits after the merger (since other investments could give the same results), but rather in the characteristics of the resulting income streams to the merged firm's stockholders and bondholders.

Diversification

By their nature, conglomerate mergers would normally be expected to combine two streams of operating profits that are not perfectly correlated, producing a diversification effect on the shareholders' earnings. For example, suppose firm A has an expected return to shareholders of $E(r_A)$, with a standard deviation of σ_A, and firm B has an expected return of $E(r_B)$ with a standard deviation of σ_B. For simplicity, suppose $E(r_A) = E(r_B)$, $\sigma_A = \sigma_B$, and that the correlation coefficient of the returns of the two firms A and B, ρ_{AB}, is less than unity. It can then be shown that, while the expected return to the shareholders of the merged firm, $E(r_M)$, is the same as the expected returns of the two original firms, the standard deviation of this return, σ_M, is lower than either σ_A or σ_B. This can be written as:

$$E(r_M) = E(r_A) = E(r_B) \tag{1}$$

$$\sigma_M < \sigma_A, \sigma_B, \quad \rho_{AB} < +1 \tag{2}$$

In general, we can say that as long as ρ_{AB} is less than one, the expected return on the merged firm's stock is equal to the weighted average of $E(r_A)$ and $E(r_B)$, but the standard deviation of that return is less than the weighted average of σ_A and σ_B. It would therefore appear, at first glance, that the merger must make the shareholders better off as long as they are risk-averse. In other words, the merger would appear to produce a diversification that helps the firm's shareholders. This, in turn, would cause the market value of the merged firm's shares to be greater than the sum of the market values of the shares of A and B, since the market places a premium on the diversification.

In perfect capital markets, however, the diversification of earnings from the merger will not have the above effect. The merger is not doing anything for the shareholders of the two firms that they could not have duplicated themselves.

Mossin has demonstrated this result in a general framework, using the principles of the Capital Asset Pricing Model (CAPM) developed by Sharpe, Lintner, and others.[9] Briefly, the CAPM provides an expression for the equilibrium one-period expected rate of return on asset i, $E(r_i)$, as a function of the one-period rate on a riskless asset, rf, and the expected return on a portfolio of all assets in the market, $E(rm)$. It can be written as

$$E(r_i) = r_f + \beta_i[E(R_m) - r_f] \qquad (3)$$

where $\beta_i = \dfrac{\text{cov}(r_i, r_m)}{\text{var}(r_m)} \cdot \beta_i$ which is often referred to as the ith asset's undiversifiable risk, is a measure of the contribution of one unit of asset i to the variance of the market portfolio. It is the same for all risk-averse individuals and is the appropriate measure of the risk of the investment.

The CAPM as described here is a one-period model, developed using the assumptions of 1) homogeneous expectations, 2) a risk-free asset with rate of return rf, at which investors can borrow and lend as much as needed, and 3) investors' ability to judge each investment solely on the basis of its expected rate of return and standard deviation.

Under the CAPM assumptions, all risk-averse investors hold the riskless bond and a portfolio of all available assets (both stocks and bonds), each in the proportion of its market value to the value of all assets. Rather than using this general derivation, Levy and Sarnat use a simpler example to illustrate the same result.[10] They consider three assets in a perfect capital market to show that, if two merge, the optimal proportion of an individual's risky asset portfolio invested in the merged firm is the sum of the optimal portfolio's proportions placed in the two assets prior to the merger. Therefore, the merger would merely duplicate what the investor could do, and in the CAPM framework, has already done. Any benefits from diversification of the earnings of the two firms have already been realized when the investors diversified their individual portfolios. The market will not pay a premium for the merger-induced diversification.

Returning to the previous example of the merger of firm A and firm B, we see that the reduction of the standard deviation of earnings for a given expected return will not cause the market to put a premium on the shares of the merged firm. The investors will have already duplicated the result by holding the shares of both firms. This same result holds, regardless of the number of assets available to the investor. Thus, pure conglomerate mergers in perfect capital markets will not produce any benefit related to diversification for the shareholders. The value of the merged firm is not increased by the diversification.

Levy and Sarnat then deal with the following imperfections: (1) indivisibilities of assets, and (2) costs of transactions, acquiring information, and monitoring large numbers of assets. The three-asset example is changed to recognize that an investor might be able to hold only two assets because of one or more of the imperfections above. In this case, a merger may indeed help the investor if it brings into his portfolio a new asset by merging it to one already held. For example, suppose that the cost of monitoring each investment is so large that an investor can hold only two stocks, even though the third stock would reduce the standard deviation of the portfolio without reducing its expected return. A merger of the third firm with one of the two in the portfolio then makes the investor better off. Because of the diversification, the value of the merged firm would be greater than the sum of the values of the original firms before the merger.

One condition is necessary for a merger to have such benefits: the merger must accomplish something the investor cannot feasibly duplicate. On the other hand, the merger may force a new asset on some investors. These investors are now forced to reassess their portfolios. If the investor limits the number of stocks in the portfolio because of the cost of evaluating or holding additional stocks, he has already decided that these costs outweigh any expected benefit of further diversification. Thus, a merger cannot help this investor unless the costs of merging (which are passed on to the shareholders in the form of reduced profits) are lower than the costs the investor has been avoiding. In the worst case, the merger can eliminate a previously desirable asset from the portfolio. This would make the investor actually worse off after the merger unless he can substitute another similar asset, or sell short an asset like the new addition. Azzi gives the conditions under which the investor can "undo" the merger and thus not be harmed by it.[11]

Lintner also shows that conglomerate mergers may help shareholders if the shareholders of the original firms had held stock in only one of the firms involved and had had no assessment of the other stock involved prior to the merger.[12] We must repeat: the cost of the merger must not be greater to the shareholder than the costs of information he was avoiding by not holding the investment. Lintner defines information as an economic good, making the costs of gathering information consistent with perfect capital markets. Imperfection or not, the result remains: if information is costly to obtain, a merger may have a positive effect on share value that was not possible under the assumptions of the CAPM.

Thus it becomes evident that with market imperfections the

effects of pure conglomerate mergers are not clear-cut. The merger could have beneficial or harmful effects on investors, depending on the resulting degree of diversification relative to the costs involved.

Coinsurance

Levy and Sarnat were the first to include considerations of the merger's effect on bondholders. Diversification reduces the joint probability of bankruptcy for the merged firm. This lowers the risk of default for any given level of earnings, and bondholders should lower their required rate of return accordingly. Levy and Sarnat call the subsequent reduction of capital costs a true economic gain, since it can only occur from the merger. We note that there is no requirement of perfect capital markets for this result and also that there is no mention in the paper of the resulting effect on the total value of the firm. Of course, *if all else stays the same,* a reduction in the cost of debt will increase the total value of the firm, i.e., the market value of the sum of its debt and equity components. A pure conglomerate merger would then produce a benefit, even in perfect capital markets.

Lewellen's analysis of conglomerate mergers explicitly considers two market imperfections: bankruptcy costs and taxes.[13] He begins with the Modigliani-Miller result which states that the equilibrium of the firm is an increasing function of its debt.[14] This can be written as

$$V_L = V_U + tD_L \qquad (4)$$

where V_U is the market value of an unlevered (no-debt) firm, V_L is the market value of an identical firm with debt in its capital structure, t is the corporate tax rate, and D_L is the value of the debt in the levered firm. Equation (4) implies that the higher the leverage used, the higher the value of the firm.[15] The firm receives a tax "subsidy" on debt because of the deductibility of interest payments. From (4), the optimal capital structure would appear to be one of total debt, and yet firms do not often operate with an extremely high percentage of debt. It is the added consideration of bankruptcy costs that puts a maximum value on the amount of debt that can be effectively used.

Together, taxes and bankruptcy costs imply two things. First, there is an optimal capital structure at which the value of the firm is maximized. Second, the higher the amount of debt possible in the optimal capital structure, the higher the value of the firm, all else being constant. Lewellen considers these two factors in evaluating the effect of conglomerate diversification on the firm's value. He states that the diversification has two results. The merger produces a lower probability of bankruptcy because of the diversification of earnings—which he calls the "coinsurance of debt"—leading to (1) a lower cost of debt at any given level of leverage, and (2) a higher optimum level of debt. He concludes that the value of the firm will therefore increase as new debt is added, resulting in higher quality values.

Rubinstein repeats the Levy and Sarnat discussion on reduction of the probability of bankruptcy and adds another consideration not covered by Levy and Sarnat or Lewellen: the limited liabilities of the two firms are no longer separate.[16] He uses the example of two firms that have merged and discusses those times when one of the two firms would have been bankrupt, but the second would not. In those time periods, some of the returns of the second firm's equity would go to meet the would-be defaulted portion of the first firm's debt obligations, and vice versa. In other words, the merger will reduce the number of times that at least some of the shareholders could have neglected to pay off their creditors because of limited liability. Rubinstein argues, without a formal proof, that even in perfect capital markets this consequence of mergers offsets the lower costs of debt, leaving the shareholders with no more and no less than before the merger.

Higgins and Schall replicate the Mossin, Levy-Sarnat, Rubinstein result using a more general proof based on eliminating arbitrage profits in perfect capital markets.[17] Focusing on the total value of the firm, they demonstrate that the "value additivity principle" first described by Mossin holds regardless of diversification effects when there is costless bankruptcy and no taxes.[18] The "value additivity principle" simply states that the value of the merged firm is equal to the sum of the values of the firms before the merger whenever there is no earnings synergy. They emphasize the importance of understanding that the value additivity applies only to the total value of the firm. It does not differentiate between stock and debt value. Their analysis shows that the value of debt is increased over pre-merger values because of the lower default risk, but that the value of the equity must decline by the same amount. There is no economic gain or lowering of *average* capital costs from the merger in perfect capital markets, so the total value of the firm is unchanged. The diversification from the conglomerate merger merely results in a transfer of wealth from stockholders to bondholders. Rather than benefiting from diversification, stockholders actually lose under these conditions. This result certainly does not appeal to one's intuition regarding–risk-averse investors. It is due partly to the limited liability of shareholders, which Rubinstein mentioned. More will be said about this later, in the discussion of the options pricing model.

Higgins and Schall then examine possible sources of shareholder gain. Recalling their value additivity principle and its implications, they show that if the conglomerate does not change its debt on merging, shareholders will lose to bondholders, as in the case of perfect markets; in this scenario, the shareholders are not taking advantage of the imperfections. Furthermore, if the conglomerate does increase debt to a new optimum level, there may not be enough of an increase in shareholder wealth from taxes to offset the coinsurance.[19] Thus, Lewellen's result is not general. With taxes and bankruptcy costs, the value of the firm increases from merger. A merger that permits a higher optimal debt level will increase the total value of the securities that are merged, but shareholders may still lose to bondholders; on the other hand, both groups may gain from the merger. In any case, a reduction of expected bankruptcy costs may produce an economic gain that is not possible without the merger.

Application of the options pricing model (OPM) has given greater clarity to the concept that shareholders lose wealth because of the effects of diversification. A clear exposition on this topic is found in Galai and Masulis, who deal with the question of corporate stock risk. Their work builds on the OPM developed by Black and Scholes, who first described the way in which common stock may be viewed as a call option to buy the company back from the bondholders.[20]

A call option gives the owner the option to purchase a share of stock at a given price—the exercise price—by a given date. The price of the call option is called the premium. Common stock gives the owner the option to purchase the firm by retiring the debt at its face value by the date of the debt's maturity. Therefore, a share of common stock can be seen as a call option on the firm in which the exercise price is the face value of the debt; the given date is the maturity of the debt; and the premium is the price of the stock itself.

The development of the options pricing model as it applies to common stock requires the following assumptions:

1. Capital markets are perfect (including the absence of bankruptcy costs, taxes).
2. There is a constant short-term, risk-free interest rate, equal for both borrowers and lenders.
3. Short-selling is allowed with no penalties.

4. The distribution of the firm's possible end-of-period asset values is log-normal, the variance of the rate of return on the firm being constant. And,
5. The firm makes no coupon payments.[21]

The OPM provides an expression for the value of a European call option, which is written as:[22]

$$S = VN(d_1) - Ce^{-r_f(t*-t)}N(d_2) \qquad (5)$$

where, when applied to common stock, S is the value of a share of common stock, V is the value of the firm's assets, C is the face value of the firm's debt at maturity, time $t*$, $(t*-t)$ is the time to maturity of the debt, r_f is the risk-free interest rate

$$N(x) = \frac{1}{\sqrt{2\pi}} \int_{-\infty}^{x} e^{-1/2y^2} dy$$

$$d_1 = \frac{\ln(V/C) + (r_f + \frac{1}{2}\sigma^2)(t* - t)}{\sigma\sqrt{t* - t}}$$

$$d_2 = d_1 - \sigma\sqrt{t* - t}$$

and σ^2 = the instantaneous variance of the rate of return to the firm. From (4) we see that

$$\frac{\delta S}{\delta \sigma^2} > 0 \qquad (6)$$

The price of the stock increases with the variance of the firm's rate of return.

That the price of a call option increases with the variance of the returns to the underlying asset can be explained in the following way. The value of a call is the difference between the current stock price and the current premium, as long as this difference is positive. The owner of an option can buy the stock at the exercise price and sell it for its current price. He will do so only if he can realize a profit. If the difference is negative, the call has a zero value. When the variance of the return on the underlying stock increases, the probability of a large price rise increases, which is attractive to the owner of the call. There is a correspondingly higher probability of a large price decline, but this is of less consequence to the call owner; since the maximum loss is still only zero, the probability of an increase in gain has more impact than an equal probability of an offsetting loss in rate of return.

The situation is similar for the stockholder. As with the call option above, the minimum value of the stock is zero, because of limited liability. Like other call options, the value of the stock will decrease with a decrease in the instantaneous variance of the firm's rate of return on the total value of the firm. Galai and Masulis use the CAPM to show Higgins and Schall's value additivity principle, again showing that the pure conglomerate merger does not increase the value of the merged firm above the sum of the values of the firms before merger. The OPM is then used. Since the merger is assumed to decrease the variance of the firm's earnings, Eq. (5) shows that the value of the stock will decline.

The OPM thus provides an excellent framework for the analysis of the pure conglomerate merger. It reaffirms the findings that had begun to appear: in perfect capital markets, a pure conglomerate merger will not increase the value of the firm above the sum of the values of the original firms before merger, but, if there is any diversification effect on the earnings streams, the shareholders will actually lose to bondholders. (At this point, one important factor should be noted. Returning to the CAPM under perfect capital markets, we find that a result of the model is that all investors hold the market portfolio. This means that shareholders holding a certain percentage of the firm's stock also hold the same percentage of its bonds. A conglomerate merger will only shift wealth from the stocks in the portfolio to the bonds, changing nothing. Of course, the logical conclusion of this line of reasoning is that a shift of wealth from one firm to another has no impact on any investors, since they hold stock in every firm.) Thus, conglomerate mergers in perfect capital markets would result in a transfer payment from equity holders to debt holders.

It is only when market imperfections are considered that gains to stockholders become possible. The diversification from pure conglomerate mergers decreases the probability of bankruptcy. In a world where there are corporate taxes and costs associated with bankruptcy, the optimal amount of debt is raised because of the diversification. The resulting tax savings increase the value of the firm. The increase in value goes to the shareholders. Both the increase in leverage and the tax savings help to offset the loss to bondholders from the coinsurance from the merger. If these offsetting factors are large enough, shareholders may gain from the merger. It is therefore possible that, because of market imperfections, there is an incentive for equity-maximizing firms to engage in conglomerate mergers where there is no expected earnings synergy.

EVIDENCE

Two types of hypotheses are relevant to preceding theories. The first deals with whether pure conglomerate acquisitions provide more than a competitive rate of return to the acquiring firm. The second concerns the reallocation of wealth between shareholders and bondholders after merger. Most empirical work deals with the former.

Rate of Return on Acquisitions

Halpern's study on mergers was one of the first to make use of the "cumulative average residual" (CAR) technique developed by Fama, Fisher, Jensen and Roll.[23] The CAR technique involves the following steps. First, a model is used to describe the relationship between the return on a given asset and the return on the market. One such model, the "market model," is written as

$$r_{it} = \alpha_i + \beta_i r_{mt} + \varepsilon_{it}, \qquad i = 1, \ldots, N \qquad (7)$$

where r_{it} is the rate of return on asset i at time t, r_{mt} is the rate of return on an index of stocks representing a market portfolio, i.e., a portfolio composed of all securities outstanding in the marketplace, and ε_{it} is the disturbance for time period t. The α_i and β_i are parameters specific to asset i.

The second step is to obtain estimates of α_i and β_i from asset i's past returns. Using time periods before the event being studied, r_i is regressed on r_m, resulting in Ordinary Least Squares (OLS) estimates, α_i and β_i. Making the usual classical linear regression model assumptions about ε_{it} and r_{mt}, OLS yields estimates $\hat{\alpha}_i$ and $\hat{\beta}_i$ that, when used in the equation

$$\hat{r}_{it.} = \hat{\alpha}_i + \hat{\beta}_i r_{mt} \qquad (8)$$

provide the best prediction of r_{it} given r_{mt}. Obviously, since α_i and β_i are assumed to be unbiased estimates of α_i and β_i, respectively, then the residual, which is defined as

$$e_{it} \equiv r_{it} - \hat{\alpha}_i - \hat{\beta}_i r_{mt}$$

$$= \alpha_i + \beta_i r_{mt} + \varepsilon_{it} - \hat{\alpha}_i - \hat{\beta}_i r_{mt} \qquad (9)$$

has expected value of zero given r_{mt}, since

$$E(\hat{\alpha}_i) = \alpha_i,$$

$$E(\hat{\beta}_i) = \beta_i,$$

and $E(\varepsilon_{it}) = 0$, given r_{mt}

the last being an assumption of the classical model.

The third step is to examine the actual returns on the asset relative to its predicted returns for the time period being studied, that is, to examine the residuals, e_{it}. Let us suppose that we are studying the asset's returns over the period 10 months prior to the merger to 4 months after the merger. For simplicity, the time of the merger is standardized at $t = 0$, resulting in a correspondence of $t = -10$ to the tenth month prior to merger and $t = +4$ to the fourth month following the merger. Consequently the methodology dictates that we estimate α_i and β_i using data prior to $t = -10$ in this example, and then calculate the residuals e_{it} from $t = -10$ to $t = +4$ using the previously estimated α_i and β_i. We emphasize that α_i and β_i are obtained from data in a period disjoint from that used to calculate the subsequent residuals.

Each asset studied has an estimated residual for every time period. The average residual (AR) for a given time period is the sum of all N residuals for the period, divided by N, the number of assets being studied. The AR for time t is expressed as

$$AR_t = \sum_{i=1}^{N} \frac{e_{it}}{N} \qquad t = -10, \ldots, +4 \qquad (10)$$

The final step is to find the "cumulative average residual" for each time period. The CAR at a given time represents the sum of all the AR's calculated up to and including that time:

$$CAR_T = \sum_{t=-10}^{T} AR_t \qquad (11)$$

We would expect the CAR for any time period to be close to zero, given that $E(e_{it}) = 0$ for all i and all t. Note that during the preceding description the α_i's and β_i's were always assumed constant over the time period being studied. Therefore, a steadily increasing (or decreasing) CAR is an indication that an overall change in the returns on the assets has occurred, i.e., *either* α_i and β_i have changed, so that the predicted returns, r_{it}, are systematically understating (if the CAR is increasing) or overstating (if the CAR is decreasing) the returns, *or* some of the assets have provided a one-time jump (or decline) in return as the market responds to some new piece of information. If the CAR stops increasing or decreasing and remains steady after some period of time, it is usually taken as an indication that the parameters (α and β) were constant over the entire time period being studied and that the change in the CAR was due to effects of new information in the market. The preceding CAR technique consists of essentially the same steps, regardless of the length of the time period being studied or the model used in generating the estimates of the parameters and predicted returns.

The purpose of Halpern's study was to estimate the premium received by stockholders of all firms involved in mergers. Assuming no other possible sources of gain to the firm, such as cost reduction or increased market power from a pure conglomerate merger, Halpern claims that any abnormal gains must be due to efficiency, so that any abnormal returns of the stock reflect the market's estimate of economic gain to the firm from the merger. With such a claim he is either disregarding Lewellen's work or the possibility of the imperfections which Lewellen assumed.

The sample consists of 145 merging firms from 1950 to 1965 in which:

1. All firms concerned were listed on the New York Stock Exchange.
2. The merger involved the exchange of common stock for stock or assets.
3. None of the firms were in regulated industries.
4. Neither of the premerged firms had a merger in the year before or after the merger under consideration.
5. Data were available for at least 17 months prior to merger. The firms were characterized as large and small rather than as acquiring and acquired.

The CAR technique is used to identify the "base date" when impact of the merger is first registered in the market. Halpern used a two-index model for the estimates and residuals:

$$_JR_{it} = \alpha_i + \beta_{1J}R_{It} + \beta_{2J}R_{mt} + \varepsilon_{it} \qquad (12)$$

where $_JR_{it}$ is the "investment relative," defined as the new stock price divided by the previous month's stock price (i.e., one plus the percentage increase in the price) of asset i; $_JR_{It}$ is the "industry relative"; the relative of the index of all companies on the New York

Stock Exchange classified as being in the same industry as asset i; and $_JR_{mt}$ is the "market relative"; the relative of a market index of other firms on the Exchange, excluding those in the industry I, all during time t.

Beginning at 23 months prior to the merger date, the CARs were examined to find if and when any abnormally high returns occurred. The CAR happened to begin to increase at 7 months prior to the merger, the time up to which stability in the parameters had already been assumed. This may not be a coincidence, as Halpern may thereby have been assuming the result. If these parameters had actually changed some time before his 7-month cutoff for their estimation, we would still expect to see the CAR begin to increase (or decrease) right at that point. Halpern does not show that the CARs stopped increasing later (recalling that this would be evidence of stability in the parameters). Thus, the increasing CARs may not have been due to a reaction to merger information in the market, but rather to changing parameters.

Once the base date is established, all subsequent price appreciation of the stock—adjusted to account for general market movements—is interpreted as the market's evaluation of the economic gain from the merger. Halpern finds significant positive gains to both the large- and small-firm groups. He therefore concludes that there was an expected economic gain from the mergers studied, that the splitting of the gain was determined by the firms' relative bargaining power, and that acquisitions could therefore provide a higher-than-competitive rate of return. Unfortunately, he does not compare these gains with the normal holding period return which an investor would expect on nonmerging firms of the same risk. He has a measure of all gains rather than of abnormal ones. Thus, the study does not show that the market is expecting the economic gain which Halpern claims.

The next two studies also make use of the CAR technique with the model to be used adjusted for Black's CAPM derivation with no riskless asset, which is called the Zero Beta Model.[24] Black's equilibrium relation is:

$$E(R_{jt}) = E(R_{ot}) + [E(R_{mt}) - E(R_{ot})]\beta_j, \quad j = 1,\ldots,N \quad (13)$$

where $E(R_{jt})$ is the expected return on asset j at time t, $E(R_{mt})$ is the expected return on the market portfolio at time t, $E(R_{ot})$ is the expected return on the minimum variance asset or portfolio whose returns are uncorrelated with the market portfolio, also at time t, and β_j is cov $(Rj,R_m)/\text{var}(R_m)$. A model based on Eq. (12) is used in the CAR technique previously described.[25]

Mandelker tests two hypotheses. The first states that mergers provide a competitive rate of return to acquiring firms. The second states that stock markets are efficient and stock prices therefore adjust instantaneously to all new information.[26] The sample consists of 827 firms contained in the Federal Trade Commission listing of mergers from 1941 to 1962. The CARs are calculated from 40 months prior to the merger to 40 months after the merger for the acquiring firms, and from 40 months up to the merger for the acquired firms. The CARs derived from the testing procedure indicate that the acquiring firms' shareholders did not earn abnormal returns. On the other hand, the CARs of the acquired firms' stocks begin to increase at about 7 months prior to the merger, indicating some returns in excess of those predicted for these stocks. Shareholders of the acquired firms thus appear to earn abnormal gains beginning about 7 months before the merger. Because the β_j's are recalculated for each time period using the previous 60 months of data, allowing the β_j to change over time, Mandelker's estimation techniques avoid the problem of assuming the 7-month base date before actually finding it, as Halpern did. He then accepts the hypothesis that acquiring firms earn no more than a competitive rate of return on acquisitions, although shareholders of acquired firms seem to earn abnormal gains. The result is consistent with Halpern's study, since the gains Mandelker found for acquiring firms could have been merely the competitive rate of return from the acquisition. Mandelker also accepts the hypothesis of an efficient market in which the firm's stock price moves to reflect anticipated gains upon receiving the merger news, well before the merger itself.

Ellert attempts to evaluate the effect of antitrust complaints on returns to stockholders.[27] He hypothesizes that if there are monopolistic-expected (i.e., greater-than-competitive) gains from mergers, antitrust proceedings under Section 7 of the Clayton Act should take them away, causing a large loss to stockholders as the market reacts to the expectation of lower returns. His methodology is essentially the same as Mandelker's, but instead of looking for large positive CARs from mergers, Ellert looks for large negative CARs from divestiture or cancellation of the planned acquisition. His sample consists of large merging firms listed on the New York Stock Exchange, of which 205 companies were named as defendants in Section 7 proceedings initiated by either the Justice Department or the Federal Trade Commission. For all companies, each case must have been filed in the period between 1950 and 1972, and decided by 1974. Ellert examines the CARs of the defendants before mergers and up to and past the filing and ruling dates. Because

Ellert's sample CARs predate the merger time by longer periods than either Halpern's or Mandelker's, they provide more information on the acquired firms. His findings include:

1. Firms ordered to divest had larger CARs to shareholders than firms not ordered to divest, but for periods of up to 5 years before the merger, too long a period to reflect some market anticipation of monopolistic gains from the merger itself (but perhaps making these firms a more visible target).
2. The CARs subsequent to divestiture were reduced, but were not statistically different from firms not ordered to divest.
3. Both the sample acquiring firms and other acquiring firms not involved in Section 7 complaints experienced abnormal gains for a very long period prior to the merger.
4. There was a long history of negative returns to acquired firms' shareholders prior to the merger bid.

Based on the second finding above, Ellert rejects the hypothesis that gains to merging firms are due to anticipation of monopoly gains. Losing the acquired company seems to make little difference to the acquiring firm's returns. The findings are consistent with an alternate hypothesis that there is a "competitive market in corporate control" in which the market recognizes efficient management, and companies with efficient management earn abnormal gains in the market. The third and fourth results above indicate that the acquiring firms had efficient managements, which were taking over poorly managed firms. The takeover bid causes an increase in the acquired firms' CARs, reflecting news of better management. The acquiring firm, however, earns no more on this acquisition than on other investments, as indicated by abnormal returns that occurred before the takeover bid as well as after divestiture. This result supports the "competitive" part of the hypothesis. Although the market rewards efficient managers, enough of them may be available to take over inefficient firms, so that the price of these firms is bid high enough to reflect all the potential gain from a takeover. Although Ellert's findings differ from those of Mandelker, the conclusions are the same: acquisition does not increase the acquiring firm's CARs.

The preceding studies are good examples of the effort to find reasons for the occurrence of pure conglomerate mergers. However, further analysis of such studies is of little value. Because of the potential for reallocation of wealth between bondholders and stockholders, there are problems in drawing inferences from rate of return during acquisition of firms. Testing to see if shareholders of merging firms earn abnormal returns provides little information on the profitability of the acquisition. A competitive rate of return to the acquiring firm on its acquisition could imply returns that are lower than, equal to, or greater than normal stockholder returns for the acquiring firm. The same is true of a greater-than-competitive rate of return. If we assume efficient markets in which the price of the stock reflects all current information in the market, once the merger news becomes known all anticipated effects from mergers will immediately be reflected in the firm's stock price. These effects include the impact of any expected coinsurance, tax savings from increased leverage, and the impact of the investment itself. Therefore, the returns to shareholders of the firms involved reflect the combined—and possibly offsetting—effects of all these factors. Thus, these shareholder returns are insufficient to indicate the expected rate of return on acquisitions.

An only slightly better approach would be to compare the total market value of the merged firm with the combined market values of the original firms before merger. While an increase in value could be due to an abnormally high rate of return or a competitive rate of return plus tax savings from increased leverage, a decrease in value after merger would at least provide information. As long as the acquisition provides a minimum of a competitive return, the value of the merged firm will be at least as great as the sum of the original firms' values. If it is not, then the return on the acquisition is expected to be less than the competitive rate. Unfortunately, this result will not provide enough information to answer the question on return in a satisfactory way.

Reallocation of Wealth Between Shareholders and Bondholders

The study by Kim and McConnell is the first to investigate empirically the possibility of a wealth transfer to bondholders because of the coinsurance effect in perfect capital markets.[28] By considering the results of all possible situations, they prove that the cash flow to the merged firms' bondholders statistically dominates their cash flows without a merger. Similarly, the cash flow after merger to the firms' shareholders is statistically dominated by the cash flows before merger. Thus, unless shareholders take some type of action, the merger will result in a net transfer of expected income from shareholders to bondholders, raising the return to debt and lowering the return to equity.

The hypothesis is that if the merger results in coinsurance, firms that maximize shareholder wealth will increase financial leverage to negate this coinsurance effect. Thus, Kim and McConnell state that bondholders of the merging firms would not earn abnormal returns around the time of the merger. Two different tests are used to find abnormal returns. The first is the CAR technique, using a two-index model similar to the one used by Halpern, containing an index for stock returns and an index for bond returns. The second technique they call "cumulative average differences" (CAD). Here, bonds of the merging firms are paired with bonds of nonmerging firms matching bond ratings by the *Standard and Poor's Bond Guide,* term to maturity, coupon rate, and type of firm (industry or utility). The time periods for the bonds were standardized to make the month of the merger $t = 0$, as in the CAR technique. For each matched pair of bonds, the monthly rate of return on the bond of the nonmerging firm, R^*_{it}, was subtracted from the monthly rate of return on the merging firm's bond, R_{it}. In each time period, the differences for each of the M bond pairs were added and then divided by M to form the average difference (AD) for that month:

$$AD_t = \sum_{i=1}^{M} \frac{(R_{it} - R^*_{it})}{M} \qquad t = -24, \ldots, +23 \qquad (14)$$

The cumulative average difference (CAD) for a given month was then calculated as the sum of all the ADs up to and including that month:

$$CAD_T = \sum_{t=-24}^{T} AD_t \qquad T = -24, \ldots, +23. \qquad (15)$$

The assumption in using this CAD is that if the paired bonds should provide equivalent returns, then the CAD should have a mean of zero. Any upward (or downward) trend in the CAD over time is assumed to indicate windfall gains (or losses) to the bondholders of merging firms.

The sample consists of 39 firms having 44 bonds outstanding where (1) the firm was engaged in only one complete major merger between 1960 and 1973,[29] (2) the bonds were outstanding for the 48 months surrounding the merger, and (3) the merger was classified as "conglomerate" by the Federal Trade Commission. The control bonds to be paired to the sample were chosen from the *Standard and Poor's Bond Guide.*

Kim and McConnell find no evidence of abnormal returns to bondholders of merging firms from either the CARs or the CADs. In addition, they claim that leverage of the merging firms increased significantly. In the absence of coinsurance, they state that the CARs and CADs should have decreased with the increase in leverage, and the fact that they did not is quoted as evidence of the coinsurance effect. Thus, they do not reject the null hypothesis: a coinsurance effect exists, but firms increase leverage upon merging to protect shareholders' wealth.

Some factors are not made clear by this study. First, if coinsurance is anticipated in an efficient market, then anticipated gains to bondholders would be realized at the time of the news of the merger, well before any increased debt is introduced. The absence of gains to bondholders before the merger implies that either the market anticipates no coinsurance effects, or that it also foresees the offsetting leverage. The second factor not considered is corporate taxes. Shareholders gain from increased leverage after the merger, not only from the reduction in coinsurance, but also from the increased tax subsidy from the new debt. Therefore, it might not be necessary for the shareholders to negate coinsurance effects totally before gaining in wealth. In fact, there may be a point beyond which the costs of issuing more debt are higher than the resulting reduction in coinsurance and increased tax benefits. It may not be optimal for shareholders to attempt to negate completely the coinsurance effect. Thus, with taxes and bankruptcy costs, it is possible for both bondholders and shareholders to gain from a conglomerate merger. In view of these two factors, the case in which the merger produces coinsurance but there are no gains to the bondholders involved seems to be very restrictive.

It would also be interesting to know the effects of these mergers on returns to the stockholders involved. In perfect capital markets, no abnormal returns to bondholders would imply no abnormal losses to shareholders, but no abnormal gains either. Thus, if the stockholders actually earned abnormal gains, we would have further support of (1) a coinsurance effect, since the bondholders did not lose from the increase in leverage, and (2) offsetting benefits from the market imperfections first discussed by Lewellen.

SUMMARY

We have seen that there are two possible incentives for pure conglomerate mergers.

The first is to provide the acquiring firm with an investment—the acquired firm—that earns at least a competitive rate of return. However, there is no incentive for the firm to enter into a conglomerate merger rather than to expand in its own business-related areas unless the acquisition provides a higher-than-competitive rate of return.

The second incentive for conglomerate mergers concerns the diversification of earnings. In perfect capital markets, shareholders of the firms involved do not benefit from the earnings diversification. The value of the firm is merely the sum of the values of the firms involved. Furthermore, the resulting coinsurance of bondholders' payments can actually cause a transfer of wealth from stockholders to bondholders.

It is only when the merger can accomplish something which the shareholders cannot duplicate, because of market imperfections, that the shareholders might benefit from the merger's diversification. The best-known of such market imperfections are corporate taxes and bankruptcy costs. If the coinsurance effect creates a higher optimal level of debt than would be possible without the merger, shareholders will gain the tax subsidy from increasing their leverage after the merger. Therefore, these market imperfections mean that shareholders of merging firms can receive an increase in wealth—even if acquisitions do not provide abnormally high returns; this holds as long as the shareholders are able to increase the leverage in the merged firm by enough so that the higher tax benefits at least offset the coinsurance effect at that level of debt.

Evidence on rates of return provided by acquisitions is inconclusive and may remain so because of the compounding effects from coinsurance and taxes on the stock of the firms. Furthermore, while there is some evidence that shareholders of acquired firms earn abnormal returns from the merger, this is not an incentive for acquiring firms to seek mergers. Kim and McConnell's paper does give preliminary evidence that shareholders at least do not lose from coinsurance to bondholders. It is therefore possible that they expect gains from being able to increase leverage after the merger.

In sum, shareholders may expect gains from pure conglomerate mergers—even if acquisitions provide no earnings synergy—by avoiding some bankruptcy costs and reducing taxes in a way that only such mergers can provide.

NOTES

1. J. Lintner, "Expectations, Mergers and Equilibrium in Purely Competitive Securities Markets," *American Economic Review* 101 (1971).
2. Note 1 *supra*, p. 106.

3. A perfect capital market is defined as one in which: (1) all investors have equal, costless access to all relevant information, (b) no one buyer or seller can affect the price of an investment, and (c) there are no transactions costs or differential taxes on different methods of distributing income.
4. The appropriate measure of risk is the "B" of the investment, described below.
5. For simplicity we may assume throughout that the acquiring firm buys all the stock and assumes the debt of the acquired firm. If the value of the stock after the merger equals the sum of the values of the stocks before merger, the shareholders have not gained, since the value of their shares has increased by exactly the amount paid for the acquired firm's stock.
6. M. Miller and F. Modigliani, "Dividend Policy, Growth, and the Valuation of Shares," *Journal of Business* 411 (1961).
7. Rubinstein shows that there will be an upward revision (greater than the amount of earnings retained) of the firm's share price only if the investment yields an expected rate of return higher than the equilibrium expected return for the investment's risk (M. Rubinstein, "A Mean-Variance Synthesis of Corporate Financial Theory," *Journal of Finance* 165 (1973)).
8. R. Sherman, "How Tax Policy Induces Conglomerate Mergers," *The National Tax Journal* 521 (1972).
9. J. Mossin, "Equilibrium in a Capital Asset Market," *Econometrica* 768 (1966); W. Sharpe, "Capital Asset Prices: A Theory of Market Equilibrium Under Conditions of Risk," *Journal of Finance* 425 (1964); J. Lintner, "The Valuation of Risk Assets and the Selection of Risky Investments in Stock Portfolios and Capital Budgets," *The Review of Economics and Statistics* 13 (1965).
10. H. Levy and M. Sarnat, "Diversification, Portfolio Analysis, and the Uneasy Case for Conglomerate Mergers," *Journal of Finance* 795 (1970).
11. C. Azzi, "Conglomerate Mergers, Default Risk, and Homemade Mutual Funds," *The American Economic Review* 161 (March 1978).
12. Lintner, note 1 *supra.*
13. W. Lewellen, "A Pure Financial Rationale for the Conglomerate Merger," *Journal of Finance* 521 (1971).
14. F. Modigliani and M. Miller, "Corporate Income Taxes and the Cost of Capital: A Correction," *The American Economic Review* 433 (1963).
15. For a thorough discussion of this and other issues related to the valuation of the firm, see F. Arditti; "A Survey of Valuation and the Cost of Capital," in *Research and Finance*, H. Levy, ed. (vol. 2), JAI (forthcoming).
16. Rubinstein, note 7 *supra.*
17. R. Higgins and L. Schall, "Corporate Bankruptcy and the Conglomerate Merger," *Journal of Finance* 93 (1975).
18. Costless bankruptcy means that there are no transactions costs incurred in transferring ownership to the creditors, such as court or reorganization costs.
19. The expression showing the benefits is given in Higgins and Schall (note 17 *supra*, p. 106) with no bankruptcy costs. It is possible for shareholders to protect their position if they buy back the premerger debt at its premerger value and reissue new debt after the merger (Higgins and Schall, note 17 *supra, n.* 16). But this assumes that the market cannot foresee the shift of wealth from the merger, or it would have already raised the value of the debt to the postmerger value in anticipation.
20. D. Galai and R. Masulis, "The Option Pricing Model and the Risk Factor of Stock," *Journal of Financial Economics* 53 (1976); F. Black and M. Scholes, "The Pricing of Options and Corporate Liabilities," *Journal of Political Economy* 637 (1973).

21. If dividend and coupon payments are assumed to occur on the same dates, this assumption will be met in-between these dates.
22. A European option is one which cannot be exercised before its expiration date.
23. P. Halpern, "Empirical Estimates of the Amount and Distribution of Gains to Companies in Mergers," *Journal of Business* 554 (1973); E. Fama, L. Fisher, M. Jensen, and R. Roll, "The Adjustment of Stock Prices to New Information," *International Economic Review* 1 (1969).
24. F. Black, "Capital Market Equilibrium with Restricted Borrowing," *Journal of Business* 444 (1972).
25. The model is $R_{jt} = \gamma_{0t} + \gamma_{1t}\beta_j + u_{jt}$. The second step of the CAR technique must be altered slightly. Referring to the model, $E(\gamma_{1t})$ corresponds to $[E(R_{mt}) - E(R_{0t})]$ in (12). Since R_{0t} cannot be observed, γ_{1t} must be estimated along with γ_{0t} and β_j. The statistical procedures for estimating γ_{0t} and γ_{1t} are found in E. Fama and J. MacBeth, "Risk, Return and Equilibrium: Empirical Tests," *Journal of Political Economy* 607 (1973).
26. It is interesting to note that if this second hypothesis is true, it would be difficult to measure Halpern's economic gain unless the measurement starts before the base date for each firm. Any gain would be realized instantaneously at that time. G. Mandelker, "Risk and Return: The Case of Merging Firms," *Journal of Financial Economics* 303 (1974).
27. J. Ellert, "Mergers, Antitrust Law Enforcement and Stockholder Returns," *Journal of Finance* 715 (1976).
28. E. H. Kim and J. McConnell, "Corporate Mergers and the Co-Insurance of Corporate Debt," *Journal of Finance* 349 (1977).
29. To be complete, the acquiring firm had to acquire all of the other firm's stock, and the debt of both companies had to be taken over by the merged firm.

Chapter 8

The Relevance of the Relevant Market in a Section 7 Analysis of Conglomerate Mergers (Whatever Those Are)

Ira Horowitz

INTRODUCTION

Since *Standard Oil*[1] and *Corn Products*,[2] delineation of product and geographic markets within which to analyze alleged violations of Section 2 of the Sherman Act[3] and Section 7 of the Clayton Act[4] has been *de rigeur*.[5] Markovits did not exaggerate when he remarked that "the market definition issue is probably more hotly contested and time-consuming than any other in horizontal merger litigation."[6] He therefore recommended that "instead of utilizing a lot of resources to aggregate this data into a crude market definition that does little more than waste much of the information the data provides, we should perform our analysis with the disaggregated data itself. For example . . . we should look directly at the frequency with which they were each other's closest competitors."[7] The purpose of this chapter is to explore the way in which the market definition issue *should* relate to antitrust enforcement and litigation under Section 7 of the Clayton Act. The exploration leads

The helpful criticisms of Professors Roger Blair and Joseph Brodley, Dr. Ted Gebhard, Mr. Hays Gorey, and especially Professor David D. Martin, are, with the usual disclaimer, gratefully acknowledged.

to the conclusion that the relevant-market concept will remain relevant for antitrust analysis in general and for judging the anti-trust implications of conglomerate mergers in particular.

The ensuing discussion, however, finesses by neglect three related issues of varying interest and importance, the first of which is the definition of a conglomerate merger. In the main, this particular neglect is laudatory, since, as observed elsewhere, "[t]he number of definitions of conglomerate mergers is but slightly exceeded by the number of writers on the subject,"[8] and in the present antitrust context any new definition I might propose would be bound to combine economic and legal logic, with debatable results.[9] Happily, the definitional issue becomes irrelevant to the present discussion[10] as a result of the decision to neglect a second related issue: namely, whether conglomerates (whatever those are) are "bad" per se, once they attain a certain size.[11] That is, since this discussion is not concerned with any real or imagined evils associated with concen-tration and agglomeration of economic power, I accord all mergers, including those resulting in these "irrationally integrated enter-prises," like analytical treatment.[12]

The third neglected issue is how to define the relevant market. This issue is ignored (except parenthetically) for two reasons: first, because it is an important and difficult topic in and of itself and one that I am dealing with elsewhere; and second, because the narrower focus of this paper is on how the market-definition issue, once resolved, *should* relate to Section 7 litigation. The narrower focus also permits all but parenthetical neglect of the related issues of whether or not (a) there are meaningful submarkets within markets,[13] (b) markets and industries must be carefully distin-guished from one another,[14] and (c) markets are gerrymandered for antitrust purposes.[15]

The paper presents two principal arguments: first, that the critical antitrust issue in *any* merger is whether a market can be discovered in which the merger increases the likelihood that a (not necessarily proper) subset of the sellers (or buyers, where relevant) electing to do so can act in concert so as to effect anticompetitive results; and, second, as implied by the preceding, that the empirical issue and economic question is whether the conditions in the market are such as to abet either tacit or overt collusion by this subset of sellers. Although the arguments are not unique, considered in tandem and with reference to previous market-definition proposals, they provide an interesting perspective on market definition and antitrust analysis.[16]

MARKET DEFINITION AND THE CLAYTON ACT: A BRIEF HISTORICAL PERSPECTIVE

Section 7 of the Clayton Act, which has provided the legal foundation upon which the antitrust authorities have based their attacks on the conglomerate firm, intends to proscribe mergers and acquisitions whose effects "may be substantially to lessen competition or to tend to create a monopoly . . . in any line of commerce . . . in any section of the country."[17] Like the Sherman Act that preceded it,[18] the Clayton Act "does not contain the word 'market.'" It is clear, however, that 'line of commerce' signifies a product market and 'section of the country' refers to a geographic market."[19] The fact that the Clayton Act "was not intended to reach every remote lessening of competition is shown in the requirement that such lessening must be substantial."[20] The latter implies that not only must a substantial *share* of the market be affected,[21] but that the *absolute size* of the market must be substantial as well.[22] Until the 1950s, however, the existence of "the market" was essentially taken for granted by the courts; only scattered clues were given as to how to discover it.[23] Nonetheless, by that time "it," at least in the geographic sense, was recognized to be "the area of effective competition" between the companies involved.[24] The Court further acknowledged that "[t]he 'market,' as most concepts in law or economics, cannot be measured by metes and bounds."[25]

With regard to the product market, the Sherman Act legal tests to bound the market, which had become focused on "reasonable interchangeability" by consumers for the same purpose,[26] and the Clayton legal tests of "sufficient peculiar characteristics and uses"[27] seemingly differed. The difference, however, was asserted to be more apparent than real, and the two tests were subsequently described as "but different verbalizations of the same criterion."[28] *Brown Shoe* further homogenized the legal tests by setting forth some "practical indicia" for bounding the product and geographic markets,[29] and *Grinnell* affirmed that comparable market definitions are required under both Acts.[30] The alleged practicality of the *Brown* criteria notwithstanding, relevant-market definition remains a thorny and arguable issue, especially where it is the geographic market that is in dispute.[31] The time dimension can also be important in market definition,[32] but whether the antitrust laws call for a short- or long-term market definition remains unresolved by the courts.[33] Further, there has been no clear attempt to tie this issue to the seemingly related time dimensions of monopoly power;[34] namely, the power to raise price, which is essentially short-run in nature, and the power to limit the freedom to compete, which is essentially long-run in nature.[35]

The multidimensional aspects of relevant-market definition, and the fact that distinctions cannot necessarily or ordinarily be sharply drawn on any one dimension, virtually assure that relevant-market delineation will in no small degree remain arbitrary.[36] If the phrase "to prove" is read literally, this arbitrary characteristic is in sharp contradistinction with the demands imposed upon plaintiffs by the courts, which call upon them "adequately to define and to prove the relevant market, which is 'a necessary predicate' for evaluating claims under these provisions (sections 7 and 2) of the antitrust laws."[37] In what we can point to *ex post*, if not necessarily *ex ante*, as the conglomerate merger cases under Section 7, delineation of the relevant market has been no less important. This is so because of the plaintiff's need to "prove" a market in which at least one of the following could be shown: (1) either the acquiring or acquired firm was a perceived[38] or actual potential competitor[39] of the other; or (2) the resulting entity's size and economic power, and the existing position of one of the merging parties, raised the spectre of entrenchment;[40] or (3) the alleged evils of reciprocity would make themselves felt.[41] Absent an antimerger law that specifically aims at conglomerates on the basis of their absolute size or their effects on aggregate concentration, there is no reason to expect that in the future relevant-market definition will become any less of a requisite in the adjudication of conglomerate merger cases brought under Section 7.[42] The issue, then, centers on the exact role that the relevant market should play in a conglomerate merger case. We suggest here that this role is no different from that which the relevant market should play in any other type of merger case.

The historical role of the relevant market—beyond satisfying the legal requirement of specifying a product or service, and the geographical area to house the alleged antitrust violations—has been to provide for a well-defined set of data on the basis of which to compute sellers' or buyers' concentration ratios. When for such market-share data *Alcoa's* 33 percent (no), 60 percent (doubtful), and 90 percent (enough) guidelines for the identification of monopoly[43] are placed in apposition to the less strenuous *Brown Shoe* and *Von's Grocery* standards[44] and the Court's awareness that the weight given to concentration ratios should depend upon their surrounding settings,[45] the risk of creating a "high concentration implies monopoly, low concentration may imply monopoly" antitrust mentality becomes very real. This, despite the fact that a "low concentration implies competitive behavior, high concentration is compatible with competitive behavior" philosophy is at least as apt.[46]

The corollary of the latter philosophy is that because concentration ratios provide only *signals* of possible anticompetitive behavior and potential monopoly (or the lack thereof), they should not be treated as direct evidence upon which a *prima facie* case of anticompetitive behavior and monopoly can be built. Instead, the concentration ratio should be just one of several inputs that must be introduced into a probabilistic framework intended to satisfy congressional concern "with probabilities, not with certainties."[47] Under this philosophy, the concentration ratio assumes both a signaling and supporting role. Delineation of the relevant product and geographic markets remains a critical consideration, but the defendant's tactical need to dispute the plaintiff's proffered definition would in principle be ameliorated.[48] It becomes *incumbent* upon the plaintiff to define the market appropriately, because a too-broad market definition that yields persistently low levels of concentration would effect a procompetitive inference; alternatively, a too-narrow market definition that yields persistently high levels of concentration would be vulnerable to a potential-competition defense. The potential competition would come, in particular, from other product and geographic markets.[49] As discussed in the next section, this view also subsumes the various legal views of market definition and, given the earlier disclaimers, encompasses the analysis of conglomerate mergers.

MARKET DEFINITION AND ANTITRUST: AN OFFERED APPROACH

The seller that has a monopoly exerts "control over supply."[50] In this economic sense, it is always possible to define a market sufficiently narrow to be monopolized or sufficiently broad to be otherwise. Indeed, as Turner has commented, "the traditional two-step legal approach of first defining the market and then deciding whether monopoly power exists" is open to the economist's criticism that "the question of the extent of the power will often be answered in the process of deciding what the market is, so that

market definition becomes redundant."[51] Moreover, every firm has
control over its own supply and in this sense has a monopoly over
the markets for the products that it in particular supplies. Thus,
upon occasion plaintiffs have succumbed to the temptation to
discover anticompetitive behavior or monopoly power behind every
bush, not merely by astutely gerrymandering markets, but more
basically by defining them on an individual-seller basis.[52] This
unhappy practice is so patently silly as to make the market-
definition process more ridiculous than redundant. Yet, a purposeful
antitrust policy demands that the market-definition process be
neither.

Section 7's concern is with whether a particular merger or
acquisition will lessen competition or tend to create a monopoly.
This initially translates into a concern with whether either merging
party sells in a candidate market wherein, as one of the merger's
outgrowths, the sellers' incentives *and* ability to raise price over a
series of future short runs, or to exclude rivals over the long run, will
be enhanced.[53] The lattern concern, which can only be dealt with
through probabilistic statements, is immediately expandable into
two alternative questions. First, does the merger substantially
enhance the opportunities and incentives for the sellers to act in
concert, as well as the possible costs to them of failing to act in
concert? And, second, if the sellers do act in concert, will this have
the probable effect of achieving a sustainable price increase or the
exclusion of rivals from the market?

The second and third questions follow directly from the first. It
can therefore be directly inferred that antitrust enforcement in the
spirit of Section 7 would proscribe those mergers for which the
answers to these two questions are in the affirmative. It does not
also follow, however, that the successful prosecution of a Section 7
suit would require evidence from which one could infer either tacit or
overt collusion in the market. The implication, rather, is that there is
a need to ask yet a fourth, and in many ways more imposing,
question: notably, are the *conditions* favorable to collusion present
in the market and will the merger strengthen them. The two-
dimensional goal of the antitrust authorities should be to prevent
only those mergers for which the latter question can be answered
affirmatively.[54] On the one hand, this goal would seem to condemn
mergers on the fragile grounds that the *opportunity* for concerted
action exists, while leaving moot the issue of whether the market
has ever actually been plagued by concerted action. On the other
hand, this goal is fully compatible with existing antimerger policy.
Moreover, its implementation requires the consideration of several

market conditions that either include or subsume the factors and indicia that have traditionally been used to define the relevant market and assess a merger's impact. It is these conditions that keep the relevant market relevant, because they can only be assessed empirically within the framework of a particular product and geographic market definition, and with respect to a specific time dimension.

A not inconsiderable advantage to this approach to Section 7 enforcement is that by and large there is agreement on the set of market conditions favorable to collusion.[55] Students of the collusive arts disagree only on the size of the set. This harmony does not exist where the degree of competition among market rivals is assessed by reference to the traditional indicia of competitive performance: e.g., advertising and research expenditures, the rate of technological innovation, and the degree of product proliferation. While most economists and lawyers would agree that these variables are reflective of competitive activity, whether the reflection is positive or negative is unclear and in dispute.[56]

The more formidable lists of the market conditions favorable to the formation and maintenance of either formal or informal collusive groups are marked by double-counting or overlap; that is, one condition either directly implies or is a prerequisite for another. To all intents and purposes, however, it is commonly accepted that the sellers in a market will be more encouraged to act in concert: (1) the lower is the price elasticity of demand for the sellers' product at the competitive price; (2) the higher is the elasticity of each seller's marginal cost curve in the competitive-output range; and (3) the fewer are the number of sellers.[57]

The time dimension first enters the analysis through the back door of market definition because two markets that are "clearly" separate and distinct over a short term will not necessarily be so over a longer term. The time dimension makes a front door reappearance through the conditions favorable to collusion. Specifically, we have to be concerned with both the short- and long-run elasticities, as well as with the number of sellers that will obtain in the market in the short and long runs.

The short-run price and marginal cost elasticities are what affect the sellers' incentives to collude in order to raise price (and restrict output); the long-run price and marginal cost elasticities affect the inducements to exclude rivals. The number of sellers determines the feasibility of forming and maintaining a collusive group over any given period. In particular, and in brief, when short-run demand is price inelastic at the competitive price, colluding rivals are able to achieve relatively substantial price boosts without severely restricting their individual output rates, while simultaneously avoiding the deleterious price effects that would ensue should one or more attempt to expand production and sales. Similarly, when short-run marginal costs are relatively elastic, absent collusion each seller has the cost incentive to expand production considerably, at the market price, with the subsequent adverse price effects of their attempts to dispose of the incremental output being suffered by all.[58] Analogously, when long-run demand is price inelastic, or with elastic long-run marginal costs, attempts by outside firms to enter the market will, in the former instance, only succeed if the in-market sellers either severely curtail production and absorb losses in market share, or if the losses in market share are accompanied by substantial price, as opposed to output, reductions. In the latter instance, where all firms have the incentive to build "large" plants and produce at "high" output rates, given the demand conditions, each additional seller's market impact is unlikely to be negligible. In either event, the in-market sellers have the incentive to collude, say through limit pricing, in the attempt to discourage new entry. Still further, to the extent that the short-run elasticity conditions initially encourage collusion to raise price, they will secondarily encourage collusion to exclude *potential* entrants to the market, the collusive group, or both. That is, the sellers will prefer not to divide the spoils of the collusion among a larger group, nor will they want to risk weakening the collusion by increasing the number of participants.

With respect to the overlap among the conditions, consider, for example, the marginal cost elasticity. When the short-run marginal cost curve is highly elastic, the long-run marginal cost curve is necessarily more so.[59] Hence, collusion to effect both aspects of monopoly power is encouraged. It can, however, also be inferred from the short-run elasticity condition that the sellers will be more inclined to collude the greater is the ratio of fixed costs to variable costs in the industry's production process. But, higher fixed costs imply higher barriers to entry to the industry and a consequently lower rate of entry, as well as smaller differences in the total costs of production among the sellers and a greater tendency for them to produce what is generally acknowledged to be a standardized product. The latter in turn induces price competition to move up on the scale of the sellers' competitive alternatives and makes the sellers more likely to use like marketing practices. The correspondence may not always be perfect, but the imperfections, such as they are, are minor.[60] Indeed, it could further be argued that the fewness-of-sellers condition will always be satisfied when the long-run elasticity conditions are satisfied. That is, when the long-run demand elasticity is low and the long-run marginal cost elasticity is high, competitive realities will assure that only a few sellers survive in the market. In fact, the limiting case of a downward-sloping long-run marginal cost curve (and consequently a falling long-run average cost curve) up through the "higher" rates of demand is how natural monopoly was born.

In general, the two elasticity conditions are sufficient but not necessary to effect their somewhat less technical counterparts. The fewness of sellers, however, is so fundamental to collusion that even if the other conditions were not "right" for collusion, once this one is satisfied concerted action becomes viable. As Adam Smith forewarned us: "If [this] capital is divided between two different grocers, their competition will tend to make both of them sell cheaper, than if it were in the hands of one only: and if it were divided among twenty, their competition would be just so much greater, and the chance of their coming together, in order to raise price, just so much the less."[61] One need not be versed in the theory of the core to take the next step and recognize that markets with few sellers will also be highly concentrated.[62] The converse, however, is not necessarily true, since highly concentrated markets might have many sellers, the preponderance of whom constitute Posner's fringe of small sellers.[63]

Nonetheless, highly concentrated many-seller markets will be unsupportable over the long term whenever the sellers have highly elastic long-run marginal cost curves. This condition evolves when the industry's production process is characterized by technological economies of scale over a wide range of outputs relative to market size and these are not totally dominated by pecuniary diseconomies.[64] Since markets with few sellers, each of whom enjoys the benefits of a highly elastic long-run marginal cost curve, will be highly concentrated, knowledge of the former two facts makes knowledge of the latter fact redundant. By the same token, when many sellers in a highly concentrated market enjoy those elastic-marginal–cost-curve benefits, there is no apparent need for concern over their incentive to compete. This is so, since in the long run each seller would be induced to extend production and sales by any market price in excess of long-run marginal cost. Under these circumstances, that marginal cost would approximate average cost and the competitive price throughout a wide output range. In the few-seller case, then, the sellers' concentration ratio provides no new information as to competitive behavior; and in the many-seller case the information provided by the sellers' concentration ratio can lead to erroneous judgments as to competitive behavior. In either event, the concentration ratio serves little purpose beyond either signaling markets for which a more serious and detailed study of the number of significant sellers and the circumstances under which they produce and sell might prove to be provocative, or, given a candidate market that has been nominated for study for reasons independent of the concentration ratio, entering as one element in determining the number of significant sellers.[65]

Unfortunately, determining the number of significant sellers in a market is more readily accomplished than is determining their marginal cost curves.[66] Nonetheless, the effort is worth making, even though data constraints that cannot be relaxed might well prevent attacking the problem with the econometrician's preferred degree of sophistication, or of resolving it with anything other than a wide-range estimate. To be sure, more often than not it might be necessary to fall back on a fixed-to-variable-cost ratio, say, as a form of proxy for the short-run marginal cost elasticity; and, even that ratio will be open to definitional manipulation. Still, that proxy would better serve the antitrust laws than does the use of the concentration ratio as the proxy for monopoly power.

Our interest in determining the price elasticity of market demand must be subject to a similar understanding.[67] It is, however, an interest to which we must cater. Situations in which short-run market (as opposed to firm) demand is relatively inelastic at the competitive price are of concern because they encourage concerted behavior. In addition, however, the price elasticity of market demand is reflective of the competition, both actual and potential, of other products and/or geographic markets, at any market price. It also reflects the potential competition of other sellers in both the present and, for delayable purchases, the future.[68] Over the long run, this potential competition becomes actual competition. Thus, if the boundaries of the market are drawn *inappropriately* narrow, market demand will be price elastic, say because of the out-of-market competition, whereas *inappropriately* broad market boundaries will effect, *ceteris paribus*, relatively inelastic estimated demand elasticities.[69] In the former instance, the sellers will have no demand-induced incentive to collude. Still further, the pressures of the potential competition of the out-of-market sellers will make illusory any apparent monopoly power enjoyed as a group by the in-market sellers.[70] In the latter instance, the market power enjoyed by the group will not be illusory, but the size of the group will be sufficiently great to preclude a sustainable collusion. In either event, the defendant's interests in an antimerger suit are protected against any inappropriate market definition proposed by the plaintiff and accepted by the court.

The proposed merger analysis procedure is thus a three-stage process. The first stage in the process requires the definition of the relevant market. In the second stage, the status of the three market conditions basic to the formulation and maintenance of collusive groups is determined for *that* relevant market, both premerger and postmerger.[71] In the third stage, an assessment is made, based on the second-stage data, as to whether the merger "substantially" enhances and/or gives rise to a "dangerous probability" that the sellers in the market can, and not necessarily do or will, act in concert. Those mergers would be blocked for which the assessed probability does in fact attain the "dangerous probability" standards established by the court. This procedure would deal with the conglomerate merger as it would with any other. At first blush, it might be inferred from this that the "pure conglomerate" merger would only be proscribed when both parties to it competed in markets that satisfied the conditions favorable to collusion *and* when the resulting business entity was a firm that would rival one that also competed in both markets. Otherwise, the postmerger opportunities for collusion would not seem to differ from the premerger opportunities.[72] Nonetheless, at the same time that he forewarned us of the dangers of few sellers, Smith also sounded his oft-quoted alert as to how the consumer is likely to be affected when businessmen get together.[73] It is an alert that was not lost on Edwards when he developed his own concerns about conglomerates.[74]

It is also an alert that is especially pertinent in a world in which firms tend to acquire working relationships with one another and market niches,[75] and where the *informal* ties that emerge among firms, including their buyer-seller relationships, can raise questions about the actual independence of some supposedly independent business entities.[76] Still further, as Andrews and Brunner have pointed out, in our world "[e]ach firm will tend to specialize in what it does best. In this way, complementary relationships between businesses may be as important as directly competitive ones."[77] A direct consequence of the latter is the emergence of inherent market-division arrangements whereby, for example, large-scale producers in seemingly well-defined markets will cater to a broader clientele than, and choose not to seriously compete with, small-scale producers that confine their efforts to the more specialized needs of a unique clientele. It may be impractical to exclude the specialty producers and purchasers from "the market," but it is important to recognize that their presence tends to effect an upward bias to the perceived "competitiveness" of the market in which they sell and buy. Similarly, it reduces the number of sellers required for a successful collusion.

In what amounts to a strong potential-competition argument, the conglomerate merger can be looked upon as a market-sharing agreement between the merging parties in which they *formally* agree not to compete with one another, irrespective of their prior intentions. The antitrust concern is with whether the temptations and opportunities for collusion in a market will be enhanced through the formal agreement not to compete or, where the *precise* manner in which collusion will occur in that market can be demonstrated, through the alleged sources of conglomerate power.[78] Any known and unknown informal relationships as might exist among sellers and potential sellers can only intensify the concern.

Consider, for example, the brewing industry. Here, the leading eight sellers account for 80 percent of beer sales in the national beer market; the leading three sellers account for more than 60 percent of that market. Further, previous studies indicate that both the short- and long-run elasticity conditions conducive to collusion are satisfied.[79] *Ceteris paribus*, then, the proposed procedure might be expected to enjoin a merger between, say, the fifth and eighth leading brewers. This is so because such a merger would, by decreasing the already small number of leading sellers, enhance their ability to coordinate activities and orchestrate the market, with the fringe of smaller sellers dancing to their tune. The *ceteris paribus* qualifier allows for either or both of two possibilities: the merging parties might be able to demonstrate that absent the merger one or both would fail and disappear from the market; alternatively, they might be able to demonstrate that the emergence of a strong fourth seller in a market that is dominated by three rather than eight sellers will reduce the likelihood of concerted market behavior. That is, whether or not the three leading sellers are acting in concert, either tacitly or overtly, the competitive pressures imposed by the newly created entity will lessen the likelihood of their doing so.[80]

How the rumored acquisition of the third-leading brewer, Schlitz, by the tobacco-selling R. J. Reynolds Co. would be dealt with by the proposed procedure is somewhat less clear.[81] The earlier arguments would suggest that because (a) the conditions favorable to collusion obtain in the market, (b) one of the sellers that would necessarily be included in that collusion is involved in the merger, and (c) the other merging party already comes in contact with another of the leading sellers (Miller) through its rivalry with Philip Morris in the tobacco market, then (d) the acquisition could at best leave unaltered, but might well increase, the potential for collusion. On the surface, the procedure would therefore look askance at this acquisition. If we probe a bit more deeply, however, the declining fortunes of Schlitz are easily demonstrable. It can even be questioned whether the injection of new capital and management can reverse the decline. A case might therefore be made that the persistent erosion in Schlitz's market position will enhance the potential of the other industry leaders to effect a successful collusion. This collusion would include a fewer number of members, each one of whom would have more to lose by failing to collude. Insofar as the merger can indeed reverse the Schlitz trend, it reduces the likelihood that the brewing market will evolve into one that is dominated by only two sellers, Anheuser-Busch and Miller, the number at which a collusion is most readily achieved. The acquisition, it can therefore be argued, is actually *pro*competitive.

Although without a detailed analysis it is not clear how the proposed approach would resolve a Reynolds-Schlitz merger, it is quite clear that it would give its blessings to the marriage of Reynolds to, say, a strong regional brewer such as Genesee. The lines along which the analysis would take place are also clear. And, by most standards, either merger would be considered to be conglomerate.

CONCLUSIONS

We have not attempted to prescribe any standards for proscribing conglomerate mergers. Rather, in recognition of the fact that we can disagree as to what constitutes a conglomerate merger, the suggestion has been made that all mergers be dealt with within the same general framework. The particular framework proposed here would focus on the conditions conducive to collusion. This chapter argues that once the focus of antitrust proceedings turns from a preoccupation with market shares as such, to a strict concern with the preconditions for firms to act in concert, the perceived need of the adversaries in a merger suit to debate the market-definition issue will be less urgent if not absent.

More specifically to the mandate of this paper, although the "relevant market" is in any event arbitrary, its definition is important. This is so because we require *some* market definition as a frame of reference within which the market demand price elasticities, the marginal cost elasticities, and the number of sellers can be determined. The closer the definition comes to some ideal, the more likely it becomes that we will correctly answer the question of whether the merger under attack should be proscribed. The approach nonetheless fails to satisfy the desideratum of providing management with a precise set of preconditions under which mergers, conglomerate or otherwise, will be approved or denied. It thus suffers from a defect common to all procedures that are forced to recognize the arbitrary and subjective nature of the judgmental process in an uncertain world.

NOTES

1. Standard Oil Co. v. United States, 221 U.S. 1, 61 (1911) wherein the Court wrote as follows: "The commerce referred to by the words 'any part' construed in the light of the manifest purpose of the statute has both a geographical and a distributive significance, that is it includes any portion of the United States and anyone of the classes of things forming a part of interstate or foreign commerce."
2. United States v. Corn Products Refining Co. et. al., 234 Fed. 964 (1916).
3. 15 U.S.C. Section 2 (1976).
4. 15 U.S.C. Section 18 (1976).
5. This statement is somewhat exaggerated. Before 1950, market definition was not crucial in Clayton Section 7 cases, where competition *between* the acquiring and acquired firms, rather than competition in a market, was of principal concern (D. D. Martin, "The Bethlehem-Youngstown Case and the Market-Share Criterion: Comment," 52 *American Economic Review* 526 (1962); "The Brown Shoe Case and the New Antimerger Policy," 53 *American Economic Review* 347 (1963)). Allegations of monopoly or the attempt to monopolize in violation of Sherman Section 2 are treated somewhat differently from allegations of combinations to monopolize, but it has now seemingly been established that Sherman Section 2 and Clayton Section 7 complaints require comparable relevant-market definitions (United States v. Grinnell Corp., 384 U.S. 563, 570-76 (1966)). There are, however, still some vestiges of courtroom sympathy for the minority view that in Section 2 cases "the relevant market is 'not in issue.'" (Lessig v. Tidewater Oil Co., 327 F.2d 459, 474 (9th Cir. 1946)). That is "[s]pecific intent to monopolize is the heart of a conspiracy charge, and a plaintiff is not required to prove what is the 'relevant market.'" (Salco Corp. v. General Motors Corp., Buick Motor Div., 517 F.2d 567-76 (10th Cir. 1975)).
   As regards Sherman Section 1, it "outlaws unreasonable restraints on interstate commerce, regardless of the amount of commerce affected" (United States v. Yellow Cab Co., 332 U.S. 218, 225 (1947)).
6. R. S. Markovits, "Predicting the Competitive Impact of Horizontal Mergers in a Monopolistically Competitive World: A Non-Market-Oriented Proposal and Critique of the Market Definition-Market Share-Market Concentration Approach," 56 *Texas Law Review* 595 (1978).
7. Note 6 *supra*, p. 603.
8. J. P. Loughlin, "A Lawyer's View of Conglomerate Mergers," 44 *St. John's Law Review* 677 (1970).

9. I have elsewhere ("The Perceived Potential Competitor: Antitrust Sinner or Saint,"*The Antitrust ·Bulletin* (forthcoming)) questioned the government's likely attitude towards the rumored acquisition of the Schlitz Brewing Company, the nation's third leading brewer, by the R. J. Reynolds Tobacco Company, in light of the immense success enjoyed by the then seventh-ranked, but now second-ranking Miller Brewing Company following its acquisition by Philip Morris in 1969. In particular, I questioned whether the precedent of the latter acquisition and its well-known success might strengthen arguments to the effect that R. J. Reynolds is a potential entrant, albeit through merger, to the brewing industry, and that more procompetitive options are available to it. My naive presumption at the time of writing was that the merger of a tobacco company with a brewery would by anybody's standards be classified as conglomerate. I have subsequently discovered that Kaldor considered an analogous situation a half-century ago. As a result, he posed the following: "If the demand for cigarettes in a particular village shop is more affected by the price of beer in the opposite publichouse than by the price of cigarettes in the shop at the nearest town, which of the two would Mrs. Robinson lump together into 'one industry': the seller of cigarettes plus the seller of beer in the village, or the seller of cigarettes in the village plus the seller of cigarettes in the town?" (N. Kaldor, "Mrs. Robinson's 'Economics of Imperfect Competition,' " 1 *Economica* 340 (1934)). To Kaldor, then, it would not be as "obvious" as it is to me that such a merger is conglomerate.

Alternatively, a merger that brought under one roof Chef Pierre's frozen pies and Sara Lee's frozen pies, which on the surface does not strike me as conglomerate, was said to be in the main "the merger . . . of complementary, not competing companies," because Chef Pierre's strength is in the institutional side of the frozen pie business whereas Sara Lee's strength is on the retail side, and the "record does not contain any indication of substantial competition between fresh and frozen pies on the retail side . . . [but] . . . by contrast, there is compelling evidence in favor of a finding that fresh and frozen pies are fiercely competitive" (United States v. Consolidated Foods Corp., 455 F. Supp. 108, 126, 137 (1978)).

10. This is not strictly true insofar as a prerequisite of the more common definitions of conglomerates is the definition of the markets of the merging firms. For example, a conglomerate merger has been defined as: "any merger of companies in unrelated markets" (Loughlin, note 8 *supra*, p. 677); "the fusion of two firms showing no common competitive market between them and bearing no vertical relationship to one another of supplier-customer" (R. C. Clark, "Conglomerate Mergers and Section 7 of the Clayton Act," 36 *Notre Dame Lawyer* 256 (1961)); "put[ting] together companies that are not competitors" (R. Bork, "Antitrust in Dubious Battle," 44 *St. John's Law Review* 670 (1970)); "mergers of firms which supply products in different markets" (M. A. McLaughlin, "The Propriety of the Single Firm's Product as the Relevant Market in Attempt to Monopolize Cases," 29 *Baylor Law Review* 225 (1979)); "[d]iversifying acquisitions [that] have no immediate effect on market structure; the market shares before and after such an acquisition are precisely the same, only the *identity* of the firms comprising the market undergoes change" (J. W. Markham, *Conglomerate Enterprise and Public Policy* (1973), p. 3.); "produc[ing] a firm having a number of external markets equal to the sum of the premerger external markets of the acquiring and the acquired firms" (J. C. Narver, *Conglomerate Mergers and Market Competition* (1967), p. 3); and perhaps most popularly, any merger that is not of the product extension, market extension, or horizontal and/or vertical variety

(M. G. Jones and E. J. Heiden, "Conglomerates: The Need for Rational Policy Making," 44 *St. John's Law Review* 244-45 (1970)).

11. Clark has suggested that Section 7's legislative history shows an intent to "fashion . . . a weapon against the conglomerate merger" (note 10 *supra*, p. 261). D. D. Martin's legislative history of Section 7 (*Mergers and the Clayton Act* (1959), pp. 20-56, 221-53) indicates that interfirm rivalry was the authors' critical concern, but that the amended version reflects a more general concern with increasing economic concentration.

Quite early in the antitrust game (1902), ex-Speaker of the House Thomas B. Reed is quoted as saying: "An indefinable something is to be done in a way nobody knows how and at a time nobody knows when. That, as I understand, is the programme against the trusts" (E. F. Nolan, *Combinations, Trusts and Monopolies* (1904), p. 1). Nonetheless, for the classic explanation see C. D. Edwards, *Maintaining Competition* (1949).

12. J. A. Rahl, "Conspiracy and the Anti-Trust Laws," 44 *Illinois Law Review* 768 (1950).

13. Economists have long disagreed on the issue. For example, after first asserting that "[t]he imprecision of the market concept—Marshall's 'industry'—is well known and needs none of the fatuous over-elaboration from which Stigler and Fellner have rescued us" (M. A. Adelman, "The Measurement of Industrial Concentration," 33 *Review of Economics and Statistics* 271 (1951), Adelman inveighs against the "pathetic illusion that the market is whatever the courts choose to call it. The market, like the weather, is simply there, whether we only talk about it or do something. . . . The evidence that sustains any of . . . three market concepts necessarily condemns the others" ("The Anti-Merger Act, 1950-60," 51 *American Economic Review* 237 (1961)). See also M. A. Adelman, "Economic Aspects of the Bethlehem Opinion," 45 *Virginia Law Review* 426 (1959); R. B. Heflebower, "Towards a Theory of Industrial Markets and Prices," 44 *American Economic Review* 552-53 (1954). Marshall's "fatuous over-elaboration" begins with the suggestion that "a 'market' refers to a group or groups of peoples, some of whom desire to obtain certain things, and some of whom are in a position to supply what others want" (A. Marshall, *Industry and Trade* (1923), p. 182) and goes on from there. By contrast, Chamberlin points to the possibility of having "a monopoly of Chateau d'Yquem, of all Sauternes, of all white wines from the Bordeaux region, or all Bordeaux wines, or of all white wines, of all wines, of all beverages, and so on indefinitely until we reach the limit of all economic goods. And whatever the area monopolized, the monopolist will always face competition in some degree from the wider area beyond the limits" (E. H. Chamberlin, "Measuring the Degree of Monopoly and Competition," in *Monopoly and Competition and Their Regulation*, E. H. Chamberlin, ed. (1970), p. 255). That is, any lines are indefensible as such (E. H. Chamberlin, "Product Heterogeneity and Public Policy," 60 *American Economic Review* 87 (1950)). From an antitrust standpoint, Brown Shoe Co., Inc. v. United States (370 U.S. 294, 325 (1962)) firmly established the relevance of submarkets whose boundaries "may be determined by examining such practical indicia as industry or public recognition of the submarket as a separate economic entity, the product's peculiar character and uses, unique production facilities, distinct customers, distinct prices, sensitivity to price changes, and specialized vendors," although "[f]or a submarket to exist . . . not all of the Brown Shoe criteria must be met" (United States v. Black and Decker Mfg. Co. 430 F. Supp. 729, 739 (1976)). For a discussion and supporting view see Martin (1963), note 5 *supra*.

14. Perhaps more pertinently, the Section 7 concept of a market is not "necessarily the same as the economist's concept of the market" (United States v. Bethlehem Steel Corp., 168 F. Supp. 576, 588 (1958)). More generally it has been argued that the term "market," which "does not appear in any of the antitrust laws is solely a term of judicial construction" (R. W. Werth, "Comment: Determination of the Relevant Product Market," 26 *Ohio State Law Journal* 241 (1965)).

For one economist's objections to the Bethlehem (and presumably the latter) philosophy, see Adelman (1959), note 13 *supra*. For a second view see D. D. Martin, "The Bethlehem-Youngstown Case and the Market-Share Criterion," 52 *American Economic Review* 522 (1962). Economic literature in the main seemingly accepts as "certain that there cannot be two prices (or values) for goods of the same quality, in the same market and at the same time (G. P. Scrope, *Principles of Political Economy* (1833), p. 171) because of the competition of buyers and sellers. Indeed, "the market" is commonly discussed in terms of its principal distinguishing "tendency for the same price to be paid for the same thing at the same time, . . . allowance . . . made for the expense of delivering the goods to different purchasers" (Marshall, note 13 *supra*, p. 325), which tells us what we can expect in the *competitive* market once we discover it, but not how to discover it to begin with. Moreover, as Mill has cautioned, "[t]here is no proposition which meets us in the field of political economy oftener than this—hat there cannot be two prices in the same market . . . yet every one knows that there are, almost always, two prices in the same market" (J. S. Mill, *Principles of Political Economy* (1848), p. 246). In fact, the uniform-price characteristic, which has been called "an *obsolete* superstition" (W. S. Woytinsky, *Market and Prices* (1906), pp. 182–83), is apparently of questionable empirical validity (J. W. Pratt, D. A. Wise, and R. Zeckhauser, "Price Differences in Almost Competitive Markets," 93 *Quarterly Journal of Economics* 189 (1979)). In actual litigation, as well as in most economic writing, the distinction between markets and industries tends to be overlooked, although the distinction can be crucial in assessing competitive behavior and impacts. Building on Andrews' view of "an 'industry' as any grouping of individual manufacturing businesses which is relevant when we study the behavior of any one such business" (P. W. S. Andrews, "Industrial Analysis in Economics," *Oxford Studies in the Price Mechanism*, T. W. Wilson and P. W. S. Andrews, eds. (1951) p. 168; see also P. W. S. Andrews and E. Brunner, *Studies in Pricing* (1975), p. 36), Nightingale has distinguished an industry as "any grouping of firms which operate similar processes and could produce technically identical products within a given planning horizon" from a market, which is "the institution within which a firm attempts to sell his output or buy an input" (J. Nightingale, "On the Definition of 'Industry' and 'Market,'" 27 *Journal of Industrial Economics* 35 (1978)). And, as Mrs. Robinson has observed in a related vein: "Questions relating to competition, monopoly and oligopoly must be considered in terms of markets, while questions concerning labour, profits, technical progress, localization and so forth have to be considered in terms of industries [which are] groups of firms having certain technical characteristics in common" (J. Robinson, "The Industry and the Market," 66 *Economic Journal* 360-61 (1956)). In the latter spirit, the focus of the present paper is on markets as distinguished from industries.

15. Numerous writers have been aggrieved by what they see as the government's unfailing tendency as plaintiff to define and defend a market definition that will be least favorable to the defendants when, in particular, market shares are taken into account in assessing anticompetitive impacts (J. Davidow, "Conglomerate

Concentration and Section 7: The Limitations of the Anti-Merger Act," 63 *Columbia Law Review* 1237 (1968); G. E. Hale and R. D. Hale, "A Line of Commerce Market Definition in Anti-Merger Cases," 52 *Iowa Law Review* 426 (1966a) and "Delineating the Geographic Market: A Problem in Merger Cases," 61 *Northwestern University Law Review* 552-53 (1966b); M. Handler and S. D. Robinson, "A Decade of Administration of the Cellar-Kefauver Anti-Merger Act," 61 *Columbia Law Review* 649-50 (1961); T. M. Lewyn and S. Mann, "Some Thoughts on Policy and Enforcement of Section 7 of the Clayton Act," 50 *ABA Journal* 156 (1964); C. J. Steele, "A Decade of the Celler-Kefauver Anti-Merger Act," 14 *Vanderbilt Law Review* 1056-57 (1961); and Werth, note 14 *supra*, p. 292). It has also been suggested that "the market may vary depending on what interests the court is primarily seeking to protect" so that "[o]ne can never be sure . . . whether the market was deliberately defined to conform to an overall conceptual scheme or whether *ex post facto* examinations of a case merely rationalize opinions which may not have been analytically consistent" (S. Mann and T. M. Lewyn, "The Relevant Market Under Section 7 of the Clayton Act: Two New Cases—Two Different Views," 47 *Virginia Law Review* 1019-20 (1961); see also note 46 *infra*).

The argument is well taken that such market gerrymandering, for whatever purpose, is unfortunate because it makes judicial results unpredictable (Hale and Hale (1966b), p. 550), and therefore causes merging parties unnecessary uncertainty. By the same token, once we break the binds of thinking that market shares are necessarily reflective of monopoly power and anticompetitive behavior, it is the *plaintiff* that will suffer the consequences of proposing an especially narrow or broad, and, in either event, ill-conceived market definition. The binds, however, are strong indeed.

16. In particular, see F. Machlup, *The Political Economy of Monopoly (1952)*, p. 116; R. A. Posner, *Antitrust Law* (1976).
17. 15 U.S.C. 18 (1976).
18. See note 1 *supra*.
19. United States v. Bethlehem Steel Corp., 166 F. Supp. 576, 588 (1958).
20. Standard Co. v. Magrane-Houston Co., 258 U.S. 346, 357 (1922).
21. Standard Oil v. United States, 337 U.S. 293, 315 (1949).
22. United States v. DuPont & Co., 353 U.S. 586, 595 (1957).
23. Handler and Robinson, note 15 *supra*, pp. 641-42.
24. Standard Oil v. United States, 337 U.S. 293, 300 (1949); Transamerica Corp. v. Board of Governors 206 F.2d, 163, 167 (3rd Cir. 1953).
25. Times-Picayune v. United States, 345 U.S. 594, 611 (1953). The Court went on to remark (note 42 *infra*, at 612) that "[f]or every product, substitutes exist. But a relevant market cannot meaningfully encompass that infinite range. The circle must be drawn narrowly to exclude any other product to which, within reasonable variations in price, only a limited number of buyers will turn; in technical terms, products whose 'cross-elasticities of demand' are small." The Court, unfortunately, subsequently asserted that such cross-elasticities are "called for" (United States v. DuPont & Co., 351 U.S. 377, 394 (1956)). Thus, although it is widely recognized that cross-elasticities (and to a lesser degree price elasticities) are neither readily interpretable (Posner, note 16 *supra*, p. 48); readily (or otherwise) measurable (Machlup, note 16 *supra*, pp. 9, 522-23), nor necessarily of uniform size when taken in either direction (F. M. Scherer, *Industrial Market Structure and Economic Performance* (1971), p. 483), any event, constrained in absolute size by the price elasticities (R. L. Bishop, "Elasticities, Cross-Elasticities, and Market

Relationships," 62 *American Economic Review* 788 (1952); Machlup, note 16 *supra*, p. 487), leading authorities in the area of antitrust continue to perpetuate the gratuitous notion that wherever possible cross-elasticities of demand as well as supply should be employed in defining the relevant market (P. Areeda and D. F. Turner, *Antitrust Law* (1978), pp. 349-50).

26. United States v. DuPont & Co., 351 U.S. 377-395 (1956).
27. United States v. DuPont & Co., 353 U.S. 586, 593-4 (1957).
28. United States v. Columbia Pictures, 189 F. Supp. 152, 183-4 (1960).
29. See note 13 *supra*.
30. See note 5 *supra*.
31. As discussed in detail in K. G. Elzinga and T. F. Hogarty, "The Problem of Geographic Market Delineation in Antimerger Suits" (18 *The Antitrust Bulletin* 45 (1973)), the courts have tended to delineate geographic markets on the basis of a limited number of exports of the product or service from the candidate area (see, e.g., United States v. The Philadelphia National Bank, et. al., 374 U.S. 321 (1963)) or, alternatively, on the basis of a limited number of imports of the product or service into the candidate area (see, e.g., United States v. Pabst Brewing Company, 384 U.S. 546 (1966)). Not surprisingly, as Elzinga and Hogarty point out, the two candidate areas so delineated will not necessarily coincide. This prompts their suggestion that the two approaches be combined so that, for example, the *average* of the percentage of imports and exports from a candidate area should not exceed a predetermined figure for the candidate to qualify as a relevant geographic market (K. G. Elzinga and T. F. Hogarty, "The Problem of Geographic Market Delineation Revisited: The Case of Coal," 23 *The Antitrust Bulletin* 1 (1978).

I have suggested elsewhere that geographic markets can be delineated, on a sound theoretical basis, by the educated deployment of price correlations between various geographic areas (I. Horowitz, "On Defining the Geographic Market in Section 7 Cases," *Bank Structure and Competition* 169 (1977)). That suggestion, which has roots at least as far back as Jevons (W. S. Jevons, *The Principles of Economics* (1965, 1905), p. 148) (and more recently see, for example, Adelman (1959), note 25 *supra*, pp. 352-53; P. Areeda and D. F. Turner, "Conglomerate Mergers: Extended Interdependence and Effects on Interindustry Competition as Grounds for Condemnation," 127 *University of Pennsylvania Law Review* 1093 (1979); G. W. Stocking, "The Rule of Reason, Workable Competition, and Monopoly," 64 *Yale Law Journal* 1141 (1955)), is neither novel nor beyond attack since, "[l]ike the Lord, competition may well work in mysterious ways so that prices or their changes alone are an inadequate guide to the operations of the 'unseen hand' " (J. M. Lishan, "The Cellophane Case and the Cross-Elasticity of Demand," 4 *The Antitrust Bulletin* 598 (1959)).

32. I. R. Barnes, "The Primacy of Competition and the Brown Shoe Decision," 51 *The Georgetown Law Journal* 728 (1963); Werth, note 14 *supra*, p. 242).
33. The short-term view that " 'any part' [of commerce] may have a significance of limitation in time" was adopted in Peto v. Howell (101 F.2d 353, 358 (9th Cir. 1938)), but the courts have also shown their longer-term interest in "present and prospective competitive conditions in this country" (United States v. Standard Oil of New Jersey, 47 F. 2d 288, 311 (D.C. E.D. Missouri, 1931)). For specific recognition of the time factor, also see American Crystal Sugar Co. v. Cuban-American Sugar Co., (259 F.2d 524, 530 (2nd Cir. 1958)) and United States v. Continental Can Co. (378 U.S. 441, 455, 465 (1964)), as well as discussions in A. R. Burns, *The Decline of Competition* (1936), p. 346; J. E. Cairnes, *Political*

Economy (1874), p. 104; D. MacDonald, "Product Competition in the Relevant Market Under the Sherman Act," 53 *Michigan Law Review* 78-79, 86 (1954); J. C. Narver, "Supply Space and Horizontality in Firms and Mergers," 44 *St. Johns Law Review* 321 (1970).

34. E. S. Mason, "Monopoly in Law and Economics," 47 *Yale Law Journal* 34-49 (1937). Although I am unaware of any instance of the correlation approach carrying the day in the courtroom, evidence of coincidental price movements in product oranges in Florida and California was introduced by the defendant in Case-Swayne Co. v. Sunkist Growers, Inc. (369 F.2d 449 (9th Cir. 1966)) in an effort at establishing a wider geographic market than that proposed by the plaintiff. The court, however, refused to make the inference of a single geographic market, concluding instead that Southern California-Arizona constituted the relevant geographic market. The message of *Columbia Pictures* (189 F. Supp. 153, 185 (1960))—"Statistical evidence can rarely, if ever, supply all the facts needed for a definitive judgment"—will undoubtedly be modified over time, as attorneys and judges become increasingly comfortable with, and sophisticated in the use of statistical techniques, especially correlation and regression analysis.

35. R. Schmalensee, "On the Use of Economic Models in Antitrust: The *Realemon* Case," 127 *University of Pennsylvania Law Review* 1044 (1979).

36. In addition to the product, geographic, and time dimensions, it has also been suggested that the buyers and sellers that make up the demand and supply dimensions, respectively, of the market, provide two more of what are at least five essential dimensions of the market (Barnes, note 32 *supra*, p. 728). In effect, we cannot necessarily achieve agreement on even as fundamental an issue as the appropriate market dimensions.

37. Fount-Wip, Inc. v. Reddi-Wip, 568 F.2d 1296, 1301 (9th Cir. 1978).

38. See, for example, the following: United States v. Penn-Olin, 378 U.S. 158; (1964); United States v. El Paso Natural Gas Co., 376 U.S. 651 (1964); Kennecott Copper Corp. v. FTC 467 F.2d 67 (10th Cir. 1972), *cert. denied*,416 U.S. 909 (1974); and United States v. Falstaff Brewing Co., 410 U.S. 526 (1973). Assuredly, even *ex post* the acquisition of one brewer by another is difficult to recognize as purely conglomerate, but for those who would classify so-called product extension and market extension acquisitions as being in the conglomerate category, it is. The marriage of Chef Pierre to Sara Lee (see note 9 *supra*) suffers from a comparable problem.

39. See, for example, the following: FTC v. Atlantic Richfield Co., 549 F.2d 289 (4th Cir. 1977); FTC v. Tenneco Inc., 433 F. Supp. 105 (1977); and United States v. Hughes Tool Co., 415 F. Supp. 637 (1976).

40. See, for example, the following: United States v. Aluminum Company of America, 233 F. Supp. 718 (1964); Ekco Products v. FTC, 347 F.2d 745 (7th Cir. 1965); and General Foods Corp. v. FTC, 386 F.2d 936 (3rd Cir. 1967); United States v. Wilson Sporting Goods Co., 288 F. Supp. 543 (1968).

41. See, for example, the following: United States v. Ingersoll-Rand Co., 320 F.2d 509 (3rd Cir. 1963); FTC v. Consolidated Foods, 380 U.S. 592 (1965); United States v. Northwest Industries Inc., 301 F. Supp. 1066 (1969); and United States v. International Tel. and Tel. Corp., 324 F. Supp. 19 (1970).

42. See, e.g., United States v. LTV Inc., 315 F. Supp. 1301, 1306, 1309 (1970).

43. United States v. Aluminum Co. of America, 148 F.2d 416, 424 (2d Cir. 1945).

44. In Brown Shoe Co. v. United States (370 U.S. 294, 343-34 (1962)) the court evinced concern with the merging parties' 5 percent share, and in United States v. Von's Grocery Co. (384 U.S. 270, 281 (1966)) the court was concerned about the merging parties holding a 9 percent share when the market leader held an 8 percent share.

45. United States v. Columbia Steel Co., 334 U.S. 495, 527-28 (1948).
46. Indeed, this is the philosophy that underlies the courts' handling of potential-competition cases. The Court has held that the "potential-competition doctrine has meaning only as applied to concentrated markets" (United States v. Marine Bancorporation, 418 U.S. 602, 630 (1974)), in effect making concentration a precondition for subsequent analysis.
47. Brown Shoe Co. v. United States, 370 U.S. 294, 323 (1961). For the gory details as to how this would be accomplished see I. Horowitz, "A Bayesian Interpretation of Concentration Data," 1 *Industrial Organization Review* 205 (1973) and "A Bayesian View of Post-Acquisition Evidence and Antitrust," 22 *The Antitrust Bulletin* 757 (1977).
48. Nevertheless, where the need to do so presents itself, I suspect that counsel for the defense, like H. L. Mencken's well-known, if anonymous, political contemporary will "learn to rise above principle. When the water reaches the upper deck, follow the rats."
49. The too-broad market definition that yields persistently high levels of concentration would only involve a defendant that did not itself have a substantial market share (otherwise the plaintiff would attempt to narrow the market). This definition would therefore be vulnerable to the defense that, by effecting an additional strong rival for the market leaders, the merger is actually procompetitive.
50. Chamberlin, note 13 *supra*, p. 255.
51. D. F. Turner, "Antitrust Policy and the Cellophane Case," 70 *Harvard Law Review* 309 (1956).
52. See note 20 *supra*. In *United Shoe,* the court argued that "[t]o define a market in terms of what the most important producer offers does not involve circular reasoning. For the problem of defining a market turns on discovering patterns of trade which are followed in practice" (United States v. United Shoe Machinery Corp., 110 F. Supp. 295, 302 (1953)). More narrowly, the franchising movement of recent decades has provided the strongest fuel for the one-firm-market inspiration, but we can probably look forward to its more widespread application. For a discussion see Mason, note 34 *supra*, and for illustrations of the practice in action, see Submeyer v. Coca Cola Co. (515 F.2d 835 (5th Cir. 1975)) and ILC Peripherals v. International Business Machines (458 F. Supp. 423 (1978)).
53. The subsequent discussion is confined to sellers' competition as opposed to buyers' competition, but analogous arguments can be made in the latter context. When the terms short and long run are used, they are used in the economist's sense of reflecting the degree of variability of resources. While time is an element, there is only a single long run and the shortest of short runs (when all resources are fixed), but there are a myriad of intermediate runs for any market and industry. More particularly, the length of time required for the long run will differ among industries. The terms short and long term, by contrast, are strictly time-related notions.

    The subsequent discussion implicitly treats the sellers *as if* they were the single-product firms of neoclassical theory, unplagued by problems of joint costs and distribution. This is done in order to make the major point that I want to make, and without any pretense that, for example, the measurement problems, in particular the separation of joint costs, are easily solved; that antitrust problems do not exist outside of manufacturing; that products mysteriously move from plants to the homes of consumers without frictions or effort; or that secondary, rental, and aftermarkets do not play a role in durable goods industries.
54. The merger that creates a monopolist with elastic marginal costs in a market with

less than perfectly elastic demand is considered to effect the ideal collusive "group"—a single unit—and would be proscribed. When the monopolist can neither raise price nor be induced to reduce output, the merger would not be proscribed.

55. See note 59 *infra.* Empirical verification of these conditions in price-fixing cases, in particular verification that the fewness of sellers, high concentration, and a homogenous product tend to be present when price fixing occurs and endures, is presented in G. A. Hay and D. Kelley, "An Empirical Survey of Price Fixing Conspiracies," 17 *Journal of Law and Economics* 13 (1974).

A not inconsiderable concern is with whether the relevant preliminary analysis can be accomplished in a short, say 20-day period of time. With the use of appropriate proxies, it would seem so. The choice between doing that which is correct but which may take time and effort, and that which is quick and easy but which may be misleading, is not always easy.

56. For a discussion of the various pros and cons see Scherer, note 25 *supra*, pp. 284-399.

57. G. S. Becker, "Crime and Punishment: An Economic Approach," 76 *Journal of Political Economy* 206 (1968); W. J. Liebeler, "Market Power and the Competitive Superiority in Concentrated Industries," 25 *UCLA Law Review* 1286 (1978); Posner, note 16 *supra.*

58. The most immediately apparent case is that of rival sellers each of whom has large plants and substantial excess capacity. In this event, each seller may be able to achieve considerable increases in output with comparatively little additional expenditure beyond the fixed costs already incurred. Thus, each seller has an incentive to expand output, but each would have to reduce price in order to sell the output, which would result in a price-cutting war detrimental to all sellers. The impetus to collusion is clear.

59. Marshall remarks on this fact (note 13 *supra*, p. 187), but also and erroneously suggests that, irrespective of time, demand elasticity is either "high" or "low" (note 13 *supra*, p. 186). The error is important since, as indicated below, inelastic short-run demand can encourage short-term collusion that cannot be maintained over the long term, say because of potential competition that effects elastic long-run demand.

60. Posner (note 16 *supra*, pp. 55-61) discusses the following "conditions favorable to collusion": (1) market concentrated on the selling side, (2) no fringe of small sellers, (3) inelastic demand at the competitive price, (4) entry takes a long time, (5) many customers, (6) standard product, (7) the principal firms sell at the same level in the chain of distribution, (8) price competition more important than other forms of competition, (9) high ratio of fixed to variable costs, (10) demand static or declining over time, (11) sealed bidding, and (12) the industry's antitrust 'record.' In addition to Posner's (3), (6), and (9), Liebler (note 57 *supra*) lists (13) a strong and active industry trade association and (14) little difference between the costs of the different firms within the industry; and, rather than (10), the static or declining demand, he suggests (10') great demand fluctuations. This view is consistent with Mrs. Robinson's argument that great demand fluctuations cause periodic excess capacity during which "there is a strong pressure to break through the tensions which preserve the individualism of firms and to resort to overt collusion to defend the level of profits," (J. Robinson, "The Impossibility of Competition," in *Monopoly and Competition and Their Regulation*, E. H. Chamberlin, ed. (1954), p. 524) with the pressures increasing when the managements are risk averse.

In a related vein, Phillips has singled out five variables as being particularly important determinants of rivalry among firms: (1) the number of firms, (2) the distribution of power among them, (3) the homogeneity of their value systems, (4) the power of firms external to the group to break down coalitions within the group, and (5) the formality of the interfirm organization (A. Phillips, "Policy Implications of the Theory of Interfirm Organization," 51 *American Economic Review* 246 (1961)). In addition to reiterating or restating the earlier market conditions, these also imply (specifically (2), (3), and (5)) the importance of the costs of collusion; that is, the costs of reaching an agreement and preventing chiseling (Posner, note 16 *supra*, p. 51). An additional cost is the *expected cost of getting caught.*

In contrasting mid-nineteenth-century views, McCulloch remarked that even combinations "formed for the accomplishment of improper objects . . . will, when let alone, inevitably cure themselves," the reason being "that the motives which individuals have to break off from the combination are so numerous and powerful that it can seldom be maintained for any considerable period: (J. R. McCulloch, *A Treatise on the Circumstances which Determine the Rate of Wages and the Condition of the Labouring Classes* (1851), p. 88), in contrast to which Mill suggested that "[i]n many trades the terms on which business is done are a matter of positive arrangement among the trade, who use the means they always possess of making the situation of any member of the body, who departs from its fixed customs, inconvenient or disagreeable" (note 14 *supra*, p. 247). Clark very early raised the issue of whether "a half dozen or less [sellers] would not, even without forming a trust, act as a quasi-monopoly" (J. B. Clark, *Essentials of Economic Theory* (1907), p. 201) with only potential competition to constrain it; and, Marshall, too, suggested that all producers that can impact significantly on the market but that do not hold absolute monopolies will be "tempted to restrictive combination" (note 13 *supra*, p. 401).

More recently, it has been suggested that collusion is too difficult to effect so that it doesn't actually occur (M. D. Blechman, "Conscious Parallelism, Signaling and Facilitating Devices: The Problem of Tacit Collusion Under the Antitrust Laws," 24 *New York Law School Review* 881 (1979); Y. Brozen, "The Concentration-Collusion Doctrine," 46 *ABA Antitrust Law Journal* 826 (1977); Burns, note 33 *supra*, p. 3). (But, see Hay and Kelley, note 55 *supra*.) Others have suggested that it may be occurring, but even if known to exist it is difficult to detect (Edwards, note 11 *supra*, p. 32; Rahl, note 12 *supra*). The trust of the present approach, however, is with the *inducements.* Whether they in fact suffice to effect a collusion is irrelevant.

61. A. Smith, *An Inquiry Into the Nature and Causes of the Wealth of Nations* (1973), p. 342.
62. A guide to what might be meant by this rather vague expression is the Kaysen and Turner definition of a concentrated Type I oligopoly as one in which the leading eight firms control 50 percent of the market (C. Kaysen and D. F. Turner, *Antitrust Policy* (1959), p. 30).
63. Posner, note 16 *supra*, p. 56.
64. The possibility that each of many sellers is given the long-run pecuniary benefits of a supplying industry's technological economies warrants mention, but not digression.
65. The second of the two purposes in particular might be better served by a concentration measure such as the Herfindahl index or entropy measure from which a numbers-equivalent can be directly determined. The latter reflects the number of equal-sized firms that would provide a level of concentration equiva-

lent to that in the candidate market (M. A. Adelman, "Comment on the 'H' Concentration Measure as a Numbers-Equivalent," 49 *Review of Economics and Statistics* 99 (1969)).

66. For a classic, but well-wearing survey of the early attempts and the issues involved, see A. A. Walters, "Production and Cost Functions: An Econometric Survey," 31 *Econometrica* 1 (1963).

67. The difficulties in estimating the price elasticity are not as great as those in estimating the cross-elasticity. Econometric estimates of the latter require a more fully specified model than is required in order to estimate the former, and both the data demands and the statistical problems are correspondingly greater.

As with the marginal cost elasticity, but somewhat less satisfactorily, we might consider some proxies for the demand elasticity. Taken in combination, for example, small fluctuations in total sales revenue and units sold, comparatively fixed per capita unit sales to buyers, low rates of entry by sellers, and large swings in market price would hint at inelastic market demand.

68. Thus, if *supply* substitutability for firms that are not in the market acts as a constraining force on the in-market rivals, and if consumers are aware of the supply substitutability possibilities, this too should be reflected in the elasticity of demand, at least as perceived by the in-market sellers. Put otherwise, supply substitutability, in effect, makes the price elasticity of market demand greater than it would be in the absence of supply substitutability. It is therefore unnecessary to consider the supply substitutability possibilities in initially *defining* the relevant market (see, e.g., United States v. Columbia Steel Co., 334 U.S. 495 (1948)), since these are most properly reflected through (adjusted) price elasticities.

The courts have been mixed in their views of supply substitutability and production flexibility as important elements in market definition (see B. A. Karish, "The Role of Supply Substitutability in Defining the Relevant Product Market," 65 *Virgina Law Review* 129 (1979) and Werth, note 14 *supra*, for discussions, and P. E. Griffin and J. W. Kushner, "Geographic Submarkets in Bituminous Coal: Defining a Southeastern Submarket," 21 *The Antitrust Bulletin* 67 (1976) for a supply-oriented definition). The positive position adopted in The Papercraft Corp. (78 F.T.C. 1352, 1390 (1971)) contrasts nicely with the negative position adopted in Fruehauf Trailer Company (67 F.T.C. 878, 906 (1965)) and reasserted in The Budd Co., (86 F.T.C. 518, 555-56 (1975)).

In this same general vein, it is also interesting to look at all the various factors that the courts traditionally look into in defining markets. These can be conveniently divided as follows. (O. K. Ames, "Evidentiary Aspects of Relevant Market Proof in Monopolization Cases," 26 DePaul Law Review 533-44 (1977)). Customer factors: physical characteristics, end use of products, attractiveness to buyers, cross-elasticity of demand, relative prices, public recognition of the product, and distinct customers. And, manufacturing factors: influence of sellers' costs, methods of production, unique production facilities, cross-elasticity of production facilities, entry barriers, specialized vendors, and industry recognition of product. That is, the factors that the courts use to define markets are the same factors that determine the elasticities of demand and marginal cost, as well as the number of sellers that the market will attract. Thus, the present approach to the antitrust analysis of a merger does not ignore the factors that have traditionally concerned the courts. Instead, it deals with them in a different manner and at a different point.

69. Even if the market boundaries are drawn "appropriately," there remains an irreducible amount of arbitrariness about the whole matter. In a two-commodity world, for example, the commodities are necessarily substitutes so that, in a cross-elasticity sense, only a single market exists. Hence, any merger of firms in that world, even firms producing "different" commodities, would under current Section 7 policy be a horizontal merger. Yet, should a third commodity be discovered, what was previously a horizontal merger could now become conglomerate. The thrust of this observation is that we should do the best job we can of appropriately defining the relevant markets, and then let the elasticity chips fall where they may.

70. As indicated by the inverse of the elasticity of demand as a measure of monopoly power (A. P. Lerner, "The Concept of Monopoly and the Measurement of Monopoly Power," 1 *Review of Economic Studies* 157 (1934)). The point has also been implied by Martin (note 11 *supra*, p. 322).

71. It is interesting to consider in this context the market-definition proposals of Areeda-Turner and Boyer. The former suggest that "a 'market' embraces one firm or any group of firms which, if unified by agreement or merger, would have market power in dealing with any grour of buyers" (Areeda and Turner, note 25 *supra*, p. 347); the latter proposes "to define the industry in which a firm operates as the ideal collusive group" (K. D. Boyer, "Industry Boundaries," in *Economic Analysis and Antitrust Law* T. Calvani and J. Siegfried, eds. (1979), p. 88). The present proposal would imply that antitrust analysis based on a collusive-group market definition would contain more than its fair share of circularity.

72. For more extensive arguments along this line see Areeda and Turner, note 31 *supra*, particularly p. 1102.

73. Smith, note 61 *supra*, p. 128.

74. Edwards, note 11 *supra*, p. 32.

75. Heflebower, note 13 *supra*, p. 124.

76. K. MacMillan and D. Farmer, "Redefining the Boundaries of the Firm," 27 *Journal of Industrial Economics* 277 (1979).

77. P. W. S. Andrews and E. Brunner, note 14, *supra*, p. 36.

78. Edwards, note 11 *supra*, pp. 99-108.

79. See, for example, C. F. Keithahn, *The Brewing Industry* (1978).

80. The risk of increased competition "forcing" the rivals to collude is one that antitrust enforcement will simply have to accept.

81. Except for the fact that the effects on the *tobacco* market would not be at issue. See note 13 *supra*.

Chapter 9

Statistical Measurement of the Conglomerate Problem

George Hay and Charles Untiet

Whatever the nature of the concern with conglomerate corporations, the seriousness of any problem that may exist is usually thought to be related to the level of so-called "aggregate concentration," i.e., the share of the economy's activity that is attributable to the largest firms. This chapter is intended simply to provide some background by presenting and comparing various measures of aggregate concentration.[1]

An obvious preliminary question is why there is more than a single measure of aggregate concentration. There are several answers. First, there is no consensus on the appropriate measure of a firm's contribution to aggregate concentration—sales, assets, value-added, profits, and employment have each been used. Second, several agencies or organizations compile statistics on which any measure might be based, and they frequently differ in their coverage or methods of compilation. For example, some of the best (and most widely used) "aggregate concentration" data cover only the manufacturing sector.

Many of the numbers presented here were prepared for Assistant Attorney General John Shenefield's testimony before the Senate Judiciary Committee on March 8, 1979. Any editorial comments made herein, however, represent the personal views of the authors.

MANUFACTURING

Much of the statistical work that has been done relates solely to manufacturing (or sometimes mining and manufacturing combined). Conceivably (although doubtfully), the focus of concern about the conglomerate problem is restricted to the manufacturing sector. Alternatively, one might speculate that what is true in manufacturing mirrors what is going on in the rest of the economy. In any event it is important to point out that manufacturing, while the largest sector of the economy, comprises only about 27 percent of private GNP. Within manufacturing, concentration can be measured in terms of assets, sales, value-added, and employment, to list the most common measures.

Assets

The Federal Trade Commission is a primary source of data on concentration of corporate assets. These data are presented in Table 9.1. The FTC has constructed the recent entries of its series from data collected for its *Quarterly Financial Report* (QFR), although for prior years they used data from *Moody's* and the IRS.[2] The following comments pertain to the FTC data.

1. The QFR collects data at the company level, not at an establishment level like Census. Therefore it will include nonmanufacturing establishments of principally manufacturing corporations and exclude manufacturing establishments of principally nonmanufacturing corporations. Data collected on the company level, as opposed to the establishment level, will tend to overstate manufacturing concentration. There are two reasons for this possible tendency. First, to the extent that the largest manufacturing corporations are more diversified into other industrial sectors than small manufacturing firms, the inclusion of nonmanufacturing assets will tend to overstate manufacturing concentration.[3] Second, the FTC denominator will tend to approximate the true denominator to the extent that included nonmanufacturing assets cancel excluded manufacturing assets. On the other hand, the FTC numerator will tend to exceed the true numerator due to the inclusion of nonmanufacturing assets. Of course, the FTC may reclassify a true numerator firm as a principally nonmanufacturing corporation. However, this firm will be replaced in the FTC numerator by another giant corporation. An asset loss from such a

Table 9.1.   Percent of Assets Accounted for by Largest Manufacturing Corporations 1947–1977

Year	100 Largest	200 Largest
1947	39.3%	47.2%
1948	40.3	48.3
1949	41.1	49.0
1950	39.8	47.7
1951	39.4	47.7
1952	40.6	49.2
1953	41.7	50.3
1954	43.3	52.1
1955	44.3	53.1
1956	45.0	54.1
1957	46.3	55.6
1958	47.1	56.6
1959	46.3	56.0
1960	46.4	56.3
1961	46.6	56.3
1962	46.2	56.0
1963	46.5	56.3
1964	46.5	56.6
1965	46.5	56.7
1966	46.4	56.7
1967	48.1	59.3
1968	49.1	60.8
1969	48.2	60.1
1970	48.5	60.4
1971	48.9	61.0
1972	47.6	60.0
1973	44.7	56.9
1974	44.4	56.7
1975	45.0	57.5
1976	45.4	58.0
1977	45.9	58.5
1978	45.5	58.3
1979	46.1	59.0

Source: Federal Trade Commission *Economic Report on Corporate Mergers*, p. 173; *Statistical Abstracts.*
Note: Data not comparable with years prior to 1973 due to internal changes.

reclassification is likely to be dominated by the asset gain from nonmanufacturing sectors.

2. Prior to 1974, the QFR classified a firm as a manufacturer if 50 percent of its gross receipts came from manufacturing. Since 1974, the QFR classifies a firm as a manufacturer if its manufacturing gross receipts exceed the gross receipts from any other industrial sector.

3. The QFR covers all U.S. corporations, both public and privately owned. It does not cover noncorporate businesses. The FTC's exclusion of noncorporate business will cause it to overstate concentration, since the top 200 firms are unlikely to include any unincorporated businesses. In recent years this difference has not been large. For example, the FTC reported the 200-firm concentration ratio for corporate assets in 1968 was 60.9 percent; for total assets it was 60.4 percent. The discrepancy becomes more important as one goes backward in time; in 1947 the difference in the 200-firm concentration ratios was 2.2 percentage points.[4] For this reason, therefore, one overstates the growth of aggregate concentration.

4. Since the final quarter of 1973, the QFR has done a good job in consolidating subsidiaries with its parent companies. A domestic, nonfinancial subsidiary is consolidated with its parent corporation if it is majority-owned (more than 50 percent) by the parent or its majority-owned subsidiaries. The assets of a parent company will include only the net equity position of its banking and other financial subsidiaries. If a corporation is owned equally by two independent companies, it is considered independent. Prior to 1973, a corporation was able to file a separate report for a majority-owned subsidiary. This effect in itself would understate concentration.

5. Since the final quarter of 1973, the QFR has excluded foreign operations. The QFR data do not include foreign companies, foreign branches, and foreign subsidiaries of U.S. companies, nor do they include U.S. companies operating only abroad. The assets of a U.S. parent company include the net equity of foreign subsidiaries. Before 1973, a corporation could include its foreign operations in its report to the FTC. This effect would overstate concentration, since the larger firms probably allocate a greater proportion of their assets to foreign operations. Given that foreign investment grew in the period 1947–1973, the FTC overstated the growth of concentration for this period. The FTC changed its rules on both domestic consolidation and foreign exclusion at the same time. It appears that prior to 1973, the upward bias of foreign consolidation dominated the downward bias of nonconsolidation of domestic operations. For example, under the old methodology the 200-firm concentration for 1973 is 59.7 percent. Under the new rules, the concentration is 56.9 percent.[5]

6. In 1969 the QFR reclassified the newspaper industry into manufacturing. This change lowered concentration since newspaper companies do not rank among the top manufacturing corporations. The effect of the change on the 200-firm concentration for 1969 is as follows:

Current Method, including newspapers   60.1
Former Method, exluding newspapers   60.7[6]

7. The QFR sample of corporations is a probability sample: not every small corporation is included. Instead, small corporations are assigned a sampling weight. However, the sample includes with certainty all corporations with assets of $10M or more. This guarantees that the top 200 corporations in terms of assets are included in the QFR sample.

A second source for measuring asset concentration is the Internal Revenue Service. Table 9.2A shows the percent of total corporate assets accounted for by the 50, 200, 500, and 1000 largest corporations. The universe data (the denominators) are from the Internal Revenue Service Statistics of Income, Corporate Income Tax Return.[7] The total assets for the large corporation (the numerators) are from a tabulation prepared for the Department of Justice from the Corporate Tax Model File. In Table 9.2B we show the percent of total business assets of the largest corporations. Total business assets are the sum of total assets for corporations and partnerships. (Assets for sole proprietorships are not available from IRS.)

Table 9.2A. Percent of Total Corporate Assets Accounted for by Largest Manufacturing Corporations, 1968–1976

Year	50 Largest	200 Largest	500 Largest	1000 Largest
1968	36.6%	57.2%	68.6%	75.7%
1970	37.7	59.8	71.6	78.5
1972	37.5	59.7	71.9	78.9
1974	38.0	60.5	73.2	80.1
1976	38.7	60.1	72.4	79.0

Sources: Based on data from Internal Revenue Service Statistics of Income, Corporate Income Tax Returns, and unpublished Internal Revenue Service data.

Table 9.2B   Percent of Total Business Assets Accounted for by Largest Manufacturing Corporations, 1968–1976

Year	50 Largest	200 Largest	500 Largest	1000 Largest
1968	36.4%	57.0%	68.2%	75.3%
1970	37.6	59.5	71.3	78.1
1972	37.3	59.4	71.6	78.5
1974	37.8	60.2	72.9	79.7
1976	NA	NA	NA	NA

Sources: Based on data from Internal Revenue Service Statistics of Income, Corporate Income Tax Returns, and unpublished Internal Revenue Service data.

The main advantage of IRS data is that it is collected for all industrial sectors, not just manufacturing. For the manufacturing sector the IRS is similar to the FTC in that it collects data on a company level, not on an establishment level. Therefore the IRS shares the FTC's tendency to overstate concentration in a given industrial sector. However, in many other respects the IRS data are inferior to the FTC data for the manufacturing sector. In particular the following comments are appropriate.

1. For the purpose of measuring concentration in a given industrial sector, the IRS procedure for industrial classification is not as precise as the FTC procedure. Instead of classifying firms into broad industrial sectors (e.g., manufacturing), the IRS classifies firms into small, disaggregate "minor industries." A firm is assigned to the minor industry that accounts for the largest portion of its total receipts. The firm is then assigned to the industrial sector that includes its principal "minor industry." Therefore, the IRS could classify a firm as a mining corporation even though it obtained most of its receipts from manufacturing, if its manufacturing receipts were spread over a number of different industries.

2. The IRS collects data on all types of business organizations: public corporations, private corporations, partnerships, and sole proprietorships. For corporations, the IRS has data on receipts, total assets, physical assets, profits, and net worth. Whenever a publicly owned corporation neglects to report its assets, the IRS obtains the figures from *Moody's* or other public sources. For partnerships the IRS collects data on receipts. and total assets. However, for sole proprietorships it has data only on receipts. (The IRS does not collect data on employment or value-added.)

3. The data reported to IRS are data for tax purposes. The tax law may allow firms to capitalize certain nonexistent assets or to depreciate assets in an unrealistic fashion.[8]

4. The IRS consolidation of multicompany corporations is neither as consistent nor as complete as the current FTC procedures. The fundamental unit of business organization for the IRS is the tax return. IRS data will consolidate a group of subsidiaries if the parent company files a consolidated return. The current eligibility requirements for filing a consolidated return are rather strict—each group member must be 80 percent owned by the group. Furthermore, even if group members satisfy these requirements, the decision to file a consolidated return is still voluntary.[9] Due to the confidentiality of IRS data we are unable to determine how companies report their operations. Incomplete consolidation will of course understate

concentration. The tax laws pertaining to consolidated returns have changed in the postwar period. For example, prior to 1963 a 2 percent surcharge was imposed on a consolidated return; the Revenue Act of 1963 repealed the surcharge. This created an incentive to file consolidated returns.[10] Such changes in the tax laws could weaken historical comparisons of aggregate concentration ratios based on IRS data. However, according to the IRS, incomplete consolidation is not a serious problem for the period covered in our tables, 1968-1976. In these years almost all large firms filed consolidated returns, and the eligibility requirements remained constant.

5. IRS data currently include foreign operations to a greater extent than the FTC and Census data sets. A U.S. corporation may include assets and receipts of foreign subsidiaries and foreign branches in its tax return. Furthermore, IRS data include U.S. corporations operating solely abroad and foreign corporations operating within the United States. As a result, total corporate manufacturing assets according to the IRS are significantly larger than the FTC figure. For 1975 the figures were $945 billion and $811 billion, respectively.[11] Given that large companies probably invest relatively more abroad, the IRS data may lead to greater estimates of concentration than will the FTC data.[12]

6. A firm may file a "part-year" return if it has been in operation for less than one year, if it is changing its accounting year, or if it is merging or liquidating. If the firm files a part-year return because it has changed its accounting year, the IRS will assign zero assets to the return.[13]

Fortune magazine publishes annual lists of the largest publicly owned corporations. One list includes the top 1000 industrial corporations (mining and manufacturing). *Fortune* ranks companies on the basis of sales rather than assets, so the *Fortune* list must be revoked if it is to be on the same basis as the other measures of aggregate concentration.

The Conference Board has attempted to rework the *Fortune* list to delete nonmanufacturing firms and to reorder by asset size. The resulting aggregate concentration figures are presented in Table 9.3. For comparison, concentration figures based on the *Fortune* list without any deletions or adjustments are presented for selected years in Table 9.4. The denominator has assets for all mining and manufacturing corporations.

The obvious advantage of the *Fortune* list is that it is published annually with only a short time lag. However, in other respects the list has some drawbacks:

1. *Fortune* does not provide any aggregate statistics; therefore the denominator in any concentration ratios must come from an independent source. This may create problems of incompatibility. (See the comments on the sales data below).
2. *Fortune* obtains its data from annual reports of publicly owned corporations; it does not have any data from privately held corporations or unincorporated businesses.
3. *Fortune* data will include foreign operations if they are included in a firm's annual report.
4. *Fortune* data do not include data from controlled subsidiaries if the parent company does not consolidate these subsidiaries in its annual report.

Table 9.3. **Percent of Assets Accounted for by Largest Manufacturing Corporations, 1947–1972**

Year	50 Largest	100 Largest	200 Largest
1947	31%	39%	46%
1954	33	43	51
1963	37	47	57
1972	37	48	60
1973	38	49	61

Source: The Conference Board, *Aggregate Concentration (1979).* The Conference Board used the *Fortune* lists and *Moody's Industrial Manual* to form the numerators in both categories. Total U.S. manufacturing sales and assets came from the *Quarterly Financial Report.*

Table 9.4. **Percent of Total Assets Accounted for by 200 Largest Manufacturing and Mining Corporations for Selected Years**

Year	200 Largest
1955	53.1%
1960	54.5
1972	60.1
1973	62.5
1974	62.2
1975	61.7
1976	61.6
1977	62.4

Sources: Statistical Report on Mergers and Acquisitions, Federal Trade Commission, Bureau of Economics, November 1977. Data for 1977 preliminary. Data for the years 1974–77 have been adjusted to compensate for changes in reporting procedures.

The *Fortune* Directory, of 500 Largest U.S. Industrial Corporations (May 8, 1978) and various editions of the *Statistical Abstract of the United States.* Companies included in the *Fortune* Directory of Industrials must have derived more than 50 percent of their sales from manufacturing and/or mining.

One additional table is relevant. As the Conference Board study points out, all the usual tables rank the top 200 for each year presented. Obviously the top 200 firms in, say, 1972 are different from the top 200 in 1947. To the extent there is considerable turnover from year to year in the identity of the top firms, the "power" associated with being large in any given year may be diminished.

To demonstrate the impact of turnover, the Conference Board has attempted to trace the top firms in 1947 forward to 1972, and to trace the top firms in 1972 back to 1947. Concentration figures based on the shares of each of the two groups of firms over the period 1947-1972 are presented in Tables 9.5A and 9.5B. It is obvious from Table 9.5A that the group of 200 firms that were the largest in 1947 has not increased its share of total assets over the period.

Table 9.5A. Percent of Total Assets Accounted for by Largest Manufacturing Firms in 1947, for Selected Years, 1947–1972

Year	50 Largest	100 Largest	200 Largest
1947	31%	39%	46%
1954	33	41	49
1963	34	43	52
1972	30	40	49

Source: The Conference Board, *The Relativity of Concentration Observations* (1978), p. 4.

Table 9.5B. Percentage of Total Assets Accounted for by Largest Manufacturing Firms in 1972 for Selected Years, 1947–1972

Year	50 Largest	100 Largest	200 Largest
1947	26%	34%	41%
1954	30	39	47
1963	35	44	54
1972	37	49	61

Sources: The Conference Board, *"The Relativity of Concentration Observations* (1978), p. 5.

In Figure 9.1, we attempt to bring the FTC, IRS, and *Fortune* measures of asset concentration together for ready comparison.

Sales and Shipments

While the FTC's QFR collects data on sales, it does not publish any sales data for the top 100 or 200 firms. (Indeed, even the asset data are not routinely published for the top 100 or 200 firms. The material in Table 9.1 was prepared for the FTC's *Economic Report on Corporate Mergers* and, for more recent years, provided directly to the *Statistical Abstract.*) This is somewhat unfortunate. Since the FTC's data are collected on a company basis, they will not include intracompany transfers. For this reason, QFR sales data may be better than Census data.

The IRS collects data on total corporate receipts and total business receipts. Business receipts are the sum of total receipts for corporations and partnerships and business receipts for sole proprietorships.[14] The universe data for receipts are published. The numerators come from a special run provided by the IRS. Concentration figures based on these data are presented in Tables 9.6A (corporate receipts) and 9.6B (total business receipts).

Table 9.6A. Percent of Total Corporate Receipts Accounted for by Largest Manufacturing Corporations, 1968–1976

Year	50 Largest	200 Largest	500 Largest	1000 Largest
1968	29.1%	47.0%	58.4%	65.7%[a]
1970	28.9	48.6	60.4	67.8[b]
1972	30.4	49.4	61.5	68.8
1974	36.5	55.2	66.7	73.5
1976	35.5	54.4	66.3	73.2

Sources: Based on data from Internal Revenue Service Statistics of Income, Corporate Income Tax Returns and Business Income Tax Returns and unpublished Internal Revenue Service data.

[a]1,010 companies

[b]1,001 companies

Table 9.6B. Percent of Total Business Receipts Accounted for by Largest Manufacturing Concerns, 1968–1976

Year	50 Largest	200 Largest	500 Largest	1000 Largest
1968	28.6%	46.1%	57.3%	64.5%[a]
1970	28.5	47.8	59.4	66.7[b]
1972	29.9	48.6	60.6	67.8
1974	36.0	54.5	65.8	72.5
1976	NA	NA	NA	NA

Sources: Based on data from Internal Revenue Service Statistics of Income, Corporate Income Tax Returns and Business Income Tax Returns and unpublished Internal Revenue Service data.

[a]1,010 companies

[b]1,001 companies

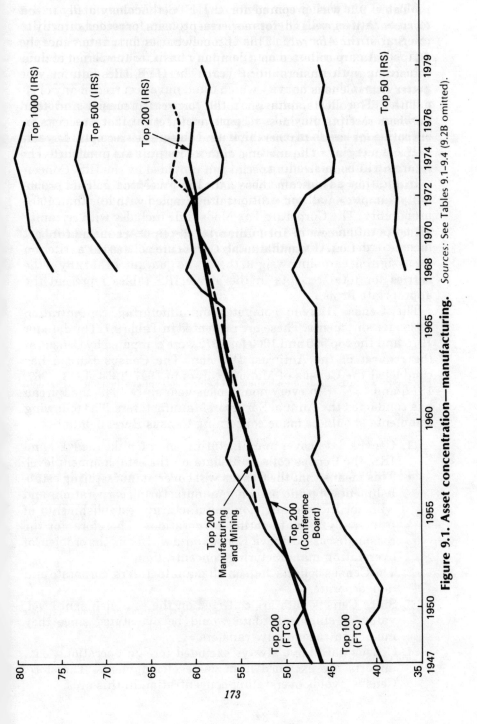

Figure 9.1. Asset concentration—manufacturing. *Sources:* See Tables 9.1–9.4 (9.2B omitted).

Most of our earlier comments on IRS methodology apply to the receipts data as well. There is a special problem for receipts since the interval of time for which the IRS collects its data is not sharply defined. A corporation must file a tax return for the period of time coinciding with its accounting year. Therefore, IRS data for any given year includes activity which could have occurred in any of 23 months. The IRS emphasis on the tax return presents another problem. A firm may file a "part-year" return if it has been in operation for less than one year, if it is changing its accounting year, or if it is merging or liquidating. Hence receipts data from part-year returns will be misleading.[15]

In addition, as indicated above, the IRS Tax Model File is a probability sample; small corporations are sampled with less than 100% probability. The Corporate Tax Model File includes with certainty all corporations with $10 million in assets or $1 million in net income or deficit. Given that total receipts are not used as a criterion for assigning sampling weight, there is no guarantee that any of the entries for total receipts in the above IRS tables represent the appropriate firms.

The Census Bureau computes manufacturing concentration ratios for shipments. These are presented in Table 9.7. The data for 1976 and the top 500 and 1000 for 1972 were computed by Census at the request of the Antitrust Division. The Census Bureau has conducted the Census of Manufacturers in 1947, 1954, 1963, 1967, 1972, and 1977.[16] In every non-Census year since 1949, the Bureau has conducted the Annual Survey of Manufacturers. The following comments should be made concerning Census Bureau data.[17]

1. Census data cover manufacturing only. Unlike the FTC and IRS, the Census collects its data on the establishment level. This means that the Census will cover manufacturing establishments of principally nonmanufacturing corporations and will not include any nonmanufacturing establishments of principally manufacturing corporations. Therefore, for the reason discussed above, Census data will avoid the problem of overstating manufacturing concentration.

2. The Census collects data on all manufacturers, corporate and noncorporate.

3. Since Census data are collected on the establishment level, value of shipments data would be overstated since they include intracompany transfers.

4. Census data have always excluded foreign operations, e.g., imports are excluded from value of shipments. Therefore, Census avoids overstating concentration in this area.

Table 9.7. Percent of Value of Shipments[a] Accounted for by the Largest Companies,[b] 1967, 1972, 1976

Year	50 Largest	100 Largest	200 Largest	500 Largest	1000 Largest
1969	25%	33%	43%	N.A.	N.A.
1972	24.3	32.5	43.2	56.8	65.2
1976	24.9	33.9	45.6	59.5	67.9

Source: Bureau of the Census, Department of Commerce, based on 1967 and 1972 Census of Manufacturers and 1976 Annual Survey of Manufacturers.

[a]Includes a substantial, but unmeasurable, amount of duplication because of shipments of materials and products among manufacturing establishments for further processing.

[b]Company rank based on value added by manufacture.

5. Unlike the FTC, the Census' accounting, classification, and sampling procedures have remained relatively constant over time. For this reason, Census data are probably the best for historical comparison. Beginning in 1958, the Census changed its definition of value of shipments. Value of shipments now includes resales (i.e., products bought and sold without further processing). Census people have stated that the 1958 changes have had little effect on concentration ratios. Another source of historical discontinuity in Census data has been the revisions in SIC classifications. However, these discontinuities are present in FTC and IRS data as well. Furthermore, they are probably not important for the broad economic sectors presented here.

6. The Census of Manufacturers is a complete enumeration of all manufacturing establishments. Therefore, for 1972 the top 1000 manufacturing companies are included in the sample. The Annual Survey of Manufacturers is based on a probability sample drawn from the previous Census. This probability sample will include with certainty all companies that employed 250 or more persons at the time of the previous Census; smaller companies are assigned a sampling weight. The 1976 ASM samples is extensive enough to include the top 1000 companies of 1972. However, the top 1000 companies in the 1976 ASM sample include some that were sampled at less than 100 percent probability. The Bureau of Census is confident that the top 200 firms in the 1976 ASM sample are the true top 200; they are less certain about the smaller companies. However, they argue that this potential downward bias on 1976 aggregate concentration is very small.

Sales concentration can also be computed from the *Fortune* data. As with the asset data, the *Fortune* list includes both mining and manufacturing firms. Table 9.8 presents the Conference Board's attempt to provide an all-manufacturing sales concentration series; Table 9.9 uses the *Fortune* list as is. The bigger numbers in the later years for Table 9.9 (as compared to Table 9.8) reflect the larger sales of the oil companies being added to the numerator.

As indicated earlier the fact that the denominators for Tables 9.8 and 9.9 come from independent sources presents some problems of incompatibility. For example, in Table 9.9 the sales data in the denominator is the sum of value of shipments from individual U.S.

Table 9.8. Percent of Sales of All Manufacturing Firms Attributable to Largest Firms, Selected Years, 1947–1972

Year	50 Largest	100 Largest	200 Largest
1947	22%	29%	36%
1954	28	36	45
1963	30	39	48
1972	31	41	52
1973	31	41	52
1974	33	43	54

Source: The Conference Board, *Aggregate Concentration* (1979). The Conference Board used the *Fortune* lists and *Moody's Industrial Manual* to form the numerators in both categories. Total U.S. manufacturing sales and assets came from the *Quarterly Financial Report.*

Table 9.9 Percent of Manufacturing Sales Attributable to 200 Largest Industrials, 1955–1977

Year	200 Largest
1955	41.8%
1960	44.7
1972	58.9
1973	60.9
1974	66.3
1975	67.1
1976	66.7
1977	66.6

Sources: 1955, U.S. Bureau of Economic Analysis, *Business Statistics, 1973;* thereafter, *Survey of Current Business* (January 1977). Taken from *Statistical Abstract of the United States* (1977), p. 559 and *Survey of Current Business* (November 1978).

The *Fortune* Directory of the 500 Largest U.S. Industrial Corporations (May 8, 1978) and various editions of the *Statistical Abstract of the United States.* Companies included in the *Fortune* Directory of industrials must have derived more than 50 percent of their sales from manufacturing and/or mining.

manufacturing establishments. The numerator is total worldwide sales in all industrial sectors of giant corporations which operate primarily in the combined manufacturing and mining sector. See also our earlier comments on the *Fortune* data.

As for assets, The Conference Board has constructed a series that traces forward the sales of the firms that were the largest in 1947 and traces backward the firms that were the largest in 1972. Sales concentration figures based on these data are presented in Tables 9.10A and 9.10B.

Table 9.10A. Percent of Sales of Largest Manufacturing Firms in 1947, for Selected Years, 1947–1972

Year	50 Largest	100 Largest	200 Largest
1947	22	29	36
1954	27	34	42
1963	27	34	43
1963	27	34	43
1972	26	32	42

Source: The Conference Board, *The Relativity of Concentration Observations* (1978), p. 4.

Table 9.10B. Percent of Sales of Largest Manufacturing Firms in 1972, for Selected Years, 1947–1972

Year	50 Largest	100 Largest	200 Largest
1947	18	23	30
1954	26	32	40
1963	28	36	46
1972	31	41	52

Source: The Conference Board, *The Relativity of Concentration Observations* (1978), p. 5.

In Figure 9.2, we bring these measures of sales concentration together for purposes of comparison.

Value-Added, Employment

The Census Bureau computes manufacturing concentration ratios indicating the shares of total value added by the largest companies.[18] These are reported in Table 9.11. The data for 1976 and for the 500 and 1000 largest companies in 1972 were computed by Census at the request of the Antitrust Division. The top companies are ranked by value added. Refer to our earlier comments on the

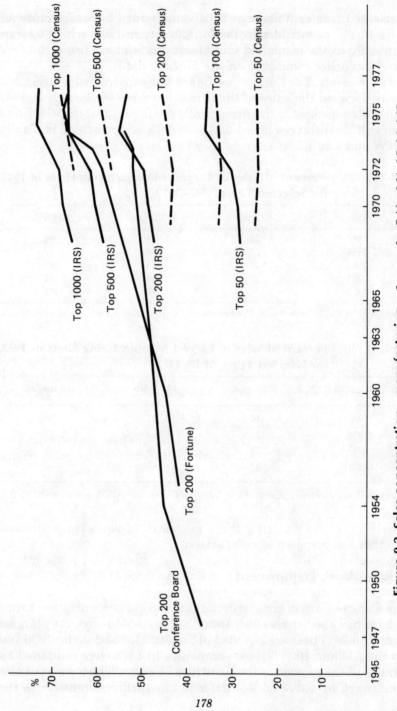

Figure 9.2. Sales concentration—manufacturing. *Sources: See Tables 9.6A, 9.7, 9.8, 9.9B.*

Top 1000 (Census)

Top 500 (Census)

Top 200 (Census)

Top 100 (Census)

Top 50 (Census)

Top 1000 (IRS)

Top 500 (IRS)

Top 200 (IRS)

Top 50 (IRS)

Top 200 (Fortune)

Top 200 Conference Board

Table 9.11. Percent Share of Total Value Added by Manufacture Accounted for by the 50, 100, 150, 200, 500, and 1000 Largest Manufacturing Companies, for Selected Years

Year	50 Largest	100 Largest	150 Largest	200 Largest	500 Largest	1000 Largest
1947	17%	23%	27%	30%		
1954	23	30	34	37		
1958	23	30	35	38	NA	
1962	24	32	36	40		
1963	25	33	37	41		
1966	25	33	38	42		
1967	25	33	38	42		
1970	24	33	38	43		
1972	24.5	33.1	38.8	43.1	56.1	64.4
1976	24.4	33.5	39.5	44.0	57.6	66.1

Source: U.S. Department of Commerce, Bureau of the Census.
NA: Not available

Census shipments data. In addition the following comments are pertinent:

1. For the purpose of constructing concentration ratios for value-added, the Census consolidates all manufacturing establishments under one "control." The Census definition of "control" is not clear, but it usually means majority ownership. If two firms each own 50 percent of a third company, the third company is considered independent.[19]

2. Beginning in 1958, the Census changed its definition of value-added. Value-added now includes the following two items: value added by merchandising (i.e., the increase in the value of products bought and sold without further processing); and the increase in the value of inventories. Census people have stated that the 1958 changes have had little effect on concentration ratios.

Once again, The Conference Board has traced forward the contribution to value-added of the largest firms in 1947, and traced backward the contribution of the largest firms in 1972. These figures are presented in Table 9.12A and B.

Figure 9.3 presents the Census value-added concentration data in a graphical context. While the value-added numbers probably show the most pronounced trend toward concentration of all the data series, the calculation of value-added is very much affected by the degree of vertical integration. To the degree that the largest

Table 9.12A. **Percent of Value-added Attributable to Largest Manufacturing Firms in 1947, for Selected Years, 1947–1972**

Year	50 Largest	100 Largest	200 Largest
1947	17	23	30
1954	21	27	NA
1963	21	28	NA
1972	17	24	NA

Source: The Conference Board, *The Relativity of Concentration Observations* (1978), p. 4.

Table 9.12B. **Percent of Value-added Attributable to Largest Manufacturing Firms in 1972, for Selected Years, 1947–1972**

Year	50 Largest	100 Largest	200 Largest
1947	12	17	NA
1954	19	25	NA
1963	22	29	NA
1972	25	33	43

Source: The Conference Board, *The Relativity of Concentration Observations* (1978), p. 5.

companies increase the internal production of raw materials, value-added will increase even where the largest companies' final sales simply keep pace with the rest of the manufacturing sector. This is not to say that value-added is a defective measure of "control," simply that the significance attached to any trend must be tempered by an understanding of the underlying process.

Census also collects data on various aspects of employment. These are gathered in Table 9.13 for the years 1967, 1972, and 1976.

ALL INDUSTRY

As indicated earlier, the FTC and Census cover only manufacturing industries. More of the concern about aggregate concentration, however, seems to relate to a broader segment of the U.S. economy. Data sources here are more limited.

Assets

The IRS is our primary source of data for sectors other than manufacturing and for the broad "all industry" grouping. (IRS sectors include: agriculture, forestry, and fishing; mining; construction; manufacturing; transportation, communication, and electric, gas,

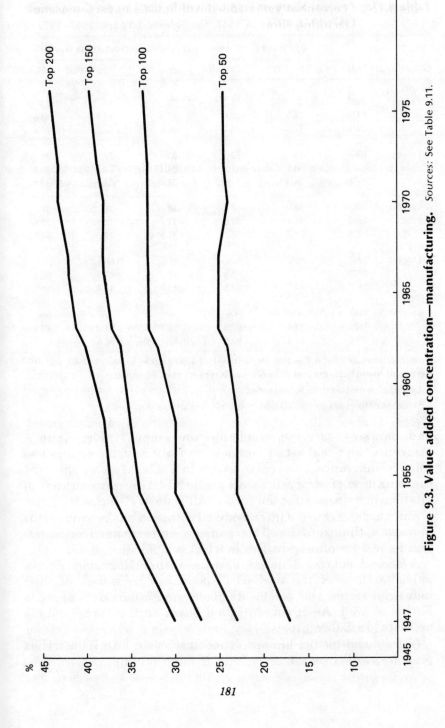

Figure 9.3. Value added concentration—manufacturing. *Sources:* See Table 9.11.

Table 9.13. **Percent Share of Employment in the Largest Companies:** 1967, 1972, 1976

Group[a]	Year	All Employees[b]		Production Workers		
		Number	Payroll	Number	Work-Hours	Wages
50						
Largest	1967	20 %	25 %	18 %	18 %	23 %
	1972	18.3	24.0	17.5	17.9	23.6
	1976	17.5	23.7	16.6	16.9	23.4
100						
Largest	1967	26	32	23	24	29
	1972	24.4	30.9	23.4	24.0	30.5
	1976	24.0	31.0	23.0	23.5	30.8
200						
Largest	1967	34	40	30	31	37
	1972	32.7	39.8	31.7	32.5	39.6
	1976	32.5	40.2	31.5	32.0	40.4
500						
Largest	1967	NA	NA	NA	NA	NA
	1972	45.7	52.3	44.1	45.0	52.3
	1976	44.9	52.8	43.7	44.4	53.1
1,000						
Largest	1967	NA	NA	NA	NA	NA
	1972	53.4	60.2	52.1	53.2	60.2
	1976	53.1	60.8	51.7	52.5	61.0

Source: Bureau of the Census, Department of Commerce, based on 1967 and 1972 Census of Manufacturers and 1976 Annual Survey of Manufacturers.

[a]Company rank based on value-added.

[b]Excludes employees of central administrative and auxiliary offices.

and sanitary services; wholesale and retail trade; finance, insurance, and real estate; services and all industry sectors less finance, insurance, and real estate).[20] In Table 9.14A we show the concentration of corporate assets and in 9.14B the concentration of total business assets for the broad "All Industry" sector.[21]

Since a major cause of increased concentration has been due to the increase in the size of the oil companies, we present asset concentration figures for mining in Tables 9.15A and 9.15B.

A second source of assets data is *Forbes Magazine. Forbes* publishes lists of the top 500 corporations regardless of their industrial sector. Our comments about the *Fortune* data apply to *Forbes* as well. Asset concentration based on the *Forbes* data is presented in Table 9.16.

A graphical picture of asset concentration for "All Industry" is presented in Figure 9.4.

Table 9.14A. Percent of Total Corporate Assets of Largest Corporations, for Selected Years

Year	50 Largest	200 Largest	500 Largest	1000 Largest
1968	20.8%	34.3%	45.9%	54.5%
1970	21.4	35.5	47.3	55.9
1972	21.4	35.3	47.1	56.0
1974	23.1	36.9	48.6	57.6
1976	22.1	36.2	47.7	56.8

Sources: Based on data from Internal Revenue Service Statistics of Income, Corporate Income Tax Returns and unpublished Internal Revenue Service data.

Table 9.14B. Percent of Total Business Assets, Corporations and Partnerships, for Largest Firms, for Selected Years

Year	50 Largest	200 Largest	500 Largest	1000 Largest
1968	20.1%	33.2%	44.3%	52.6%
1970	20.5	34.0	45.2	53.6
1972	20.3	33.5	44.6	53.1
1974	21.9	35.0	46.1	54.6
1976	NA	NA	NA	NA

Sources: Based on data from Internal Revenue Service Statistics of Income, Corporate Income Tax Returns, and unpublished Internal Revenue Service data.

Table 9.15A. Percent of Total Corporate Assets of Largest Corporations, for Selected Years

Year	50 Largest	200 Largest
1968	56.1%	75.5%
1970	56.6	74.5
1972	60.7	78.4
1974	65.7	80.7
1976	67.4	80.6

Sources: Based on data from Internal Revenue Service Statistics of Income, Corporate Income Tax Returns and unpublished Internal Revenue Service data.

Table 9.15B. Percent of Total Business Assets, Corporations, and Partnership, for Largest Firms, for Selected Years

Year	50 Largest	200 Largest
1968	52.8%	71.1%
1970	52.5	69.1
1972	56.3	72.7
1974	59.7	73.3

Sources: Based on data from Internal Revenue Service Statistics of Income, Corporate Income Tax Returns and unpublished Internal Revenue Service data.

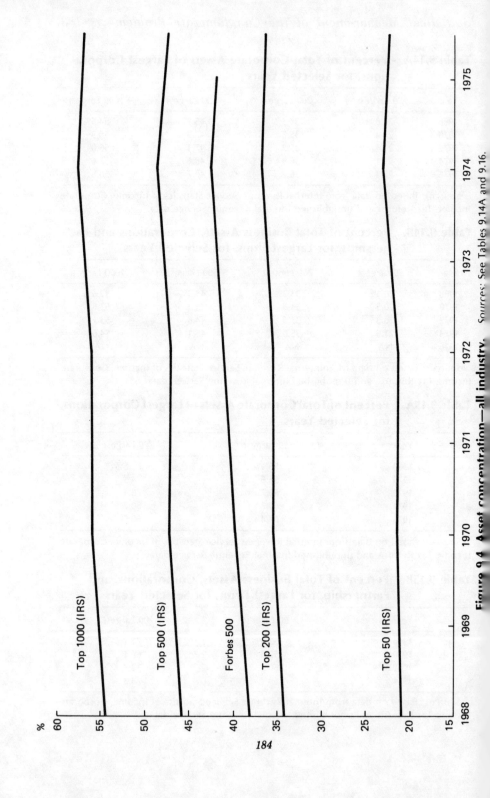

Figure 9.4. Asset concentration—all industry. Sources: See Tables 9.14A and 9.16.

Table 9.16.   Forbes 500 as Percent of All Corporate Total Assets, for for Selected Years

Year	500 Largest
1968	38.3%
1970	39.6
1974	42.3
1975	41.8

Sources: Dept. of the Treasury, Internal Revenue Service; *Statistics of Income, Corporation Income Tax Returns,* 1968, 1970, 1974. Data for 1975 preliminary. Taken from *Statistical Abstract of the United States,* 1971, 1973, 1977; *Forbes,* May 15 issues of 1969, 1971, 1975, and 1976

Sales

Once again our sources are IRS and *Forbes.* Sales concentration from IRS data is presented in Tables 9.17A and 9.17B for the "All Industry" sector and in 9.18A and 9.18B for Mining. Sales concen-

Table 9.17A.   Percent of Total Corporate Sales by Largest Corporations, for Selected Years

Year	50 Largest	200 Largest	500 Largest	1000 Largest
1968	15.5%	26.4%	35.2%	41.8%[a]
1970	15.1	26.5	36.0	42.8
1972	15.4	26.4	35.8	42.6
1974	19.2	30.8	40.6	47.3
1976	18.1	29.7	39.6	46.6

Sources: Based on data from Internal Revenue Service Statistics of Income, Corporate Income Tax Returns and unpublished Internal Revenue Service data.
[a] 1,001 companies

Table 9.17B.   Percent of Total Business Sales; Corporations, Partnerships and Sole Proprietorships; by Largest Corporations, for Selected Years

Year	50 Largest	200 Largest	500 Largest	1000 Largest
1968	12.9%	21.9%	29.3%	34.8%[a]
1970	12.7	22.3	30.3	36.0
1972	13.1	22.4	30.4	36.2
1974	16.7	26.7	35.2	41.1
1976	NA	NA	NA	NA

Sources: Based on data from Internal Revenue Service Statistics of Income, Corporate Income Tax Returns and Business Income Tax Returns, and unpublished Internal Revenue Service data.
[a] 1,001 companies

tration based on *Forbes'* 500 biggest corporations is presented in Table 9.19.

A graphical picture of sales concentration for "All Industry" is presented in Figure 9.5.

Table 9.18A. **Percent of Total Corporate Sales by Largest Corporations, for Selected Years**

Year	50 Largest	200 Largest
1968	52.8%	NA
1970	55.3	70.7[a]
1972	60.3	75.5[b]
1974	76.0	84.3[c]
1976	74.1	82.7[d]

Sources: Based on data from Internal Revenue Service Statistics of Income, Corporate Income Tax Returns, and unpublished Internal Revenue Service data.

[a]229 companies

[b]218 companies

[c]204 companies

[d]203 companies

Table 9.18B. **Percent of Total Business Sales; Corporations, Partnerships and Sole Proprietorships, by Largest Corporations, for Selected Years**

Year	50 Largest	200 Largest
1968	45.7%	NA
1970	47.9	61.3[a]
1972	52.9	66.3[b]
1974	68.8	76.3[c]
1976	NA	NA

Sources: Based on data from Internal Revenue Service Statistics of Income, Corporate Income Tax Returns and Business Income Tax Returns and unpublished Internal Revenue Service data.

[a]229 companies

[b]218 companies

[c]204 companies

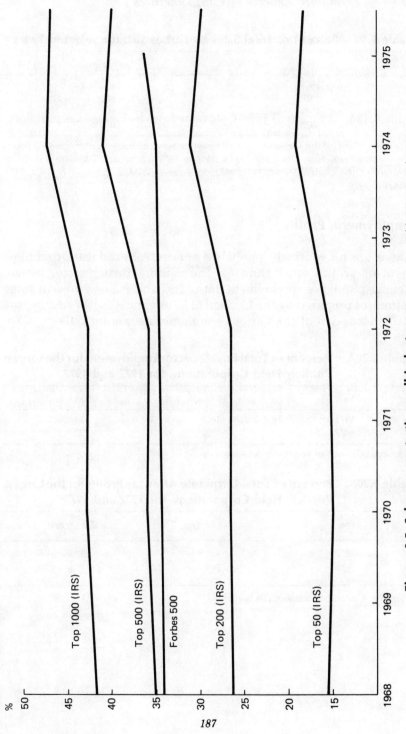

Figure 9.5. Sales concentration—all industry. *Sources:* See Tables 9.17A and 9.19.

Table 9.19. Percent of Total Sales by Forbes 500, for Selected Years

Year	500 Largest
1968	34.3%
1970	34.2
1974	34.7
1975	36.2

Sources: Dept. of the Treasury, Internal Revenue Service; *Statistics of Income, Corporation Income Tax Returns,* 1968, 1970, 1974. Data for 1975 preliminary. Taken from *Statistical Abstract of the United States,* 1971, 1973, 1977; *Forbes,* May 15 issues of 1969, 1971, 1975 and 1976.

Employment, Profits

There are no routinely published concentration data for employment or profits other than for the manufacturing sector (where Census publishes employment data). In Table 9.20 we present some estimates prepared by the Council of Economic Advisors during the 1979 discussion of the various conglomerate merger bills.

Table 9.20A. Percent of Total Private Sector Employment for the Largest Publicly Held Corporations, for 1972 and 1977

Year	100 Largest	200 Largest
1972	18.2%	23.9%
1977	17.3	22.7

Source: Council of Economic Advisors

Table 9.20B. Percent of Total Corporate After Tax Profits for the Largest Publicly Held Corporations, for 1972 and 1977

Year	100 Largest	200 Largest
1972	46.8%	59.8%
1977	45.8	57.8

Source: Council of Economic Advisors

APPENDIX: THE CONTRIBUTION
OF MERGERS TO AGGREGATE
CONCENTRATION

Since most proposed policies to deal with "the conglomerate problem" limit their focus to preventing conglomerate mergers, it is useful to inquire what role mergers have played in reaching the current level of aggregate concentration. To deal with this question we relied on a report prepared by the FTC that examined the 200 largest manufacturing and mining firms in 1975 and compiled a list of their acquisitions in each year from 1948. The raw data is contained in Table 9.A1. From 1948 to 1977, the top 200 acquired $54 billion in assets, compared to current assets of $662 billion. Hence, in one sense 8.2 percent of current (1977) assets are the result of acquisitions.

These numbers must be used with care. For one thing, we cannot be sure how the acquired assets were entered on the books of the acquiring companies. More generally, absent replacement-value accounting, the time path of acquisitions relative to the time path of internal expansion in new facilities will influence the current level of reported assets. Finally, some part of the current assets may be the result of internal growth by the "acquired" part of the company. If the source of this growth is the capital-raising (or reinvesting) capability of the acquired entity, the share of current assets that is attributable to the earlier mergers is greater than is reflected in the 8.2 percent calculation.

Of course for policy purposes it would be presumptuous to conclude that if acquisitions by the largest firms had been prohibited since 1948 the level of aggregate concentration would be less (by eight percentage points or more) than it is today. To reach any conclusion on that score we would have to make some assumptions about the internal growth that the largest companies would have resorted to in the face of a ban on using their capital-expanding capability to acquire other companies.[22]

Table 9.A1.   Large Acquisitions[a] in Manufacturing and Mining by Firms Ranked Among the 200 Largest Manufacturing Firms in 1975, by Year, 1948–1977

(in millions of dollars)

Year	Value of Assets Acquired
1948	$ 63.2
1949	45.3
1950	20.0
1951	160.1
1952	195.0
1953	457.9
1954	919.9
1955	1,148.7
1956	1,246.5
1957	693.4
1958	682.1
1959	687.9
1960	689.4
1961	1,480.7
1962	1,205.6
1963	1,871.7
1964	1,075.7
1965	1,815.7
1966	1,929.5
1967	5,252.8
1968	7,717.1
1969	6,054.5
1970	3,260.2
1971	960.6
1972	739.1
1973	1,767.0
1974	1,874.6
1975	2,592.0
1976	2,809.1
1977	5,236.9
Total	$54,203.3

Sources: Statistical Report on Mergers and Acquisitions, Federal Trade Commission, Bureau of Economics, November 1977, Table 22. Data for 1977 preliminary.

Fortune Director of the 500 Largest Industrial Corporations, Fortune, August 1961, May 15, 1976 and May 8, 1978.

Note: Not included in the above tabulation are companies for which data were not publicly available. There were 164 such companies with assets of $5.2 billion for the period 1948–1976 (and an unknown number and amount in 1977), which were acquisitions by the 200 largest companies.

[a] Acquired firms with assets of $10 million or more.

NOTES

1. There is no shortage of previous commentary on this topic. Important references include M. Adelman, "The Measurement of Industrial Concentration," 33 *The Review of Economics and Statistics* 269 (1951); J. Farkas and D. Weinberger, "The Relativity of Concentration Observations," published by The Conference Board (1978); Federal Trade Commission *Economic Report on Conglomerate Mergers* (1968); D. Penn, "Aggregate Concentration: A Statistical Note," 21 *Antitrust Bulletin* 91 (1976); and P. Steiner, *Mergers* (1975). The most recent study of which we are aware is "Aggregate Concentration" by B. Bock, J. Farkas, and D. Weinberger, released by The Conference Board in May 1979.
2. See FTC, *Economic Report on Corporate Mergers* (1968), pp. 716-29.
3. For example, suppose all corporations with manufacturing establishments are defined by the FTC to be principally manufacturing corporations. Considering only manufacturing assets, suppose that the 100-firm concentration ratio is r. Suppose also that these 100 firms have a greater share than r of all nonmanufacturing assets held by principally manufacturing corporations. In this case the inclusion of nonmanufacturing assets will raise the 100 firm concentration ratio. Moreover, to the extent that diversification generally has increased over time, the FTC will overstate the growth in concentration.
4. FTC, note 2 *supra*, p. 173, presents the two series of concentration ratios for 1947-1968.
5. Penn, note 1 *supra*.
6. Penn, note 1 *supra*, p. 96.
7. For a general description of the IRS data, see *Statistics of Income.*
8. For a somewhat dated discussion, see Senate Antitrust Subcommittee, hearings on Economic Concentration, Pt. 1 (1964), testimony of J. M. Blair, pp. 383-85.
9. *Statistics of Income* (1974), p. 187.
10. See FTC, note 2 *supra*, p. 734.
11. *Statistical Abstract of the U.S.* (1978), pp. 572, 578.
12. For example compare Tables 9.1 and 9.2 for 1974.
13. *Statistics of Income*, note 9 *supra*, pp. 1, 213.
14. Total receipts are collected but are not available from IRS for sole proprietorships. Total receipts exceed business receipts in that they include interest income, rents, and royalties.
15. *Statistics of Income*, note 9, *supra*, pp. 1, 213.
16. Concentration data from the 1977 Census will not be ready until later this year.
17. For a description of Census data, see U.S. Bureau of Census, Census of Manufacturing (1972) *Special Report Series:* Concentration Ratios in Manufacturing, MC72 (SR)-2 (1975); and U.S. Bureau of Census, Annual Survey of Manufacturers, *General Statistics for Industry Groups and Industries* (annually).
18. Value-added is essentially sales revenue minus the cost of raw materials. Value-added represents the output of the firm that is subsequently distributed to its workers and its owners.
19. Senate Antitrust Subcommittee, note 8 *supra*, p. 82.
20. *Fortune* has "top 50" lists for commercial banking, life insurance, diversified financial, retailing, transportation, and utilities.
21. See our previous comments on the IRS data.
22. For studies that attempt to estimate the contribution of mergers to aggregate concentration, see Dennis Mueller, "The Effect of Conglomerate Mergers" 1 *Journal of Banking and Finance* 315-47 (1977), especially pp. 336-39 and references cited therein.

PART IV

Antitrust and the Conglomerate Firm

Chapter 10

The Burger Court and Conglomerate Mergers

Howard R. Lurie

INTRODUCTION

Eleven years have passed since Richard W. McLaren (at hearings on his nomination to be Assistant Attorney General, Antitrust Division) told the Committee on the Judiciary of the United States Senate that he disagreed with the view of his predecessors, Dr. D. Turner and Mr. E. Zimmerman, that new legislation was necessary "in order to make section 7 [of the Clayton Act] apply to conglomerates." "Personally," he said, "I am not persuaded that such legislation is needed.

> Insofar as the conglomerate merger trend is contributing to [economic concentration], I believe that the antitrust laws, and more particularly, section 7 of the Clayton Act, are able to reach conglomerate mergers. . . . [A]s far as the pure conglomerate is concerned, I do not think we know the answer. . . . [But] I am not persuaded that it cannot be reached or that we must have new legislation.[1]

A few months later Mr. McLaren told the House Ways and Means Committee:

> My predecessors at the Antitrust Division took the position that "purer" forms of conglomerate mergers could not be reached under

Section 7 because, in their view, where merging firms are commercially unrelated, proof cannot generally be made of a reasonable likelihood of a substantial lessening of competition as called for by the Act's provisions. They suggested that conglomerate mergers which threaten undue concentration of economic power should be dealt with through new legislation.

At the Senate Judiciary hearing on my confirmation in January, I stated that I was not persuaded that Section 7 will not reach purer types of conglomerate mergers than have been dealt with by the courts thus far.[2]

Doubts as to the applicability of Section 7 to conglomerate mergers arise from its express language:

No corporation engaged in commerce shall acquire, directly or indirectly, the whole or any part of the stock or other share capital and no corporation subject to the jurisdiction of the Federal Trade Commission shall acquire the whole or any part of the assets of another corporation engaged also in commerce, where in any line of commerce in any section of the country, the effect of such acquisition may be substantially to lessen competition, or to tend to create a monopoly.[3]

The Act does not prohibit all mergers and acquisitions; it prohibits only those that have a particular effect. The literal language of the Act proscribes only those mergers that may have the effect of substantially lessening competition or tending toward the creation of a monopoly. Horizontal mergers may have this effect because they eliminate actual competition between the merging firms. Vertical mergers may have this effect because they allegedly foreclose markets to competitors, thus depriving rivals of a fair opportunity to compete.[4] The evils of conglomerate mergers are not so easily determined.

Since by definition a conglomerate merger does not combine rivals, it does not eliminate actual competition in a market. The alleged primary vice of a pure conglomerate merger is a feared concentration of economic and political power in fewer hands.[5] This vice, however, is not one against which Section 7 of the Clayton Act protects in the absence of an injury to competition.[6] Thus, opponents of conglomerate mergers have had some difficulty in devising theories upon which conglomerate mergers may be challenged under Section 7 of the Clayton Act. At his confirmation hearings McLaren had listed three theories for attacking conglomerate mergers: (1) reciprocity, (2) entrenchment, and (3) elimination of potential competition. Each of these had received judicial recognition by the Warren Court.

When Mr. McLaren's predecessors expressed the view that new legislation was needed to reach conglomerate mergers, they were simply acknowledging the adverse competitive effect touchstone of Section 7. McLaren did not deny the necessity of satisfying this adverse competitive effect touchstone. Rather, he simply disagreed with the view that it could not be satisfied under the precedents.

But President Richard M. Nixon, who had appointed McLaren to head the Antitrust Division, also appointed Warren Burger to replace Earl Warren, Harry Blackmun to replace Abe Fortas, Lewis Powell to replace Hugo Black, and William Rehnquist to replace John Harlan. President Ford later appointed John Paul Stevens to replace William Douglas. Whether the Court, as presently constituted, shares the views of McLaren regarding conglomerate mergers is the subject of this paper.

It is my contention that the present Supreme Court will not view challenges to conglomerate mergers with much sympathy. When I use the term "conglomerate merger" I am referring to all mergers and acquisitions between two companies other than those which are principally horizontal or vertical. Included in my usage of the term, therefore, are "geographic extension mergers," "product extension mergers," and "pure conglomerate mergers." The antitrust decisions of the Burger Court lead me to believe that the Court will not indulge in the kind of presumptions as to anticompetitive effects that will be essential to a finding of illegality under Section 7. First, this Court does not appear likely to invalidate a conglomerate merger in the absence of an anticompetitive effect. Second, this Court appears to demand proof of a kind that will seldom, if ever, be possible in the real, as opposed to the theoretical, world of business. Finally, I am not very sanguine about the effectiveness against conglomerate mergers of new legislation providing an escape for mergers that produce "substantial efficiencies" or "enhanc[e] competition."[8]

REQUIREMENT OF AN ANTICOMPETITIVE EFFECT

Even though conglomerate mergers do not necessarily produce anticompetitive effects, they do raise serious questions regarding "the distribution of power in our society."

Conglomerate mergers, which unite even purely unrelated business ventures into a single corporation, present a direct challenge to the balance of institutional power because there is almost no limit to the size a firm can achieve through such mergers. The fear is that these huge private organizations will increase their power at the expense of smaller and less organized groups and of the individual.[9]

Is it possible, therefore, that the Court, recognizing this danger, will apply Section 7 to invalidate a merger or acquisition, in the absence of a demonstrated anticompetitive effect? Based upon the Court's reluctance to apply Section 7 in a purely remedial fashion, I believe it highly unlikely that the Burger Court would do so. The Burger Court, in sharp contrast to the Warren Court, has not shown any inclination to extend the reach of Section 7 of the Clayton Act to proscribe even allegedly anticompetitive acquisitions that arguably do not meet the jurisdictional requirements of the Act.

As originally enacted, Section 7 had prohibited only corporate *stock* acquisitions where the effect of the acquisitions tended to "lessen competition between the corporation whose stock is so acquired and the corporation making the acquisition, or to restrain commerce in any section or community, or tend to create a monopoly of any line of commerce."[10]

This language was felt by many to limit Section 7 to *horizontal* acquisitions, because only in such cases could there be a lessening of competition between the corporation whose stock is acquired and the corporation making the acquisition. The first case to present the question of the applicability of Section 7 to *vertical* acquisitions to the Supreme Court was *United States* v. *duPont de Nemours & Co.*, decided in 1957.[11] In question was the 1917 purchase by duPont of a 23 percent stock interest in General Motors Corporation (GM). The Warren Court held that the "tend to create a monopoly" language of Section 7 allowed it to reach vertical acquisitions.

In 1950, Congress amended Section 7 to extend its reach to corporate *assets* acquisitions for corporations subject to the jurisdiction of the Federal Trade Commission (FTC), and to all acquisitions where "the effect of such acquisition may be substantially to lessen competition, or to tend to create a monopoly," thus clarifying the reach of Section 7 to vertical mergers and acquisitions.[12]

In 1963 the Warren Court decided *United States* v. *Philadelphia National Bank*. This case presented the Court with another significant question regarding the jurisdictional reach of Section 7. The case involved a proposed merger between the second and third largest commercial banks in the Philadelphia metropolitan area.

The banks argued that Section 7 did not apply to bank mergers. If viewed as an *assets* acquisition, the merger would not be within the purview of Section 7, since that section reaches only those acquisitions made by corporations subject to the jurisdiction of the FTC, and banks are not. On the other hand, since the merger was technically a statutory consolidation—a transaction in which both the existing corporations disappear and a new corporation emerges—it could not accurately be viewed as a *stock* acquisition. Conceding that a bank merger did not fit neatly into either category, the Court rejected the bank's assertion that Section 7 was inapplicable.

> Congress contemplated that the 1950 amendment would give § 7 a reach which would bring the entire range of corporate amalgamations, from pure stock acquisitions to pure assets acquisitions within the scope of § 7. Thus, the stock-acquisition and assets-acquisition provisions, *read together,* reach mergers which fit neither category perfectly but lie somewhere between the two ends of the spectrum.... So construed, the specific exception for acquiring corporations not subject to the FTC's jurisdiction excludes from the coverage of § 7 only assets acquisitions by such corporations when not accomplished by merger.[13]

In *United States* v. *Penn-Olin Chemical Co.,* the Warren Court rejected the argument that Section 7 does not apply to joint ventures.[14] The defendants had argued that a newly formed corporation not yet conducting business was not "engaged in commerce" for the purpose of Section 7.

The Burger Court's restrictive application of Section 7 is evidenced by *United States* v. *American Building Maintenance Industries.* In the context of an acquisition (by one of the largest suppliers of janitorial services in the country) of the largest supplier of janitorial services in Southern California, the Court was presented, for the first time, with the question of whether the acquisition of an intrastate corporation by an interstate corporation was within the prohibition of Section 7. Both the acquired and acquiring corporations supplied janitorial services in the same geographic market—Southern California—to customers engaged in interstate commerce. The Court concluded that regardless of the acquisition's *effect* on interstate commerce, Section 7 requires that both corporations "be directly engaged in the production, distribution, or acquisition of goods or services in interstate commerce."[15]

The Court asserted that its decision was compelled by the literal language and legislative history of the Clayton Act and prior decisions interpreting the "in commerce" language. Justice Stewart took pains to characterize the Court's action as nothing more than a literal construction of the "in commerce" requirement of Section 7.[16] Contrary to the Court's assumption, however, nothing in the *language* of Section 7 suggests that the "commerce" language of Section 7 was intended by Congress to have a meaning different from the "commerce" language of Section 1 of the Sherman Act. Section 1 of the Sherman Act proscribes contracts, combinations, and conspiracies "in restraint of trade or commerce among the several States, or with foreign nations."[17] Section 1 of the Clayton Act defines "commerce" as "trade or commerce among the several States and with foreign nations...."[18] Justice Stewart dismissed the virtually identical language of the two statutes by simply stating: "The phrase 'in commerce' does not, of course, necessarily have a uniform meaning whenever used by Congress."[19]

The government in *American Building Maintenance* had contended that "it would be anomalous for Congress to have strengthened the antitrust laws by curing perceived deficiencies in the Sherman Act and at the same time to have limited the jurisdictional scope of those remedial provisions. . . ."[20] Justice Stewart, however, justified the Court's restrictive interpretation of the reach of Section 7 by noting the explicit congressional limitation of that section to corporate acquisitions.[21] The Court noted that although the Sherman Act reaches contracts, combinations, and conspiracies by partnerships and natural persons as well as by corporations, Section 7 clearly does not apply to the "allegedly anticompetitive acquisition[s] of partnership assets.[22] According to the Court, Congress clearly intended Section 7 to reach only certain types of acquisitions, and there was no justification for disregarding these limitations.

Since Section 7 purports to prohibit only those acquisitions which have the proscribed anticompetitive effect, it is inconceivable that the Burger Court would be willing to strike down a merger or an acquisition which did not result in some injury to competition. If, therefore, a conglomerate merger does not lessen competition, it is unlikely that the Burger Court would hold it unlawful even though it resulted in a concentration of political power in fewer hands.

PROOF OF AN ANTICOMPETITIVE EFFECT

The burden of demonstrating that a particular merger or acquisition results in the necessary anticompetitive effect, however, can be substantially eased if a court is inclined to do so. The Warren Court, I submit, was inclined to do so. The Burger Court is not.

In *Philadelphia National Bank* the Warren Court announced its "simplified test of illegality." It said that the ultimate question under Section 7—whether the effect of the merger "may be substantially to lessen competition" in the relevant market—clearly:

> is not the kind of question which is susceptible of a ready and precise answer in most cases. It requires not merely an appraisal of the immediate impact of the merger upon competition, but a prediction of its impact upon competitive conditions in the future; this is what is meant when it is said that the amended Section 7 was intended to arrest anticompetitive tendencies in their "incipiency."

Emphasizing the business community's need to be able to "assess the legal consequences of a merger with some confidence," and the "danger of subverting congressional intent by permitting a too-broad economic investigation," the Court concluded that "in any case in which it is possible, without doing violence to the congressional objective embodied in Section 7 to *simplify the test of illegality,* the courts ought to do so in the interest of sound and practical judicial administration." (Emphasis added.) Thus, the Court said it could, in certain cases, dispense "with elaborate proof of market structure, market behavior, or probable anticompetitive effects."[23]

The Warren Court's application of that "simplified test of illegality" was what ultimately led Justice Stewart to remark in 1966 that, in litigation arising under Section 7 of the Clayton Act, "the sole consistency that I can find is that . . . the Government always wins."[24]

The Warren Court's simplified test of illegality, amounting to a rule of presumptive illegality, stopped only a step short of declaring mergers unlawful per se.[25] With the ascendency of the Burger Court, a different antitrust philosophy achieved dominance.[26] This shift in antitrust philosophy has serious implications for conglomerate mergers, since the new majority is not willing to presume an anticompetitive effect without an examination of market structure and market behavior.

In the new majority's first merger case, *United States* v. *General Dynamics Corp.,* it made clear that proof of an anticompetitive effect was no "simple" task.[27] Essentially, the case involved a merger between the Freeman Coal Mining Corporation and United Electric Coal Companies.

The primary issue on appeal to the Supreme Court concerned the validity of the district court's finding that the evidence did not show that the acquisition substantially lessened competition between Freeman and United Electric in any product or geographic market. The government had sought to establish a Section 7 violation through the use of statistics showing that the coal industry was concentrated among a small number of large producers, that the concentration was increasing, and that the acquisition in question would contribute to the trend toward concentration. In a remarkable example of judicial candor, Justice Stewart conceded:

> In prior decisions involving horizontal mergers between competitors, this Court has found prima facie violations of Section 7 of the Clayton Act from aggregate statistics of the sort relied on by the United States in this case. . . .
> The effect of adopting this approach to a determination of a "substantial" lessening of competition is to allow the government to rest its case on a showing of even small increases of market share or market concentration in those industries or markets where concentration is already great or has been recently increasing, since "if concentration is already great, the importance of preventing even slight increases in concentration and so preserving the possibility of eventual deconcentration is correspondingly great."[28]

Nevertheless, despite the government's statistics, the Court was satisfied that the district court did not err when it found there was no substantial lessening of competition. The Court, relying on *Brown Shoe* v. *United States* emphasized that, while statistics were significant, they "were not conclusive indicators of anticompetitive effects." Therefore, the Court agreed with the district court that other factors, such as the decrease in coal consumption in recent years, the increase in coal use by the electric utility industry, and the increase in the number of long-term requirements contracts, were to be given great weight.[29]

Considering those other factors, the Court agreed with the district court that United Electric was simply not a viable competitive force in the market.

> A . . . significant indicator of a company's power effectively to compete with other companies lies in the state of a company's uncommitted reserves of recoverable coal. . . . *In a market where the availability and price for coal are set by long-term contracts rather than immediate or short-term purchases and sales, reserves rather than past production are the best measure of a company's ability to compete.* (Emphasis added.)[30]

In light of the district court's findings that United Electric's coal reserve prospects were "unpromising" and that United Electric was unable to acquire additional reserves,[31] the Court concluded that the district court's dismissal was proper.[32]

Theoretically, the Court's decision is correct. The elimination by merger of a firm that has ceased to be a significant competitive factor in the market cannot substantially lessen competition. It is like subtracting a zero.

The principle had been accepted by the Supreme Court many years before in *International Shoe* v. *FTC*. In that case, the Court had held that the purchase of the capital stock

> of a corporation with resources so depleted and the prospect of reha-
> bilitation so remote that it faced the grave probability of a business
> failure . . . by a competitor (there being no other prospective purchaser)
> . . . does not substantially lessen competition. . . .[33]

Thus was born the "failing company" doctrine.

That defense had been severely restricted, however, by the Warren Court just five years prior to *General Dynamics*. In *Citizen Publishing Co.* v. *United States,* the Court had held that the

> failing company doctrine cannot be applied in a merger . . . case unless
> it is established that the company that acquires the failing company
> . . . is the only available purchaser. For if another person or group
> could be interested, a unit in the competitive system would be
> preserved. . . .[34]

The Court also imposed "the burden of proving that the conditions of the failing company doctrine have been satisfied . . . on those who seek refuge under it."[35]

In *General Dynamics* the Government had argued that the "defense of inadequate resources rests on the same economic premise as the failing company defense . . ." (i.e., the acquired company is a competitive zero) and must be tested by the general legal standards that govern that defense.[36] The Court rejected that argument, however, on the ground that the district court did not premise its failure to find a violation of Section 7 by reason of United Electric's being a failing company. The Court stated that

> the District Court's conclusion was not . . . identical with or even
> analogous to such a finding. The failing company defense pre-
> supposes that the effect on competition and the "loss to [the

company's] stockholders and injury to the communities where its plants were operated," . . . will be less if a company continues to exist even as a party to a merger than if it disappears entirely from the market. It is, in a sense, a "lesser of two evils" approach, in which the possible threat to competition resulting from an acquisition is deemed preferable to the adverse impact on competition and other losses if the company goes out of business. The respondents' demonstration of United's weak reserves position, however, proved an entirely different point. Rather than showing that United would have gone out of business but for the merger with Material Service, the finding of inadequate reserves went to the heart of the Government's statistical prima facie case based on production figures and substantiated the District Court's conclusion that United Electric, even if it remained on the market, did not have sufficient reserves to compete effectively for long-term contracts. The failing company defense is simply inapposite to this finding and the failure of the respondents to meet the prerequisites of that doctrine did not detract from the validity of the court's analysis.[37]

Two interpretations of the failing company defense are possible: (1) that where the acquired company is failing it is a competitive zero, and for that reason its acquisition does not substantially lessen competition; or (2) that even when the acquisition results in a substantial lessening of competition, there is no violation of Section 7 if the acquired company was failing and would have gone out of business.

The Court in *International Shoe* had never said that *even if* there is a substantial lessening of competition there is no violation of Section 7 when the acquired company is failing. Before it discussed the failing condition of the acquired company, it had already determined that there was no basis to conclude that the acquisition "would probably result in a substantial lessening of competition."[38] The "failing company" discussion was a second basis on which the Court concluded that there was no violation of the Act.

In *Citizen Publishing Co.* the Warren Court did not expressly state which of the two views of the failing company defense it was accepting. Instead it focused solely on the loss of "a unit in the competitive system." The Warren Court clearly placed the burden of proof on the acquiring company to show that the acquired company could not be preserved. The acquired company's prospects for reorganization would have "to be dim or nonexistent to make the failing company doctrine applicable to this case."[39]

If the Warren Court accepted the first view, it would mean that a company would not qualify as a competitive zero unless it could not be reorganized or purchased by someone other than the defendant. Or, to put it another way, it is not a competitive zero if it can be reorganized or purchased by someone other than the defendant. This view suggests that as a matter of law, an anticompetitive result must necessarily follow from the acquisition by a competitor of a firm that is more than a competitive zero.

Arguably, the Warren Court was accepting the second view of the doctrine, i.e., that it is an affirmative defense to be proved by the defendant after the government establishes that the merger has the necessary anticompetitive effect to render it illegal. However, it seems inconsistent with that view for the Court to impose upon the defendant the burden of proving that the acquired company's prospects for reorganization are "dim or nonexistent." It seems to me that to the extent that the defendant is able to meet its burden of proof as to the dim prospects for continuation of the acquired firm, the government's showing of an anticompetitive effect is diminished.

The Court's treatment of the defense under either view makes sense only if the burden upon the government to show an anticompetitive effect is satisfied merely by a statistical showing as to market shares. Only then does it make sense to impose upon "those who seek refuge under [the failing company doctrine] the burden of proving" that its conditions have been satisfied.[40]

My analysis seems consistent with the government's approach in *General Dynamics*. The government made a statistical showing sufficient under prior decisions of the Court to establish a *prima facie* case. The burden of proof as to the affirmative defense should then have been on the defendant.

However, in *General Dynamics,* the Burger Court felt that United's inadequate reserves made it a competitive zero, and placed on the government the burden of proving that United was not a zero, and could obtain additional coal reserves.[41] The loss to the market of an independent decision-maker was apparently of no significance to the Court.

Clearly, the Burger Court had rejected the first view of the failing company doctrine and accepted the second. The first view, which described the situation of United, was not, according to the Court, a situation for the application of the doctrine. Therefore, since the government had not shown that the acquisition was likely to lessen competition substantially, the defendant did not have to meet the prerequisites of the failing company defense imposed by the *Citizen Publishing Company* Court.

General Dynamics has some very significant implications. In a horizontal merger not producing a tendency toward monopoly, a finding of a lessening of competition is merely a conclusion reached by the mind. Thus, the Warren Court had concluded in *Philadelphia National Bank* that

> a merger which produces a firm controlling an undue percentage share of the relevant market, and results in a significant increase in the concentration of firms in that market is so inherently likely to lessen competition substantially that it must be enjoined *in the absence of evidence clearly showing that the merger is not likely to have such anticompetitive effects.* (Emphasis added.)[42]

The Court in *General Dynamics* seems to concede that the government made a satisfactory *prima facie* showing. Yet the Court did not require the defendant to show that the merger was not likely to have an anticompetitive effect. Rather, the Court seems to say that the burden is on the government to show that the acquired company has the resources "to compete effectively."[43]

The Court's treatment of the failing company defense in *General Dynamics* has serious implications for conglomerate mergers. The Court seems to assume that if the burden of proving the prerequisites of the defense were on the defendant, they were not satisfied. Thus, if the burden had been on the defendant, the showing that was made was insufficient to exculpate from condemnation under Section 7. However, since the burden was placed on the government, that same showing was sufficient to defeat illegality. Obviously, the government's ante has been raised. In the absence of a willingness on the part of the court to presume an anticompetitive effect as a result of market shares and market structure, a court is less likely to find conglomerate mergers anticompetitive. Thus, as the burden of proof on the government to prove an anticompetitive effect without the use of presumptions increases, the likelihood of finding an anticompetitive effect decreases.

Since the government, in *General Dynamics,* was arguing that United could in the future acquire new coal reserves or the expertise to mine deep reserves, it was in effect arguing that the acquisition eliminated the potential for future competition. The Court viewed this argument as a "mere possibility." The Court seems to require that the government prove that *but for* the acquisition, competition would improve over what it is at the time of the trial. This view is more clearly expressed in *United States* v. *Marine Bancorporation* and has serious implications for the potential competition doctrine.[44]

Marine Bancorporation involved a challenge to the proposed merger between the National Bank of Commerce of Seattle (NBC) and the Washington Trust Bank of Spokane (WTB). The home cities of the two banks were almost 300 miles apart, at opposite ends of the state. The banks were not in direct competition to any significant degree in Spokane, nor in any other part of the state of Washington. Thus, the merger could be viewed as conglomerate. The government argued that "the acquisition may substantially lessen competition in the Spokane market, in Eastern Washington, and in the State as a whole."[45] Relying exclusively upon the "potential competition" theory, the government contended that the acquisition of WTB eliminated NBC both as an actual competitor and as a perceived potential entrant into the Spokane banking market.[46] The district court held against the government on all aspects of the case, and the Supreme Court affirmed.

One of the issues before the Supreme Court involved the determination of the relevant geographic market. Although the government had stipulated prior to trial that the Spokane area was one relevant market, it also contended that the entire state was an appropriate "section of the country." The Court, however, rejected the government's argument as contrary to precedent.

Without exception the Court has treated "section of the country" and "relevant geographic market" as identical, and it has defined the latter concept as the *area in which the goods or services at issue are marketed to a significant degree by the acquired firm*. In cases in which the acquired firm markets its products or services on a local, regional, and national basis, the Court has acknowledged the existence of more than one relevant geographic market. But in no previous Section 7 case has the Court determined the legality of a merger by measuring its effects on areas where the acquired firm is not a direct competitor. . . . We hold that *in a potential-competition case like this one, the relevant geographic market or appropriate section of the country is the area in which the acquired firm is an actual, direct competitor*. (Emphasis added.)[47]

This ruling is significant because it appears to require proof of an anticompetitive effect in a *particular* geographic market. In all probability, the Court will take a similar approach with respect to the product market. If so, it is extremely doubtful that an anticompetitive effect can be demonstrated in a conglomerate merger. The likelihood that the Court would combine two geographic or product markets into a single market is remote, considering what the Court said in *United States* v. *Connecticut National Bank,* decided the

same day as *Marine Bancorporation*.[48] The district court in the
Connecticut National Bank case had ruled that the state as a whole
was an appropriate geographic market within which to measure the
alleged anticompetitive effect of a merger between two banks that
were not competing directly.[49] The Supreme Court disagreed,
however, stating:

> The State cannot be the relevant geographic market... because... [the
> two banks] are not direct competitors.... The two banks do not operate
> statewide, nor do their customers as a general rule utilize commercial
> banks on that basis.... Although the two banks presumably market a
> small percentage of their loans to large customers on a statewide or
> broader basis, it is undoubtedly true that almost all of their business
> originates locally....
>
> As indicated by our opinion today in *Marine Bancorporation,* the
> relevant geographic market of the acquired bank is the localized area
> in which that bank is in significant, direct competition with other
> banks, albeit not the acquiring bank.[50]

Thus, the Court held in *Marine Bancorporation* and *Connecticut
National Bank* that the rules governing direct competitor mergers
and nondirect competitor cases should be different. Where parties
compete directly with one another, the elimination of competition
between them as a result of a merger may be sufficient to tend to
lessen competition substantially within the area where they do
business; but where the parties are not actual competitors, the
merger does not eliminate any competition between them. Consequently, the Court in these two cases must necessarily be concluding
that if no competition is eliminated between the parties themselves,
the merger cannot tend to lessen competition in *any* area except the
one in which the acquired bank does business.

This reasoning has very serious implications for conglomerate
mergers for it goes to the very heart of the "potential competition"
doctrine, which recognizes that a merger between two companies,
one inside and the other outside a given market, may have an anticompetitive effect within the market even though the number of
actual competitors remains the same. Since the acquired and
acquiring companies are not direct competitors, the anticompetitive
effect, if any, must be measured vis-a-vis either or both of the
merging companies and the other competitors in the market.

The Court in *Marine Bancorporation* construed the potential
competition doctrine to be applicable only to concentrated markets
where the dominant firms in the target market are "engaging in

interdependent or parallel behavior and with the capacity effectively to determine price and total output of goods or services." The Court agreed that the government had adequately demonstrated that the Spokane commercial banking market was structurally concentrated. Indeed, it acknowledged that "*all* banking markets in the country are likely to be concentrated," making them subject to the potential competition doctrine.[51] As the Court recognized, however, the chief factor that makes the banking market concentrated—regulatory barriers to entry—also renders demonstration of an actual anticompetitive effect difficult.

Entry barriers protect existing firms from new competition. Since they perceive no potential competitors where there are barriers to entry, the existing firms are not likely to act anticompetitively in an effort to forestall market entry. In effect, there are no "perceived potential competitors" in such a barricaded market. Hence, the acquisition of a firm within the market by a firm outside the market cannot eliminate any procompetitive element, and therefore cannot substantially lessen competition.

Such an acquisition would be unlawful only under a theory that Section 7 bars a merger whose sole effect upon competition is the preclusion of the procompetitive effect that would result from *de novo* entry or a toe hold acquisition. This issue, which the Court left unresolved in *United States* v. *Falstaff Brewing Corp.* constituted the government's main argument in *Marine Bancorporation.*[52] Once again, the Court declined to rule on the validity of this theory on the ground that the preconditions of the theory were not met.

According to the Court, in order for the theory to operate it must be determined that (1) there is a feasible means for *de novo* or toehold entry into the target market, and (2) "those means offer a substantial likelihood of ultimately producing deconcentration of that market or other significant procompetitive effects." There was considerable disagreement between the parties in *Marine Bancorporation* as to the feasibility of *de novo* or toehold entry into the Spokane banking market. But nowhere did the Court hold that such entry was not possible; rather the Court said that even assuming *arguendo* that such entry were possible, it did not follow that such "entry would be reasonably likely to produce any significant procompetitive benefits" or "long-term market-structure benefits."[53]

The acquisition of WTB by NBC would merely substitute NBC for WTB in the Spokane area, leaving the number of competitors in the market unchanged. Absent an allegation that the merger would produce entrenchment in the Spokane market, there could be no adverse competitive effect resulting from the merger in *Marine*

Bancorporation except under the potential competition doctrine. The Court's decision thus turned on a question of judgment.

The Court clearly felt that the merger would not have an adverse competitive effect. The impact of a potential entrant on competition within a market is, of course, difficult to prove. Inevitably, the more competitive the market is, the less the impact will be. As the Court conceded, only in the case of a concentrated market is there likely to be an impact at all. Moreover, that impact can range only from no effect to a beneficial effect upon competition. It simply cannot be adverse. Thus, when a firm's status as a potential entrant is eliminated by an acquisition within the market, there are two possible effects. At best, the acquisition has no impact on competition. This occurs only if there was no market effect when the acquiring firm maintained the posture of a potential entrant. In this situation, one firm merely replaces another as a competitor in the market. At worst, the acquisition has an anticompetitive effect. This is the outcome if the acquiring firm exerted a procompetitive effect as a potential entrant, because its entrance into the market eliminates this beneficial impact. Moreover, assuming that a potential entrant does not exert a procompetitive effect, the impact of a "toehold" acquisition can also range only from no effect to a beneficial effect. If the market is already concentrated, the strengthening of one of the weaker competitors is likely to be beneficial to some extent. Entry by a "toehold" acquisition is, therefore, more beneficial than entry by acquisition of a market leader. Finally, the effect of *de novo* entry is beneficial because it clearly adds a new competitor to the market. *De novo* entry, therefore, must necessarily be more beneficial than entry by acquisition of a market leader.

Thus, when the *Marine Bancorporation* Court suggested that the government simply had not established the preconditions for the potential competition theory, it was really saying that the government has not proved an adverse competitive effect. But, assuming the validity of the theory reserved in *Falstaff,* the logical effect of the acquisition had to be adverse. As a result, the Court must have been deciding either that the theory was wrong or that the adverse effect of the acquisition was not "substantial." Since the Court expressly refused to rule on the merits of the theory, it was clearly concluding that the substantiality requirement of Section 7 had not been satisfied. Indeed, the Court indicated that the second precondition of the theory had not been met when it stated that the government had failed to demonstrate that the alternate means of entry offered a "reasonable prospect of long-term structural improvement or other benefits in the target market."[54] As in *General Dynamics,* the Court seems to be saying that the government must prove that competition will be enhanced by prohibiting the merger.

United States v. *Citizens and Southern National Bank* provides additional support for the view that under Section 7 the Burger Court demands proof of an actual lessening of competition.[55]

The state of Georgia restricted city banks from opening suburban branches. To circumvent the restrictions, the Citizens and Southern National Bank (C&S) in Atlanta formed a bank holding company, which embarked on a program of forming de facto branches in the suburbs.[56] Under the program, five percent of the stock of the de facto branches was to be owned by the holding company, and the remaining stock was to be placed in the hands of parties friendly to C&S.[57] The branches were permitted to use the C&S "logogram" and banking services and were subject to close C&S supervision and governance. When Georgia law was changed in 1970 to allow de jure branch banking countywide, C&S sought to absorb the 5-percent branches as true branches.[58] The government brought suit, alleging that the acquisitions would lessen competition in the relevant banking market in violation of Section 7. The government also charged that the relations between C&S and the 5-percent banks constituted unreasonable restraints of trade in violation of Section 1 of the Sherman Act. The district court held against the government on all issues, and the Supreme Court affirmed.[59]

The government alleged that the relationship between C&S and the de facto branches violated Section 1 of the Sherman Act because the branches did not compete with C&S even though they were legally distinct corporate entities.[60] It was conceded by the Court that C&S's de facto branches did not behave as active competitors, with respect either to each other or to C&S and its majority-owned affiliates.[61] The Court also granted: "Were we dealing with independent competitors having no permissible reason for intimate and continuous cooperation and consultation as to almost every facet of doing business, the evidence adduced here might well preclude a finding that the parties were not engaged in a conspiracy to affect prices."[62] Recognizing that the de facto branches were "a direct response to Georgia's historic restrictions on *de jure* branching," the Court observed that "the question ... remains whether restraints of trade integral to this particular, unusual function are unreasonable."[63] This statement alone is of enormous antitrust significance for it suggests that certain practices—such as price fixing— heretofore regarded as per se offenses, are now to be examined under the rule of reason.[64]

The Court then concluded that C&S's de facto branching program was plainly procompetitive, since it provided competition for the other suburban banks. Therefore, the Court held: "in the face of the stringent state restrictions on branching"—which must be viewed as anticompetitive—"C&S's program of founding new de facto branches, and maintaining them as such, did not infringe Section 1 of the Sherman Act."[65]

Having found no Section 1 Sherman Act violation, the Court then allowed C&S to lift itself by its own bootstraps to avoid a Section 7 Clayton Act violation as well. Given the lack of competition between the 5-percent banks and C&S before the transformation into de jure branches, the Court stated that it "indisputably follows that the proposed acquisitions will extinguish no present competitive conduct or relationships."[66] With respect to the acquisition's possible elimination of future competition, the Court simply remarked that there was no "realistic prospect that denial of these acquisitions would lead the defendant banks to compete against each other."[67]

Inherent in the Court's approach was the idea that, if C&S could legally have established de jure branches at the outset without running afoul of the Sherman or Clayton Acts, there was no reason for the Court to find an antitrust violation simply because C&S could not legally branch into the suburbs at the time it established the 5-percent banks.[68] Since the economic effect was the same, the Court apparently felt that the manner in which the branching was accomplished was not determinative.

This reasoning has serious implication for the entrenchment theory in attacking conglomerate mergers. If, as in *C&S National*, the acquiring and acquired companies do not compete with each other, the acquisition cannot lessen competition between them. If there is no realistic prospect that the acquiring and acquired corporations would compete with each other in the future, the acquisition cannot eliminate or lessen future competition. And, if the acquiring corporation could have entered the market of the acquired company on a grand scale *de novo* without running afoul of the Sherman or Clayton Acts, there would be no reason for the Court to find an antitrust violation simply because the acquiring company enters the market via an acquisition, even of a market leader. In other words, if one believes that there is no harm in allowing a bull into a china shop it does not matter whether he is allowed in through the front door or the back door.

Implicit in the Court's decision in *C&S National* is a willingness on the part of the Court to examine a situation for procompetitive effects. The Court saw Georgia's antibranching law as making suburban bank customers a captive market for small unit banks. Thus, "[b]y providing new banking options to suburban Atlanta customers, while eliminating no existing options, the *de facto* branching program of C&S has plainly been procompetitive."[69]

It is worth noting that new banking options are viewed as procompetitive by the Court so as to defeat a charge of illegality, whereas when the government suggests that *de novo* or toehold entry would be more competitive than the acquisition being challenged, the Court experiences difficulty in concluding that the procompetitive effect is likely to be significant.

This willingness on the part of the Court to find procompetitive benefits in challenged conduct has serious implications for the Court's treatment of conglomerate mergers. There are some who believe that conglomerate mergers are not necessarily anticompetitive but may actually promote competition, as for example, "where the conglomerate enterprise displaces a stagnant or inefficient firm in an industry dominated by a few powerful firms."[70] Accordingly, it is informative to note that the Court does not seem to require the same measurable substantiality for the procompetitive effects it accepts as for the anticompetitive effects it requires.

This willingness on the part of the Court to find procompetitive effects of certain conduct and to balance those procompetitive effects against the asserted anticompetitive effects is not limited to merger cases. A significant nonmerger case is *Continental T.V. Inc. v. GTE Sylvania.*

Sylvania is the only antitrust case in which the Burger Court has expressly overruled a Warren Court decision, *United States. v. Arnold, Schwinn & Co.*[72] In each case a manufacturer revised its marketing strategy and reorganized its method of distribution. In each case the manufacturer decided to distribute its products through a limited number of franchised dealers. And in each case in order to reduce competition among their respective retailers, the manufacturers imposed certain restrictions on their franchises. Schwinn's restrictions prohibited franchised retailers from selling Schwinn products to unfranchised retailers. Sylvania's restrictions prohibited franchised retailers from selling Sylvania products from locations other than those specified in the agreements.

In *Schwinn,* the Court had held the restrictions per se illegal with respect to those bicycles Schwinn sold to the dealers. As to those bicycles distributed to dealers under the Schwinn Plan and consignment and agency arrangements, the Court held that the rule of reason applied.

In *Sylvania* the Court said:

> In intent and competitive impact, the retail customer restriction in
> *Schwinn* is indistinguishable from the location restriction in the
> present case. In both cases, the restrictions limited the freedom of the
> retailer to dispose of the purchased products as he desired. The fact
> that one restriction was addressed to territory and the other to
> customers is irrelevant to functional anti-trust analysis. . . .[73]

Since the Court could not distinguish the cases, it felt that
Schwinn should be reconsidered, and upon reconsideration, overruled. "Per se rules of illegality," said the Court, "are appropriate
only when they relate to conduct that is manifestly anticompetitive." Apparently, the Court did not view vertical restrictions as
"manifestly anticompetitive," since they "promote interbrand
competition by allowing the manufacturer to achieve certain
efficiencies in the distribution of his products." Thus, the loss in
intrabrand competition is outweighed by the gain in interbrand
competition. The manufacturer's self-interest will maintain "as
much intrabrand competition as is consistent with the efficient
distribution of their products," and the Court suggests that ". . . the
manufacturer's interest necessarily corresponds with that of the
public. . . ." The "economic utility" of vertical restrictions led the
Court to conclude that they were unlikely to have a "pernicious
effect on competition" or that they lacked "any redeeming virtue."[74]
Accordingly, the per se rule stated in *Schwinn* was overruled.

Sylvania is an especially significant case because it illustrates the
economic philosophy of the Burger Court majority. The crucial issue
raised in *Sylvania,* whether the courts should attempt to weigh
against the loss of intrabrand competition caused by vertical
restrictions the gains in interbrand competition, had been presented
to the Court before in *United States* v. *Topco Associates, Inc.* and
firmly rejected.[75]

Topco involved "a cooperative association of approximately 25
small and medium-sized regional supermarket chains which
operate[d] stores in some 33 states."[76] The basic function of the
association was to serve as a purchasing agent for its members. In
this capacity, it procured and distributed to its members food and
nonfood items under brand names owned by Topco. These items
were not manufactured, processed, or warehoused by Topco, but
were procured by Topco for members and shipped directly to them
by the packer or manufacturer. Topco brand products thus
constituted the private brand of Topco members just as "each

national and large regional chain had its own exclusive private label products in addition to the nationally advertised brands which all chains sell."[77]

The association, the common stock of which was owned entirely by its members, imposed upon its members restrictions on the sale of Topco brand products. No member could sell these products outside the territory in which it was licensed. The government maintained that the territorial restrictions prohibited "competition in Topco brand products among grocery chains engaged in retail operations" in violation of Section 1 of the Sherman Act.[78]

Topco argued that the territorial restraints were essential in order to enable Topco members to compete with the larger national and regional chains.

The district court agreed with Topco. It concluded that

[w]hatever anticompetitive effect these practices may have on competition in the sale of Topco private label brands is far outweighed by the increased ability of Topco members to compete both with the national chains and other supermarkets operating in their respective territories.[79]

The district court held that Topco's practices, being procompetitive, were consistent with the purposes of the antitrust laws, and, therefore, not unlawful.

The Supreme Court did not necessarily disagree with the district court's conclusion regarding the procompetitive effect of Topco's restrictions. Rather, the Court concluded that the district court "used an improper analysis in reaching its results."

Whether or not we would decide this case the same way under the rule of reason used by the District Court is irrelevant to the issue before us. The fact is that courts are of limited utility in examining difficult economic problems. Our inability to weigh, in any meaningful sense, destruction of competition in one sector of the economy against promotion of competition in another sector is one important reason we have formulated *per se* rules.

There have been tremendous departures from the notion of a free enterprise system as it was originally conceived in this country. These departures have been the product of congressional action and the will of the people. If a decision is to be made to sacrifice competition in one portion of the economy for greater competition in another portion this too is a decision which must be made by Congress and not by private forces or by the courts. Private forces are too keenly aware of their own interests in making such decisions and courts are ill-equipped and ill-situated for such decision-making. To analyze, interpret, and evaluate the myriad of competing interests and the endless data which would surely be brought to bear on such decisions, and to make the delicate judgment on the relative values to society of competitive areas of the economy, the judgment of the elected representatives of the people is required.[80]

Here we see not only the essential difference between the Warren and Burger courts, but also the antitrust philosophy of the Burger Court, which will guide it in deciding the legality of conglomerate mergers under Section 7. The *Topco* Court was unwilling to allow a court to weigh a gain in interbrand competition against a loss in intraband competition. The Burger Court in *Sylvania* was not only willing to engage in the weighing, but held that it must be done.

Two conclusions with significant implications for the Burger Court's treatment of conglomerate mergers can be drawn from these cases. One is that the Court has abandoned the "simplified test of illegality" of the Warren Court. In its place the Court has adopted a rigorous requirement that the government demonstrate that a lessening of competition is more than a theoretical possibility. The Court seems to insist upon "elaborate proof of market structure, market behavior, [and] probable anticompetitive effects."[81]

The second conclusion is that the Court is less likely to view the evidence as demonstrating an anticompetitive effect than was the Warren Court and may be willing to look for competitive benefits.[82]

With these conclusions in mind, I turn to a consideration of Mr. McLaren's theories for attacking conglomerate mergers.

THEORIES FOR CHALLENGING CONGLOMERATE MERGERS

Reciprocity

"Reciprocity in trading as a result of an acquisition violates Section 7, if the probability of a lessening of competition is shown." So said the Supreme Court in 1965, in *FTC* v. *Consolidated Foods Corporation*.[83] The case involved the acquisition of Gentry, Inc., a manufacturer of dehydrated onion and garlic, by Consolidated Foods Corporation, a food processor and owner of a network of wholesale and retail food stores. The Court described the acquisition as a conglomerate one, since Gentry and Consolidated neither competed with each other nor bought or sold to each other. Gentry sold dehydrated onion and garlic to food processors who used it in preparing and packaging foods sold to Consolidated and others. The FTC alleged that the acquisition gave Consolidated the ability to foreclose to competitors of Gentry a substantial share of the market for dehydrated onion and garlic by the use of Consolidated's buying power. This leverage was "an irrelevant and alien factor" that intruded into the choice among competing products and gave to Gentry "a priority on the business at equal prices."[84]

The Court did not say that every probability of reciprocal buying as a result of an acquisition violates Section 7. In order to violate Section 7, the acquired company must command "a substantial share of a market."[85] The Court thus seemed to be saying that a substantial lessening of competition is proved by showing that (1) the acquired company has a substantial share of a market and (2) there is a probability of reciprocal buying. Immediately prior to its acquisition Gentry had "about 32% of the total sales of the dehydrated garlic and onion industry."[86] Apparently, that share of the market is "substantial."

The opinion in *Consolidated Foods Corporation* is somewhat unclear as regards how the requirement of a "probability of reciprocal buying" was satisfied. The Court says that "[r]eciprocity was tried over and again and it sometimes worked."[87] The Court of Appeals did not think it worked very well, since it concluded that the Commission had failed to show a probability of a lessening of competition based upon ten years of postacquisition evidence. While Gentry did increase its share of the dehydrated onion market by 7 percent, its share of the dehydrated garlic market decreased by 12 percent. While saying that the Court of Appeals gave too much weight to postacquisition evidence, the Supreme Court also saw the postacquisition evidence as confirming, rather than casting doubt upon, the probable anticompetitive effect of the acquisition. Mere speculation is relied upon to support the conclusion that Gentry was able to protect its market share by the use of reciprocity. Because Gentry was able to expand its share of onion sales in a rapidly expanding market with an admittedly inferior product, the Court felt that the Commission was justified in attributing this increase to reciprocity. The *decline* in market share in garlic was also viewed as proof of the success of reciprocity. The FTC had rejected Consolidated's argument that "[t]he decline in its share of the garlic market proves the ineffectiveness of reciprocity. We do not know that its share would not have fallen still farther, had it not been for the influence of reciprocal buying."[88] The Court said that the Commission was on "safe ground" in reaching that conclusion.[89]

The Court's approach in *Consolidated Foods* was described by Mr. McLaren's Director of Policy Planning, Roland W. Donnem, as "the use of inference on the basis of limited evidence," and he concluded that it was a useful weapon in the use of Section 7 to attack conglomerate mergers.[90]

The Burger Court has not yet decided a case involving reciprocity, nor has it commented on this theory. Justice Stewart, however, a pillar of the Burger Court majority, concurred in the decision in *Consolidated Foods Corporation.* His comments, therefore, may be a significant guide to how the Burger Court would react to a Section 7 challenge of a conglomerate merger on the grounds of reciprocity. I set out below some of his comments.[91] Most need no elaboration.

> The Clayton Act was not passed to outlaw diversification.

> Clearly the opportunity for reciprocity is not alone enough to invalidate a merger under § 7.

> Before a merger may be properly outlawed under § 7 on the basis solely of reciprocal buying potentials, the law requires a more closely textured economic analysis.

> Certainly the mere effort at reciprocity cannot be the basis for finding the probability of a significant alteration in market structure. ... [S]ome standard must be established for determining how effective reciprocity must be before the merger is subject to invalidation.

> The touchstone of § 7 is the probability that competition will be lessened. But before a court takes the drastic step of ordering divestiture, the evidence must be clear that such a probability exists.

If these comments reflect the thinking of the Burger Court, then it is doubtful that a conglomerate merger could be successfully enjoined on a reciprocity theory. Prior to the consummation of a merger, there can be only a possibility of reciprocity. Stewart says that this is not enough. Before a merger is unlawful for reciprocity it must reach some threshold of effectiveness. The obstacles to proof of such effectiveness seem almost insurmountable in the absence of an extensive period of time during which reciprocity is practiced. Stewart joined in the result in *Consolidated Foods* only because *ten years* of postacquisition evidence produced a record containing "just enough" to support invalidation of the merger.[92]

Entrenchment

The term "entrenchment" is used to describe a situation "where an acquiring firm's market power, existing capabilities, and proposed merger partner are such that the merger would produce an enterprise likely to dominate the target market."[93] In such situations, an anticompetitive effect is alleged to result in the target market firm substituting for the acquired company "an acquiring firm of substantially greater economic power."[94]

The supposed anticompetitive effect of entrenchment results from the competitive advantages of access to a "deep pocket" and intimidation of competitors. The "deep pocket" or "rich parent" theory argues that competition is injured by a firm which has a "grossly disproportionate capacity to accept the reduced profits of market price wars."[95] Smaller competitors are also likely to be discouraged in their efforts to engage in vigorous competition by fear of overwhelming retaliation on the part of the dominant firm.

Acceptance of the concept of entrenchment as an anticompetitive effect is found in *FTC* v. *Procter & Gamble Co.* The case involved the acquisition of Clorox Chemical Company, the leading manufacturer of household liquid bleach, by Procter & Gamble, a large, diversified manufacturer of household products. Procter & Gamble did not manufacture liquid bleach. The Court felt that the anticompetitive effects of the acquisition could "easily be seen." The competitive structure of the industry would be reduced "by raising entry barriers and dissuading the smaller firms from aggressively competing."[96]

Entrenchment as a result of a pure conglomerate merger is probably the least likely theory to be accepted by the Burger Court for finding a violation of Section 7 for at least two reasons: (1) the anticompetitive effects of entrenchment are entirely speculative and (2) a conglomerate merger resulting in entrenchment may also produce significant economies.

The anticompetitive effects of entrenchment, if any, result from fear. The fear is, according to Turner, that "existing competitors [will] restrain their competitive efforts for fear of the retaliation or financial power of the merged firm, [and] . . . new entry [will be] significantly deterred." He suggests that these feared adverse competitive effects are "highly speculative."

> [W]hen the acquisition yields significant economies and the acquirer, competing vigorously but fairly, takes full advantage of them, . . . smaller competitors, whether fearful or not, will be under heavy pressures to improve, rather than worsen, their competitive perfor-

mance. They will be forced to cut costs, to improve their products, to lower their price in order to survive.

There are some instances, according to Turner, where

> there seems good reason to surmise that the smaller competitors will become more timid in initiating lower prices, in some instances to the point that the conglomerate firm will become the sole price leader. They may overassess the likelihood of severe disciplinary price cuts by the large firm.

Even in these situations, however, he acknowledges that "there is no way of assessing how substantial the effect is likely to be...."[97] Fear of entrenchment is essentially fear of bigness. Indeed, fear of entrenchment is fear of fear, for the sole anticompetitive effect, if any, results from fear. Thus, the anticompetitive effect cannot be measured. Unlike a horizontal merger, there is no automatic increase in market share. Unlike a vertical merger, there is no market foreclosure. Absent a loss of potential competition, there is no measurable anticompetitive effect. The adverse competitive effects are entirely speculative and theoretical.

The Burger Court has not shown much receptivity to arguments that require the Court to accept speculative anticompetitive effects. In *Marine Bancorporation* the government had argued that the acquired bank could "expand outside its base in Spokane and eventually develop into a direct competitor with large Washington banks in other areas of the State." The Court said the record supported the district court's finding that the government had failed to establish the existence of "any reasonable probability" that the acquired bank would expand into other banking markets. Accordingly, the Court dismissed the government's argument about the acquired bank's potential for expansion outside its market as "little more than speculation."[98]

Likewise, in *Citizens & Southern National Bank* the government had argued that a conventional correspondent relationship between C&S and the 5-percent banks would have been more competitive than the actual relationship. The Court dismissed this more-competition argument as "mere speculation on the present record." As to the Clayton Act, the Court said that it "is concerned with 'probable' effects on competition, not with 'ephemeral possibilities.'"[96]

Another difficulty with the entrenchment argument is the difficulty in attributing the anticompetitive effects to the acquisition itself. The feared evils of entrenchment do not result from "a danger to competition peculiar to mergers."[100] In *Brunswick* v. *Pueblo Bowl-O-Mat, Inc.*, the Court held that a competitor seeking to recover treble damages on account of a Section 7 violation

> must prove more than injury causally linked to an illegal presence in the market. Plaintiffs must prove *antitrust* injury, which is to say injury of the type the antitrust laws were intended to prevent and that flows from that which makes defendant's acts unlawful. The injury should reflect the anticompetitive effect either of the violation or of anticompetitive acts made possible by the violation. It should, in short, be "the type of loss that the claimed violations . . . would be likely to cause.[98]

In this case the plaintiffs, bowling center operators, claimed to be injured as a result of the acquisition by Brunswick of several bowling centers competing with plaintiffs. Allegedly, the competing bowling centers would have gone out of business but for the acquisitions. The Court said:

> If the acquisitions here were unlawful, it is because they brought a "deep pocket" parent into a market of "pygmies." Yet respondent's injury—the loss of income that would have accrued had the acquired centers gone bankrupt—bears no relationship to the size of either the acquiring company or its competitors. Respondents would have suffered the identical "loss"—but no compensable injury—had the acquired centers instead obtained refinancing or been purchased by "shallow pocket" parents. . . . Thus, respondent's injury was not of "the type that the statute was intended to forestall.[102]

The implication that I draw from this case is that if the alleged injury in the market of the acquired firm is one that would have resulted if the acquired firm had obtained the resources of a "deep pocket" other than by its acquisition, Section 7 has not been violated. In other words, the acquisition is only "causally linked" to the anticompetitive effects.

A merger producing entrenchment may also result in significant economies. While the Warren Court took the position that "economies cannot be used as a defense to illegality,"[103] the Burger Court may be more receptive to the argument. In *Sylvania,* the Burger Court expressly overruled the *Schwinn* per se rule regarding vertical territorial restrictions, because the Court believed that "[v]ertical restrictions promote interbrand competition by allowing the manufacturer to achieve certain efficiencies in the distribution of his products."[104]

Potential Competition

The potential competition doctrine is the only one of the three theories suggested as useful in attacking conglomerate mergers that the Burger Court expressly accepted in principle. However, the Court's treatment of the doctrine does not suggest that it will be a useful tool against conglomerate mergers.

The Warren Court had developed the doctrine to reach those mergers where no actual competition was eliminated or lessened and no actual competitors foreclosed from a market. In *United States* v. *El Paso Natural Gas Co.*, the Warren Court held that Section 7 was violated by the acquisition of Pacific Northwest Pipeline Corporation (Pacific Northwest) by El Paso Natural Gas Company (El Paso). At the time, El Paso was the sole out-of-state supplier of natural gas to California. Prior to the acquisition, Pacific Northwest had been attempting to enter the rapidly expanding California market, but it did not have a pipeline into California or regulatory approval to enter the California market.[105] It was, therefore, merely a potential competitor, not an actual one. Nonetheless, on review of the record, the Court considered that "Congress used the words [in Section 7] '*may be* substantially to lessen competition' to indicate that its concern was with probabilities, not certainties."[106] In holding that there was a Section 7 violation, the Court explained:

> Pacific Northwest, though it had no pipeline into California, is shown by this record to have been a substantial factor in the California market at the time it was acquired by El Paso. . . .
> . . . We would have to wear blinders not to see that the mere efforts of Pacific Northwest to get into the California market, though unsuccessful, had a powerful influence on El Paso's business attitudes within the state. We repeat that one purpose of Section 7 was "to arrest the trend toward concentration, the *tendency* to monopoly, before the consumer's alternatives disappeared through merger. . . ."
> The effect on competition in a particular market through acquisition of another company is determined by the nature or extent of that market and by the nearness of the absorbed company to it, that company's eagerness to enter that market, its resourcefulness, and so on. Pacific Northwest's position as a competitive factor in California was not disproved by the fact that it had never sold gas there.[107]

Later in the same year, in *United States* v. *Penn-Olin Chemical Co.*, the Court elaborated upon the "potential competition" theory.[108] In that case, Pennsalt Chemicals Corporation (Pennsalt) and Olin Mathieson Chemical Corporation (Olin) jointly formed the Penn-Olin Chemical Company (Penn-Olin) in order to produce and sell sodium chlorate in the southeastern United States. Prior to this time, Olin had never produced sodium chlorate. Although Pennsalt had produced the chemical and had sold it in the southeastern United States, it maintained no processing plants in that area. One issue before the Court, therefore, was whether the joint agreement to build a plant in the relevant geographic area of the southeastern United States would tend substantially to lessen competition within the meaning of Section 7. The district court found that "Pennsalt and Olin each possessed the resources and general capability needed to build its own plant in the southeast and to compete . . . in that market. Each could have done so if it had wished."[109] The district court also determined that "the forecasts of each company indicated that a plant could be operated with profit."[110] However, the district court held that these considerations were not of controlling significance except "as a factor in determining whether, as a matter of probability, *both* companies would have entered the market as individual competitors if Penn-Olin had not been formed. Only in this event would potential competition between the two companies have been foreclosed by the joint venture."[111]

The Supreme Court disagreed and held that the district court's conclusion was erroneous. Mr. Justice Clark, writing for the Court, commented:

> Certainly, the sole test would not be the probability that *both* companies would have entered the market. Nor would the consideration be limited to the probability that one entered alone. There still remained for consideration the fact that Penn-Olin eliminated the potential competition of the corporation that might have remained at the edge of the market, continually threatening to enter. Just as a merger eliminates actual competition, this joint venture may well foreclose any prospect of competition between Olin and Pennsalt in the relevant sodium chlorate market.[112]

In the Court's view, potential competition was important to preserve because it could serve as a valuable substitute for actual competition and even compensate to some extent for the shortcomings of actual competition.

> The existence of an aggressive, well equipped and well financed corporation engaged in the same or related lines of commerce *waiting anxiously to enter an oligopolistic market* would be a substantial

incentive to competition which cannot be underestimated. (Emphasis added.)[113]

Thus, the Supreme Court remanded *Penn-Olin* to the district court to determine whether, absent the joint venture, there was a reasonable probability that one of the corporations would have built a plant in the southeast market while the other would have remained a significant potential competitor.

In *FTC* v. *Procter & Gamble Co.*, the potential competition theory was asserted as a reason to void a merger which, among other things, eliminated the acquiring firm as a prospective market entrant. The FTC there charged that Procter & Gamble (P&G) had violated Section 7 by acquiring the assets of the Clorox Chemical Company. Prior to the merger, Clorox was the leading manufacturer of household liquid bleach, while P&G produced none. P&G had determined, however, that it was advisable for it to enter the liquid bleach industry. Moreover, the FTC found, and the Court agreed, that

> Procter was the most likely prospective entrant, and absent the merger would have remained on the periphery, restraining Clorox from exercising its market power. If Procter had actually entered, Clorox's dominant position would have eroded and the concentration of the industry reduced.[114]

Therefore, in spite of the refusal of the Sixth Circuit to enforce the FTC's divestiture order on the ground that the finding of illegality had been based on "mere conjecture," possibility, and suspicion, the Supreme Court reversed and remanded the case with instructions to enforce the order.[115]

In none of these cases did the Warren Court suggest that the acquisitions would be unlawful only if it could be shown that the acquiring firm exerted a significant "beneficial influence on competitive conditions in [the] market"[116] or that the prohibition of the acquisition offered a "reasonable prospect of long-term structural improvement or other benefits in the target market."[117] In each of these cases, the Warren Court seemed concerned only with the question of whether a potential competitor had been eliminated by the acquisition or joint venture.

The Burger Court has not been willing to assume that competition is necessarily injured by the elimination of an actual or a potential competitor. Instead, the Court has insisted upon proof of a significant injury to competition.

The Warren Court had apparently recognized the difficulty of proving that competition was likely to be lessened substantially by an acquisition. Its adoption of the "simplified test of illegality" was a necessary response for a Court bent on prohibiting mergers. A Court intent on upholding mergers is likely to insist on greater proof of the likelihood that competition will be substantially diminished. Economists have difficulty drawing the Plimsoll line with respect to actual competitors in a market. To expect greater precision when dealing with potential competition is to expect the impossible.

In *Marine Bancorporation* the Burger Court limited the applicability of the potential competition doctrine to concentrated markets. Only in such markets are the participants likely "to fashion their behavior to take into account the presence of a potential entrant."[118] Thus, the doctrine cannot be used at all to attack conglomerate mergers in nonconcentrated markets. And, in concentrated markets, the possibility of *de novo* or toehold entry by the acquiring firm will invalidate a merger only if one of these methods would be likely to produce significant deconcentration. Such a requirement is a contradiction of concepts. Small or insignificant entry is unlikely to produce any significant deconcentration. Entry *de novo* on a grand scale in a concentrated market is inconceivable.

CONCLUSION

Third Circuit Judge Ruggero Aldisert related recently in one of his dissenting opinions that his "late colleague Abraham Freedman was fond of saying at decision conferences, 'The way you come out in this case depends on how you go in.'"[119] I have stated elsewhere that I believe the present Burger Court harbors an antienforcement bias with regard to the antitrust laws, especially in the area of mergers.[120] If my belief is correct, then it is unlikely that the Burger Court will see the alleged evils of conglomerate mergers manifesting themselves in anticompetitive effects.

Each of the major theories suggested as useful in attacking conglomerate mergers under Section 7 calls for a greater willingness on the part of the courts to infer from market conditions that a substantial lessening of competition is a reasonable probability as a result of the acquisition than is required for horizontal or vertical mergers. Given the Burger Court's basic reluctance to engage in presumptions as to anticompetitive effects, it is extremely unlikely that the Court would conclude that a conglomerate merger is unlawful under Section 7.

Arguably, Mr. McLaren was wrong, and new legislation is needed to deal with conglomerate mergers. However, to the extent that such legislation provides an escape for acquisitions with demonstrable procompetitive effects, a court predisposed to find such effects—as the Burger Court seems to be—will do so, and such legislation will be ineffective.

NOTES

1. Hearing, Committee on the Judiciary, United States Senate, 91st Congress, 1st Sess., Department of Justice Nominations, January 29, 1969, p. 36.
2. Statement by Richard W. McLaren, Assistant Attorney General, Antitrust Division, U.S. Department of Justice before the Committee on Ways and Means, House of Representatives Hearings on House Bill 7489. Hearings March 12, 1969. 401 Antitrust & Trade Regulation Report X-16 (March 18, 1969).
3. Clayton Act, ch. 1184, 64 Stat. 1125 (1950), 15 U.S.C. § 18 (1976).
4. Brown Shoe Co. v. United States, 370 U.S. 294, 323–24 (1962).
5. Pertschuk and Davidson, "What's Wrong with Conglomerate Mergers?" 48 *Fordham Law Review* 1, 2 (1979).
6. Brown Shoe Company v. United States, 370 U.S. 294, 319–20 (1962).
7. A geographic extension merger is one involving companies operating in the same product market but in different geographic areas. A product extension merger is one in which the companies operate in the same geographic market but in different, although related, product markets. A pure conglomerate merger is one between companies operating in completely unrelated businesses.
8. S. 600, § 3(a). 96th Cong. 1st Sess.
9. Pertschuk and Davidson, note 5 *supra*, p. 2.
10. Clayton Act, ch. 323, § 7, 38 Stat. 730 (1914).
11. 353 U.S. 586 (1957).
12. Clayton Act, ch. 1184, 64 Stat. 1125 (1950), 15 U.S.C. § 18 (1976).
13. 374 U.S. 321, 335–36, 342–43 (1963).
14. 378 U.S. 158 (1964).
15. 422 U.S. 271, 283 (1975).
16. *Id.* at 275–83.
17. 15 U.S.C. § 1 (1976).
18. 15 U.S.C. § 12 (1976).
19. 422 U.S. at 277.
20. *Id.* at 278.
21. *Id.* at 279.
22. *Id.*
23. 374 U.S. 321, 362–63 (1963).
24. United States v. Von's Grocery Co., 384 U.S. 270, 301 (1966) (Stewart, J. dissenting).
25. H. R. Lurie, "Mergers Under the Burger Court: An Anti-Antitrust Bias and Its Implications," 23 *Villanova Law Review*, 213, 239 (1978).
26. In March 1974 the new majority consisted of Chief Justice Burger and Justices Blackmun, Powell, Stewart, and Rehnquist. Justices Douglas, Brennan, White, and Marshall became the new minority.
27. 415 U.S. 486 (1974).

28. *Id.* at 496–97, quoting United States v. Aluminum Co. of America, 377 U.S. 271, 279 (1964).
29. 415 U.S. at 498, 499.
30. *Id.* at 502.
31. 341 F. Supp. at 559, 560.
32. 415 U.S. at 503–4.
33. 280 U.S. 291, 302 (1930).
34. 394 U.S. 131, 138 (1969).
35. *Id.* at 138–39.
36. Brief for the United States at 65.
37. 415 U.S. at 507–8.
38. 280 U.S. at 299.
39. 394 U.S. at 138–39.
40. *Id.*
41. 415 U.S. at 509.
42. 374 U.S. at 362–63.
43. 415 U.S. 506.
44. 418 U.S. 602 (1974).
45. Brief for the United States at 54.
46. 418 U.S. at 626.
47. *Id.* at 620, 620–22.
48. 418 U.S. 656 (1974).
49. United States v. Connecticut Nat'l Bank, 362 F. Supp. 240, 283 (D. Conn. 1973).
50. 418 U.S. at 667 (citation omitted).
51. 418 U.S. at 630.
52. 410 U.S. 526 (1973).
53. 418 U.S. at 633, 636, 638.
54. *Id.* at 638–39.
55. 422 U.S. 86 (1975).
56. A de facto branch bank is a bank that is legally a separate corporate entity, but is operated as, and, in many respects, functions as, a branch bank of the sponsoring bank.
57. 422 U.S. at 89. This amount of stock ownership represented the maximum allowed by state law. See Ga. Code Ann. § 13-207(a)(2) (1967 & Supp. 1974) (current version at Ga. Code Ann. § 13-207.1 (Supp. 1977)).
58. 422 U.S. at 94, citing Ga. Code Ann. § 13-203.1(a) (Supp. 1974). A de jure branch bank is a legal branch that is not incorporated separately from the parent bank.
59. United States v. Citizens & S. Nat'l Bank, 372 F. Supp. 616 (N.D. Ga. 1974).
60. 422 U.S. at 112. The government asserted that the branching arrangements "actually encompassed at least a tacit agreement to fix interest rates and service charges, so as to make the interrelationships—to that extent at least—illegal 'per se.' "
61. *Id.* The Court noted that, if the branches had been de jure branches of C&S, the entire group of relationships would have been beyond attack. *Id.*
62. *Id.* at 113–14.
63. *Id.* at 116; *Id.,* citing Chicago Bd. of Trade v. United States, 246 U.S. 231 (1918).
64. See, e.g., United States v. Socony-Vacuum Oil Co., 310 U.S. 150 (1940). In Socony, the Court unequivocally stated: "[F]or over forty years this Court has consistently and without deviation adhered to the principle that price-fixing agreements are unlawful per se under the Sherman Act. . . ." *Id.* at 218.
65. 422 U.S. at 119–20.

66. *Id.* at 121.
67. *Id.*
68. *Id.* at 111-12, 117-18.
69. *Id.* at 119.
70. ABA, Antitrust Developments 68 (1968).
71. 433 U.S. 36 (1977).
72. 388 U.S. 365 (1967).
73. 433 U.S. at 46.
74. *Id.* at 49-58.
75. 405 U.S. 596 (1972).
76. *Id.* at 598.
77. *Id.* at 604, quoting Answer, App. 11.
78. *Id.*
79. 319 F. Supp. 1031, 1043 (1970).
80. 405 U.S. at 606, 609-613.
81. 374 U.S. 321, 362-63 (1963).
82. That different minds can reach different conclusions as to whether or not an anticompetitive effect has been shown is amply demonstrated by the three opinions in United States v. Container Corp. of America, 393 U.S. 335 (1969). The case involved the exchange of price information among competitors. For Justice Douglas, writing for the majority, "the inferences are irresistible that the exchange of price information has had an anticompetitive effect in the industry. . . ." *Id.* at 337. Justice Fortas did not feel that the price exchange was per se unlawful, but that the evidence in the record, "although not overwhelming," was sufficient "to show an actual effect on pricing" (*Id.* at 339 (Fortas, J., concurring opinion)) and that it "did in fact substantially limit the amount of price competition in the industry." *Id.* at 340. Justice Marshall, on the other hand, could not "agree that the agreement should be condemned, either as illegal per se, or as having had the purpose or effect of restricting price competition in the . . . industry. . . ." (*Id.* Marshall, J., dissenting opinion)).
83. FTC v. Consolidated Foods Corporation, 380 U.S. 592, 595 (1965).
84. *Id.* at 594; *Id.*, citing International Salt Co. v. United States, 332 U.S. 392, 396-97 (1947).
85. 380 U.S. at 600.
86. *Id.* at 595.
87. *Id.* at 600.
88. 62 F.T.C. 929 (1963).
89. 380 U.S. at 599.
90. Roland W. Donnem, Address to American Management Association Briefing Session, 436 ATRR X-7 (1969).
91. 380 U.S. at 603-5 (Stewart, J., dissenting opinion).
92. *Id.* at 607.
93. 418 U.S. 602, at 623 n.23 (1974).
94. Bauer, "Challenging Conglomerate Mergers Under Section 7 of the Clayton Act: Today's Law and Tomorrow's Legislation," 58 *Boston University Law Review* 199, 226 (1978).
95. *Id.* at 227.
96. 386 U.S. 568, 578 (1967).
97. Turner, "Conglomerate Mergers and Section 7 of the Clayton Act," 78 *Harvard Law Review* 1313, 1352, 1355, 1356 (1965).
98. 418 U.S. 640, 641 (1974).

99. 422 U.S. 86, 119, 122 (1975).
100. Bork, *The Antitrust Paradox* (1978), p. 251.
101. 429 U.S. 477, 489 (1977).
102. *Id.* at 487-88.
103. FTC v. Procter & Gamble Company, 386 U.S. 568, 580 (1967).
104. Continental T.V., Inc. v. GTE Sylvania, Inc., 433 U.S. 36 (1977); United States v. Arnold, Schwinn & Co., 388 U.S. 365 (1967); 433 U.S. at 54.
105. 376 U.S. 654 (1964).
106. *Id.* at 658, quoting Brown Shoe Co. v. United States, 370 U.S. 294, 323 (1962).
107. *Id.* at 658-60, quoting United States v. Philadelphia Nat'l Bank, 374 U.S. 321, 367 (1963).
108. 378 U.S. 158 (1964).
109. United States v. Penn-Olin Chem. Co., 217 F.Supp. 110, 129 (D. Del. 1963).
110. *Id.*
111. *Id.* at 130.
112. 378 U.S. at 173.
113. *Id.* at 174.
114. 386 U.S. 568, 575 (1967).
115. FTC v. Procter & Gamble Co., 358 F.2d 74, 83 (6th Cir. 1966).
116. United States v. Falstaff Brewing Corp., 410 U.S. 526, 532-33 (1973).
117. United States v. Marine Bancorporation, 418 U.S. 602, 638-39 (1974).
118. *Id.* at 630.
119. Larry V. Muko, Inc. v. Southwestern Pennsylvania Building and Construction Trades Council, 609 F.2d 1368, 1377 (dissenting opinion) (3d Cir. 1979).
120. Lurie, note 23 *supra.*

Chapter 11

Antitrust Presumptions: Some History About Prophecy

Stephen Rubin

The judicial development of rules of presumptive illegality ranks among the most distinctive features of American antitrust law. By defining various categories of violation in terms of easily identified operative facts, the rules impart a high degree of structure and predictability to antitrust analysis. The alternative in such cases, an extensive inquiry into the specific market context and competitive consequence of each challenged practice, historically has appeared to judges to be unnecessary and largely unworkable.[1]

Yet the rules do more than decide cases; they decide cases in a particular way. With increasing effect, critics charge that the rules arbitrarily focus on factual indicia judges can readily comprehend, such as collusion and coercion, and greatly overstate the importance of small business units and independent enterprises as policy goals.[2] The rules are said to ignore essential but more complex factual questions regarding economic efficiency and market performance, questions whose resolution may at times vindicate superficially anticompetitive business behavior.[3] Especially during the decades when the antitrust opinions of Justices Black and Douglas anchored the Warren Court's populist tradition, the expansion of the rule of per se illegality seemed to many the outward expression of the Court's antibusiness philosophy.

PER SE TODAY

Misgiving about the use of presumptive rules is now evident
in the Supreme Court's own decisions. Most notably in *Continental
T.V., Inc.* v. *GTE Sylvania, Inc.,* the *Schwinn* per se condemnation
of all postsale territorial and customer allocation arrangements was
overturned by a "new majority," whose attention is "upon demonstrable economic effect rather than—as in *Schwinn*—upon
formalistic line drawing."[4] Nearly as dramatic is the Court's
announcement in *United States* v. *General Dynamics Corp.*[5] that
henceforth a horizontal merger "had to be functionally viewed, in
the context of its particular industry."[6] Justice Stewart, who wrote
for the five-member majority, had been an outspoken critic of the
Court's previous presumptive approach to horizontal mergers. One
Stewart dissent carries the celebrated line: "The sole consistency
that I can find is that in litigation under § 7, the Government always
wins."[7]

Consistency has troubled the Court in another way. Once a
presumption becomes rooted, the judicial task is reduced, in the first
instance, to a determination of whether the litigated activity falls
within the condemned category. Warning in *Broadcast Music, Inc.*
v. *Columbia Broadcasting System, Inc.,* that "easy labels do not
always supply ready answers," the Supreme Court rebuked the
court of appeals for its "literalness" in concluding that an agreement to fix prices constitutes "*per se* price fixing." Instead,

> in characterizing this conduct under the *per se* rule, our inquiry must
> focus on whether the effect and, here because it tends to show effect,
> see *United States* v. *United States Gypsum Co.,* 438 U.S. 422, 436, n. 13
> (1978), the purpose of the practice are to threaten the proper operation
> of our predominantly free-market economy—that is, whether the
> practice facially appears to be one that would always or almost
> always tend to restrict competition and decrease output, and in what
> portion of the market, or instead one designed to "increase economic
> efficiency and render markets more, rather than less, competitive."[8]

Goldfarb v. *Virginia State Bar* suggests that restraints of trade
engaged in by professionals may also confound the "easy labels" of
the per se approach. "The public service aspect, and other features of
the professions," the Court cautioned, "may require that a
particular practice, which would properly be viewed as a violation of
the Sherman Act in another context, be treated differently."[9]

How differently remains unclear. When an absolute ban on professional bidding was before the Supreme Court in *National Society of Professional Engineers* v. *United States,* it escaped the per se treatment normally accorded price-fixing agreements. The Court's application of a reasonableness standard, however, did not embrace the one defense the Society could muster: that price competition for engineering services was not in the public interest. The Court explained:

> In sum, the Rule of Reason does not support a defense based on the assumption that competition itself is unreasonable. Such a view of the Rule would create the "sea of doubt: on which Judge Taft refused to embark in *Addyston* ... and which this Court has firmly avoided ever since.[10]

The turnabout in treatment of antitrust presumptions reflected in the Supreme Court's latest decisions profoundly affects not simply the existing decisional apparatus, of which the per se principle is an integral part. It also places in doubt current proposals to establish broad prohibitory rules in conglomerate acquisition and monopolization cases through new legislation.[11] If the Court's opinions are properly read as a repudiation of traditional presumptive rules in favor of "economic realism," as some believe,[12] then no effort by Congress to impose new legal presumptions on an unwilling Court is likely to succeed. An entirely new adjudicatory mechanism may be required, as the late Senator Hart maintained—virtually alone— in his Industrial Reorganization Act.[13] Indeed, just this assessment of the Supreme Court attitude toward the Sherman Act[14] following the *Standard Oil*[15] and *Tobacco*[16] decisions of 1911 resulted in passage of the Clayton Act,[17] with its specific enumeration of unlawful practices, and the Federal Trade Commission Act,[18] which established an alternate forum for antitrust litigation.[19]

If the Court's current opinions can be harmonized with earlier precedent, however, Congress may yet have a framework within which to create new prohibitory rules that will accurately express national policy and serve the practical needs of antitrust compliance and enforcement. The history of the per se rules, considered in the context of the institutional and ideological wellsprings of the common law process, suggests that such a synthesis is possible. Rather than weaken the usefulness of presumptions, in fact, careful restructuring of the per se concept may well provide necessary flexibility during a period when opinions concerning antitrust are once again in a state of flux.[20]

To understand this latest phase of antitrust transformation, it is necessary to move away from the detail of individual cases until the full history becomes visible. The years marked by the ascendency of per se rules—from *United States* v. *Socony-Vacuum Oil Co.* in 1940 to *United States* v. *Topco Associates, Inc.* in 1972—comprise only one-third of the ninety-year federal antitrust experience. The half-century preceding *Socony* records the Supreme Court's beginning struggle with the indefinite language and sweeping intent of the antitrust laws.[21] The result was not a tightly woven construct. It never will be. Antitrust development has never assumed the patterned logic of economic or legal formalism.[22] Its growth reflects, instead, the untidy accommodations of particularized litigation, pliable precedent, and the inevitable changes in philosophy that come with new Court membership. The modern period of Supreme Court revision mirrors the cycles of reform of previous years. Indeed, the present effort to refine the per se concept thus far has been more restrained than it was during the period when the rules were first set in place.

The unique features of antitrust law suggest that periodic judicial rethinking will always be with us. They also explain why presumptive rules are a logical outgrowth of antitrust enforcement policy.

THE PREMISES OF PRESUMPTIONS

One distinct feature of antitrust analysis has already been mentioned: the extraordinary discretion (or lack of guidance) given federal judges in construing the language and legislative policy of the laws. Senator Sherman acknowledged as much when he opened the debate on his antitrust bill in 1890.[23] The organic nature of the laws, their central importance in ordering economic affairs, and the fundamental philosophical themes that weave through the congressional history eventually blossomed into Chief Justice Hughes' dictum: "As a charter of freedom, the [Sherman] act has a generality and adaptability comparable to that found to be desirable in constitutional provisions."[24] In the hands of Justice Black, this premise would grow to full height,[25] resulting in the equation of antitrust with the liberty and opportunity values of the Bill of Rights.[26]

Recent decisions appear to be pulling back from the full force of this conviction.[27] Yet it is true that antitrust will never squeeze comfortably into a one-dimensional economic bottle after its long association with constitutional reasoning. The present Supreme

Court, moreover, seems disinclined to press antitrust reform that far.[28]

The "soft" political and social goals of antitrust policy are thus unavoidable. Although they derive some legitimacy from the congressional history, their perpetuation is more accurately understood in terms of the realities of the decisional process. In construing laws of such direct importance to business performance and economic well-being, judges inevitably are influenced by their private vision of the role of government, the proper etiquette of industry, and the function of market capitalism. It is futile to argue for the neutral principle of decisions based on economic science.[29] For one thing, economic theory is hardly as normatively neutral as some claim.[30] But more basically, it is a misreading of the judicial process to believe that judges and jurors can shed their ideological baggage at the courtroom door. The true dilemma for the Supreme Court is whether to make such biases explicit and uniformly applicable through conclusive presumptions[31] or, rather, to leave them largely unsaid, giving reign to the presuppositions of individual judges.[32] Their contrasting responses to this issue may well mark the most significant difference in antitrust approach between the Supreme Court of Chief Justice Warren and that of Chief Justice Burger.

A second prominent feature of antitrust, related to the first, is the fact that the acknowledged touchstone of analysis, competition, does not submit to precise legal definition or accurate legal measurement.[33] The staged focus of the adversary process, with its custom of bi-polar issues and deductive classification, no doubt contributes to this. Nearly a century of antitrust case law is devoted to a search for evidentiary surrogates by which courts can more readily identify illegal behavior. Emphasis on competitors, one component of competition theory, was an obvious and early choice.[34] Structural indicia—the number or size of competitors in the affected market— could be measured with a fair degree of certainty and consistency. If the court found a decrease in numbers or an increase in size, then anticompetitive effect could be predicted with reasonable assurance.[35] The power, purpose, and effect underlying a challenged agreement would similarly substitute for the seemingly endless task of trying to measure the impact on market performance of particular business combinations.[36] Ultimately, the question of intent would be subsumed in judicial reasoning under the more easily demonstrated power and effect determinants.[37]

To be sure, evidentiary surrogates only roughly approximate the true economic consequences of specific practices. In particular, they tend to ignore factors like efficiency and consumer welfare maximization, factors which have now become respectable subjects of judicial attention.[38] But a complete investigation of challenged conduct often requires fact-finding and expertise beyond the normal limits of the adversary process or juror comprehension.[39] This is the flaw in the reasonableness inquiry outlined by Justice Brandeis in *Chicago Board of Trade* v. *United States.*[40] The required information is difficult and costly to produce and may go beyond evidence available to the involved litigants.[41] Once assembled, the information will likely point in a number of directions.[42] Variables must be accounted for.[43] Connecting assumptions must be made and tested. In the end, burdens of proof and rules of evidence, more than systematic investigation and economic analysis, will determine the victor. As an intellectual exercise, it has been little more satisfying when attempted than invocation of the conclusive presumptions of the per se rule.[44]

The tripartite scheme of enforcement constitutes a third unique aspect of antitrust law. The selection and timing of cases brought to trial is a defining element in the common law process of synthesis. The law might appear quite different today if *United States* v. *International Telephone & Telegraph Corp.* or *Telex Corp.* v. *International Business Machines Corp.* had not been settled by the parties at the doorstep of the Supreme Court, if the Federal Trade Commission (FTC) had not been transfixed by the Robinson-Patman Act in the 1950s and 1960s, and if private litigants had not been able to bring the *Schwinn* doctrine to the Supreme Court for reconsideration.[45]

The interplay of the diverse enforcement strategies of the Department of Justice,[46] the FTC,[47] and private plaintiffs (including state attorneys general)[48] is becoming increasingly important in the formulation of antitrust doctrine. Indeed, the fact that for the first time all three enforcement elements are now actively involved in antitrust litigation may well reduce the future attractiveness of broad presumptive rules. As a practical matter, the rules shift major responsibility for the assessment of liability from the courts to the plaintiff. Until recently, the Antitrust Division of the Department of Justice was the primary plaintiff in antitrust suits, and the Supreme Court could rely on prosecutorial discretion to develop the per se power with appropriate caution. That this condition no longer obtains can be seen in the wave of private litigation which followed the per se holding in *Schwinn.*[49] A similar situation appears to be developing in tying-arrangement cases and may develop in other areas.[50]

The elimination of per se precedents in the most common areas of private antitrust litigation undoubtedly would be a serious inhibiting factor. Not only would it increase the already formidable costs of discovery and trial, but it would also significantly reduce plaintiff's probability of success. Unlike the proenforcement policy of the Supreme Court in previous years, however, the present Court may well find a decrease in enforcement highly desirable. It has already made plain its reluctance to open federal-court doors to private litigation in antitrust and other fields of legal complexity.[51] A further opportunity to reduce federal litigation by discouraging a substantial portion of the numerous private antitrust suits filed each year, therefore, is likely to appeal to the Court for reasons beyond antitrust theory.

Ironically, resource constraints traditionally have molded judicial analysis in a different direction. Because business relationships and market forces are highly fluid, standards based on the reasonableness or economic effect of each anticompetitive practice would necessitate "continuous administrative supervision and readjustment in light of changed conditions."[52] The endless oversight required of regulatory commissions in nonmarket rate, entry, and performance decisions has been reason enough to encourage federal judges to formulate conclusive standards of antitrust illegality in the form of broad prohibitory rules.

Still another distinctive feature of antitrust that does not fit neatly into existing theoretical models is the high incidence of lower court disavowal of Supreme Court enforcement precedent. Judge Will's treatment of horizontal territorial and customer-allocation agreements before and after the Supreme Court opinion in *United States* v. *Topco Associates, Inc.,* is one of many illustrations.[53] The formulation of conclusive presumptions of illegality by the Supreme Court is one of the few effective means available to forestall this disavowal. That the Court's per se opinions often contain hortatory and absolutist phrases can be understood not only as a warning to potential offenders, but also as a warning to errant district judges who comprise the first level of doctrinal implementation. Without such rules, the trial courts are likely to find for defendants in all but the most blatant cases, despite the Supreme Court's call for balanced analysis.

A final aspect of antitrust theory contributing to its mutable nature is the element of prediction required in decision making. This is made explicit in the substantive provisions of the Clayton Act, which are intended to reach "incipient" violations.[54] It is also an important feature of most Sherman Act and Federal Trade

Commission Act adjudication.[55] Prediction occurs at multiple levels. Prediction regarding the likelihood of detection and probable penalties guides the decisions of firms contemplating anticompetitive activity. Prediction about the probability and cost of obtaining a favorable judgment influences the enforcement decisions of government prosecutors and private plaintiffs. Because of the difficulty often encountered in linking anticompetitive conduct with provable effects on overall market competition, prediction often will guide the fact-finder in determining whether challenged activity "lessens competition" or "restrains trade" in an unlawful manner. Prediction, finally, directs the court's selection of the most appropriate means of enjoining the future anticompetitive effects of past behavior.

It is unclear whether Congress could remove the predictive quality of antitrust analysis if it desired. It certainly has not done so. Instead, Congress has consciously avoided the inclusion of bright-line determinants in antitrust legislation out of concern that the law might become ossified and easily evaded. Yet without fixed points, any law surrenders the benefits of voluntary compliance and effective enforcement. The special dynamics of antitrust law serve only to compound this problem. The rules of per se illegality are thus not simply a judicial gloss that can easily be peeled away, exposing an equally functional statutory frame beneath. As we have seen, the several antitrust per se rules respond to a number of correlated institutional and analytical needs that are critical to the successful operation of the law.

How likely are the per se rules to fulfill these historic requirements if they are reduced in scope and encumbered by factually complex exceptions? Recent court opinions and legislative proposals raise this question. They also offer the beginnings of an answer.

CURRENT ANTITRUST RULEMAKING

To measure the impact of the new approaches to the per se concept, one must have the contours of the present scheme in mind.

Each of the categories of per se illegality evolves through several stages. The decisional tree is defined by the "rule of reason." After several initial skirmishes, Chief Justice White established the rule in the 1911 *Standard Oil* case as the overarching test of Sherman Act legality.[56] All subsequent antitrust enactments have also come within its broad province.

As formulated and later refined, the rule of reason divides into branches.[57] The first and conceptually dominant branch is the standard of reasonableness. Agreements and practices not previously examined, or those that customarily may be ancillary to a primary procompetitive or legitimate business interest, are measured by this scale. The novel practice may be found to impose no cognizable restraint.[58] If it does restrain competition, nonetheless, it may be upheld due to its ancillary and limited character. Or it may be unreasonable, and a violation, if its primary purpose or effect is to eliminate competition. So, too, with conventional practices that may or may not be reasonable, depending on their particular facts.[59]

The main contours of the reasonableness test were established by Justice Brandeis writing several years after *Standard Oil* in *Chicago Board of Trade* v. *United States:*

> The true test of legality is whether the restraint imposed is such as merely regulates and perhaps thereby promotes competition or whether it is such as may suppress or even destroy competition. To determine that question the court must ordinarily consider the facts peculiar to the business to which the restraint is applied; its condition before and after the restraint is imposed; the nature of the restraint and its effect, actual or probable. The history of the restraint, the evil believed to exist, the reason for adopting the particular remedy, the purpose or end sought to be attained, all are relevant facts.[60]

The *Board of Trade* promise of rational analysis was difficult to fulfill. The undeveloped state of economic knowledge, the impossibility of measuring many of the proposed criteria, and the absence of suggested weight to be given different findings contributed to the problem. Had trial judges been forced to solve the problem, antitrust enforcement likely would have ground to a halt. But they were not.

The second branch of the rule of reason provided the escape. Certain restraints, Chief Justice White wrote in 1911, "because of their inherent nature or effect"[61] create "a conclusive presumption which brought them within the statute. . . ."[62] Into this category would eventually go:

> certain agreements or practices which because of their pernicious effect on competition and lack of any redeeming virtue are conclusively presumed to be unreasonable and therefore illegal without elaborate inquiry as to the precise harm they have caused or the business excuse for their use.[63]

At its zenith, the per se classification contained horizontal and vertical price fixing (including the setting of maximum prices),[64] horizontal and vertical nonprice territorial and customer restrictions (the latter no longer),[65] tying arrangements,[66] group boycotts,[67] exclusive dealing (for a brief period),[68] horizontal mergers (but no longer),[69] monopolization (for a fleeting moment),[70] and something Justice Douglas once identified as reciprocity.[71]

No agreement or practice is placed in the per se group on first reading. "It is only after considerable experience with certain business relationships," Justice Marshall asserted in Topco, "that courts classify them as per se violations of the Sherman Act."[72] Experience is relative, of course. Price-fixing cartels were viewed as inherently restrictive from the start. Then, too, the Court gained enough experience in the four years between White Motor and Schwinn to include postsale territorial and customer restrictions within the presumptively illegal designation.[73] More important than experience in a literal sense is the Court's conception of "pernicious effect" and "redeeming virtue," terms sufficiently elastic to be molded by the dynamic forces of antitrust law already described.

In theory, once an arrangement was conclusively presumed to be illegal, it would be shunted to the per se branch of decision without passing through the reasonableness evaluation. Practice has been something else. The process of classification has always been the core of the per se rule. For example, when price fixing became conclusively illegal, litigation shifted to the meaning of "price fixing." Was vertical price fixing to be treated the same as horizontal agreements?[74] Was the exchange of price information by competitors price fixing?[75] A comparison of the underlying factual predicates convinced the Supreme Court that they were.

Like price fixing, market division among competitors has been condemned as unreasonable per se since the time of Addyston Pipe.[76] Three-quarters of a century later, the Supreme Court reaffirmed this when presented with a market division agreement in United States v. Topco Associates, Inc.[77] The market division classification left the Court little choice. If the frame of reference, instead, had been on the group boycott aspects of the Topco practice, the case law would have permitted a wider range of holdings.[78]

Tying arrangements offer another illustration. They, too, have long been in the condemned class, but the many more definitional elements of a tie-in diminish the clarity of the per se rubric and provide significant range for defensive maneuver.[79] Moreover, tying arrangements now have a "soft core"; in United States v. Jerrold

Electronics Corp.[80] a new entrant defense was sustained. Similarly, in group boycotts, an exception to the per se rule exists for boycotts undertaken to enforce necessary association rules.[81] In both instances, the defense is gauged by the reasonableness test.

Some conclusive presumptions are built on rebuttable presumptions. The existence of a patent, copyright, or trademark for the tying product is presumptive proof of leverage in tie-in cases. But it may be rebutted by the defendant.[82] Price uniformity over a prolonged period is presumptive of price fixing. It, too, is subject to defense rebuttal.[83]

It is in this context that the decisions of the Burger Court must be considered. In only one instance has the Court frontally overturned a per se rule. In that case, *Continental T.V., Inc.* v. *GTE Sylvania Inc.,* the rule prohibiting postsale territorial and customer restrictions was so consumed by exceptions devised by lower courts as to have become untenable.[84] Lower court disavowal is one of the dynamic forces always at work in antitrust, but here it was coupled with an unprecedented outpouring of scholarly criticism. Moreover, the development of economic science appeared to the Court to have reached a level at which the *Board of Trade* reasonableness inquiry might produce principled distinctions and measurable benefits. Although a basis for decision narrower than the uprooting of the *Schwinn* per se doctrine was available in *Sylvania,* this may have seemed to the Court the best opportunity to trim the use of conclusive presumptions by demonstrating the merit and feasibility of a return to the reasonableness approach.

The greatest significance of *Sylvania* lies in the fact that the Supreme Court did not—perhaps could not—articulate how postsale distribution restraints were to be evaluated under the reasonableness standard. The Court provides neither economic compass nor procedural lantern, thrusting the parties back to a freewheeling *Board of Trade* inquiry. Only weeks before its *Sylvania* decision, the Court was sufficiently concerned with the judicial capacity to undertake refined economic analysis to deny relief to plaintiffs in *Illinois Brick Co.* v. *Illinois.*[85] Why a similar incapacity does not result from *Sylvania*'s required balancing of intrabrand and interbrand competitive effects is never explained. Moreover, although the Court leaves open the possibility of maintaining the per se approach for some forms of distributional restriction, there is not a hint as to what conditions might warrant this special treatment.[86]

Others have begun to formulate decisional models in an effort to make the *Sylvania* holding operational.[87] Necessarily, burden-shifting rebuttal presumptions are liberally employed to provide structure and conclusiveness to the analysis. But are these the sets of presumptions the Supreme Court will endorse? Until the Court or other governmental authority makes clear the mode of desired legal reasoning, doctrinal consistency and enforcement effectiveness will remain in doubt.

Similar problems exist with the Supreme Court's dilution of the conclusive presumption historically applied to price fixing. In *Goldfarb* v. *Virginia State Bar* and *National Society of Professional Engineers* v. *United States* price fixing, or its near equivalent, by professional associations is apparently exposed to a reasonableness analysis, although the Court fails to illustrate the conditions under which such a practice would ever be reasonable.[88] The Court seems either unconcerned about the possibility of price fixing in *United States* v. *Citizens & Southern National Bank,* or willing to excuse it based upon "market practicality" in *Broadcast Music, Inc.* v. *CBS, Inc.* or "controlling circumstance" in *United States* v. *United States Gypsum Co.*[89]

In the past, political considerations such as the "extra-governmental" nature of price-fixing cartels and group boycotts persuaded the Court to issue blanket prohibitions.[90] Consonant with modern analysis, economic factors can justify private market manipulation in some contexts. But by what criteria are trial judges to identify the appropriate cases? The Supreme Court is correct in attempting to refine antitrust analysis to incorporate contemporary economic tools, but it has failed to provide a methodology which will translate the generalities of economic realism into the practical necessities of litigated cases. The resultant doctrinal instability, joined with the dynamic features of antitrust policy and enforcement, suggests that the current Supreme Court approach is transitional. Either the Court will revert to administrable presumptions, such as those that assign burdens of proof, or Congress will likely intervene to require this result.

THE FUTURE OF PRESUMPTIONS

Some measure of the future can be taken in legislative proposals involving oligopoly markets,[91] monopolization,[92] and conglomerate acquisitions.[93] Each of the proposals defines a violation in terms of data. While not without evidentiary difficulty, these structural indicia afford relative clarity and certainty.[94] In each proposal, only the government may institute suit; one measure creates a special enforcement commission and adjudicatory tribunal.[95] The rationale of each proposal is also similar: to simplify the initial burden of proof by establishing a rebuttable presumption of antitrust illegality. Proof that relief would result in a substantial loss of efficiencies is the primary defense.[96]

Basically, the reform legislation combines the historic advantage of legal presumptions with the flexibility of limited defenses based on current economic thinking. By placing the burden of rebuttal on the defendant, the legislation rests evidentiary responsibility on the party typically in command of the relevant data. To the extent that the efficiencies defense requires a showing of substantiality, the law would be generally enforced. Only exceptional cases would be excluded. The defendant's burden is indeed great; it bears the main responsibility for theoretical or empirical ambiguity. In this, the legislative proposals continue to reflect the emphasis given noneconomic goals in the implementation of antitrust policy.

Difficulties now present in mounting an efficiencies defense are addressed by the legislative scheme in two ways. First, by acknowledging the validity of the efficiency factor, the proposals encourage efforts by industry and the academic community to formulate administrable criteria by which the defense may be gauged. Second, the proposals encourage or require government prosecutors to issue explanatory guidelines or rules setting forth enforcement standards and procedures. This will do much to focus litigation and to remove some of the uncertainty of the judicially-uncharted economic efficiencies concept.

The several legislative proposals and recent Burger Court opinions have some resemblance. Both seek to open the per se approach to greater realism and flexibility, while retaining the benefits of its clarity and enforcement efficiency. But where the Burger Court has yet to find a methodology that accommodates these objectives in a functional manner, the legislative proposals have established what may be the beginning of a workable solution. They formulate strong but rebuttable presumptions that steer the process of litigation. Furthermore, the details of analysis and implementation are not exclusively the preserve of the courts; interested parties are encouraged to formulate guidelines in the more appropriate context of administrative rulemaking.[97]

It is a measure of the advance of economic learning that courts no longer invoke per se rules with confidence. Yet theory must still be molded to meet the needs of national enforcement policy and the limitations of the judicial process. Until national policy is altered, or an alternative to litigation is created, the tension between the economic and legal themes of antitrust will continue to transform the law. Presumptions that facilitate identification of illegal practices but allow for the development of administrable economic defenses in appropriate cases, respond to the modern interface of these competing values. It is difficult to predict whether this will mark antitrust's future path. That the law will continue to change is certain.

NOTES

1. Representative are the statements of then Circuit Judge Taft in United States v. Addyston Pipe & Steel Co., 85 F. 271, 283-284 (6th Cir. 1898), *aff'd*, 175 U.S. 211 (1899); Justice Stone in United States v. Trenton Potteries Co., 273 U.S. 392, 397 (1927); Justice Black in Northern Pacific Ry. Co. v. United States, 356 U.S. 1, 4-5 (1958); and Justice Marshall in United States v. Topco Associates, Inc., 405 U.S. 596, 607-10 (1972).
2. See, e.g., Bork and Bowman, "The Crisis in Antitrust," 65 *Columbia Law Review* 363, 369-70 (1965); Stigler, "The Economic Effects of the Antitrust Laws," 9 *Journal of Law and Economics* 225, 235 (1966).
3. See, e.g., Posner, "Antitrust Policy and the Supreme Court: An Analysis of the Restricted Distribution, Horizontal Merger and Potential Competition Decisions," 75 *Columbia Law Review* 282 (1975).
4. 433 U.S. 36 (1977); United States v. Arnold, Schwinn & Co., 388 U.S. 365 (1967). The "new majority" of the "Burger Court" has been charged with displaying its own set of philosophical prejudices in the field of antitrust. See, e.g., Lurie, "Mergers Under the Burger Court: An Antitrust Bias and Its Implications," 23 *Villanova Law Review* 213 (1978). 433 U.S. at 59.
5. 415 U.S. 486 (1974). See also United States v. Marine Bancorporation, Inc., 418 U.S. 602 (1974). Justice White began his dissent in *Marine Bancorporation:* "For the second time this Term [*General Dynamics* is the first], the Court's new antitrust majority has chipped away at the policies of § 7 of the Clayton Act." *Id.* at 642.
6. 415 U.S. at 498, quoting Brown Shoe Co. v. United States, 370 U.S. 294, 320-21 (1962).
7. United States v. Von's Grocery Co., 384 U.S. 270, 301 (1966).
8. 441 U.S. 1, 8, 9, 19-20, *n.* 16 (1979).
9. 421 U.S. 773, 788-89 *n.* 17 (1975).
10. 435 U.S. 679, 696 (1978).
11. See, e.g., S. 600, 96th Cong., 1st Sess. (1979) (prohibiting mergers between firms of a specified size); "FTC Statement to NCRALP on Legislation to Eliminate Requirement under Sherman Act § 2 of Proving Some Objectional Conduct," 891 *BNA Antitrust and Trade Regulation Report* F-1 (1978).
12. See, e.g., Bork, "Vertical Restraints: Schwinn Overruled," *Supreme Court Review* 171, 172 (1977).
13. S. 1167, 93d Cong., 1st Sess. (1973).
14. Act of July 2, 1890, 26 Stat. 209, as amended, 15 U.S.C. §§ 1-7 (1976).
15. Standard Oil Co. of New Jersey v. United States, 221 U.S. 1 (1911).
16. United States v. American Tobacco Co., 221 U.S. 106 (1911).
17. Act of Oct. 15, 1914, c. 323, 38 Stat. 730, as amended, 15 U.S.C. §§ 12-27 (1976).

18. Act of Sept. 26, 1914, c. 311, 38 Stat. 717, as amended, 15 U.S.C. §§ 41-58 (1976).
19. See generally W. Letwin, *Law and Economic Policy in America: The Evolution of the Sherman Antitrust Act* (1965), ch. 7.
20. See Director and Levy, "Law and the Future: Trade Regulation," 51 *Northwestern University Law Review* 281 (1956). As later developed in this paper, however, the Supreme Court has yet to find the middle ground between the rigidity of the per se approach and the uncertainty of an unstructured reasonableness standard.
21. 310 U.S. 150 (1940); 405 U.S. 596 (1972).
22. See generally Demsetz, "Economics as a Guide to Antitrust Regulation," 19 *Journal of Law and Economics* 371 (1976); Tribe, "Trial by Mathematics: Precision and Ritual in the Legal Process," 84 *Harvard Law Review* 1329 (1972).
23. "I admit that it is difficult to define in legal language the precise line between lawful and unlawful combinations. This must be left to the courts to determine in each particular case. All that we, as lawmakers, can do is to declare general principles, and we can be assured that the courts will apply them so as to carry out the meaning of the law." 21 *Cong. Rec.* 2460 (1890).
24. Although the legislative history has been variously interpreted, the most comprehensive analysis remains H. Thorelli, *The Federal Antitrust Policy: Origins of an American Tradition* (1955), p. 227, describing multiple and interrelated political, social, and economic aims. Appalachian Coals Inc. v. United States, 288 U.S. 344, 359-60 (1933).
25. Northern Pacific Railway Co. v. United States, 356 U.S. 1, 4-5 (1958).
26. United States v. Topco Associates, Inc., 405 U.S. 596, 610 (1972); Kauper, "The 'Warren Court' and the Antitrust Laws: Of Economics, Populism, and Cynicism," 67 *Michigan Law Review* 325 (1968).
27. See, e.g., the dissent of Justice Stevens in Broadcast Music, Inc. v. Columbia Broadcasting System, Inc., 441 U.S. 1, 25, 32-33 (1979).
28. See, e.g., National Society of Professional Engineers v. United States, 435 U.S. 679, 692 (1978).
29. Indeed, a similar plea in the somewhat analogous field of constitutional law has gone largely unheeded. See Wechsler, "Toward Neutral Principles of Constitutional Law," 73 *Harvard Law Review* 1 (1959).
30. Compare Posner, "The Chicago School of Antitrust Analysis," 127 *University of Pennsylvania Law Review* 925 (1979), with Nelson, "Comments on a Paper by Posner" 127 *University of Pennsylvania Law Review* 949 (1979).
31. See, e.g., United States v. Philadelphia National Bank, 374 U.S. 321, 371 (1963).
32. See, e.g., Continental T.V., Inc. v. GTE Sylvania, Inc., 433 U.S. 36, 59 (1977) (White, J., concurring). The problem of statutory vagueness, which may render the antitrust laws unconstitutional, exists just beneath the surface of this issue. See R. Bork, *The Antitrust Paradox: A Policy at War with Itself* (1978), pp. 73-79.
33. See, e.g., Bernhard, "Competition in Law and Economics," 12 *Antitrust Bulletin* 1099, 1104 (1967).
34. The first Supreme Court opinion to evidence this focus is United States v. Trans-Missouri Freight Ass'n, 166 U.S. 290, 323 (1897). See also Brown Shoe Co. v. United States, 370 U.S. 294, 344 (1962); United States v. Aluminum Co. of America, 148 F.2d 416, 428-29 (2d Cir. 1945).
35. See, e.g., Brown Shoe Co. v. United States, 370 U.S. 294, 339-46 (1962).
36. See, e.g., United States v. Trenton Potteries Co., 273 U.S. 392, 307-98 (1927). Cf. Posner, "Oligopoly and the Antitrust Laws: A Suggested Approach," 21 *Stanford Law Review* 1562 (1969).

37. This is made explicit in civil conspiracy cases. See, e.g., Interstate Circuit, Inc. v. United States, 306 U.S. 208 (1939). Compare United States v. United States Gypsum Co., 438 U.S. 422 (1978) (criminal intent can be inferred but not presumed). But see United States v. Gillen, 599 F.2d 541 (3d Cir. 1979).
38. See Continental T.V., Inc. v. GTE Sylvania, Inc., 433 U.S. 36, 54–56 (1977).
39. See generally Panel, "Critical Evaluation of the Preparation and Trial of Cases Involving Complex Antitrust Issues," 47 *Antitrust Law Journal* 869 (1979).
40. 246 U.S. 231, 238 (1918). See text accompanying note 60 *infra*.
41. On this asserted ground, the Supreme Court extended the pass-on theory to bar recovery to plaintiffs involved in private damage litigation. Illinois Brick Co. v. Illinois, 431 U.S. 720, 731–33 (1977).
42. Compare Horowitz, "Decision Theory and Antitrust: Quantitative Evaluation for Efficient Enforcement," 52 *Indiana Law Journal* 713 (1977), with Brodley, "The Possibilities and Limits of Decision Theory in Antitrust: A Response to Professor Horowitz," 52 *Indiana Law Journal* 735 (1977).
43. See, e.g., Schmalensee, "On the Use of Economic Models in Antitrust: The Realemon Case," 127 *University of Pennsylvania Law Review* 994 (1979).
44. A classic illustration is the *Cellophane* case. United States v. E. I. duPont de Nemours & Co., 351 U.S. 377, 391–400 (1956).
45. 324 F.Supp. 19 (D. Conn. 1970); 367 F.Supp. 258 (N. D. Okla. 1973), *rev'd per curiam*, 510 F.2d 894 (10th Cir. 1975). The government has not filed a nonprice vertical distribution restraint case since *Schwinn* was decided in 1967. The Federal Trade Commission has been only slightly more active. See, e.g., Adolph Coors Co. v. FTC, 497 F.2d 1178 (10th Cir. 1974), *cert. denied*, 419 U.S. 1105 (1975).
46. S. Weaver, *Decision to Prosecute: Organization and Public Policy in the Antitrust Division* (1977).
47. See *Report of the ABA Commission to Study the Federal Trade Commission* (1969); Pertschuk, "Report from the Federal Trade Commission," 47 *Antitrust Law Journal* 765 (1979).
48. See Reiter v. Sonotone Corp., 442 U.S. 330 (1979); K. Elzinga and W. Breit, *The Antitrust Penalties: A Study in Law and Economics* (1976), chs. 4, 5.
49. Representative cases are collected in Continental T.V., Inc. v. GTE Sylvania, Inc., 433 U.S. 36, 48 n.14 (1977).
50. See, e.g., Austin, "The Individual Coercion Doctrine in Tie-In Analysis: Confusing and Irrelevant," 65 *California Law Review* 1143, 1176–77 (1977). Resale price maintenance agreements are an example. Cf. Albrecht v. The Herald Co., 390 U.S. 145 (1968).
51. The Court's decisions are somewhat mixed. Compare Illinois Brick Co. v. Illinois, 431 U.S. 720 (1977), and Brunswick Corp. v. Pueblo Bowl-O-Mat, Inc., 429 U.S. 477 (1977), with Reiter v. Sonotone Corp., 442 U.S. 330 (1979), and Pfizer, Inc. v. Government of India, 434 U.S. 308 (1978).
52. United States v. Socony-Vacuum Oil Co., 310 U.S. 150, 221 (1940).
53. 319 F.Supp. 1031 (N.D. Ill. 1971), *rev'd*, 405 U.S. 596 (1972), *on remand*, 1973 Trade Cas. ¶74,485 (N.D. Ill.), *aff'd per curiam*, 414 U.S. 801 (1973). Judge Wyzanski pointedly observed that disavowal may not always be avoidable: "[A] District Judge knows that he cannot give any authoritative reconciliation of opinions rendered by appellate courts. And in connection with the Sherman Act, it is delusive to treat opinions written by different judges at different times as pieces of a jig-saw puzzle which can be, by effort, fitted correctly into a single pattern." (United States v. United Shoe Machinery Corp., 110 F.Supp. 295, 342 (D. Mass. 1953), *aff'd per curiam*, 347 U.S. 521 (1954)).

54. See Brown Shoe Co. v. United States, 370 U.S. 238, 323 (1962); Standard Oil Co. of California (Standard Stations) v. United States, 337 U.S. 293, 310 *n*.13 (1949).
55. See Fashion Originators' Guild of America v. FTC, 312 U.S. 457, 466–467 (1941).
56. For an interpretation of the major pre-1911 cases and judicial viewpoints consult M. Handler, *Antitrust in Perspective: The Complementary Roles of Rule and Discretion* (1957); Bork, "The Rule of Reason and the Per Se Concept: Price Fixing and Market Division (I)," 74 *Yale Law Journal* 775 (1965). Standard Oil Co. of New Jersey v. United States, 221 U.S. 1, 60 (1911).
57. See United States v. United States Gypsum Co., 438 U.S. 422, 474, 476 (1978) (Stevens, J., concurring and dissenting).
58. See White Motor Co. v. United States, 372 U.S. 253 (1963); Missouri v. National Organization of Women, Inc., — F.2d — (8th Cir. 1980) (958 *BNA Antitrust and Trade Regulation Report* F-1) (Apr. 3, 1980).
59. See, e.g., Tampa Electric Co. v. Nashville Coal Co., 365 U.S. 320 (1961).
60. 246 U.S. 231, 238 (1918).
61. United States v. American Tobacco Co., 221 U.S. 106, 179 (1911).
62. Standard Oil Co. of New Jersey v. United States, 221 U.S. 1, 65 (1911).
63. Northern Pacific Railway Co. v. United States, 356 U.S. 1, 5 (1958).
64. See, e.g., United States v. Container Corp. of America, 393 U.S. 333 (1969) (horizontal information exchange); Albrecht v. The Herald Co., 390 U.S. 145 (1968) (vertical price ceiling).
65. See, e.g., United States v. Topco Associates, Inc., 405 U.S. 596 (1972) (horizontal); Continental T.V., Inc. v. GTE Sylvania Inc., 433 U.S. 36 (1977), reversing, United States v. Arnold, Schwinn & Co., 388 U.S. 865 (1967) (vertical).
66. Compare Fortner Enterprises, Inc. v. United States Steel Corp. (Fortner I), 394 U.S. 495 (1969), with United States Steel Corp. v. Fortner Enterprises, Inc. (Fortner II), 429 U.S. 610 (1977).
67. See, e.g., Klor's, Inc. v. Broadway-Hale Stores, 359 U.S. 207 (1959).
68. Compare Standard Oil Co. of California (Standard Stations) v. United States, 337 U.S. 293 (1949), with Tampa Electric Co. v. Nashville Coal Co., 365 U.S. 320 (1961).
69. Compare United States v. Von's Grocery Co., 384 U.S. 270 (1966), with United States v. General Dynamics Corp., 415 U.S. 486 (1974).
70. See United States v. Griffith, 334 U.S. 100 (1948). Cf. Areeda and Turner, "Predatory Pricing and Related Pratices Under Section 2 of the Sherman Act," 88 *Harvard Law Review* 697 (1975).
71. FTC v. Consolidated Foods Corp., 380 U.S. 592, 594 (1965).
72. United States v. Topco Associates, Inc., 405 U.S. 596, 607–8 (1972).
73. White Motor Co. v. United States, 372 U.S. 253 (1963); United States v. Arnold, Schwinn & Co., 388 U.S. 365 (1967).
74. Professor Bork argues that the Supreme Court's affirmative reply to this question is one of the greatest "missteps" in antitrust law (R. Bork, *The Antitrust Paradox: A Policy at War with Itself* (1978), p. 32).
75. The Court concluded it was in the factual context of United States v. Container Corp. of America, 393 U.S. 333 (1969).
76. United States v. Addyston Pipe & Steel Co., 85 F. 271 (6th Cir. 1898), *aff'd*, 175 U.S. 211 (1899).
77. 405 U.S. 596 (1972).
78. Compare Deesen v. Professional Golfers Ass'n of America, 358 F.2d 165 (9th Cir.), *cert. denied*, 385 U.S. 846 (1966), (PGA member boycott reasonable under circumstances), with Blalock v. Ladies' Professional Golf Ass'n., 359 F.Supp.

1260 (N.D. Ga. 1973) (LPGA member boycott based on unreasonable discrimination).

79. See United States Steel Corp. v. Fortner Enterprises, Inc. (Fortner II), 429 U.S. 610 (1977).
80. 187 F.Supp. 545 (E.D. Pa. 1960), *aff'd per curiam*, 365 U.S. 567 (1961).
81. See note 78 *supra*.
82. See generally United States Steel Corp. v. Fortner Enterprises, Inc. (Fortner II), 429 U.S. 610 (1977).
83. See, e.g., FTC v. Cement Institute, 333 U.S. 683 (1948).
84. 433 U.S. 36, 48 *n*.14 (1977).
85. 431 U.S. 720, 741–43 (1977).
86. 433 U.S. at 58–59.
87. See, e.g., Zelek, Stern & Dunfee, "A Rule of Reason Decision Model After Sylvania," 68 *California Law Review* 13 (1980).
88. 421 U.S. 773 (1975); 435 U.S. 679, 692 (1978). The Court of Appeals for the Ninth Circuit has attempted to fill this void. Boddicker v. Arizona State Dental Ass'n, 549 F.2d 626, 632 (9th Cir. 1977).
89. 422 U.S. 86 (1975); 441 U.S. 1 (1979); 438 U.S. 422 (1978).
90. See Fashion Originators' Guild of America, Inc. v. FTC, 312 U.S. 457, 465 (1941); United States v. Socony-Vacuum Oil Co., 310 U.S. 150, 227 (1940).
91. Industrial Reorganization Act, S.1167, 93d Cong., 1st Sess. (1973).
92. "FTC Statement to NCRALP on Legislation to Eliminate Requirement under §2 of Proving Some Objectional Conduct," 891 *BNA Antitrust and Trade Regulation Report* F-1 (Nov. 30, 1978).
93. Small and Independent Business Protection Act of 1979, S.600, 96th Cong., 1st Sess. (1979).
94. See generally Brodley, "Potential Competition Mergers: A Structural Synthesis," 87 *Yale Law Journal* 1 (1977).
95. Industrial Reorganization Act, Titles II & III, note 91 *supra*.
96. See generally, Williamson, "Economies as an Antitrust Defense Revisited," 125 *University of Pennsylvania Law Review* 699 (1977).
97. Although not without its limitations, administrative rulemaking similar to that undertaken for the FTC's Premerger Notification Guidelines, and having a format comparable to the Justice Department's 1968 Merger Guidelines, appears preferable to development through adversary litigation.

Chapter 12

In Defense of Presumptive Rules: An Approach to Legal Rulemaking for Conglomerate Mergers

Joseph F. Brodley

Conglomerate mergers are the least enforced of the extensively litigated antitrust fields. Since the views of the Burger Supreme Court majority have become clear, the government has lost all fully-litigated conglomerate merger cases. The reason is traceable to the type of legal rule the Court has adopted, a nonpresumptive rule that has proved intractable in the courts.

This is not a stable situation, for it has created a wide discrepancy between what Congress intended in Section 7—a viable policy for conglomerate mergers—and the current level of antitrust enforcement.[1] Bills have been introduced in Congress and hearings held on new conglomerate merger legislation.[2] Indeed, these proposals, reflecting the freedom of choice implicit in the legislative as compared with the judicial process, have stimulated a broad reconsideration of appropriate legal rules for conglomerate mergers.

This chapter is an inquiry into legal rulemaking for conglomerate mergers. In it are discussed the relative advantages of legal and

This paper has benefited from the comments of my colleagues, including James A. Henderson, Alan L. Feld, David M. Phillips, Richard N. Pearson, William Page, and the participants in the Boston University Corporate and Tax Law Workshop. I am also indebted for research assistance to Jody Acford, a third-year student at Boston University School of Law.

economic analysis in this task, emphasizing the specific constraints that the legal system imposes on feasible antitrust rules. Rejecting the simple dichotomy between per se and rule-of-reason rules, this chapter suggests a more discriminating classification system for rule feasibility, based on tractability of legal proof and the confidence level of legal advice. Finally, the chapter outlines specific rules for various types of conglomerate mergers and applies a cost-benefit analysis to each proposed rule. I do not attempt here to provide a detailed justification for the noneconomic social goals underlying antitrust policy for conglomerate mergers.[3] Rather, the focus is on the selection of feasible rules, given basic policy assumptions.

THE DIVISION OF LABOR BETWEEN LAW AND ECONOMICS

Both law and economics have zones of relative advantage in antitrust rule formation. The design of antitrust rules involves a three stage process: (1) designation of the social goals to be served by the rule, (2) selection of an appropriate rule, utilizing cost-benefit analysis, and (3) articulation of the rule in legally effective terms.

Designation of Relevant Social Goals

Designation of the social goals served by the Clayton Act is essentially a legal task. Here the lawyer's training as a policy generalist and synthesizer gives him a relative advantage. Most economic analysis of antitrust law is confined to allocative efficiency—appropriately so since economics has little to say outside its accustomed domain. But there is no social theorem that limits economic legislation to purely economic goals. While legal analysts themselves differ on the extent to which the Clayton Act incorporates noneconomic goals, essentially that is a question to be settled within the legal system by customary legal analysis. There is nevertheless a limited economic role even here. If it could be shown that the consumer welfare costs of pursuing any particular social goal were extremely large, this would become a factor in the legal assessment of the statutory policy. Thus, if it could be established that significant deterrence of conglomerate mergers would cause a large decline in consumer welfare, the courts could, and no doubt would, give that finding significant weight—not controlling weight, however, since Congress could choose to prevent mergers, whatever the social costs, if that were its desire.

Selection of Appropriate Rule

Economic analysis has a key role to play in rule evaluation. Indeed, in selecting the optimal rule to serve legally established social goals, we follow the classic economic procedure of cost-benefit analysis. This was expressed generally by Baumol and Quandt, formulated for legal rulemaking by Posner, applied in detail to an antitrust problem by Joskow and Klevorick, and is further explored in recent papers by Schwartz and by Reynolds.[4] The benefit from a legal rule is the undesirable social behavior prevented. The costs of a legal rule flow from two sources: (1) the prevention of desirable behavior to the extent that the rule is over-inclusive; and (2) the transaction and avoidance costs generated by the rule itself.

Lawyers are, of course, also deeply involved in the rule-evaluation process. They are in the best position to estimate the purely legal costs, and—most important—their advice on the efficacy of other possible legal approaches and policy-defeating avoidance techniques is crucial. Thus, selection of an appropriate rule requires an interdisciplinary partnership.

Formulating the Legal Rule

The final step in rule selection is to formulate the precise wording of the legal rule. Since such formulations provide working instructions to lawyers and judges, this is essentially a legal task.

THE CONSTRAINTS IMPOSED BY THE LEGAL SYSTEM

Economists are likely to be more optimistic about the capabilities of the legal system than are lawyers, who have had direct experience with the limited complexity that can actually be managed in a courtroom or before an administrative agency (compare Areeda and Turner with economists who have entered the debate on predatory pricing).[5] The effect of the legal process on a contested factual inquiry is similar to the application of a magnifying glass of high focal power. Issues spring up where they seem not to have existed; simple questions are transformed into matters of high complexity; and that which begins as complex becomes wholly unmanageable.[6] All of this takes place in a verbal battle, one level removed from the facts under examination. The flavor was captured forty years ago by Hamilton and Till in their description of an antitrust proceeding:

> Every move, every witness, every fact, every document becomes a counter in a legal game. "The record" has come to do vicarious duty for an analysis of the industry in operation; and every item, favorable to one side, can win admission only against the heavy cross-fire of the other. Every procedural device which may arrest or speed action, flank or snip the verbal minions of the enemy, color the conduct on parade with innocence or guilt, is called into play. The campaign is lost in its events.[7]

Thus, an effective legal rule in antitrust can emerge only when the constraints of legal inquiry are carefully and explicitly recognized.

Specific Constraints

As applied to the particular problem of selecting a rule for conglomerate mergers, at least five specific limitations must be recognized:

1. The subjective intent of a corporation with respect to specific future actions is incapable of rational proof.
2. Even using objective performance measures, e.g., competitiveness, efficiency, and innovation, the future economic performance of a corporation cannot be effectively proved.
3. Additional factors or elements of proof beyond a very small number increase the chance of legal error and irrational decision.
4. The length and complexity of a legal proceeding increases not only with the complexity of the legal rule, but also with the resources of the participants.
5. The social-political values inherent in the antitrust laws (e.g., limiting discretionary economic authority and equality of economic opportunity) are necessarily nonquantifiable "soft values." That is to say their benefits cannot readily be estimated in monetary or other quantitative terms so as to permit a simple cost comparison; and, therefore, cannot be made the subject of direct proof.

The fourth and fifth constraints will be intuitively obvious to those familiar with the legal system. The others, while perhaps equally apparent, can be briefly developed as follows.

1. Subjective Intent of Corporation Incapable of Rational Proof. The intent of a corporation—an inanimate institution—is, of course, a fiction. It can be proved only by the past writings or present testimony of individuals within the corporation. But which individuals reflect the corporate intent, and to what extent, when each corporation has its own decision-making apparatus? When the issue relates to future corporate action, is the relevant intent that of the individuals formerly in office, those presently in office, or those who will be in office in the future? How can even individual testimony be reliable when the witness or maker of the document knows that his expressions can be outcome-determinative in an important corporate matter?

The difficulty is illustrated in the recent *Atlantic Richfield* case involving a potential competition merger. In that case the court disregarded prelitigation documentary evidence showing that Arco was a potential entrant into the relevant market in favor of post-litigation testimony by Arco's managers denying that there had been any "specific commitment at Arco's top managerial level to enter the copper markets by original entry or toehold acquisition . . ."[8] The conjunction of litigation interest, fallibility of memory, and absence of risk of perjury prosecution (difficult enough even as to objective facts) inevitably distorts the evidence. But even if truthful, its significance is inherently ambiguous as a guide to future institutional behavior.[9]

2. Future Economic Performance Cannot Be Proved Even by Objective Facts. Assessment of socially desirable economic performance, which raises issues of competitiveness, efficiency, and innovation, is a complex undertaking even when it does not relate to the future or involve legal proceedings.[10] The difficulty is compounded in the courtroom, as seen in recent potential-competition cases when issues of past economic performance arose,[11] and under the old Public Utility Holding Company Act.[12]

Proof of *future* economic performance adds a new dimension of difficulty, for future economic performance depends on a business environment, external and internal, that can scarcely be perceived, much less be made the basis of courtroom proof.[13] In potential-

254 / *Antitrust and the Conglomerate Firm*

competition cases future performance is a necessary element of proof in the government's case; for the government must establish that in the absence of the merger the acquiring firm would by a future entry into the target market create a significantly procompetitive effect. Not surprisingly, the government has been uniformly unable to meet its burden of proof on this issue.[14] Attempts under the British merger law to prove another aspect of future performance (future economic efficiency) have also been assessed as unsuccessful.[15] None of this should be surprising: testimony as to future competitiveness and efficiency, even when offered by expert witnesses, can be no more than conjecture or opinion. There is no objective means of verifying the proof. Even an actual occurrence will provide no verification, since a single event can neither prove nor disprove a previous statement as to its probability.[16]

3. Multiplying Factors of Proof Beyond Small Number Increases Chance of Irrational Decision. When decisional-choice factors are multiplied without criteria for weighting them, the result is simply to overload the decision maker. The psychological tendency, as Derek Bok illustrated in his analysis of the *Brillo* merger case, is to increase possibilities of error in logic and inference and to move toward less rational decision making.[17] That is to say, we must recognize the "bounded rationality" of legal as well as business decision makers.[18]

Impact of Constraints on Cost-Benefit Analysis of Conglomerate-Merger Rule

The above constraints severely limit the cost-benefit analysis of a conglomerate-merger rule. This will be apparent in the particular discussion of the various rules. Suffice to say here that benefits, whether in terms of soft values or competitiveness cannot be assessed with respect to individual cases, but at most only for general classes of transactions. The same limitation holds for efficiency losses and other economic costs of an over-inclusive rule. Transactions costs, consisting of both legal costs and avoidance costs, are more accessible to analysis, but even those can be discussed only in rather general terms.

ANALYSIS OF ANTITRUST RULES

Simplicity and Complexity in Antitrust Rules: The Per Se–Rule-of-Reason Controversy

The debate between advocates of per se and rule-of-reason approaches to antitrust rulemaking has obscured more than it has illuminated. Despite the attractions of the legal mind for two-valued issues, more than two-valued logic is needed to explain the simplicity and complexity of antitrust rules. That is why the concepts of rule-of-reason and per se are so illusive. There is no operational definition of the rule-of-reason, and per se itself has no fixed meaning, but, rather, differing interpretations depending on the doctrinal and factual context. What is involved is a continuum between simplicity and complexity, or somewhat more precisely, tractability and intractability, with many possible stopping points. The essence of the problem was captured by Edward Mason, when he wrote in 1957 that the difference between per se and rule-of-reason is the difference between considering factor "a" alone (per se) or factors "a+b" (rule-of-reason).[19] But the point can be amplified.

The tractability of an antitrust rule depends on the following factors: (1) the number of legal elements; (2) the difficulty of proving individual legal elements, which in turn is a function of factual complexity, concept ambiguity, and time reference;[20] (3) the need to engage in balancing between legal elements, e.g., weighing loss of competition in one market as against increase in competition in another.

If the above factors are divided into two broad categories— number of legal elements and complexity of legal elements—a simple three-dimensional diagram is illustrative. Number of legal elements is plotted on one axis, and the other two factors, combined into a single dimension—Complexity of Elements—is plotted on the second axis. The degree of legal difficulty is the height of the resulting surface, which I shall call the Intractability Index. (See Figure 12.1.)

The Confidence Level of Legal Advice

The effectiveness of an antitrust rule in influencing behavior depends on the confidence level of legal advice—the ability of lawyers to advise clients as to the legal risks of contemplated action.

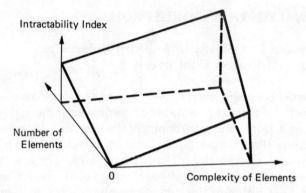

Figure 12.1. Intractability Index.

This is particularly vital in the merger field where there is no criminal penalty or fine and ordinarily no damage award (although litigation costs would remain to provide some deterrent factor).[21] The more confidently the lawyer can advise his client as to the likely outcome of legal action challenging a merger, the greater the influence of the legal rule.

The relation between rule intractability and the confidence level of legal advice is *not* one-directional. The confidence level is highest for rules that are at extremes on the intractability scale. Thus, the very simple rule allows for a high confidence level of advice that defined conduct will lead to liability. Less obviously, the same result obtains when an antitrust rule has high intractability. The reason is that as intractability increases, and both the number of elements and their complexity increase, the burden of proof becomes outcome-determinative.[22] Thus, location of the proof burden (generally placed on the government) suffices to predict the legal result when legal rules become intractable. The relationship appears roughly as shown in Figure 12.2.

It is urged below that the intractability of conglomerate merger rules is high. This in turn leads to a high confidence level of legal advice, and in view of the nature of that advice, a low level of enforcement.

Classification of Existing Antitrust Rules in Terms of Intractability or Rule Complexity

We have seen that a more discriminating assessment of the levels of difficulty posed by antitrust rules is needed than that provided by the simple per se–rule-of-reason dichotomy. While to some extent the

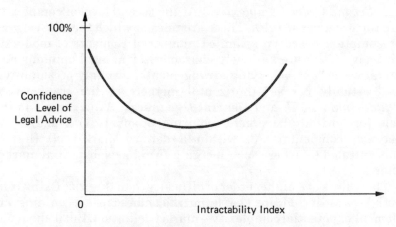

Figure 12.2. Confidence level of legal advice.

number of categories is arbitrary, a five level classification scheme seems most useful.

1. First-Order Complexity. The simplest type of legal rule contains one or a very small number of legal elements, each of which is subject to proof by objective and simply-verified facts. An example is the traffic rule that a motor vehicle shall come to a full stop before a stop sign. Even this rule can be viewed as subject to the rule-of-reason since extenuating circumstances may justify deviations. The simplest antitrust role is more complex than this, for it contains elements that can pose substantial difficulties of proof. Thus, the per se rule against horizontal price fixing requires proof of the following: (1) an understanding or agreement (2) with respect to prices (3) between competitors.

The rule can generate difficulties in resolving whether observed conduct actually amounted to an "agreement," whether the agreement involved prices directly or indirectly, and whether the defendants are competitors.[23] Even when the legal elements are present, it is left to the defendant to show that application of the rule is not sensible on the particular facts, and that can involve a far more intricate inquiry than what is likely in the stop sign case.[24] In actuality, therefore, the per se rule is no more than presumptive, and its application is far from simple in all circumstances. We call the rule "per se" because there is a broad category of transactions in which rebuttal of the presumption is improbable and application of the rule is highly predictive; hence, the confidence level of legal advice is high.

2. Second-Order Complexity. At the second level of complexity are the weak per se rules. These are rules in which there is a strong presumption based on a limited number of elements of moderate difficulty. They are variously characterized in legal opinions and literature as "per se," (tying arrangements), strongly presumptive, or "virtually per se" (horizontal mergers in the era between *Philadelphia Bank* and *General Dynamics).*[25] An example is the rule for horizontal mergers requiring proof of: (1) a merger (2) between competitors (3) within a defined market (4) that is concentrated (5) where each merging firm has substantial market share.

This rule is of a higher order of difficulty than the price fixing rule, both because it contains more elements and because it contains one element of potential complexity—market definition. But it should be noted that the difficulty is of intermediate level only, for the facts relating to market definition are essentially *past* economic facts; moreover, under the *Brown Shoe* rule that permits proof of submarkets within larger markets, it is unnecessary to search for the single most appropriate market, but only to establish that the market is one among several alternative submarkets.[26] The manageability of the concept is seen in the frequency with which adverse parties are willing to stipulate all or part of the market definitions.[27]

A quite different rule, but within the same order of difficulty, is the vertical merger rule after *Brown Shoe.* While this was never described as a presumptive rule (in contrast to the rule for horizontal mergers), the proof rested on an objective and manageable factual showing. Thus, the substantial foreclosure of outside suppliers that constituted the crucial element of proof in a vertical merger case was inferred from the market share of the supplying merger partner.[28]

Although second-order rules do not rank as high on the legal advice confidence level as first-order rules, they nevertheless permit informed advice to participants in mergers, or at least they did so prior to *General Dynamics,* which established a broad permissiveness to rebut the inference drawn from market share statistics.

3. Third-Order Complexity. The conglomerate merger rules applied by the Supreme Court and most lower courts in the Warren Court years were of limited complexity despite the inherent difficulty of the theories on which they rested—potential competition, entrenchment, and reciprocity. The reason is that the Warren Court was willing to find a conglomerate merger in a concentrated market to be unlawful on a showing of a merely possible anticompetitive effect. Thus, in *Procter & Gamble,* which involved the acquisition by Procter of the dominant firm in the liquid bleach industry, the merger was unlawful because it was *possible* that in the absence of the merger Procter would have entered the liquid bleach market, and because it was *possible* that following the merger Procter would use its large resources to entrench Clorox in the market.[29] Under a standard of merely possible anticompetitive effect, lawyers were able to make viable predictions of the outcome of conglomerate merger cases, although at lower confidence levels.[30]

4. Fourth-Order Complexity. *Marine Bancorporation* and subsequent conglomerate merger decisions involve a higher order of complexity. The class of suspect transactions is identified by a structural presumption, but evidence of conduct and performance regarding one or more elements is permitted. This is seen in *Marine Bancorporation* where the elements of proof were as follows:[31]

1. The target market is highly concentrated, and hence presumptively oligopolistic,
2. but such presumption can be rebutted by a showing of competitiveness.
3. The acquiring firm is a probable entrant.
4. Entry of the acquiring firm would be significantly procompetitive.
5. The acquiring firm is perceived to be an entrant, and
6. such perceptions modified oligopolistic behavior.

The *Marine Bancorporation* elements are not only numerous, but involve difficult issues of competitiveness and future firm behavior and performance, actual and perceived. Thus, the Intractability Index is high, but the Legal Advice Confidence Level is also high, since it has proved impossible for the government to sustain the burden of proof on these elements in litigated cases.[32]

Affirmative defenses contained in proposed conglomerate merger bills, relating to efficiency and future competitiveness, are similarly difficult and equally predictive.[33] In this event, however, since the burden of proof is placed on the defendants, the basic merger legislation may prove to be highly enforceable. Indeed, unless the courts intervene decisively, the defenses will serve mainly to give prosecutorial discretion to the enforcement agencies and an opportunity for defendants to protract litigation.

Modern rule-of-reason cases under the Sherman Act also tend to fit within this category. Rather than open-ended inquiries, recent rule-of-reason cases tend to consider a finite list of elements and to draw some inferences from market structure. They continue, however, to require complex evaluations of the competitiveness of behavior.[34]

5. *Fifth-Level Complexity.* The open-ended rule-of-reason approach in which all conceivable facts are relevant—"facts peculiar to the business . . . condition before and after . . . nature of restraints . . . effects . . . history . . . evil believed to exist . . . reason . . . purpose . . . all relevant facts"—is the most expansive rule of all.[35] It contains a virtually open-ended set of elements, and these include issues of great complexity. This was the state of merger law before *Philadelphia Bank* and *Brown Shoe,* as most particularly exemplified in the *Columbia Steel* merger case.[36] This gave the determined litigant much scope for protraction of the proceedings. The outcome was highly predictive, however, when the burden of proof was on the government and the defendants could freely spin out theories to show that the transaction viewed in detail was beneficial on some overall competitive or other social ground. No doubt this is why Professor Posner termed the old rule of reason "a euphemism for non-liability."[37]

CHOOSING THE OPTIMAL RULE
FOR CONGLOMERATE MERGERS

Rule Characteristics and Level of Complexity

The conclusion to be drawn from the above analysis is that there is a limited zone of feasible conglomerate merger rules. The characteristics of an optimal rule can be defined as follows:

1. The rule must effectively recognize antitrust values, which include both competitive and social-political values.
2. The rule must not be so inclusive as to seriously inhibit the marketability of controlling interests.
3. The rule should be sufficiently predictive that lawyers can advise their clients with reasonable confidence as to the legality of a merger.
4. The rule should be enforceable without inducing excessive transaction costs.

An effective legal rule for conglomerate mergers must be below fourth-level complexity *(Marine Bancorporation),* and thus cannot include intractable issues as to future performance and future behavior. The appropriate level of lower order complexity depends on the type of conglomerate merger. I will discuss in turn potential-competition, pure conglomerate, and entrenchment-effect mergers.

Potential Competition Mergers

In my 1977 analysis of potential-competition mergers, I proposed a legal rule of third-order complexity.[38] It is similar in some respects to the "two-tier" approach recently proposed by Joskow and Klevorick for predatory pricing, consisting of a first structural-presumptive tier and a second behavioral tier.[39] My proposal differs, however, in being more parsimonious in the factors to be considered. Joskow and Klevorick seek to avoid the costs of over-inclusion by allowing rebuttal of presumptions by unrestricted factual proof, but this leads to multiplication of elements, inclusion of complex issues, and hence intractability. I would seek to prevent over-inclusion by more narrowly confining the presumption itself. If proof of complex issues of future economic performance is not tractable in a legal proceeding, my method appears superior since transaction costs are less.

The proposed rule is presumptive, but subject to rebuttal. The presumption rests on four structural elements. A merger satisfying such elements would be presumptively unlawful. The burden would then shift to the defendants to justify the acquisition, but only by means of designated factors of proof that are deemed manageable.

Merger Presumptively Unlawful:
1. The Acquiring Firm Is in Close Proximity to the Target Market. Proximity or closeness of markets in terms of information and capabilities becomes the manageable proxy for probable market entry. Use of the proxy is plausible because firms are more likely to enter markets about which they are knowledgeable than those with which they are unfamiliar. Proximity, which has both a geographic and product market dimension, is to be assessed on the basis of (i) similarity of production methods, (ii) marketing similarity, and (iii) observed entry (a) into the target market from the proximate market, or (b) by the acquiring firm into a market similar to the target market.[40]

2. The Acquiring Firm Would Be a Significant Entrant into the Target Market. Significance of entry is presumed from the acquiring firm's size, either as a leading firm in a proximate market, or as one of the 200 largest firms in the country with a significant (but not necessarily leading) market share in the adjacent market.

3. The Structure of the Target Market is Significantly Oligopolistic. Oligopolistic structure of the target market would be established by high concentration, infrequent entry, and persistent substantial profits.

4. The Target Firm Has Significant Market Share. Only acquisitions of leading target market firms would be included in the presumptive rule. A leading firm may be defined as a firm having market share exceeding 10 percent.

Rebuttal of Presumption: The presumption having been established that the merger would injure competition, the burden would shift to the defendants to rebut the presumption. Rebuttal would be permitted, however, only by means of manageable types of proof. Thus, any of the following affirmative defenses would effectively rebut the presumption: (1) existence of other markets of closer or equivalent proximity to the target market; (2) lack of entry capability by the acquiring firm; or (3) beneficial changes in the structure of the target market, either before or after the merger (in cases where merger is allowed to proceed), sufficient to justify the conclusion that the target market will eventually become nonoligopolistic in structure (e.g., significantly decreasing concentration, substantial new entry).

Other behavioral and performance factors would be excluded from consideration, including future market competitiveness, oligopolistic behavior, economic efficiency or synergy, innovation or progressiveness, and corporate intent and perceptions.

Cost-Benefit Analysis: The proposed rule for potential-competition mergers is admittedly a crude instrument, but nevertheless justified on a cost-benefit analysis. Substantial inclusion benefits are present, and over-inclusion and transaction costs are constrained.

1. Inclusion Benefits. Two fundamental social policies are served by potential-competition merger enforcement: (1) promoting competitiveness of oligopolistic markets and (2) limiting further concentration through merger of discretionary economic authority. The basic presumptive rule thus defines the intersection of two classes. No merger is included within the presumptive rule unless there is basis for assuming that both policies will be served. More specifically, firms will be subject to the potential-competition rule only when they share the following characteristics: (a) presumed market entrants are knowledgeable concerning the production and technology of the market to be entered; (b) presumed entrants comprise those firms most capable of financing entry by internal expansion, since their financial endowments are the largest; (c) presumed entrants comprise those firms most likely to enter new markets *de novo* since the largest firms have been a prime source of new market entry; (d) mergers included within the presumptive rule would include prior cases in which courts have found potential competition injury (thus utilizing whatever information past legal experience can contribute in defining the presumptive rule); and (e) the presumptive rule is limited to acquisitions by the largest firms in American industry, defined in an absolute sense and in terms of market size in adjacent markets.

2. Over-Inclusion Costs. Over-inclusion costs result when a legal rule includes transactions *not* within the purposes of the rule. The limited class of transactions included in the potential competition rule, together with the defenses allowed even in those cases, substantially limits over-inclusion costs. Thus, with respect to the competitiveness objective of the rule, over-inclusion costs are constrained in the following ways. First, only a limited class of firms is covered by the presumption that excludes lesser firms in proximate markets as well as large firms in nonproximate markets; the result is to leave most firms, including most large firms, unaffected by the rule. Second, the affirmative defenses allowed to defendants are effectively provable since they rest on objective facts either peculiarly within the defendant's knowledge (lack of entry capability), or at any rate capable of courtroom proof (existence of other markets of closer or equivalent proximity and beneficial changes in the structure of the target market). Third, a presumptive rule would give substantial protection from antitrust challenge to transactions outside the rule, thereby preserving potential for capture of whatever efficiencies may be available from conglomerate mergers.

Over-inclusion with respect to the social-political objectives of the rule is more difficult to assess. It might be urged that any inclusion of a weak or faltering firm is an over-inclusion, since a firm in such condition presumably lacks discretionary authority. But that is not the case. A firm dominating a substantial market or of large aggregate size has important and socially far-reaching decisional

264 / Antitrust and the Conglomerate Firm

choices so long as it survives, and thus has discretionary authority corresponding to the scope of such decisions. If one accepts the legitimacy of a social-political goal for conglomerate merger policy, the issue of over-inclusion becomes one essentially of not impacting so many transactions as to substantially impede the capital transactions market. But this seems most unlikely from a potential-competition merger rule that after all restricts firms from acquisitions only in markets closely proximate to their own.[41]

3. Transaction Costs. Transaction costs in connection with a legal rule are of two types: *legal costs,* which consist of the costs of generating and enforcing the legal rule,[42] and *avoidance costs,* the costs of less preferred strategies to which a firm may move when first-choice strategies are legally barred.[43] Both types of transaction costs will be larger under an effective conglomerate merger rule, but the absolute level would still appear modest.

Legal costs with respect to potential-competition (and other large conglomerate) mergers probably cannot fall much below their present level. It has been argued that the present rules do not significantly deter conglomerate mergers, and, thus, the present level of cost depends primarily on government enforcement budgets. Antitrust enforcement budgets are necessarily formulated in response to Congressional and Executive Office expectations, and these have, under the administrations of both parties, included substantial efforts against conglomerate mergers, a situation that will probably continue.[44] The number of private merger cases is more variable, being subject to the general level of merger activity.[45] Private actions are constrained in their expense, however, because they typically last for only a limited time, usually terminating with the grant or denial of a preliminary injunction.[46]

The proposed presumptive rule for potential-competition mergers would increase legal costs in several ways. The new rule being of intermediate complexity would lower the confidence level of legal advice with respect to potential-competition mergers since prediction of the legal result would become more difficult than under the present rule in which a prediction of nonliability is typically justified. Moreover, some increase in antitrust litigation in contested takeovers could be expected since the target firm's case would be strengthened.[47] Finally, because of the substantial freedom of litigants to control the length of the trial by the level of expenditures they are willing to commit, a simpler legal rule will not necessarily shorten litigated cases.

Nevertheless, additional litigation costs are constrained by the fact that not many transactions would be included within the presumptive rule. Thus, even if all included mergers were litigated, the cost would not be outrageous since (a) some mergers would be litigated under existing doctrines, (b) the preliminary injunction-setting of the litigation sharply limits pretrial as well as trial proceedings, (c) if the injunction is granted, the transaction will frequently be abandoned, thus stopping further legal costs,[48] (d) if the injunction is denied and the merger consummated, the case is likely to be settled with, at best, partial relief if it is a government suit and voluntarily dismissed if it is a private action,[49] and (e) the (usual) unavailability of damages in merger cases lessens the incentive to litigate.

Avoidance costs or strategic adaptation costs result when firms barred from first-choice mergers move to less preferred possibilities such as other mergers or some other use of available funds. We are, of course, concerned with the social costs of moving to less preferred possibilities and not to purely private costs, which might only reflect a loss of anticompetitive advantages.[50]

A presumptive rule of limited application leaves much range for alternative merger moves, but when the effect is to force firms away from proximate market entry to acquisitions in markets where they lack information advantage, an avoidance cost might be anticipated. The point has most force if, as Blair and Peles have asserted at this conference, conglomerate mergers are to be viewed primarily as efficiencies-capturing transactions for reallocating production between related markets.[51] The possible efficiency loss is substantially ameliorated, however, when the alternative to the merger is entry into the same market by internal expansion or acquisition of a smaller firm; for then the information advantage is preserved. Moreover, if near-market acquisitions were an important source of synergies, one would expect to observe both greater returns and higher acquisitions premiums being paid in such mergers; but I know of no such evidence.

There would appear to be no means to clearly circumvent the presumptive rule, although some avoidance techniques appear possible. When market proximity requires that a firm have only a relatively small part of its operations in close proximity to the target market, the firm—in anticipation of the merger—might divest itself of the proximate business; but this is not undesirable if the business so divested is carried on with equal vigor. Similarly, the firm might desist from entering, in advance of the merger, a market similar to the target market (in order not to create evidence of observed entry). Since new entry is generally desirable, this is a perverse incentive, but it could be removed by limiting the observed entry test to entry by firms other than the acquiring firm.[52]

Thus, the proposed presumptive rule offers important benefits, particularly when one includes social-political goals as well as competitiveness among antitrust values. Over-inclusion costs are limited by the confined scope of the rule and by the limited but effective defenses recognized. And transaction costs, both legal and avoidance, appear moderate.

Entrenchment Effect Mergers

The economic concept of entrenchment is that an acquisition of a dominant or leading firm in an oligopolistic market would further strengthen and solidify that firm's margin of advantage over both competitors and potential competitors. To establish an entrenchment effect requires proof that (1) the target firm is the largest and dominant firm in a highly concentrated market, (2) the acquiring firm dwarfs in size the target firm and other firms in the affected market, (3) the acquiring firm is itself a leading firm in its own market, and (4) the merger would give the target firm an advantage likely to further entrench its dominant position.[53]

Recent merger cases considering issues of entrenchment have required proof of a specified anticompetitive advantage that would accrue to the target firm as a result of the merger. In the face of determined opposition by defendants such proof—either in advance of the merger or after the merger, but while litigation is pending— has proved impossible for litigants to establish.[54] For reasons previously discussed, such a rule places an intractable litigation burden on the government, with the result that there is presently no effective enforcement of the entrenchment doctrine.

This result is at odds with the historic development of the entrenchment doctrine, which in my view rests primarily on a social-political rationale, to wit: a firm holding market leadership in a highly concentrated market, and being already one of the largest firms in the country, has sufficient discretionary authority that it ought not be permitted to augment that authority further by achieving a ranking position in a related market, through merger.[55] So viewed, the entrenchment doctrine is a limited expansion of the potential-competition rule. In fact, the acquiring firm in entrenchment cases has inevitably been a leading firm in a related or proximate market; and the courts have rarely, if ever, found an entrenchment effect unless there was also a potential competition effect.[56] The connection is plausible since the most entrenching acquisition is likely to be one where the acquiring firm not only directly strengthens the target firm by the availability of its superior resources, but indirectly by removing itself as a potential entrant to the market. An entrenchment rule thus harmonizes with a proximity approach to potential competition, in effect extending the presumptive rule from markets of close proximity to markets of moderate proximity, while at the same time restricting covered transactions to acquisitions of market-dominating target firms.[57]

Presumptive Rule:

1. The Acquiring Firm Is in Proximity to the Target Market. This is similar to the proximity requirement for potential-competition mergers except that the market similarly need not be as close. Thus, multiple markets might be found in proximity to the target market.

2. The Acquiring Firm Is Among the 100 Largest Firms and is a Leading Firm in the Proximate Market. This narrows the test followed for potential-competition mergers. Both entrenchment and significant potential-competition factors are most apt to be present in acquisitions by firms that are large in both an absolute and a market-based sense.

3. The Structure of the Target Market is Significantly Oligopolistic. This is identical to the potential-competition requirement.

4. The Target Firm is the Leading Firm in a Market in Which Total Sales or Assets Are at Least $100 Million and Itself Has a Market Share of At Least 20 Percent. This is designed to exclude nonsignificant markets.

Rebuttal of Presumption: The presumption, which would shift the burden of proof to defendants, could be rebutted by showing either of the following affirmative defenses:

1. beneficial changes in the structure of the target market, either before or after the merger, sufficient to justify the conclusion that the target market will eventually become nonoligopolistic in structure (e.g., significantly decreasing competition, substantial new entry); or
2. the acquiring firm has voluntarily divested itself of assets comparable to those acquired in the form of one or more viable firms.

The first defense is identical to one of the defenses under the proposed potential-competition rule. The second defense, not available in potential-competition cases, is appropriate here because of the primary social-political thrust of an entrenchment rule (see cost-benefit discussion below). Two other defenses available in a potential-competition case would not be allowed: (1) a showing that other markets were in close or equal proximity, and (2) lack of entry capability by the acquiring firm. The first is unnecessary since it is not required that proximity be uniquely close. The second is not worth the additional complexity that it would introduce, since in any event potential entry is only weakly indicated by a market proximity that is not close and immediate. As in the potential-competition rule, other behavioral and performance factors would be excluded as overly burdensome, and this would include any showing of entrenching advantages conferred on the target firm.

Cost-Benefit Analysis: The entrenchment-effect rule seems less justified on a cost-benefit analysis than the potential-competition rule, but still beneficial on balance if primacy is given to political-social values. Particularly would this be so if successful operation of a more modest potential-competition rule had previously been demonstrated.

1. Inclusion Benefits.   Inclusion benefits are similar to those for the potential-competition rule, encompassing (1) promotion of competitiveness in oligopolistic markets, and (2) limitation of further concentration, through merger, of discretionary economic authority. But the weight that can be assigned to these benefits differs. The entrenchment rule promotes the second objective much more clearly than the first.[58] It is thus an intermediate point on the road to a pure conglomerate merger rule. But unlike a pure conglomerate rule, it ties the promotion of social-political goals to a plausible theory of competitive benefit; and the rule is subject to rebuttal if defendants can show on manageable evidence that it does not promote competition. Nevertheless, justification for finding a competitive benefit is weaker than it was for the potential competition rule. To compensate, the class of included firms is narrowed to firms that are both among the 100 largest firms and are also leading firms in the proximate market. This serves to strengthen the social-political justification for the rule, as well as strengthen, moderately, the competition rationale. Even so, the case for significant benefits from an entrenchment-effect rule must rest primarily on the social-political case. If that is accepted as an important benefit, an entrenchment rule provides a limited, essentially cautious, forward step.

2. Over-Inclusion Costs. Over-inclusion costs might include the blocking of efficiency-producing mergers and possible inclusion of so many mergers as to seriously inhibit the market for controlling interests. But under the rule formulated above, these risks appear minimal. Efficiency-producing mergers would not be barred since a firm would be able to proceed with an otherwise prohibited entrenchment acquisition if it was prepared to divest itself of comparable assets. The larger the efficiency or synergy gain, presumably the more attractive this choice would become. Moreover, the rule would leave firms ranking below the top 100 uninhibited so that unless the cross-market synergies were peculiar to the combination of the acquiring firm and the target firm, synergies could be achieved by an alternative route.

With respect to impact on capital markets, there is perhaps some risk that proximity would be defined so loosely as to apply to any dominant-firm acquisition by the largest 100 firms. But even in this event, spinoffs are still possible. In addition, the rule would affect only acquisitions by the 100 largest firms, thus leaving all other firms uninhibited. Finally, a loose construction of proximity should be resisted, and instead an actual information proximity insisted upon. This would allow acquisitions by the 100 largest firms to proceed in unrelated markets without meeting the spin-off requirement.

3. Transaction Costs. The rule would clearly entail additional legal costs, but less than one might initially think. Absence of an effective rule for entrenchment effect mergers does not mean an absence of litigation, since in contested mergers, litigation has a delaying function for the party opposing the merger. Thus, an entrenchment issue is frequently introduced into current merger litigation, however unlikely ultimate success.[59] The proposed entrenchment rule would be of manageable complexity, the most difficult issues being market definition and, in some instances, determination of the adequacy of a divestiture of comparable assets.[60]

Avoidance costs appear limited under an entrenchment rule. In potential-competition mergers avoidance costs might result, as we saw, if the rule caused a shifting of merger investment from markets where the firm was most knowledgeable to those where it was less informed. Whatever such risks in potential-competition cases, the risks would be less under an entrenchment rule. This is because the entrenchment rule applies to mergers of weaker proximity than the potential-competition rule; thus, the informational advantage of the acquiring firm will, in general, be less, and as a result any displacement of merger activity will be less costly. The somewhat greater avoidance-cost risk is that acquiring firms, approaching statutory size limits that would subject them to the entrenchment rule, would desist from growth by internal expansion in order to remain outside the rule, or would simply divert funds to foreign acquisitions in order to prevent further growth in domestic size. But this seems a far-fetched strategy under a rule that places no overall cap on growth by merger; it could operate, however, when an acquiring firm has already resolved on a particular future acquisition. Nevertheless, on balance avoidance costs appear moderate under an entrenchment rule.

Pure Conglomerate Mergers

No antitrust rule presently constrains pure conglomerate mergers. But two pending legislative proposals raise issues concerning the appropriate content for such a rule.[61] One proposal would apply to all kinds of conglomerate mergers, the other only to those in the petroleum industry.[62]

A rule for pure conglomerate mergers is by necessity a general rule, applying to all types of conglomerate mergers. It differs in a fundamental way from more specific conglomerate merger rules: it includes no theory of competitive restraint in particularized markets; instead it rests almost entirely on the social-political values of antitrust. Some competitive benefits may nonetheless flow from the rule since it would necessarily include in its general survey many potential-competition and entrenchment situations. In resting on a social-political basis, the pure conglomerate rule represents a break in the antitrust tradition, and proponents have sought to maintain the antitrust duality of values by introducing economic considerations of competition and efficiency as affirmative defenses. Thus, the proposed conglomerate merger statutes can be said to differ from traditional antitrust rules only in shifting the burden of proof with respect to economic issues to the defendant. The defendant is required to justify the merger as promoting economic values (competition or economic efficiency) in contrast to the usual requirement that the plaintiff establish that the merger is anticompetitive. This preserves the doctrinal symmetry of antitrust policy, but difficulties of proof render these defenses illusory in most situations. This is unsatisfactory, since it would defeat the condition for an optimal conglomerate merger rule requiring that competitive as well as social-political values be considered. As suggested below, one approach shows promise for preserving the historic antitrust duality—the spin-off defense.

In form, a pure conglomerate rule is much simpler than the rules for other types of conglomerate mergers because it contains a per se type of prohibition, based on asset size or total sales of the merging firms.[63] Thus, in its primary statement, a pure conglomerate rule is of first-order complexity. Higher levels of complexity are introduced when affirmative defenses are allowed. These defenses can lead to high levels of intractability since they involve issues of future competitiveness and efficiency from organizations yet to be formed. But with the burden of proof placed on the defendant, the confidence level of legal advice remains high for the same reason that obtains under the present regime of conglomerate merger rules: the burden is generally not sustainable in the courtroom.

A more feasible approach to an economic justification defense for conglomerate mergers is the spin-off defense.[64] This would permit consummation of an otherwise impermissible merger when the acquiring firm was prepared to divest itself within a limited time of assets comparable in magnitude to the acquired assets. The spin-off defense provides a self-administered approach to the efficiency problem, since the merging firms would be allowed to proceed with the merger when they anticipate that the expected return on the new assets will exceed the return on the assets to be divested; the higher the differential in return, the greater the incentive to use the spin-off option.

A rule of the generality suitable for pure conglomerate mergers lacks the incremental quality of more specific conglomerate merger rules. This is a disadvantage since incrementalism is a generally desirable characteristic of a legal rule.[65] An incremental rule permits policy reversal or modification at relatively low cost, as each successive step yields feedback from the new cases and other effects generated.[66] The conglomerate merger decisions of the Warren Court can be seen as incremental steps toward a more general conglomerate merger rule. Thus, the Court's use of imaginative theories of competitive injury, e.g., reciprocity, deep pocket, and entrenchment, provided a judicial approach to incrementalism, a gradual tightening of the permissive legal policy toward conglomerate mergers. Such a policy would have made it possible to assess adverse impacts on a gradual basis.[67] But this approach was foreclosed by the decisions of the Burger Court.

Incrementalism is much more difficult to achieve under a statutory approach. Legislation is a blunt instrument, and necessarily so, since a legislature can never be certain that it will be able to speak on an issue a second time. Nevertheless, incrementalism remains a virtue even for a legislature. It is best realized by a rule that operates decisively within a confined zone. With respect to conglomerate mergers, an incremental statutory approach would confine the operation of the rule to mergers involving the largest firms in the society.

Drawing on the above considerations, the appropriate rule for pure conglomerate mergers should encompass only major acquisitions by firms of largest size. A plausible rule might thus extend to an acquisition of one of the 500 largest firms in terms of sales or assets by one of the 100 largest firms. As previously mentioned, the prohibition should not be absolute, but subject to a spin-off defense, based on voluntary divestiture of comparable assets in the form of one or more viable business units.

1. Cost-Benefit Analysis. Cost-benefit analysis is particularly difficult for a pure conglomerate rule because both costs and benefits are hard to bring into sharp focus. The prime benefit from a general conglomerate merger rule is the check it would place on the continued concentration of ownership through merger. This could have an important effect on concentration generally, since the existence of an effective horizontal merger rule has forced most large mergers into conglomerate form.[68] An additional benefit would flow from the social statement such a rule would make on the desirability of containing the concentration of industrial assets, an ideological expression that, as I have argued elsewhere,[69] is vital to a competitive, capitalist ideology.[70]

2. Over-Inclusion Costs. It has been argued that the costs of a general conglomerate merger rule would be such as to undermine the efficiency and competitive ability of American industry by preventing the transfer of unproductive assets to more efficient hands, lowering the return on investment in target firms, discouraging enterprise growth even by internal expansion, hampering the ability of U.S. firms to compete in world markets, and discouraging foreign investment in the United States.[71]

I attempted to analyze these questions in some detail in a recent article in *Ohio State Law Journal*.[72] There I conclude that while they appear to be a formidable challenge, on close analysis the claims of dire adverse effects are less compelling. Favored acquisition candidates in recent mergers have not been the lagging, floundering firms most in need of better management, but more often highly successful firms with strong market shares. Moreover, conglomerate firms have not compiled records that are superior to those of nonconglomerates. If the key to conglomerate efficiency lies in the pressure that a takeover threat imposes on existing management, it is unclear why such pressure is not equally necessary for the largest firms, whose very size insulates them from successful takeover. This point gains force when one realizes that these largely insulated firms are the very ones upon whose competitive ability our success in world markets is said to depend most vitally. In short, it remains a puzzle, for example, how a major conglomerate acquisition by one of the Big Three auto manufacturers will help in building a "world car" to recapture automobile sales lost to foreign producers.

3. Transaction Costs. Legal costs would not necessarily increase under a rule for pure conglomerate mergers, despite the fact that we would be substituting an effective legal rule for a regime in which no rule exists. This seemingly surprising result follows because even in the absence of a legal rule for pure conglomerate mergers, many are litigated on antitrust and other grounds. Thus, government and private litigants, sometimes merely for delay, attack such mergers under imaginative claims that somewhere in the widespread operations of the merging firms lurks an unlawful anticompetitive effect—horizontal, vertical, potential-competition, or entrenchment.[73] A rule for pure conglomerate mergers would obviate the tendency to resort to such theories, which, however far fetched, provide ample basis for extensive and costly litigation. Indeed, in cases where a pure conglomerate rule deterred the merger, there would be no litigation at all. Litigation might also be discouraged in cases outside the rule, for judges would probably be less tolerant of efforts to dress up pure conglomerate merger cases in conventional anticompetitive merger theories. Emergence of an effective legal rule for pure conglomerate mergers would make it the focal point for expression of social-political values in conglomerate merger policy, and other theories would be viewed primarily in competitive terms. Hence, failure to sustain a showing that the merger was anticompetitive would preclude effective challenge in most cases.

Litigation and other legal costs would be induced in borderline cases, where a merger was just within or outside size limitations. In such cases, disputes would no doubt arise as to what is the proper basis for calculating assets or sales, but experience could provide precedents and guidance. The major source of legal costs that would be induced by a rule for conglomerate mergers is the spin-off defense, as this would require a determination that comparable assets are, or will be, diverted into one or more viable firms. Perhaps the least costly procedure would be one based on advance rulings, as in tax cases; and the reviewing agency might rely on actual market values whenever available, and otherwise on a carefully prescribed appraisal procedure.

The more serious problem is with respect to avoidance costs, but benefits can also result. To the extent that firms are induced to make alternative investments in the form of internal expansion into new markets, the social return seems positive. This appears to hold even if the firm itself bears higher costs, since new productive capacity is created. But less desirable avoidance techniques may also occur in both domestic and foreign acquisitions. Domestic investment incentives would be affected adversely if, to preserve merger capacity, firms approaching statutory size limitations held off from investing in new plants. Foreign investment incentives would be altered if U.S. firms, restricted from domestic acquisition, shifted investment to foreign acquisitions; or if foreign firms either directed investment away from the United States to overseas markets or, alternatively, increased merger investments in the United States, thus taking advantage of a reduced number of large U.S. firms eligible to make acquisitions.

These are real problems, which I have attempted to deal with in another place.[74] They provide important constraints to be considered in shaping the exact contour of the legal rule and strongly suggest the desirability of a limited statutory rule with a spin-off defense. While present evidence leads me to conclude that costs can be held to acceptable levels under such a rule, I acknowledge that if one concludes otherwise, one would not be in favor of the rule. Thus, under a cost-benefit analysis of a pure conglomerate merger rule, avoidance cost appears as the critical issue.

CONCLUSION

Thurmond Arnold noted that despite the ringing rhetoric of the "trust busters," the antitrust laws have had remarkably little effect in altering the large-business structure of American industry.

The reason for this was simple enough: there was no effective rival or alternative to the large business organization.[75] This remains true, and thus it is illusionary to think the existing structure of markets can be much changed by antitrust policy—with one exception. The exception is merger policy, undeveloped in Thurmond Arnold's time, which allows antitrust to influence market structure before change is institutionalized and the costs of deconcentration become prohibitive. An effective merger policy is the only effective means by which to give substance to the antitrust ideal that private, as well as public, power should be limited in a democratic society. A strengthened antitrust policy for conglomerate mergers, utilizing presumptive rules, provides a cost-effective approach to this goal.

NOTES

1. Brodley, "Potential Competition Mergers: A Structural Synthesis," 87 *Yale Law Journal* 1, 40-45 (1977).
2. S. 600, 96th Cong., 1st Sess. (1979) ("Small and Independent Business Protection Act of 1979"); S. 1246, 96th Cong., 1st Sess. (1979) ("Oil Windfall Acquisition Act of 1979").
3. The author has elsewhere attempted to justify such policies, however. See Brodley, note 1 *supra* and "Limiting Conglomerate Mergers: The Need for Legislation," 40 Ohio *State Law Journal* 867 (1979).
4. Baumol and Quandt, "Rules of Thumb and Optimally Imperfect Decisions," 54 *American Economic Review* 23 (1964); Ehrlich and Posner, "An Economic Analysis of Legal Rulemaking," 3 *Journal of Legal Studies* 257 (1974); Joskow and Klevorick, "A Framework for Analyzing Predatory Pricing Policy," 89 *Yale Law Journal* 213 (1979); R. Reynolds, "The Economics of Antitrust Enforcement: Theory and Measurement" (1979) (unpublished); W. Schwartz, "An Overview of the Economics of Antitrust Enforcement" (1979) (unpublished).
5. Compare Areeda and Turner, "Predatory Pricing and Related Practices under Section 2 of the Sherman Act," 88 *Harvard Law Review* 697 (1975), with Scherer, "Predatory Pricing and the Sherman Act: A Comment," 89 *Harvard Law Review* 869 (1976); Williamson, "Predatory Pricing: A Strategic and Welfare Analysis," 87 *Yale Law Journal* 284 (1977); Baumol, "Quasi-Performance of Price Reductions: A Policy for Prevention of Predatory Pricing," 89 *Yale Law Journal* 1 (1979); and Joskow and Klevorick, note 4 *supra*.
6. Legal complexity has not evolved by accident. Lawyers are trained to make the apparently simple complex. As early as law school, a system of natural selection is at work by which legal ability is significantly measured by the number of legal issues that can be identified in a factual situation. In addition, many lawyers view as the highest exercise of legal talent the taking on of a simple, all but hopeless, case and then by assiduous diligence and imagination constructing a complex edifice sufficient to prevail in the contest. Such ability is highly rewarded, and it comprises much of the margin of advantage of the most successful lawyers and law firms.

7. W. Hamilton and I. Till, "Antitrust in Action," No. 16 *TNEC Monograph* 60 (1941).
8. FTC v. Atlantic Richfield Co., 549 F.2d 289, 297 (4th Cir. 1977). In its brief, Arco summarized management testimony concerning the difficulty of entry, the existence of other entrants, and the lack of intent to enter other than by acquisition. Brief for Appellees, FTC v. Atlantic Richfield Co., at 26–31, 33–36.
9. Note, "Decisionmaking Models and the Control of Corporate Crime," 85 *Yale Law Journal* 1091, 1128 (1976); Brodley, note 1 *supra* pp. 25, 54–55.
10. G. Stigler, *The Organization of Industry* 12 (1968) (no analytic basis for eliminating disagreement between competent observers on competitiveness of an industry).
11. In potential-competition cases issues of *past* economic performance arose in connection with the competitiveness of the target market. Defendants were permitted to rebut the presumption of oligopolistic conditions in the target market, a precondition to application of the potential-competition doctrine, by proof of actual market competitiveness. After a close study of the cases, I concluded that the uniform failure of the defendants to make the showing, despite repeated attempts, evidenced the inherent unmanageability of the issue. See Brodley note 1 *supra*, pp. 20–25.

In the one recent case that might be thought to be an exception, United States v. Hughes Tool Company, 415 F. Supp. 637 (C.D. Cal. 1976), the issue of market competitiveness was quite unnecessary. Since the target market was not concentrated under *Marine Bancorporation* a finding of market competitiveness was redundant under *Marine Bancorporation,* for "[t]he potential-competition doctrine has meaning only as applied to concentrated markets" (United States v. Marine Bancorporation, 418 U.S. 602, 630 (1974)).
12. In Public Utility Holding Company proceedings, loss of substantial efficiencies was a defense to the divestiture mandate for condemned holding company systems. My study of these proceedings showed that for the most part the decision-making agency avoided deciding such cases on the merits, in favor of finding some procedural defect, and as a result defendants were seldom successful in their efforts to prove substantial efficiencies loss (Brodley, "Industrial Concentration and Legal Feasibility: The Efficiencies Defense," 9 *Journal of Economic Issues* 365, 369–70 (1975)).
13. See generally, J. Leubsdorf, "Remedies for Uncertainty" (unpublished Paper, 1979) (profound difficulties in attempting to prove "what would have happened or will happen in the future as if it were a fact, to be 'found' by a judge . . .").
14. See United States v. Black & Decker Mfg. Co., 1976-2 Trade Cas. ¶61,033 (D. Md. 1976); British Oxygen Co., 86 FTC 1241, (1973-1976 Transfer Binder) Trade Reg. Rep. ¶21,063, *rev'd and remanded sub nom.,* BOC Int'l Ltd. v. FTC., 557 F.2d 24 (2d Cir. 1977); FTC v. Tenneco, Inc., 5 Trade Reg. Rep. (1977-1 Trade Cas.) ¶61,449 (D. D.C. 1977); U.S. v. Bethlehem Steel Corp., 168 F. Supp. 576 (S.D. N.Y. 1958). See also Bok, "Section 7 of the Clayton Act and the Merging of Law and Economics," 74 *Harvard Law Review* 226 (1960); Brodley, note 1 *supra*, pp. 19–25; Note, "Substantially to Lessen Competition . . . : Current Problems of Horizontal Mergers," 68 *Yale Law Journal* 1627 (1959).
15. Wasserstein, "British Merger Policy from an American Perspective," 82 *Yale Law Journal* 656, 662 (1973).
16. Viewed objectively, statements of probability are statements about classes of similar events, or in the nature of statistical hypotheses. A single observation will of course neither prove nor disprove a statistical hypothesis.

17. Unless multiple factors point in a single direction, assessing their impact on merger is difficult; inclusion of additional factors does not lead to greater precision in determining whether merger is lawful. (Bok, note 4 *supra,* pp. 293–94). Cf. Use of multiple factors in legal decision making can involve internal contradictions under choice theory (Spitzer, "Multicriteria Choice Processes: An Application of Public Choice Theory to Bakke, the FCC, and the Courts," 88 *Yale Law Journal* 717 (1979)).

18. I do not read Professor Cooper's chapter to disagree in any fundamental way with the difficulties discussed. Indeed, his chapter is eloquent in its articulation of the "enormous," "extraordinary" and even "overwhelming" difficulties confronting antitrust decision at various doctrinal levels. What Professor Cooper questions is whether workable simplification can be achieved short of draconian, over-inclusive rules. It is the burden of this chapter to show that a legal rule for conglomerate mergers can be both workable and cost-justified.

19. E. Mason, *Economic Concentration and the Monopoly Problem* (1957), p. 394.

20. Factual complexity refers to the simplicity or difficulty of proving the underlying fact (contrast, e.g., the relatively simple-to-prove fact that two firms have merged with the much more difficult-to-prove fact that a significant saving in production costs resulted from the merger). Concept ambiguity refers to concepts with no settled factual definition, e.g., progressiveness. Time reference refers to the time framework within which factual events are viewed—past, present or future.

21. When there is a penalty, behavior can be affected by increasing the penalty without changing the probability of liability.

22. Intractable rules may lead to unpredictable results in trials before juries, but merger and other nondamage cases are tried only before judges, and even in jury cases antitrust courts seem increasingly willing to reverse jury verdicts in complex cases. See, e.g., William Inglis & Sons Baking Co. v. ITT Continental Baking Co., 461 F. Supp. 410 (N.D. Cal. 1978).

23. Nonhorizontal price fixing agreements are also subject to the per se rule against price fixing, but such agreements are sufficiently different to require separate analysis.

24. See Broadcast Music v. CBS, Inc., 99 S. Ct. 1551 (1979). See also Rahl, "Price Competition and the Price-Fixing Rule—Preface and Perspective," 57 *Northwestern University Law Review* 137, 143–48 (1962).

25. U.S. v. Philadelphia National Bank, 374 U.S. 321 (1962); U.S. v. General Dynamics Corp., 415 U.S. 486 (1974).

26. Brown Shoe Co. v. U.S., 370 U.S. 294 (1962).

27. See, e.g., FTC v. Procter & Gamble Co. (Clorox), 386 U.S. 568, 571 (1967) (both product and geographic market); U.S. v. Penn-Olin Chemical Co., 378 U.S. 158, 161 (1964) (both product and geographic market).

28. See, e.g., Dept. of Justice, *Merger Guidelines* (1968) (Department will generally challenge a merger between a supplying firm with 10 percent of the market and a purchasing firm with 6 percent of the market.)

29. FTC v. Procter & Gamble Co. (Clorox), 386 U.S. 568 (1967).

30. The Bork approach to antitrust rules is at comparable levels of complexity, but the bias is reversed. An antitrust practice is permitted if it can be established that there is some possibility that it will lead to enhanced efficiency. See Bork, "The Rule of Reason and the Per Se Concept: Price Fixing and Market Division," 75 *Yale Law Journal* 373, 377–90 (1966).

31. U.S. v. Marine Bancorporation, Inc., 418 U.S. 602 (1974).

32. See Brodley, note 1 *supra,* pp. 10–25 (reviewing cases).

33. See Oil Windfall Acquisitions Act of 1979 (S. 1246), 96th Cong. 1st Sess. (1979), Small and Independent Business Protection Act of 1979 (S. 600), 96th Cong., 1st Sess. (1979).
34. See, e.g., Kestenbaum v. Falstaff Brewing Corp., 575 F.2d 564 (5th Cir. 1978) (assessment of anticompetitive effect as against procompetitive benefit or justification); Petroleum for Contractors, Inc. v. Mobil Oil Corp., 1978-2 Trade Cas. ¶62,151 (S.D. N.Y., 1978) (balancing of interbrand competition against intrabrand market power). See Zelek, Stern, and Dunfee, "A Rule of Reason Decision Model After Sylvania," 68 *California Law Review* 13 (1980) (logically ordered approach, but incorporates complex, unmanageable concepts).
35. Chicago Board of Trade v. U.S., 246 U.S. 231, 238 (1918).
36. "In determining what constitutes an unreasonable restraint, we do not think the dollar volume is in itself of compelling significance; we look rather to the percentage of business controlled, the strength of the remaining competition, whether the action springs from business requirements or purpose to monopolize, the probable development of the industry, consumer demands, and other characteristics of the market" (U.S. v. Columbia Steel Co., 334 U.S. 495, 527 (1948)).
37. Posner, "The Rule of Reason and the Economic Approach: Reflections on the Sylvania Decision," 45 *University of Chicago Law Review* 1, 14 (1977).
38. Brodley, note 1 *supra*.
39. Joskow and Klevorick, note 4 *supra*.
40. Market similarity registers the presence of information overlap between two markets based on shared production and marketing characteristics, an analytic technique that underlies the well-accepted census classification categories. The observed entry test registers whether in fact there has been actual entry from one market to the other, a test similar in strategy to the survivor test for scale economies. Thus, the first test identifies markets between which the information gap is comparatively small; the second or observed entry test confirms the inference from the first test by showing that cross-market entry has occurred. Used together, the two tests provide an objective, legally feasible basis for identifying the markets of close proximity. Both tests were satisfied in Ford Motor Co. v. United States, 405 U.S. 562 (1972), in which (1) close market similarity existed between the automobile manufacturing and spark plug markets and (2) another auto manufacturer had previously entered the spark plug market. Both tests were also satisfied in United States v. Standard Oil Company (New Jersey), 253 F. Supp. 196 (D. N.J. 1966) and in United States v. Phillips Petroleum Co., 367 F. Supp. 1226 (C.D. Cal. 1973), aff'd mem., 418 U.S. 906 (1974) (market extension case).

   Professor Cooper questions whether the acquiring firm or even a class of acquiring firms within a single market can be designated as a more probable entrant than other firms or classes of firms except by charting "the most probable lines of expansion of a large number of firms." But this misconceives the idea of proximity, which is a static concept, based on a present similarity and information overlap between markets. Proximity analysis does not attempt to assess probable lines of future expansion, an impossible task that has led to the current breakdown of potential-competition enforcement (and that would also plague the Department of Justice Merger Guidelines if they were to be implemented). Professor Cooper suggests that numerous firms might be identified as proximate. But this condition could only arise if several markets were in a comparable close and immediate proximity to the target market. This appears unlikely, but in any event, should it arise defendants can rebut the presumption from proximity on a showing that more than two or three other markets are in equal proximity or that even a single market is in closer proximity.

41. The possible cost that would be involved in deflecting acquisitions from proximate to less proximate markets, perhaps with a greater risk of improvident investment, is properly treated as a transaction cost of the avoidance type (discussed below).

42. Ehrlich and Posner, note 4 *supra*, pp. 267-71.

43. Suggesting that strategic adaptation by firms to preserve predatory pricing strategies under a marginal cost pricing test for predatory pricing would induce firms to create wasteful excess capacity (Joskow and Klevorick, note 4 *supra*).

44. The number of merger complaints has remained fairly constant over the last twenty-five years. Thus, the number of large conglomerate mergers in mining and manufacturing that were challenged have not fluctuated substantially since 1951: 1951-55 (5 challenges), 1956-60 (5 challenges), 1961-65 (8 challenges), 1966-70 (13 challenges), and 1971-77 (7 challenges) (W. Mueller, *The Celler-Kefauver Act: The First 27 Years,* Study for Subcomm. on Monopolies and Commercial Law, House Judiciary Comm., 95th Cong. 2d Sess. (1978) at 113).

45. This is seen from the following data, comparing the number of private and government merger cases:

	Private	Government
1950	0	0
1951	0	0
1952	0	1
1953	3	0
1954	0	2
1955	1	8
1956	3	18
1957	1	7
1958	2	8
1959	4	13
1960	3	24
1961	1	19
1962	3	13
1963	4	12
1964	6	21
1965	3	27
1966	0	26
1967	3	16
1968	3	34
1969	0	31
1970	2	22
1971	7	33
1972	7	24
1973	13	23
1974	7	17
1975	15	10

These data were compiled from ABA Antitrust Section, Monograph No. 1, *Mergers and the Private Antitrust Suit: The Private Enforcement of Section VII of the Clayton Act Policy & Law,* Appendices B, C and D (1977).

46. ABA Monograph, note 45 *supra*, pp. 33–35. See, e.g., Missouri Portland Cement Co. v. Cargill, Inc., 498 F.2d 851 (2d Cir.), *cert. denied,* 419 U.S. 883 (1974).

47. It should be recognized, however, that delay is one objective of private merger litigation and to a considerable extent, this requires no more than merely colorable theories of liability, which the present law clearly provides.

48. Over the 4-year period 1970–74, in sixteen cases in which injunctions were granted, eleven were terminated and only one was reported as ongoing. See ABA, *Merger Case Digest*–1976, 357–507, 524–25. See also Missouri Portland Cement Co. v. Cargill, Inc., 498 F.2d 851, 870 (2d Cir.), *cert. denied,* 419 U.S. 883 (1974) ("The grant of a temporary injunction . . . spells the almost certain doom of a tender offer."); ABA Monograph, note 45 *supra*, p. 33.

49. In private actions "when preliminary injunctive relief has been denied and the tender offer has proceeded, the lawsuit has generally not been prosecuted, for it is usually not in the interests of the management of the acquired company to continue a lawsuit against its new owners" (ABA Monograph, note 45 *supra*, p. 35). See also Filtral Corp. v. Slick Corp., 1970 Trade Cas. ¶73,035, at 88,051 (C.D. Cal. 1969), *aff'd per curiam,* 428 F.2d 826 (9th Cir. 1970). (Court noted that failure to issue preliminary injunction would frustrate Court's jurisdiction over merger because suit would not be prosecuted further.)

50. This might occur when the anticipated private gain includes higher profit from output restriction, as when the most probable potential entrant enters a market in which it is a perceived entrant, and thereby removes a restraining influence. See Reynolds and Reeves, "The Economics of Potential Competition," in *Economic Analysis and Antitrust Law,* Calvani and Siegfried, eds. (1979), p. 299.

51. Blair and Peles, "Conglomerate Mergers: Efficiency Considerations," in this volume.

52. This would not seriously weaken the test since by definition the acquiring firm will not have previously entered the target market.

53. FTC v. Procter & Gamble Co. (Clorox), 386 U.S. 568 (1967).

54. See, e.g., Emhart Corp. v. USM Corp., 527 F.2d 177 (1st Cir. 1975); U.S. v. Black & Decker Mfg. Co., 1976-2 Trade Cas. ¶61,033 (D. Md. 1976).

55. "The unarticulated rationale of the entrenchment effect cases (of the Warren Court)" (Brodley, note 1 *supra*, p. 82 and *n*.340).

56. *Id.*

57. The Kennedy bill follows a different approach to entrenchment mergers, excluding any explicit consideration of potential-competition factors. Large firms are simply barred from acquiring leading firms (20 percent market share) in markets having sales or assets exceeding $100 million.

58. Professor Cooper's assessment is consistent with this view, for in his generally negative analysis of the competitive justification for conglomerate merger rules, he finds much less basis of support for an entrenchment rule than for a potential-competition rule.

59. See, e.g., United States v. United Technologies Corp., 466 F. Supp. 196 (N.D. N.Y. 1978); United States v. Occidental Petroleum Corp., Civ. Act. Nos. C-3-78-241/242/268/288 (S.D. Ohio Oct. 13, 1978).

60. Administration and tractability of a voluntary divestiture or spin-off rule is discussed in the pure conglomerate merger section below.

61. Note 2 *supra*.

62. These are only the most recent of recurrent proposals since the late 1960s for legislation that would effectively limit pure conglomerate mergers.

63. For example, the Kennedy bill (S. 600) prohibits the merger of a firm that has

assets or sales over $2 billion with another firm that has assets or sales over $2 billion (S. 600, note 2 *supra*, Section 2a).

64. S. 600, note 2 *supra*, Section 3a.
65. See generally J. Stone, *Social Dimensions of Law and Justice* (1966), 762-63 (Introduction of a social policy modifies the environment in which the policy operates such that "knowledge required for social action" becomes adequate only by incorporating feedback from attempts to implement the policy.)
66. Incrementalism may not always be desirable, however, as when an entire regulatory scheme is to be drastically changed, and a partial approach would allow a new interest group coalition to be formed at each incremental stopping point. See Kahn, "Application of Economics to an Imperfect World," 69 *American Economic Review* 1 (1979).
67. Under an incremental approach to merger policy, successive steps might have included sequentially adopted rules for potential-competition mergers, entrenchment effect mergers, and pure conglomerate mergers.
68. In 1976, sixty-one out of seventy-one mergers in which the target firm had assets exceeding $10 million were conglomerate mergers. See 2 S. Kanwit, *The Federal Trade Commission* (1979) § 1701.
69. Brodley (1979), note 3 *supra*, pp. 871-75.
70. Professor Cooper suggests that we may have much to fear from government power, and accordingly that "social and political interest" are best served by denying government "any additional tools to defeat substantial aggregation of private power." But that is to accept a breakdown in the concept of confined powers, both governmental and private, and to assume that governmental power will be content to remain stagnant in the face of rising industrial power. It seems more likely that governmental intrusion will expand as concentration grows, and that the best way to contain both is to uphold throughout society the ideal of limited powers and bounded discretionary authority.

   It has also been suggested that the legislation would produce a positive economic benefit in terms of freeing acquisition assets for investment in new plant and equipment (*Business Week* (Nov. 14, 1977), p. 177 (statement of Arthur Burns)). See also Liman, "Has the Tender Movement Gone Too Far?" 23 *NYLS Law Review* 687, 708 (1978). (Takeovers may have distorted capital formation proceeds and unduly diverted investment banking resources); and S. 600 Subcommittee Hearings, note 2 *supra*, pp. 461-62 (Pt. 1) (statement of Michael Gort, "The Role of Conglomerate Mergers in the American Economy") (investment in a firm's existing industry is a likely alternative use of funds now used for conglomerate acquisitions, but in Gort's view a less desirable one because of its lower return). One thoughtful investment banker has recently suggested that capital spending by target firms makes them more vulnerable to takeover because of the inevitable lag created between such expenditures and subsequent increases in profitability and market value of shares (Troubh, "Takeover Strategy: The Investment Banker's Role: Characteristics of Target Companies," 32 *Business Law* 1301, 1302-3 (1977)).
71. Baker and Grimm, "S. 600—An Unnecessary and Dangerous Foray into Classic Populism," 40 *Ohio State Law Journal* 847 (1979).
72. Brodley (1979). *Limiting Conglomerate Mergers* note 3 *supra*, pp. 875-83.
73. See, e.g., U.S. v. Occidental Petroleum Corp., Civ. Act. Nos. C-3-78-241/242/268/288 (S.D. Ohio 1978).
74. Brodley (1979), note 3 *supra*, pp. 879-80.
75. T. Arnold, *The Folklore of Capitalism* (1937), pp. 207-29.

Chapter 13

The Case Against a New Presumptive Approach to Conglomerate Mergers

Edward H. Cooper

INTRODUCTION

Paradoxically enough, the arguments against controlling conglomerate mergers by presumptions are also arguments in favor of adhering to rules of legal presumption. In legal parlance presumptions come in many shapes and sizes and serve many purposes. In a very real sense, the present antitrust law of conglomerate mergers relies on presumptions. The most fundamental presumption is embodied in the rules that require the party attacking a merger to produce evidence and to persuade the tribunal of its illegality. These burdens reflect a presumption that the transaction is lawful until proved otherwise. (Beyond the burden-of-proof rules, a modest presumption has been built around potential-competition theories. The shortcomings of this presumption will be explored below.)

This paper is written to state the arguments against venturing beyond the present decisions by creating new presumptions of illegality that would narrow the range of conglomerating freedom. The common core of these arguments is a simple proposition: the balance of uncertainty between the arguments for and against greater control is too close to warrant any change from the general present course of judicial decision.

Full statement of the case against adopting new presumptions to extend control of conglomerate mergers would require repetition of all the matters that have been covered so well in the prior papers. The same raw materials underlie the case for new presumptions and the case against. Resolution of the question requires an act of wise judgment in the face of a welter of always complex, at times confusing, and often contradictory insights drawn from both abstract theory and empirical research. Great care must be taken lest judgment be controlled by undisciplined intuition or unspoken biases. No attempt will be made here to restate all of these difficulties.

The cases for and against new presumptions may also depart from another and more pedestrian common point. Experience with conglomerate merger litigation has not been happy. Blame for this can be laid impartially on economists and lawyers alike. Economists have identified many theoretical ways in which conglomerate acquisitions may harm competition, and as many ways in which they may help competition. Application of these theories to a particular case requires measurement of an enormous array of variables. Some of the variables can be measured with modest confidence in some cases, although even then expert economists are apt to be found on both sides of all issues. The simpler variables lumped under the label of "market structure" provide an example. Other of the variables cannot be measured with any plausibility at all. The actual impact of perceived potential competition seems to me a clear example. Adversary lawyers attempt to obfuscate the things that are reasonably clear and to exploit those that are hopelessly vague. It strains credulity to suppose that judges can often make much sense out of a vigorously contested case. Only the bravest champions of the Seventh Amendment believe that a jury can make any sense at all of such matters.

The case for new presumptions often starts with the observed shortcomings of full-blown litigation. It is common to add the observation that in recent years most full-blown litigation has resulted in defense victories. These observations are then combined in the proposition that there is a need for rules that are simple, rules that will prevent more mergers than are prevented under present law. The need to prevent more mergers is justified by argument from economic theory and empirical studies, by suppositions that in amending Section 7 of the Clayton Act Congress intended to bar "big" mergers on noneconomic grounds, and by urging that even apart from congressional intent big mergers should be barred on noneconomic grounds.

The case against adopting new presumptions of illegality puts the uncertain experience of actual litigation to different use. The inability to prove clearly the economic impact of any particular merger mirrors a deeper inability to assay the general economic impact of conglomerate mergers. If the only clear demonstration we have is that after trying a substantial number of actual cases we remain unable to reach firm economic judgments, we are still too ignorant to bar activity that may have important redeeming economic virtues. Noneconomic judgments are brushed aside as alien intruders that have no place in sound antitrust analysis, or are met by countervailing noneconomic arguments.

Beyond these vague starting points, the case against adopting new presumptions will be advanced in three major groups of arguments. First, there is a brief reminder of some of the reasons for encouraging conglomerate mergers. Second, there is a general statement of the ways in which presumptions can fail to achieve intended results or produce adverse results. Third, various specific presumptions will be examined in order of the categories of economic theory that have been advanced as justification. These categories include the twin theories of potential competition, entrenchment, reciprocity and tying effect, multimarket confrontation, and aggregate concentration of wealth.

BENEFITS OF CONGLOMERATE MERGERS

Orderly presentation of the case against new presumptions of illegality requires a brief reminder of the general reasons to believe that opportunities for conglomerate acquisition should be preserved.

Efficiency Advantages

Many of the arguments in favor of conglomerate mergers are framed in terms of economic efficiency. As with the contrary arguments, it is easy to provide a descriptive list and difficult to evaluate its practical importance.

Conglomerate mergers are approached by lawyers as any mergers that cannot be characterized as horizontal or vertical. They are mergers that do not change the number or market shares of firms in any identifiable market and that do not involve any identifiable relationships as buyer and seller. The only immediate impact is a change of ownership. Adverse consequences can be predicted to result from the change of ownership only on the basis of theories much more subtle than the already complex theories of oligopoly behavior and market imperfections that surround horizontal and vertical mergers. And there are many reasons to believe that the opportunity to substitute new owners for old may provide important benefits.

It is easy to observe that firms entering new markets often prefer acquisition of an incumbent firm over creation of new capacity. Some of the reasons for this preference represent desirable efficiencies. Perhaps the most common reason is that it is cheaper to acquire existing capacity than to build new capacity. In part, this phenomenon may simply represent imperfections in markets for the sale of going businesses. In part, it may reflect the basic proposition that old capacity is presumably worth less than new capacity because it has less remaining life, and may be less efficient. Even this alternative explanation may present an important opportunity to reduce the risk of entry by reducing the absolute commitment required and reducing uncertainty as to the efficiency of the business that is acquired. More important, the opportunity to enter immediately permits the new owner to seize opportunities without the delay and uncertainty of starting from scratch. There may be many entrants with something important to contribute to the market who will enter today, but not tomorrow. Beyond these concerns lies the obvious concern that creation of new capacity not needed to serve present demand may be directly wasteful. The elitist response that competition is best served by a fight for survival among firms with redundant capacity may often prove a fleeting fantasy that vanishes on the facts that entry is foregone, that victory goes to the less efficient, or that any marginal improvement in aggregate efficiency is more than offset by the creation and destruction of excess capacity.

To the extent that acquisition may facilitate entry, it is important in preserving all of the advantages of new entry that are urged by potential-competition theory. The new owners may be better able to exploit the existing capacity, to seize new opportunities, and to compete effectively than the former owners. Recognition that entry is open by way of acquisition may in turn spur all firms in the market to more vigorous competition. In addition, the fear that inefficient performance may spark a takeover may drive incumbent management to more efficient performance.

Just as acquisition facilitates entry directly, so it facilitates exit from a market. Strict rules against conglomerate acquisitions may reduce competition in the market for operating business organizations, thereby defeating many important values. In particular, it may seem desirable to maintain a market for the sale of going businesses in order to provide a "fair" reward for success. Given the choice between maintaining a market for sale by horizontal, vertical, or conglomerate acquisition, the choice may bend strongly toward conglomerate acquisition. In broader terms, sale of a going business as a unit preserves the enterprise as a functioning unit and avoids the inefficiencies that may be incurred in disbanding it. So too, it may be important to preserve the opportunity to rationalize the structure of existing firms by selling off individual operations as functioning enterprises. And, from a longer perspective, the opportunity to sell out on attractive terms may provide an important inducement to entry and expansion by small firms.

Acquisition of firms in other markets may support a variety of efficiencies within the conglomerate firm. Market- and product-extension mergers may permit integration of operations at all levels of input, manufacture, and distribution in the same way as horizontal and vertical mergers do. Even in "pure" conglomerate mergers, efficiencies may derive from optimal use of managerial resources or other services that cannot be provided as well by market transactions. Other efficiencies may draw from internalization of financial transactions. The most modest possibility is that the acquired firm has simply failed to perceive the optimal structure of equity and debt financing. In broader terms, internal financing may avoid substantial costs of uncertainty, delay, and risk compensation that are entailed in loan or outside equity transactions. It is at least arguable that the increased stability enjoyed by conglomerate firms that are not bound to the vicissitudes of any single market is itself a desirable reduction of investment risk that cannot be duplicated as efficiently by interposing financial markets and mutual fund managers between investors and a diversified portfolio.

Individual acquisitions may also be motivated by very specific purposes to increase or improve competition. The final chapters have yet to be written in the book of managerial motivations. It is possible that an aggressive firm may acquire a stagnating member of an ossified oligopoly for the sheer fractious joy of bringing competition to the market. Perhaps more likely, the acquisition may rest on a belief that the acquired firm has unexploited advantages that can provide greater profits than its current share of the oligopoly pie, or that the acquiring firm can provide such advantages. More special cases may exist as well. The producer of a legitimately monopolized product, for instance, might acquire a firm producing a complementary product in the belief that it can benefit by eliminating all oligopoly profits from the production of the complementary product.

There is no reason to suppose that these opportunities for efficiency are hidden from either party to a conglomerate merger. On the contrary, the merger may result because both parties share the perception of mutual advantage. Narragansett Brewing Company may have been as keenly aware of the advantages of national beer brewing and marketing as was Falstaff when Narragansett sold out. The transaction need not reflect divergent appraisals of the value of the acquired business; it may reflect agreement that the transaction will enhance its value.

Finally, the fact that a market may be maintained for going businesses can provide one further advantage. Some of the conglomerate acquisitions of the last big binge are now being undone. The very fact that the mistakes can be corrected, often by a different conglomerate acquisition, suggests that in various ways the markets are self-correcting. Efficient and neutral acquisitions will persist; inefficient acquisitions will be undone.

This statement of potential efficiency advantages is incomplete. More important, it is entirely abstract. There are cogent reasons to believe that the abstract possibilities are not often realized to any important extent in actual practice. Conglomerate mergers may be motivated just as easily by deliberately anticompetitive or inefficient reasons as by good reasons. Perhaps most often, they may be motivated by reasons quite unrelated to market competition or efficiency. The motivations most commonly identified are stock market performance, tax considerations, expansion of the managerial empire, access to immediate cash flows or other sources of unused capital, and simple differences in value perceptions. An abstract list of potential disadvantages cannot carry the day by itself. Stronger proof is required, at least if we retain any faith in free business decisions.

Noneconomic Advantages

Many of the arguments in favor of further limits on conglomerate acquisition draw from the supposed social and political disadvantages of large business enterprise. If the economic arguments are a matter of fair dispute, the noneconomic arguments are little more than professions of faith. The faith of those who oppose conglomerate acquisition is at least professed to be a faith in individual freedom, entrepreneurial wisdom, local control of community business, and like values. Big business is condemned for stifling initiative, suppressing innovation, callously abandoning dependent communities to a fate of desperate unemployment, and joining in unholy alliance with big government. It may even be argued that quite apart from actual effects, it is popularly perceived that big business exerts baneful effects and that new controls are needed to preserve faith in the fairness of our political processes.

Such arguments leave little room for dispassionate academic discussion. They may be profoundly right. It is fair to point out, however, that they may be terribly wrong. At the most obvious level, it may be countered that very big firms actually lose political influence—the giant integrated oil firms have not been much beloved of populace or politicians in recent years. At a more fundamental level, current conditions do not present whatever specters might be feared from control of the private economy by one or two or ten giant enterprises. Many giant enterprises are surrounded by a few hundred very large enterprises and unnumbered smaller enterprises. This broad dispersion of significant economic power may prove vitally necessary as the last effective check on the power of government. Social and political interest may be best served by denying to the government any additional tools to defeat substantial aggregation of private power. Finally, it may be urged that freedom to acquire and dispose of private property—including operating businesses—is an important part of individual liberty.

COMMON DIFFICULTIES OF PRESUMPTIONS

If it is indeed true that some conglomerate acquisitions may be desirable, the most general danger of creating new presumptions against such acquisitions is that desirable transactions will be prohibited. The most specific dangers that would be created by new presumptions are of course dependent on the specific presumption involved. Before turning to these specific dangers, however, it may prove helpful to reflect on the common difficulties encountered by most of these presumptions. The first difficulty lies in shaping the presumption itself. Once the presumption has been shaped, it may incorporate economic elements that are difficult to define or to prove. Partly as a consequence of these difficulties, the presumption may not avoid the need for protracted and uncertain litigation. The terms of the presumption, moreover, may shape conduct not only in

290 / Antitrust and the Conglomerate Firm

the ways intended but in unintended and undesirable ways as well. These four areas of difficulty will be explored in order.

Shaping The Presumption

The possible range of conglomerate presumptions is immense. Legislative action can produce very precise presumptions expressed in such terms as absolute firm size, clear market shares, or offsetting acquisitions and divestitures. It is even possible to propose that presumptions expressed in dollar terms may be continually adjusted by some such index as a gross national product deflator. The nature of the judicial process and the generality of the antitrust statutes prevent courts from achieving comparable precision. Judicial presumptions, moreover, are far more likely to be cast in terms of the economic theory that judges have found embraced by the statutes. Since the theory is complex and qualified, the resulting presumptions are far more likely to be rebuttable on a wide range of grounds. The legislature can enact that no corporation with assets in excess of $1 billion shall acquire any other business; courts are not likely to do so. The legislature can enact that no firm with assets in excess of $1 billion shall acquire any firm that has more than a 20 percent share of any market; courts are more likely to speak of acquisition of a dominant firm by a large firm and to permit rebuttal proof that any presumed ill effects are not reasonably to be feared.

However any presumption is shaped, it is likely to depend on relatively static and objective data. Market shares and distribution, trends over recent years, absolute firm size, and like information are continually suggested in shaping new presumptions. Subjective data and actual conduct or performance data are considered, if at all, to be matters of rebuttal. To the extent that the softer data are subordinated or suppressed, the resulting presumptions serve better the purpose of simplifying litigation and providing workable guides to business planners. In like measure such presumptions augment the risk of upsetting desirable plans. Two acquisitions may be totally different in purpose and effect even though they appear identical when described in terms of market shares, firm size, and like indicia. Acquisition of a maverick firm that has a 15 percent share of an otherwise comfortable oligopoly market may be supported by the intent and effect of completely disrupting the oligopoly or by the intent and effect of suppressing all competition and sharing in an enhanced collective profit. Much is lost by a presumption that insists that the two acquisitions be treated alike.

A presumption that insists that proponents of the procompetitive merger justify distinctive treatment may lose the same values, invite proponents of the anticompetitive merger to attempt the same justification, and entail all of the complex litigation that would occur without the presumption.

The example just given reflects a phenomenon common to many presumption proposals. These proposals begin with a catalogue of the economic theories that suggest possible losses from conglomerate mergers. The theories are elaborated with elegant and sophisticated detail. The difficulty of applying such complex theories in adversary litigation is then outlined, often with a description of a string of defense victories. It is then suggested that the abstract possibility of economic losses is bolstered by social and political concerns. The conclusion is that courts may properly create presumptions that are partly justified by social and political concerns but that are defined in terms of the economic theory. The plaintiff is required to prove such matters as firm size, market concentration, market shares, and market proximity. Defendants are then commonly permitted to rebut the resulting presumption by proving other matters drawn from economic theory, but not too much economic theory. Thus, a large firm in a proximate market is not allowed to acquire a firm that enjoys a substantial share in another market, unless the defendant can show such matters as actual efficiency, inability to enter by alternate means, or actual changes in market structure. The result is a curious creature. It relies primarily on the portions of economic theory that identify the dangers of conglomerate acquisition, excuses the weaknesses of the theory by reliance on noneconomic concerns, and denies the opportunity to use other parts of economic theory in the name of litigation capacity. It may indeed be necessary to concoct such rules if present antitrust statutes are to prove effective in defeating conglomerate mergers. Economic elements are introduced not to justify rules based on social and political concerns but to minimize the economic price paid for added control. Nonetheless, many lawyers will find it uncomfortable to rely on the hazy legislative history of Section 7 to justify such selective use of theory.

In short, presumptions that require proof of economic matters to establish the presumption, or that permit proof of economic matters to rebut the presumption, may lose many of the potential gains in seeking some measure of economic rationality. A few of the more common economic elements permitted in presumption proposals serve to illustrate the point.

Applying Economic Elements

Economic elements are reduced to a minimum in proposals that rely simply on firm size. It is possible to imagine modest difficulties in proving the assets or sales of firms that fall close to presumption thresholds, but most cases would be resolved easily. Somewhat greater difficulty may be encountered with proposals that permit an acquisition to be protected by spinning off assets to form a viable enterprise of comparable value. Substantial problems may be encountered in fixing an accurate value on the acquired assets, particularly if "funny paper" is not to be taken at face worth. Greater problems may be encountered in valuing the assets spun off, not only if a forced sale or even scrapping provides no more than a distorted yardstick. Efforts to ensure the viability of any new enterprise may prove even more strained. The proposals of S. 600, the Small and Independent Business Protection Act of 198?, go beyond these defenses to permit some mergers to be justified by showing that they "will have the preponderant effect of substantially enhancing competition" or "will result in substantial efficiencies." The defense that measures a preponderant effect of enhancing competition is simply incredible. Honest administration would require measurement of all the threats to competition that underlie present law and a wide variety of offsetting benefits that are largely ignored by present law. The defense of substantial efficiencies may not be completely incredible, but it still invites litigation of matters that are not yet capable of satisfactory definition or proof.

Many presumption proposals go beyond firm size to embrace elements of market structure, particularly market shares. Such presumptions begin with the still unsatisfactory task of defining and proving the market. In addition, they cannot restore any substantial economic element to the case unless there is some added element of minimum market size. To satisfy present merger law, prohibiting acquisition of a firm that has 20 percent or more of any market would have to reach rural banks, small town theaters, a startling number of retail operations, and other firms that have no place in the realms of genuine conglomerate concern. Even if some minimum market size is set to reflect this concern—S. 600 sets the figure at $100 million—it may prove surprisingly difficult to measure the total volume of sales in many markets that are defined by the legal standards of Section 7 rather than by any real-world standard.

The problem of market definition extends beyond the simple

starting point. Added difficulties arise from efforts to refine the categories of conglomeration. Such efforts may take the form of moving the merger out of the conglomerate category into a horizontal category so as to enjoy the benefit of the market share presumptions that are applied in horizontal cases. It seems impossible to find any advantage in market share figures if persistent unsuccessful efforts to make sales in a market are used to identify a firm as a present competitor with a 0 percent market share, even though horizontal analysis is otherwise proper.[1] It may prove possible to torture out some sort of market share figures if a "supply space" approach is taken to market definition, but any honest use of this approach would require identification of all firms that occupy the same supply space and calculation of their capacities.[2] Market share reasoning can be used with full force if separate products are dumped into a single market for fear that a more rational approach will defeat desired results, as was done in *U.S.* v. *Continental Can Co.*, but it should be apparent once again that honest analysis cannot accept this approach without substantial elaboration and qualification.[3]

Efforts may be made to define presumptions that depend on further distinctions within the broad category of conglomerate mergers. These efforts would be closer to the target of new presumptions. Such presumptions distinguish between pure conglomerate mergers, product-extension mergers, and market-extension mergers. The distinction rests on the sound perception that potential competition and entrenchment effects are most plausible with respect to the extension mergers. Rules that rest on this distinction, however, must undertake the chore of identifying degrees of proximity between different product and geographic markets. Here too, honest application of the distinction often requires examination of many markets beyond those involved in the actual case, to determine which markets are closest to which others. Simplified litigation, sound business planning, and clear results are not to be expected from such presumptions as these.

Presumptions that distinguish among categories of conglomeration may suffer one further defect. Many of the litigated cases show that it is possible to find small horizontal or vertical elements within the framework of much larger transactions. In hard-fought takeover contests, indeed, such elements may be created deliberately for the purpose of creating an antitrust refuge. Similarly, small elements of product or market extension may be found within the framework of much larger and otherwise purely conglomerate transactions. It would be a gross distortion to seize upon the relatively incidental elements as fit foundation for presumptive invalidation. If any adjustment is to be made to the presumptions to account for this fact, however, it may add yet one more dimension of confusion and uncertainty.

Litigation Burdens

The foregoing discussion should serve to describe in a general way the litigating burdens that will result from any economic elements incorporated into new presumptions. The greater the effort made to approach economic theory, the greater the litigating costs will be.

The prospect that the courts can develop presumptions devoid of any substantial economic content is remote. Two brief illustrations from current law serve to make the point.

If there is any clear rule in antitrust law, it is that horizontal price fixing is per se unlawful. Yet it has become painfully clear that "this is not a question simply of determining whether two or more potential competitors have literally 'fixed' a price."[4] Instead, the question is whether activity that can be characterized as price fixing falls into a pattern that courts perceive to be plainly anticompetitive and without any redeeming virtue. The per se rule does no more than to reject out of hand some of the defenses that might be offered. Other defenses remain, even if they must be accommodated awkwardly in the initial decision of whether to characterize the challenged conduct as price fixing for purposes of the per se rule. So it will be with judicial presumptions of anticompetitive effect from conglomerate mergers. Categorization, explanation, and rebuttal are almost inevitable problems.

In the area of merger doctrine, horizontal merger cases have come to rely heavily on the inferences to be drawn from market shares and concentration ratios. The underlying reliance on the economic theory of oligopoly market behavior and performance provides a ready analogy to support a similarly presumptive approach to conglomerate mergers. The decision in *U.S.* v. *General Dynamics Corp.*, however, has made it clear that at least in some circumstances sophisticated economic evidence may be adduced to rebut the inferences suggested by market share data alone.[5] The full consequences of this decision have yet to be worked out. Whatever the consequences may be in horizontal cases, the lesson is clear for any judicial presumptions in conglomerate cases. Conglomerate theories and presumptions that rest on the uncertainties of oligopoly theory and compound it with still further elaborations will surely remain open to rebuttal.

Courts are simply not prepared to adopt the drastic presumptions that would be necessary to provide substantial relief from the burdens of litigation under present conglomerate merger law. The case for judicial presumptions must rest instead on a hope for better results with no greater burdens.

Impact on Conduct

Advocates of new presumptions hope that clear rules will shape private planning in desirable ways. Presumptions will not only deter undesirable behavior, but channel conglomerate acquisitions into paths that will preserve the opportunities for efficiency. Such results may occur. At the same time, account must be taken of the contrary possibilities. Presumptions may succeed in little more than diverting acquisitions from the most efficient paths to less efficient and more undesirable paths.

Experience with the ways in which artificial legal rules can distort private transactions is provided in abundance by the Internal Revenue Code. Some conglomerate mergers may themselves be good examples. It does not seem likely that merger presumptions can produce such spectacular effects. A few illustrations should serve to show that strange transactions may nonetheless be encouraged.

The most direct risks are that efficient acquisitions must be bypassed in favor of less efficient acquisitions, internal expansion, or quite different patterns of investment or distribution of corporate profits. Efforts to avoid this result by permitting an efficiency defense will seem an illusion to the prudent and an attractive gamble to the reckless. The less efficient transactions, moreover, may be directed to markets different from the more efficient transactions. Instead of a procompetitive acquisition in a market that needs new blood, the result may be neutral or anticompetitive transactions that slip below the presumptive thresholds. The risk of such diversions is enhanced by the fact that conglomerate acquisitions may be prompted by a whole host of artificial, nonefficient, or anticompetitive motives. If an efficient transaction is discouraged, there is little reason to assume that the alternative transaction likewise will prove efficient.

Proposals that limit the size of single transactions, or require offsetting divestitures, may produce particularly inefficient effects. A firm that is engaged in a vigorously competitive market may seek to divest that business—perhaps to less competitive hands—in order to enter a stagnant market that will not benefit from the transaction at all. Alternatively, an opportunity for a single effective acquisition may be replaced by a number of smaller and less efficient acquisitions.

Even more bizarre results may occur in contested takeover settings. A hostile target firm may be able to manipulate presumptive rules by acquiring other firms adjacent to markets occupied by its suitor, by arranging a friendly alliance that crosses a minimum size threshold, or by like strategies that serve no interest beyond survival of current management.

The most perverse results that can be foreseen arise from the possibility that presumptive rules may be applied some time after a merger has been consummated. As Section 7 now stands, the transaction can be challenged "at any time that an acquisition may be said with reasonable probability to contain a threat that it may lead to a restraint of commerce or tend to create a monopoly of a line of commerce."[6] It would be absolutely devastating to hold that an acquisition that initially passed the tests of presumption could be attacked in later years as circumstances changed. An acquisition that created substantial efficiencies, for example, might be followed by valiant efforts to defeat or redirect the efficiencies so as not to rise above a forbidden market share. Whatever else may be said of presumptions, surely it is necessary to find some safe way to isolate the eternality aspects of the *du Pont/General Motors* case.

POTENTIAL COMPETITION PRESUMPTIONS

Potential competition theories have supported the most elaborate efforts to develop specific conglomerate merger presumptions. The best framework for understanding these proposed presumptions is provided by the current law they are designed to change. Current law, indeed, has at least approached the use of presumptions in this area. The difficulties of theory and proof that surround current law are set out here in some detail, followed by a shorter suggestion of the difficulties that surround some of the proposed presumptions.

Potential Competition in Gross

The cases clearly identify—and then often mingle—two distinct theories of potential competition. The first, best styled as the "actual entry" theory, is that a merger may lessen competition because without the merger one of the firms involved would have chosen a more competitive means of entering a market already occupied by the other. The second, often styled the "perceived potential-competition" theory, is that a merger may lessen competition because prior to the merger the acquiring firm spurred competition in a market it did not occupy as a result of the fear that it would enter the market. Although it is easier to combine these distinct theories into a single set of presumptions than to separate them, it is better to approach current law by stating these theories separately.

Actual Entry

Deliberate Forestalling. Theoretically, there is one relatively easy case for the actual entry theory. An acquisition may be made solely for the purpose of preventing actual entry into a market. This purpose is most easily understood if a potential entrant is acquired by a firm that is presently in the market, or by a firm that is firmly committed to actual entry. El Paso's acquisition of Pacific Northwest may well have involved such motives.[7] The decision in *U.S. v. Penn-Olin Chem. Co.* tells us that the same concern would apply to a joint venture in which one parent sought to protect its market by involving a potential competitor.[8] In *U.S. v. Continental Can Co.*, the Court suggested that one motive for the merger may have been a desire by Continental to keep Hazel-Atlas from expanding into more areas of competition between cans and bottles, and that the result thus may have been *more* anticompetitive than if Hazel-Atlas had already been entrenched in a competitive position from which Continental could not dislodge it without loss to its own new proprietary interests. *Brunswick Corp.* suggests that one of the reasons for the joint venture between Brunswick and Yamaha was that Brunswick was eager to forestall independent entry by Yamaha into the domestic market for outboard motors.[9]

Proof of deliberate forestalling motives should tell heavily against an acquisition. Clearly persuasive proof, however, is apt to be hard to come by. Speculation about such motives on the basis of circumstantial evidence is not apt to add much to more fundamental potential-competition concerns, and should offer small help. And it seems clear beyond doubt that little advantage is apt to be found in fabricating presumptions to reach such cases.

2. Forcing Procompetitive Entry. It is possible to argue that absent deliberate forestalling, Section 7 does not reach mergers that do not diminish existing levels of competition. A merger that simply defeats a hope of increased competition is not within the statutory language or purpose. This argument appeared to be rejected in the decisions in *Penn-Olin Chemical Co., FTC* v. *Procter & Gamble Co.,* and *Ford Motor Co.* v. *U.S.*[10] These cases seemed to recognize that a merger may be prohibited if it is an alternative to a more competitive form of entry by internal expansion or by acquisition and competitive expansion of a small firm. More recent decisions leave the question uncertain once more. In *Falstaff,* the Court said that it must

> leave for another day the question of the applicability of § 7 to a merger that will leave competition in the marketplace exactly as it was, neither hurt nor helped, and that is challengeable under § 7 only on grounds that the company *could* [emphasis supplied] have, but did not, enter de novo or through "toe-hold" acquisition and that there is less competition than there would have been had entry been in such a manner. There are traces of this view in our cases, . . . but the Court has not squarely faced the question, if for no other reason than because there has been no necessity to consider it.[11]

Then in *U.S.* v. *Marine Bancorporation, Inc.,* after devoting the major portion of the opinion to the conclusion that there was no reason to upset the merger on actual entry grounds, the Court said that there was no need to express a view on the question left open in *Falstaff.*[12]

The natural reading of these passages is that the Court has not yet determined whether actual entry effects are available to bar a merger under Section 7. It would be possible to read the Falstaff passage as referring only to the question of whether a merger could be barred simply because the acquiring company *could* have entered in more desirable fashion even though it *would not* have done so. This reading takes on slight added strength from the suggestions in the concurring opinions of Justices Douglas and Marshall that a merger may be blocked on actual entry grounds if a firm that today would not follow alternative paths to entry might in the future decide on actual entry. Neither reading is entirely satisfactory. The restatement of the question left open by Falstaff in the *Marine Bancorporation* opinion is itself ambiguous.

In the face of this uncertainty, lower courts and the FTC continue to treat the actual entry theory with respect. Although confident prediction is impossible, it is best to assume that the loss of actual entry by *de novo* entry or toehold acquisition remains available as a basis for attacking a conglomerate merger.

3. What is a Toehold? Acceptance of actual entry theory requires some means of identifying the modest acquisition that qualifies as a desirable procompetitive toehold rather than as a forbidden transaction. It is tempting to suggest that a presumptive approach could work in connection with this question, and indeed the FTC has suggested that a firm with less than 10 percent of a market is likely to qualify as a toehold.[13] It is clear, however, that no automatic market share test will do. In *U.S.* v. *Phillips Petrol. Co.*, the district court concluded that acquisition of the Tidewater assets, with about 6.8 percent of the market, could not qualify as a toehold. It offered a functional test, finding that an acquisition can qualify as a toehold only if there is a substantial need to build further on the basis of the acquisition.[14] Phillips was apparently content to accept 6.8 percent of the market as itself a sufficient share, so toehold treatment was unavailable. This approach may seem attractive in the abstract, but it invites artificial distinctions by encouraging the people planning the acquisition to use their foresight and craft to build a record of need and intent for vigorous expansion. And it is subject to the further danger that an acquisition that was in fact intended as a toehold may be subject to retroactive attack if original plans for expansion prove unsuccessful or are aborted without ever getting off the ground.

A particularly dangerous approach was taken by the FTC in British Oxygen Co.[15] In identifying the firms that might have qualified as alternative toehold acquisitions, the FTC stated that the sole reason they were not disqualified was because they might have large shares of regional markets for particular industrial gases. Since this case was concerned with the effects of the merger on the national market for all industrial gases, that was the sole relevant market for measuring eligibility for toehold treatment. On the surface, this approach seems very attractive. Unfortunately, it masks this fact: anyone assessing the alternative mergers would have to consider the danger that someone else might attack an alternative merger because of its effects in the small markets that did not concern the FTC at the moment of invalidating the Airco acquisition. This danger would be reduced if we could count on intelligent disregard of small markets in applying conglomerate merger doctrines, but that seems very risky.

Finally, it may be noted that in *Missouri Portland Cement Co.* v. *Cargill, Inc.*, Judge Friendly hazarded the thought that perhaps toehold acquisition doctrine should embrace the possibility of making a number of small acquisitions.[16] There is an obvious danger of horizontal merger trouble in such an alternative—see the unsuccessful claim that SKF had run afoul of the law by acquiring a failing company with 2 percent of the domestic tapered roller-bearing market and by also acquiring various foreign producers.[17] Quite apart from that, the difficulties of toehold doctrine seem compounded almost beyond endurance if we are to require exploration and exhaustion of the possibilities of putting together an effective new market force by a series of small acquisitions.

4. Showing of Market Structure & Behavior. Once it is accepted as a premise that Section 7 encompasses mergers whose only sin is denial of an opportunity to increase competition, it is difficult to know where to stop. It could be argued plausibly that there are few markets indeed that could not benefit from added competition. Clearly, the Supreme Court is not prepared to go this far.

In the *Marine Bancorporation* decision, the Court stated that there is no need to worry about the prospects of long-term deconcentration if the market is presently competitive. It built this statement into a general proposition that any potential competition theory is available only

> where there are dominant participants in the target market engaging in interdependent or parallel behavior and with the capacity effectively to determine price and total output. . . .[18]

Perhaps in tacit recognition of the difficulties of proof that might be presented by this requirement, it then went on to state that by introducing evidence that the largest firm had 42.1 percent, the next 31.6 percent, and the acquired firm 18.6 percent of the market, the government had established a "prima facie case that the Spokane market was a candidate for the potential-competition doctrine." The burden then shifted to the defendants to provide evidence of a lack of parallel behavior, disproving the natural inferences of the concentration ratios. Thus, a judicial presumption has been introduced into potential-competition doctrine. Although the market figures are obviously one illustration, it seems apparent that reasonably tight oligopoly markets are eligible for actual entry concern. At the same time, there is room for rebuttal. The Court was at least prepared to imagine a persuasive showing that actual behavior was so competitive as to disprove the need for actual entry.

The two obviously critical questions left to be resolved across a number of cases are the market structure that will raise the *Marine Bancorporation* presumption, and the showings of actual competitive behavior that will rebut it. Lower court and administrative decisions shed little light. In *U.S.* v. *Hughes Tool Co.*, the court found that potential-competition doctrine was irrelevant in both its branches, since the market was in fact highly competitive. The market had been growing rapidly, concentration had been falling, and new firms had been entering.[19] In *U.S.* v. *Black & Decker Mfg. Co.*, sufficient concentration was found with two firms sharing nearly 50 percent of the market, although falling, and four firms holding 75 percent. The presumption of benefit from actual entry was found not to have been rebutted, even though the market was growing rapidly, many new firms had entered, two of the new entrants reached the ranks of the top ten, there had been substantial product innovation and improvement, and average prices had trended downward (though this was foggy because cheaper models were selling better).[20] The merger was allowed only because actual entry by Black & Decker was found blocked. In *U.S.* v. *Consolidated Foods Corp.*, the court concluded that even if it were to treat frozen institutional pies as a relevant market, potential-competition theories must fail in face of acquisition of a firm with a 40 percent market share because there was no evidence of oligopolistic behavior—on the contrary, profits were low—and there was no showing that any incumbent firm had changed its behavior as a result of perceiving Consolidated to be a potential entrant.[21]

FTC decisions give no clearer guidance. In the Brunswick Corporation case, the FTC found that actual entry effects were important because two firms had 85 percent of the market, demand had been increasing, barriers to entry were significant, profits were high, the number of firms had declined, and actual new entry had been insignificant. In the British Oxygen case, the Commission applied the *Marine Bancorporation* decision and found that the structural presumption had been established. The four largest firms had nearly 70 percent of the market, and the big eight had more than 86 percent. Airco, the acquired firm, was third with 15.73 percent. Efforts to rebut the presumption by showing that competition was in fact vigorous were rejected, even though prices had fallen in a period of general inflation—because costs were falling. Current profit figures were not shown, but were said to be rising—as a 10 percent after-tax return by one firm on CO_2, causing it great delight; and there was a lively threat of backward integration by major customers. In other opinions, the FTC has clearly recognized that potential-competition doctrine requires examination of market structure, including attempts to measure the barriers to new entry, but it has not provided any clearer guide.

Even if the *Marine Bancorporation* presumption is not satisfied, it is possible that potential-competition concerns may remain available to upset a merger. In *Kennecott Copper Corp.* v. *FTC,* the court accepted the proposition that potential-competition concerns—apparently including actual entry effects—could be used to bar a merger into a market that was not yet even "oligopolistic," since there was a "trend toward high concentration."[22] The largest four firms in the market held almost 30 percent; the largest 68 firms had all of 70 percent. The court's approach, and the FTC, seem to compound the notion of potential competition and the notion of incipiency: it is enough to bar a merger that potential competition might become an important factor in the future. Compare the opinions of Justices Douglas and Marshall in the *Falstaff* case, which seem to embrace this notion. If this approach should be developed, judicial interpretation would be perilously close to the extreme view that on a long time horizon any market might stand to benefit from actual entry at some time in the future. Accordingly, any merger by a firm that might plausibly become an actual entrant is barred.

The logical lawyerly mind is apt to react to these problems by proposing that the strength of the initial presumption must vary with the nature of the structural showing that supports it. The more concentrated the industry, the heavier the burden of rebuttal by showing that behavior is so competitive as to defeat the claim that actual entry is needed. Tidy as this proposal may seem, it rests on unrealistic assumptions about the ability to distinguish between categories of structure. Even more important, it rests on an assumption that the strength of competitive behavior can be measured—either in terms of "conduct" or "performance"—with some degree of clarity. That assumption is marvelous indeed.

5. Entry Opportunities. Once it is shown that the market could benefit from actual entry, it remains to be shown that the merger has caused a troublesome loss of actual entry opportunity. Two major elements must be shown: that alternative entry was possible, either by internal expansion or toehold acquisition; and that the number of prospective actual entrants is so small that concern is justified over loss of one of them. In addition, it may be necessary to show that the acquiring firm would have entered by alternative means but for the merger.

In many extension acquisitions, it will be possible to show that entry by internal expansion was feasible—indeed, that is part of the reason for characterizing it as an extension from one market to a nearby market. It will be much more difficult to determine whether as a matter of sound business judgment entry would or should have occurred without the merger. In some cases, nonetheless, defendants have been successful in persuading a tribunal that the entry barriers that were so high as to justify concern with the actual entry effect were so high that the acquiring firm itself could not have entered. The arcane difficulties of entering two-cycle internal combustion engine technology were responsible for persuading the court that Black & Decker could not enter the chain saw market. The substantial difficulties of creating a network of frozen food broker-distributors helped persuade the FTC that General Mills would not enter the prepared frozen food market without an acquisition.[23] The district court in *FTC* v. *Atlantic Richfield Co.* cheerfully pointed out that the FTC had planted itself on the horns of a dilemma by showing high entry barriers that made it unlikely that if ARCO were prohibited from acquiring Anaconda it would enter copper refining by *de novo* expansion.[24] And in *United Brands Co.*, the Commission was even prepared to be impressed by the proposition that inelastic price-demand relationships would make *de novo* entry on any large scale highly unattractive for any firm.[25]

Special difficulties are presented by the toehold theory. In the British Oxygen case the FTC squarely took the position that it is enough to show that there are smaller firms in the market, without requiring any showing of whether any of them could actually be bought. Courts, at least, have been satisfied by showings that all of the potential toehold firms were either unavailable or, rather, clearly unsatisfactory as a basis for aggressive entry and expansion.[26] There is simply no satisfactory resolution of this problem. Virtually any potential toehold could be had for a sufficiently high price, and expanded with a sufficiently ruinous investment. There is a real danger that protective courtships will be required—such at least is the course of safety, although the problems are obviously enormous.

6. Number of Prospective Entrants. Apart from entrenchment effects, acquisition entry by one potential actual entrant does not reduce the possibility that other potential actual entrants will enter. Indeed, it is reasonable to suppose that in some circumstances actual entry will be encouraged: the other firms are now freed from the fear of actual entry by the acquiring firm through creation of new capacity or a combative toehold acquisition and may be encouraged to rely on the evidence that the market offers attractive opportunities for entry. Given the common statements

304 / Antitrust and the Conglomerate Firm

that even an "incipiency" statute like Section 7 requires a reasonable probability of lessened competition, it is commonly argued that loss of one potential actual entrant is accordingly a fair basis for concern only if there are very few prospective entrants. Some of the cases rely on findings, however accurate, that the acquiring firm was the most probable entrant, e.g., *Procter/Clorox; Kennecott/Peabody; British Oxygen/Airco*. Other cases find it sufficient that the acquiring firm was one of only a "small group" of firms that were highly likely to enter—the FTC was concerned with four entrants in The Stanley Works;[27] and in Bendix it was concerned that although there were twenty-three prospective entrants only a few of them approached Bendix in size and potential expansion capacities.[28]

As with edge effects, it seems very clear that identification of other prospective entrants is one of the weakest points of actual litigation. It is incredible to suppose that any careful evaluation can be made of the entire array of firms that might qualify as potential entrants. The firms that are most obvious to the defense will be identified and subjected to such investigation as is possible in the framework of a much larger suit, but the result at best will be only a crude approximation. There is nothing much to be done about this shortcoming, unless it is to be papered over by some new presumption.

7. Effect of Alternative Entry. The theory of actual entry is that *de novo* creation of new capacity or expansion of a toehold acquisition would increase competition in the market. Thus, the theory should be subjected to rebuttal by showing that entry by other means would not enable the acquiring firm to offer a significant competitive threat. The most important decision accepting this theory is the *Marine Bancorporation* case. The ultimate basis for upholding the merger was that the government had failed to demonstrate that alternative means of entry, even assuming they were possible, would "offer a reasonable prospect of long-term structural improvement or other benefits in the target market." This conclusion rested on special inhibitions state law placed on postacquisition expansion of a small bank. In *Black & Decker,* the court was persuaded that formidable technological barriers would have prevented any significant competitive effect from a toehold acquisition or internal expansion into the chain saw market. And in *Missouri Portland Cement Company,* the Second Circuit was impressed that the cost of expanding a small cement firm would be nearly as prohibitive as the costs of building new capacity. Such arguments as these are apt to be encountered only in markets that have very high barriers to entry by internal expansion, but it remains to be determined how far the burden of proving capacity for expansion will lie on the party attacking a particular acquisition.

There is one further aspect of this concern with the effects that actual entry would have on the market. The toehold theory is, in the abstract, a good one. It is so good that it deserves to be applied to some very large acquisitions. In the *Marine Bancorporation* case, the Court noted that acquisition of the third largest bank in Spokane would provide a third full-service bank to increase competition with the two larger banks and thought it anomalous that the government should be challenging the acquisition on the theory of alternative means of entry that would not have been as vigorously competitive. In the Budd case, the FTC approved acquisition of Gindy, the fourth largest firm in the van trailer market with about 8 percent, as in fact a toehold merger—there was an impressive showing that Budd was in fact able to help Gindy expand in competition with the larger firms. General Mills' acquisition of Gorton quite probably was intended to provide an entry into the much larger general market of prepared frozen foods, and calculated to make General Mills' entry a much more effective competitive force by providing a ready-made distribution system. Given the postmerger evidence that Narragansett's share of the New England beer market fell drastically, while two national sellers greatly increased their own shares, it may well be that Falstaff's acquisition of the then number one firm was in fact the most procompetitive thing that could have happened to the market.

8. The Firm That Would Not Enter. It has been noted above that it is not clear whether courts today would be willing to bar an acquisition simply on the ground that the acquiring firm *could* have entered in more competitive fashion, even though it *would not* have done so. On an abstract level, the question is simply one of taste in extending the incipiency aspect of Section 7. In light of the strong possibility that a conglomerate merger may be procompetitive, however, there is every reason to go slowly in embracing this theory. If we really believe that the firm would not have entered by any more desirable means, fear of the loss of actual entry seems self-contradictory. And the question hardly seems susceptible of a "general deterrence" theory that we can force actual entry by closing off alternative paths of acquisition. Nonetheless, the problem remains real because of the practical difficulty of determining whether the firm would in fact have entered by alternate means without the challenged acquisition. Brief attention will be directed below to the problems of measuring actual entry prospects. For the moment, it is enough to point out that a conclusion that the firm would in fact have entered in a more competitive fashion must rely in large part on an estimate of probabilities that in turn draws from a determination of the firm's capacity, interest, and incentive to enter by other means. Perhaps this will prove one area in which a form of presumption is useful: if a firm not only could enter by more desirable means, but it is shown that as a matter of sound business judgment it "should" enter by those means, we can presume that it would enter by those means at some reasonably near time. Even this approach, however, will often require an extension of the time horizons of Section 7 over a period of several years.

9. Fabricated Claims by Takeover Target. Actual entry can work both ways. It is easily possible that an acquired firm was a potential entrant into concentrated markets occupied by the acquiring firm—indeed, it was suggested above that an acquisition may be motivated solely by a desire to forestall such entry. Section 7 suits to prevent unfriendly takeovers have gone a long step beyond this possibility to the apparently deliberate creation of claims by a target company that it had plans to enter the markets of the acquiring company. Allis-Chalmers, for instance, sought to show that it intended to enter the electrical appliance market in competition with White Consolidated in terms that left the district court unpersuaded.[29] Corenco, a fat-rendering company, sought to resist a takeover by Schiavone & Sons by claiming that it was planning to enter the scrap metal business. This claim was rejected, with the wise observation that visions conjured up by resisting targets should be examined with special care.[30] Somewhat more plausible claims of the same sort have also been rejected.[31]

Whatever else may be done with presumptions, it seems clear that no presumption can deal satisfactorily with the problem of assessing entry plans that may have been fabricated for the purpose of avoiding a takeover. Certainly it cannot be presumed that such plans always represent a significant prospect of increased competition; neither is it fair to presume that such plans never represent significant potential benefits to competition.

Perceived Potential Entry

1. Procompetitive Effects. The abstract edge-effect theory is easily stated. A market that is structured so that noncompetitive behavior is possible may behave competitively solely out of fear that noncompetitive behavior will attract new entry and thus make the entry more difficult to resist. One of the most commonly emphasized theories is that of "limit pricing," which suggests that oligopoly firms may charge a price below their oligopoly profit- or safety-maximizing price to reduce the profit incentive to new entry and to serve as a warning that the prices that would prevail after entry by addition of new capacity may be lower still. In addition, incumbents may be pressured to expand capacity to keep up with expanding demand; to maintain efficiency because of a recognition that it is harder to get costs into line when challenged by new entry than it is to get prices or other behavior into line; to increase progressiveness; to improve and proliferate products and services; and generally to accomplish all the good results of competition. It may even be that some markets are better served by the fear that a large and close outside firm will enter than by actual entry of the same firm.[32]

Attractive as the theory is, it is easily possible to overestimate the practical importance of such effects. Limit-pricing, for instance, costs money in the short run: the incumbents may calculate that it is better to extract maximum short-run profits and cope with new entry later—if possible by continued oligopolistic pricing cooperation. Moreover, it is increasingly common to argue that limit pricing does not work, that likely entrants probably have such sound information about costs and demand as to understand what the opportunities are. The core of sound reason is not itself strong enough to push edge-effect concerns as far as they might be.

Finally, to the extent that edge effects may produce desirable present results, it has been recognized that such results may follow from a perception that a particular firm may enter by acquisition rather than internal expansion. If presumptive rules are to be created to limit the opportunity to make competitive toehold acquisitions, the result may be to vitiate the desirable edge effects as incumbent firms perceive that the most threatening forms of entry have been outlawed.

2. Anticompetitive Effects. Apart from the question of whether edge effects are often very important in fact, it must be recognized that perception of a potential competitor may instigate undesirable rather than desirable behavior. Incumbents may seek to forestall entry by increasing expenditures on promotion and other product differentiation ploys. Alternatively, they may seek to block access to necessary raw materials, to trained personnel, to customers, or to distribution channels by a variety of questionable or even unlawful restrictive arrangements. Technology may be blocked by a proliferation of patents. Theoretically, these concerns suggest that a fully litigated case should include a measure of adverse responses to perceived potential entry and should admit a defense that removal of a perceived potential entrant has in fact improved competition. It does not seem at all likely that this will be done. On the contrary, present thinking seems to embody a de facto presumption that on balance, edge effects are always good. Any such presumption must be justified, if at all, in the name of expediency, not clear logic.

3. Measuring Premerger Sidelines Effects. The abstract theory of edge effects might suggest that, for instance, limit-pricing theory be put to the proof of establishing the oligopoly-maximizing, or satisficing price, comparing it to the actual price, and then demonstrating that a lower actual price resulted from perception of the acquiring firm as a potential entrant. There are traces of this approach in the opinions. In *Procter/Clorox,* for instance, the Supreme Court noted that there was no showing that the price that would induce Procter to enter was above the price that would maximize the profits of existing firms. And in *Marine Bancorporation,* the Court began with the statement that in applying the edge effect doctrine,

> the Court has recognized that a market extension merger may be unlawful if the target market is substantially concentrated, if the acquiring firm has the characteristics, capabilities, and economic incentive to render it a perceived potential *de novo* entrant, and if the acquiring firm's premerger presence on the fringe of the target market in fact tempered oligopolistic behavior on the part of existing participants in the market.[33]

A few pages later, it stated that if the market is in fact behaving in competitive fashion, there is no need to worry about perceived potential entry effects; this appears in a passage that by its silence seemed to suggest that there is not even any need to undertake a determination whether present competitive behavior is in fact due to a market perception that the acquiring firm might have entered.

This approach to the edge-effect theory would create obvious and enormous litigation difficulties. Scant reflection on the task of cutting through competing expert testimony on the profit-maximizing price, and the reasons for not attaining it, is required to demonstrate that the task is unmanageable. The Court apparently recognized these problems in the Marine Bancorporation decision, for its initial statements were followed by the position already noted: a *prima facie* case for application of both actual-entry and edge-effects doctrines can be made by showing a concentrated market, leaving the burden on the defendants to show that the market is working competitively. There is no further help in guessing at just how defendants are to undertake the still very difficult task of proving the competitive nature of actual behavior. And there is no help at all on the most important question of all—how it is to be shown whether such level of competitive behavior as may be observed resulted from perception that the acquiring firm might enter the market in some threatening way. Thus, we are left without guidance on what to do after a showing that the market has been behaving in exemplary competitive fashion, whether it should be to ban the merger because the behavior can be explained only on edge-effect grounds or to allow the merger because the market is competitive. The modest presumption articulated by the Court is little help.

In the face of such inherent uncertainty, some cases have found that the market of the acquired firm was competitive for reasons intrinsic to the market, without regard to the perception of possible entry.[34] That such findings can be made does not tell us when or why they should be made.

Other cases have found that edge-effect was shown to have influenced actual behavior of the market, without enough detail to permit a sophisticated evaluation of the conclusion. In *Procter/Clorox*, the Court stated in a single paragraph that the behavior of incumbent bleach firms was influenced by the perceived threat of entry; that the barriers to entry by Procter were low; that the number of potential entrants was not so large as to deflate concern for loss of Procter's potential entry threat; and that Procter was the most likely entrant. So too other cases have found that competition was weak, but nonetheless stronger than it would have been without perception of the acquiring firm as a potential entrant (see *Bendix/Fram*). In *Phillips/Tidewater*, perhaps because the number of firms and behavior of the market made more precise findings perilous, the district court ruled that whether or not specific actions of incumbents could be shown to have been affected by perception of Phillips as a potential entrant, "it must be assumed that such influence exists where the market is concentrated." It then went on to conclude that there was in fact direct evidence of actual impact, but the evidence seems doubtful to an outside eye.

Support for the presumption approach taken in the Phillips case may well be found in the "rational beer merchant" portion of the Falstaff opinion. First, the Court stated in the text of the opinion that the Narragansett acquisition would become "suspect" if Falstaff would appear a dangerous potential entrant to "rational beer merchants in New England."[35] Next, and perhaps more important, the Court added that although there was no direct evidence of reaction to potential competition from Falstaff, "circumstantial evidence is the lifeblood of antitrust law, . . . especially for § 7 which is concerned 'with probabilities, not certainties.' "[36]

Putting these cases together, they seem likely to recognize a use of the *Marine Bancorporation* presumption that is somewhat broader than the minimum reach of the opinion. The plaintiff's burden on an edge-effect theory can be carried by showing that the market was substantially concentrated, and that the acquiring firm seemed a likely entrant because of objective factors apparent to firms actually in the market. Showing competitive behavior is not alone sufficient to rebut this case. In addition, some persuasive showing must be made to demonstrate that the competitive behavior did not result from edge effects generated by fear that the acquiring firm would enter in a more competitive manner. Even this use of presumption, however, leaves many uncertainties yet to be answered.

Among the uncertainties that remain is the proper role of subjective testimony by incumbent firms that goes directly to the edge effect. Subjective testimony can come in either direction: incumbents may testify that they in fact perceived the firm as a potential entrant and competed all the harder, or they may testify that they did not perceive it as a potential entrant or did not respond to any such perception. Subjective testimony of this sort is of course the most direct and potentially the most useful information about edge effects. At the same time, it is incredibly dangerous. Some incumbents may be tempted to react to an acquisition that has in fact stirred up unwelcome competition in the market by imagining that there had been strong edge effects before the acquisition. Others may deny edge effects because they are afraid that invalidation of the merger will be followed by a more competitive situation. Nonetheless, several decisions have relied on negative testimony of this sort. On remand of the Falstaff case, the district court found that there was no edge effect, relying in large part on testimony of actual beer merchants that Falstaff was not considered a threat, despite its well-known desire to get into the market, and that they had much more immediate competitive problems to worry about. Similar testimony by incumbents has been accepted by the FTC as disproving edge effects in a number of cases (see *British Oxygen/ Airco; Budd/Gindy; General Mills/Gorton*).

The danger of subjective edge-effect testimony is underscored by the probability that some incumbent firms may in fact perceive and react to a threat of entry, while others do not. Such a record was presented in *Black & Decker*. The court concluded that there was no edge effect without inquiring into the theoretical possibility that perception by a single substantial incumbent can be sufficient to generate an edge effect. If one firm reacts to a fear of entry, its behavior may be as effective in stirring competitive behavior by all firms as if they all had perceived the threat of entry. Reliance on the subjective testimony of a single incumbent, however, simply augments the danger of defeating a procompetitive merger.

Measuring the premerger sidelines effects attributable to the acquiring firm, in short, is an extraordinarily difficult undertaking. The very difficulty of the undertaking, however, arises from the fact that the underlying theory is itself complex. Simplifying presumptions seem possible only by ignoring the theory; convincing empirical demonstration that the theoretical complexities are of no practical importance is yet to be achieved.

4. Application To Other Firms. As with actual entry, the Achilles heel of the edge-effect theories is the care that can be taken in identifying the number of other potential entrants and measuring the height of the barriers to entry confronting each of them. In theory, removal of an acquiring firm's edge effect should justify prohibition only if it faced substantially lower barriers than others, or if the number of approximately equal entrants is very small, or perhaps if there is some combination of these factors with an entrenchment effect that raises the barriers that face other firms. In fact, it does not seem likely that great care can or will be devoted even to identifying alternative entrants, much less to the impossible task of measuring the comparative height of the individual barriers separating each of them from the market. Even if this task should be undertaken, it may be met with exaggerated concern for the importance of a single potential entrant. Bendix, for instance, was thought by the FTC to be obliged to acquire a smaller filter firm than Fram, even though twenty-three other firms had actually discussed entry by acquisition.

The intrinsic difficulty of measuring the edge effect of other firms is again exacerbated by the danger of *post litem motam* testimony. Incumbents who welcome an acquisition, for instance, both because it has removed a threat of more competitive entry and because the acquiring firm has joined or even formed the oligopoly club, could easily provide testimony that many other firms were perceived as potential entrants, and still are.

The most likely outcome of these difficulties is that insufficient care will be taken in measuring comparative edge effects. The only way to avoid a charge that this failure is an irrational inconsistency in potential-competition doctrine is to assert a presumption that the abstract possibility of edge effects is sufficient of itself to bar some mergers.

5. Potential Edge Effect. Justice Marshall's concurring opinion in *Falstaff* and the FTC's opinion in *British Oxygen* both open the possibility that an acquisition may be barred on the ground that although the acquiring firm has not yet had any impact on the market as a perceived potential entrant, it might come to have such an impact in the future. The Second Circuit opinion in *British Oxygen* may put a damper on such speculation. As a matter of manageable litigation, there seems to be little room for such a theory unless it is supported by a presumption that any firm sufficiently interested to enter a market by acquisition would some day become sufficiently interested to enter by better means. The presumption, moreover, might need to be made irrebuttable. The prospect of litigating the question of whether the company would find other alternatives more attractive over a long period of time is at best very unattractive.

Evaluating Entry Potential

Both actual entry and edge effects rely on the possibility that entry would occur. This possibility can be measured both by subjective testimony of officials of the acquiring firm as to entry plans, and by an assessment of the objective factors that make actual entry more or less likely. It is clear, in theory and in the cases, that both objective and subjective elements must be considered.

Initially, it may be quarreled that edge effects rely on the perceptions of incumbents rather than the actual probability of entry. Nonetheless, it has been seen that reliance cannot be placed exclusively on the subjective testimony of incumbent firms, even if edge-effect doctrine is limited—as it should be—to present impact. The quality of subjective testimony must itself be measured against the objective factors that make it more or less reasonable to fear actual entry. Objective and subjective testimony must be considered. Even the self-interested testimony of officials of the acquiring firm must be considered, for it is some evidence of actual business judgments that may have been shared by incumbents as well as by the acquiring firm.

As to actual entry effect, a determination of the firm's real behavior must consider its internal subjective judgments unless concern is to be placed exclusively on the objective possibility of entry. Subjective testimony after the fact is of course subject to grave credibility doubts, but it must remain a very important element. If nothing else, detailed evidence as to actual managerial processes is apt to provide at least as sound an assessment of probable behavior as the post hoc rationalizations of a judge or—heaven help us—a jury. Justice Marshall's valiant concurring opinion in the Falstaff case is itself more valuable than anything else for showing clearly how difficult it must be for courts to attempt an entirely objective measure of actual entry probabilities.

The importance and danger of subjective evidence warrant a few additional observations.

First, it seems clear that one of the defects of subjective evidence is that an acquiring firm is generally incapable of making an impartial assessment of the prospects of entry by some other means. In most cases, exploration of entry possibilities will quite properly consider all alternatives; the fact that acquisition was ultimately chosen means that at some point, the inquiry may have become tainted by gradually building conclusions in favor of acquisition. Still, there may be special cases. In *U.S.* v. *Consolidated Foods Corp.*, Sara Lee had twice tried without success to enter the sale of institutional pies.[37] Its experience suggested strongly that it would not try again, nor would it be perceived as a potential entrant. So a firm may have rejected all alternative means of entry at a time when it seemed clear that it could not make a particular acquisition, and then gained an opportunity to make the acquisition. Care must nonetheless be taken even in such circumstances; Yamaha's two unsuccessful efforts to sell outboard motors in the United States seemed likely not to discourage actual entry but to encourage entry on a much broader and more competitive scale if the joint venture with Brunswick had not occurred.

Second, it is a mistake to place too much weight on the fact that internal expansion studies have been made, or on the conclusions expressed in them. The fact that a firm has explored the possibility of internal expansion into a particular market does not warrant any conclusion about probable entry, unless all other expansion studies are also considered and a ranking of all opportunities is set against the firm's total capabilities. In many cases, this task will prove too difficult to undertake; the result is apt to be that the fact of study is given more weight than it deserves. And the cases are replete with illustrations of the fact that recommendations by middle management people should not be taken at face value. Some courts have warned that middle-management recommendations for internal expansion should not be taken as strong evidence of eventual policy, without more showing as to the probable reactions of more responsible managers.[38]

Third, it is dangerous to take seriously everything that is said in studying a potential acquisition. In *Procter/Clorox,* the Court noted that the report urging the acquisition suggested that it would be a way of achieving a "dominant position ... quickly, which would pay out reasonably well."[39] Such language, and even more excited phrases, are bound to occur, and courts would do well to recognize that many memoranda are written more to impress upper management than to inform.

Fourth, the difficulties that may be encountered in a really thorough inquiry into entry probabilities are graphically shown in *Penn-Olin* on remand. The Supreme Court set out various "objective" factors, including demonstrated interest, and concluded that "unless we are going to require subjective evidence this array of probability certainly reaches the prima facie stage." There is little reason to read the opinion as precluding a supplemental subjective inquiry. On remand, the district court in fact engaged in a detailed inquiry into the decision making processes of each company. So on Olin's part, much attention was focused on the relationships between the research and development people in the chemical division (who wanted to go into sodium chlorate) and the staff people at the corporate level, and much importance was attached to the fact that the staff was not particularly impressed with the abilities of the chemical people to spot good opportunities. Some unstated significance was even attached to the fact that there was no showing whether the board of directors was in the general habit of approving any project the staff might recommend. And on Pennsalt's side, a great deal of significance was attached to the fact that Pennsalt had an asserted corporate policy against undertaking a new investment unless the projected profit was at least 25 percent. The ensuing conclusion that there was no violation of Section 7 because the government had not proved a reasonable probability that either firm would have entered independently was affirmed, without opinion, by an evenly divided Supreme Court. Evidence of at least comparable complexity seems to be in the offing in the pending proceedings involving Exxon's acquisition of Reliance Electric Company.[40]

If it seems tempting to respond to these difficulties by creating a presumption, it must be remembered that the presumption is apt to be of little help unless it is avowedly artificial. An attempt to rely on the capacities of a disinterested tribunal to evaluate "objective" evidence alone, without illumination from actual subjective appraisal of the same factors by those immediately involved, is simply to deny one source of vitally important information. Significant relief from the burden of litigation and decision is apt to be provided only by presumptions that put aside careful appraisal of the objective factors in favor of simpler criteria. Simpler criteria, in turn, are apt to deny the rationality of sound theory in favor of easy decision.

Finally, it may be fair to remark once more that one of the greatest weaknesses of potential-competition doctrines is that the difficult and elaborate task of measuring the potential entry role of the firms involved in an actually challenged acquisition cannot be duplicated for other firms. The mere thought of applying to other potential entrants the elaborate and perilous inquiry suggested above—or any simplifying presumption—is again overwhelming. Yet unless the same careful inquiry is undertaken, or the same corrosive presumptions are applied equally across the board, decision must be conjuring with very faint shadows indeed.

Suggested Presumptions

The cases just examined show a process in which courts have attempted to litigate many of the variables that are relevant to potential competition theory, have ignored some of the variables, and have attempted to simplify some of the confusion by starting to create limited presumptions. The enormous difficulty of the task is apparent. This difficulty corresponds directly to the complexity of potential-competition theory. There is excellent reason to attempt to sort through the theory once more, asking whether some of the complexities are more theoretical than real. If it is plausible to discard some of the complexities, the immediate gains are a reduction in litigation costs and perhaps increased certainty in planning acquisitions. Beyond this immediate gain, it is possible that actual decisions may be improved by ignoring the more refined details of abstract theory. The more complex the theory and the resulting litigation, the greater the danger that actual decision will rest on uninformed intuition or worse. On a less elegant level, simplified rules may seem desirable simply because they prohibit more mergers.

The case against this simplifying process is direct. It rests on the argument that there is no sound ground for concluding that some of the theoretical complexities can be discarded without vitiating potential-competition doctrine. If anything, the cases have simplified matters too much already. There is simply not enough empirical information to justify a presumption that any market that reaches a defined level of concentration needs the spur of edge effects or actual entry, that it in fact has responded to edge effects, or that any response to edge effects or actual entry will be more desirable than undesirable. There is no basis at all for presuming that a simple distinction can be drawn between small acquisitions that may benefit competition and larger acquisitions that will not. Efforts to create presumptive or objective tests to measure the probability that an acquiring firm would have entered a market by other means invariably are reduced to an argument that a very low probability is still sufficient for antitrust purposes. Claims that efficiencies are not to be had rest on particularly thin grounds when dealing with the product- and market-extension mergers that supply the only plausible case for potential-competition analysis from the onset. And so it goes. One way of summarizing the objection is that oligopoly theory itself is sophisticated, intricate, and woefully deficient as a means of explaining or predicting actual market conduct or performance. Potential competition theory complicates oligopoly theory by adding one more layer of multifarious possibilities and uncertain measurement.

The broad challenge may be illustrated by looking at two of the most important efforts to create new presumptions out of potential competition theory. The first effort is found in paragraph 18 of the Merger Guidelines of the Department of Justice. The second effort is found in Professor Brodley's elegant article and in his chapter in this book.[41]

The Merger Guidelines are worth quoting. The Department will ordinarily challenge any merger between one of the most likely entrants into the market and:

(i) any firm with approximately 25% or more of the market;

(ii) one of the two largest firms in a market in which the shares of the two largest firms amount to approximately 50% or more;

(iii) one of the four largest firms in a market in which the shares of the eight largest firms amount to approximately 75% or more provided the merging firm's share of the market amounts to approximately 10% or more; or

(iv) one of the eight largest firms in a market in which the shares of these firms amount to approximately 75% or more, provided either (A) the merging firm's share of the market is not insubstantial and there are no more than one or two likely entrants into the market, or (B) the merging firm is a rapidly growing firm.

The method of determining whether an acquiring firm is one of the most likely potential entrants is especially remarkable:

> the Department accords primary significance to the firm's capability of entering on a competitively significant scale relative to the capability of other firms (i.e., the technological and financial resources available to it) and to the firm's economic incentive to enter (evidenced by, for example, the general attractiveness of the market in terms of risk and profit; or any special relationship of the firm to the market; or the firm's manifested interest in entry; or the natural expansion pattern of the firm; or the like).

A defense that the merger will produce economies will be accepted only in "exceptional circumstances," in light of the belief that equivalent economies ordinarily can be achieved through internal expansion or smaller acquisitions.

The first major presumptions built into these guidelines are reflected in the successive structural tests. It is presumed both that any market that meets these tests, e.g., one that has a single 25 percent firm, needs the benefits of potential competition. It is then further presumed that these benefits will not follow from the substantial acquisitions identified. There is no requirement that market performance or conduct be examined at all. A third major presumption is that there is a significant loss of edge effects and possible actual entry whenever an acquisition is made by "one of the most likely entrants"; there is no indication how small the universe of potential entrants must be, apart from the negative implication that in most cases it need not be limited to one or two firms. Allied to these presumptions is a fourth presumption that acquisition of a significant firm will not lead to enhanced competitive conduct or performance. However questionable these presumptions may seem in the abstract, moreover, it must be remembered that literally, at least, they apply to any market that passes the completely fractionalizing tests of the Guidelines. As to many of the narrowly drawn product markets and small geographic markets that would satisfy these tests, it is apparent that these presumptions are untenable; it is not to be supposed that the Department in fact intends to apply these market tests.

The virtue of the presumptions just noted is that they should be relatively simple to apply. Market definition and measurement of market shares are still required, but these tasks are at least familiar to antitrust litigation. A rather different sort of presumption is built into the identification of a probable entrant. The basic presumption must be that there is a significant probability that any firm that passes the superficially objective tests of the Guidelines either presents a significant probability of actual entry or is likely to be perceived as a potential entrant. The grounds for doubting judicial capacity to make particularly sound estimates of probable entry have been described earlier. These difficulties are enhanced if they are to rely on such slippery concepts as "the general attractiveness of the market," "any special relationship of the firm to the market," "manifested interest in entry," or "the natural expansion pattern of the firm." The presumption of potential entry that rests on assessment of such factors can be plausible only if we are willing to accept as significant a very low probability of actual entry. In addition, this presumption is drawn in terms of comparison between the acquiring firm and other firms. It can lay claim to respectability only if the very same effort is expended in measuring the relative probability of entry by as many other potential entrants as imagination can suggest. It does not seem credible to suppose that such efforts will be undertaken. If they are undertaken, the goal of simplifying litigation will be sacrificed in direct measure.

The final presumption that is worth noting in the Guidelines is that economies normally can be achieved by more desirable means. There is some support for this presumption in the fact that economists have not yet been able to identify in any rigorous way the actual regular achievement of substantial economies by conglomerate acquisition. There is further support in the very dim prospects for defending a merger under present law on the ground that it promises to achieve substantial economies. Litigation of the question, moreover, bids fair to be hopeless. To this extent, the Guidelines seem well based. At the same time, this is not a new presumption; it simply continues the probable course of general Section 7 law.

Professor Brodley's presumptive approach was based on exhaustive study of economic literature as well as the case law. After concluding that potential competition has ceased to be a viable legal policy, he urged that a structural-presumptive approach is the only means of resurrecting it. His suggested approach was drawn from the conclusion that it should not be necessary to predict whether a specific acquiring firm actually would enter the market of the acquired firm or be perceived as a potential entrant. Instead, it is enough to bar acquisitions by firms that fall into a class of most probable entrants. The key to his proposed presumptions is found in the concept of market proximity and a simplified approach to identifying the most significant potential entrants. As to market-extension mergers, the concept of proximity is direct: the geographic markets closest to the acquired firm's market are the most proximate markets. As to product-extension mergers, the concept is more complicated: proximate markets are identified either by the level of similarity in production and marketing, or by actual entry patterns. The most significant potential entrants are then identified by relying on their absolute size and their sales in the proximate market on the theory that large firms are the most likely entrants into adjacent markets.

Separate but very similar presumptions are built around these concepts for market- and product-extension mergers. These presumptions are offered as suitable for adoption by judicial decision as well as legislative action. The presumption for market-extension mergers begins with a requirement that the acquired firm have at least 5 percent of a highly concentrated market. The acquiring firm must occupy a closely proximate market, and either be one of the two largest firms in that market with a share of at least 10 percent and annual sales or assets of at least $100 million or be as large as any of the 200 largest industrial corporations and make significant sales in that market. The presumption for product-extension mergers is the same except that the acquired firm must have at least 10 percent of a highly concentrated market. The market share requirement imposed as to the acquired firm reflects a presumption that smaller acquisitions are potentially desirable toeholds. Rebuttal would be permitted to show that the acquiring firm lacked the financial resources or other capacities required for a more desirable form of entry, or to show that beneficial changes in market structure resulted from the acquisition. No rebuttal would be permitted on grounds of actual market conduct or performance, nor would a demonstration of actual efficiencies be permitted. All testimony of subjective intent would be barred.

The difficulties suggested by these presumptions may be sketched by beginning with the simpler market-extension setting. Exclusion of testimony of subjective intent is supported by the proposition that the law need not be concerned with identifying the actual prospect of entry by this particular firm. This justification either puts aside all concern with predicting any effects of the transaction, or assumes that it is enough that at some time in a sufficiently long-range future the factors favoring entry would persist unchanged and would spur actual entry or produce an edge effect. Exclusion of evidence about the actual workings of the market must rest on the judgment that any "highly concentrated" market needs the benefits of actual entry or the perception that it may occur. Reliance on the market share and size of the acquiring firm to indicate probable entry is bought at the expense of excluding any study of the alternative entry opportunities that might be more attractive. Together, these simplifications can be justified only in the terms that Professor Brodley offers. The presumption, although drawn in terms of potential entry, is simply an effort to bar acquisitions by relatively large firms in circumstances that seem to threaten the least possible interference with desirable transactions.

The market-extension presumption is also affected to some extent by an additional problem that drastically affects the presumption for product-extension mergers. The presumption is cast in terms of probable entry from "the" proximate market. It is recognized that identification of market proximity is apt to be a task somewhat more difficult than the initial task of identifying the relevant markets, and that in the end this difficulty may require still simpler presumptions. A defense is permitted by showing that other markets lie as close to the target market. There is no clear indication, however, of the yet greater difficulty encountered in any attempt to assess the relative proximity of different markets. Even if it should prove possible to achieve some measure of relative proximity between different markets and the market of the acquired firm, the next step of a complete analysis would require measurement of the relative proximity between all markets of the acquiring firm and every other nearby market. There is no such thing as a class of firms that probably will extend itself from one particular and somewhat proximate market to another market. There is only a universe of firms often engaged in various arrays of markets that are more or less close to many other markets. A judicial determination that a particular pair of markets is proximate cannot begin to picture even plausible lines of probable expansion by the acquiring firm. If there is any real concern with the importance of the acquiring firm—or some class of acquiring firms—as a more probable entrant than any other firm, moreover, it becomes necessary to measure and rank the most probable lines of expansion of a large number of firms engaged in the markets that are most proximate to the market of the acquired firm. None of these proposed measurements is feasible, and it seems likely that they are to be disregarded in applying the proposed presumptions. Without such measurements, however, the presumptions come indistinguishably close to the proposition that all large acquiring firms should be regarded as potential entrants by other means and that no potential entrant should be permitted to acquire a firm with a substantial share of any concentrated market.

These presumptions, in short, go part way toward the proposition that large acquisitions should be banned. They cannot be cogently justified by the potential-competition theory they mutilate, nor by empirical demonstration that the mayhem is merely theoretical. They retain sufficiently complex opportunities for dispute that litigation will be simplified but not much. If there is any reason to permit conglomerate mergers, it is sufficient to establish the case against such presumptions.

ENTRENCHMENT PRESUMPTIONS

Little effort has been directed toward the development of new presumptions based on the entrenchment effects of conglomerate mergers. The most prominent efforts are the very limited attempt in the Merger Guidelines of the Department of Justice and Professor Brodley's chapter in this book. The reasons that explain the lack of enthusiasm for presumptions in this area are again best illustrated by recounting the difficulties that have been encountered by efforts to apply entrenchment theory in specific cases. This review will set the stage for a brief examination of the Guidelines and Professor Brodley's proposal.

Entrenchment in General

The basic concern of entrenchment theory is that a change in ownership may give the acquired firm a new capacity to chill competition by present rivals and to deter entry by potential rivals. Ordinarily this concern is focused on acquisition of a firm that is already "dominant" in one or more markets. When Procter & Gamble acquired Clorox, Clorox had approximately half the liquid bleach market. The fear of entrenchment is that after the acquisition Clorox would be even better able to maintain or expand its position. This concern is not peculiar to conglomerate mergers; it would be present if the merger were a horizontal merger because Procter & Gamble already had a share of the liquid bleach market, or if it were a vertical merger because Procter & Gamble was a supplier or customer of Clorox. The mechanisms of entrenchment are many and varied; some of them are more likely to result from extension mergers that promise significant integration of operations, but others may result from pure conglomerate relationships. The mechanisms that are most frequently identified are sketched below.

Efficiency

One way in which a firm's market position may be entrenched is by improving its efficiency, so that it enjoys a cost advantage over its rivals. To the extent that a conglomerate merger may improve efficiency, it may correspondingly lead to entrenchment. Such results seem particularly plausible in product- or market-extension mergers.

Recognizing this theory, some cases have indicated that efficiencies generated by a merger may be used to establish illegality. Some reflections of this possibility may be found in the Supreme Court's opinion in the Clorox case. The Court was very clearly of the view that new efficiencies in advertising Clorox that might be achieved by Procter & Gamble could not be offered in defense of the merger. The opinion is less clear, but may also be read to embrace the further argument that such economies should be used as grounds for invalidating the merger.

In the most recent round of subsequent litigation, the Ninth Circuit has clearly ruled that Procter & Gamble can be held liable for treble damages if the acquisition made Clorox more efficient by providing managerial resources, advertising discounts, and technical services, so long as the increased efficiency served as part of the mechanism by which the illegal merger lessened competition. The opinion seems to contemplate that it is sufficient to show that fear of the efficiency of Clorox deterred others from entering the market or deterred Purex from competing in its preferred ways.[42] And the Third Circuit has twice indicated that increased efficiency may be counted against a merger. In *NBO Indus. Treadway Cos.* v. *Brunswick Corp.*, it explained that Brunswick's acquisition of bowling alleys could be found invalid because such a large owner could, among other things, "achieve cost-savings by investing in new equipment."[43] Earlier, in *General Foods* v. *FTC*, it ruled that General Foods' ability to advertise SOS steel wool more cheaply and more effectively should be held against the merger.[44] In several other cases, district courts and the FTC have rejected arguments that mergers should be held invalid because of promised efficiencies simply by finding that no such efficiencies were likely to occur.

On the face of things, it is difficult to understand why Section 7 should be set against the cause of economic efficiency. If, for instance, the most efficient form of production and distribution calls for integration of a wide variety of more or less obviously related functions, or for utilization of a superb management team across the full sweep of a large enterprise, so be it. Some efficiencies, nonetheless, may properly be suspect. In the Clorox case, one of the efficiencies feared was that Procter & Gamble was simply able to get better time rates from the television networks. If that was so, and if better rates reflected merely huge buying power, it may be possible to agree that the cost savings should be held against the merger. It may even be possible to find undesirable the possibility of real efficiencies in promotion if the result is to create an artificial perception of distinctions between consumer products that are physically identical, as all liquid bleaches and steel wools were thought to be. Beyond that point, vigorous efforts should be made to resist claims that mergers should be held unlawful precisely because they have created real efficiencies. The First Circuit has quite properly perceived that entrenchment doctrine does not properly block "simple improvements in efficiency."[45]

Pricing Behavior

Another possibility of entrenchment arises from the danger that undesirable pricing will result from the deep pocket, vicious motivation, or sheer ignorance of the acquiring company. Once Procter & Gamble had acquired Clorox, it would be easier for Clorox to finance a predatory war to the death against smaller rivals, or to support a program of disciplinary pricing designed to maintain oligopoly prices. Alternatively, Procter & Gamble may understand Clorox' potential better than Clorox did, and assume a new role of noncompetitive leadership. It is even possible that a large conglomerate firm will engage in pricing that is simply irrational, out of ignorance of its own true costs.

These abstract possibilities do not translate readily into specific grounds for attacking any given merger. It is conceivable that direct evidence might be found—as a result of some indiscretion or infidelity—showing that an acquisition was motivated by a purpose to engage in predatory pricing, or to use disciplinary pricing or previously unexercised power in an effort to improve the previous level of oligopoly profits. It is barely conceivable that evidence of such behavior in fact might be found after a merger and traced to the new ownership.

Apart from such bizarre cases, the abstract fear of bad pricing behavior does not furnish a convincing basis for attacking a conglomerate merger.

Returning to the Clorox case, the prospect of predatory pricing in the liquid bleach industry was approximately zero. It was clear from the record that small firms could enter the market easily, and more than 200 of them were in fact competing with the small number of larger firms. The prospect of raising the barriers to entry so high as to pay off an investment in predation seems nonexistent. So it will often be in other markets. Much modern theory suggests that predatory pricing is seldom a rational market strategy. Actual experience does not provide any convincing illustrations of actual predation, whether rational in economic theory or not.

Surely a mere deep pocket capacity to engage in irrational behavior cannot reasonably be used to attack any acquisition. And reliance on actual experience after the acquisition will require all of the perspicacity required to approach predatory pricing directly; in addition, it might require some showing of connection between the merger and the subsequent pricing behavior. These lessons are perhaps most convincingly illustrated by a case that ignores them, *Reynolds Metals Co.* v. *FTC.*[46] Initially, the court suggested that a mere capacity for undesirable pricing might well be enough to prohibit some mergers. Then it appeared to approve findings that seem to have been findings of predatory pricing in the florists' foil market without even indicating whether the price war had been started by the acquired company or someone else. Much clearer stuff than this is required for a convincing decision.

The Court may have been more concerned with disciplinary pricing than predation in the Clorox case. It cited in a footnote the "lesson" learned by Purex when Purex' attempt to enter the Erie, Pennsylvania, market was met by promotional response from Clorox. The full story of this incident is told in *Purex Corp.* v. *Procter & Gamble Co.*[47] Purex entered the market with a promotional campaign that cost it nearly $3.00 per case sold. Its total promotional expenses were nearly $22,000. Clorox responded with a campaign of price reductions and promotional sales items that cost about 90 cents per case, for a total of less than $7,000. Purex initially grabbed a 30 percent market share, which then fell to 10 percent; another brand, Austin's, managed to grow from 5 percent to 24 percent during this period. Whatever may be said of Clorox' response, it can hardly be characterized as disciplinary pricing. The Ninth Circuit, however, has concluded that Purex can recover damages for this incident if it can show that the result was to deter it from expanding by internal growth or to cause it to pay more than it otherwise would have had to pay to acquire the company it thereafter bought as a base for further expansion.

In other situations, it may be more plausible to fear that a large firm will be more willing to resort to disciplinary pricing than a small firm. The abstract possibility, however, hardly seems sufficient basis for presuming that a large firm acquisition will have such effects.

Closely related to the possibility of disciplinary pricing is the possibility that an acquiring firm may have a deliberate desire simply to lead the way to higher prices for all firms. In *United Brands Co.,* it was found that United intended to become a price leader in the lettuce market for the benefit of all sellers.[48] It was further found, however, that the market structure was so competitive that United simply could not achieve its original goal. Again, the possibility seems real, but it seems difficult to apply it in particular cases absent a direct showing of purpose and of a market structure that may support the purpose. Once again, there is no rational basis for substituting some sort of presumption about the probable behavior of large and small firms.

Finally, it has been urged at times that a conglomerate firm may engage in undesirable pricing simply because it is ignorant of its real costs, or is under such stock market performance pressures that it cannot admit its own mistakes, or is simply uninterested in maximizing profits in any individual line of business. Such possibilities are not impossibilities. Neither have they been shown to be meaningful. This prospect should not be held against any particular merger absent a specific showing of a sort difficult to foresee.

Product Differentiation

If, indeed, Procter & Gamble is able to get more bang for its advertising buck than Clorox is, the acquisition could facilitate still further artificial differentiation of the Clorox brand in consumers' eyes. There are at least four possible sources of this advantage. One is that Procter & Gamble enjoys artificial television rate advantages that are unrelated to any efficiency of doing business with it. The Court plainly thought that this was so. Another is that Procter & Gamble can achieve genuine promotional efficiencies. Such efficiencies might result because it really is more efficient for the media to deal with a large advertiser. They are more likely to result because Procter has access to more efficient forms of promotion. Joint promotion of related products would be an obvious example, as in a campaign advising people to keep their teeth really white by brushing with Crest and gargling with Clorox. A third and quite distinct possibility is that Clorox will sell better simply by its new identification with Procter & Gamble, in a nation of housekeepers who identify Procter with all that is good in household cleaning products. This third category seems to me a genuine efficiency too, at least in many circumstances. Finally, it may be that Procter & Gamble is simply more adept at advertising or at selecting advertising agencies. General Foods was found to have improved the effect of SOS advertising, in part because of better television rates and in part because it shifted to a new advertising program.

In all of these possibilities, it is virtually impossible to distinguish between socially desirable and clearly undesirable effects. Some advertising is clearly good; increased efficiency in accomplishing such advertising is equally good. So too, acquisition of a small firm and enhancement of its advertising capacities may be a desirable means of toehold entry into an imperfect market; thus in the Bendix case the FTC suggested that Bendix should acquire a smaller filter firm than Fram and use the well-established Bendix name to help expand its market share. Even if advertising is neutral or bad, it is hard to quarrel with the ability to achieve the same level of neutral or bad effects with fewer resources. In addition to this difficulty in evaluating effects, it is ordinarily very difficult to know whether a merger will have any effect at all, either as a matter of prediction at the time of the merger or as an inference after the fact.

Several cases have responded to these difficulties by rejecting product differentiation claims of entrenchment. Many of them have rested on the ground that the product involved was not subject to artificial blandishments. The products involved have included executive jets, chain saws, band uniforms, gymnastic equipment, fire control equipment, and institutional dry groceries at the wholesale level. Another ground has been that other firms in the market were large and competent advertisers that would not be threatened by the acquisition.[49]

On the other hand, the FTC found grave cause for concern that United Brand's acquisition of several lettuce growers was part of a program intended to create a differentiated, premium-commanding Chiquita brand. Although United had not been able to achieve this goal, because of its inability to secure sufficient assured lettuce supplies to support such a program, the Commission found that any such program would be a grave threat to competition in a market that had not known any strong brand differentiation. The Commission ordered United to report to it any increases in its holdings of lettuce-producing land. Just how the point of danger would be identified was not vouchsafed.

The mixed success that has characterized the differentiation concern seems at least as good as it deserves. There is nothing in these cases to suggest that any sort of simplifying presumption can be found that would warrant a generalized approach detached from the actual workings of specific markets.

E. Capital Supply

Another possible advantage accruing to acquisition by a large firm is that the parent can transfuse capital into the child at advantageous rates. Empirically, it is not at all clear whether absolute size is a significant advantage in access to capital markets, either as to availability of investment or as to its terms once a relatively small minimum firm size has been reached. It may yet happen that in times of severe distress such advantages will emerge. However that may be, there are a host of excellent reasons why a large firm can and should be able to finance its own operations from internally generated funds on terms more attractive and discerning than market borrowing. So too, a large acquiring firm may be able to utilize unused capital resources of the acquired firm more efficiently than the general market for capital. To the extent that any of these phenomena is shown, it seems to represent a genuine efficiency. Nonetheless, conglomerate acquisitions have been challenged on this ground. In *U.S.* v. *International Tel. & Tel. Corp.,* the claim was rejected on the ground that there was no showing that Grinnell had any unmet needs for capital at the time of the acquisition.[50] A like result was reached in Beatrice Foods Co.[51] It is to be hoped that this ground of entrenchment attack will be abandoned in the future. If it is not abandoned, at a minimum the theory must be supported by a specific showing that draws from the facts and dangers of a particular acquisition in particular markets. No presumption can be made that big acquisitions will produce this result.

F. Psychological Reaction

Quite apart from the specific mechanisms of entrenchment, smaller firms may react to the absolute size or reputation of a takeover firm by overestimating its capacity and desire to engage in predation, discipline, aggressive promotion, more efficient operations, or the like. They may be driven by a sense of compulsion, or drawn by a desire for protection, to follow the leadership of an absolutely large

328 / Antitrust and the Conglomerate Firm

firm where they would not follow a firm of smaller wealth but the same market share. Clorox may not have been feared—or revered—as much as Procter & Gamble.

It seems likely that this sort of entrenchment effect depends on acquisition of a reasonably "significant" firm in the market. Beyond that point, theory suggests that much must also depend on the premerger workings of the market. In his seminal article, "Conglomerate Mergers and Section 7 of the Clayton Act," Professor Turner has suggested that the area of concern is that of the market which, prior to the merger, was so structured as to make oligopoly behavior feasible, but which was nonetheless competitive in performance.[52] Then there is something to lose. Similar concerns may underlie a double assertion made by the Court in the Clorox case. First, it stated that the industry "was already oligopolistic before the acquisition, and price competition was certainly not as vigorous as it would have been if the industry were competitive." Then it concluded that there is "every reason to assume that the smaller firms would become more cautious in competing due to their fear of retaliation by Procter. It is probable that Procter would become the price leader and that oligopoly would become more rigid."

That such assertions can be made about market performance does not carry us far in determining whether really satisfactory showings can be made or should be required. As with the part of potential-competition theory that looks to actual market behavior, it may prove extraordinarily difficult to find plausible answers. In addition, theoretical grounds make one wonder whether the showing should be required. If the market is grossly noncompetitive at the time of the acquisition, it may be feared that the entrenchment effects of a merger may undo whatever prospects there might have been for loosening oligopolistic interdependence and may raise still further the barriers against competitive entry or expansion. On the other hand, it is also possible that the acquisition may shake up the stagnating industry by vigorous new competitive efforts. Given the speculative nature of this entrenchment concern, it is equally plausible to reject the argument, to require that it be supported by specific showings of actual market conduct and performance, or to adopt a presumption that acquisitions that produce some major size disparity will chill competition. Of itself, this seems scant argument for adopting the presumption approach.

Even if a presumption is to be adopted, it will remain necessary to define the size disparity that is needed to produce the chilling effect.

In addition, it will be necessary to recognize some sort of toehold threshold, so that a large outside firm can acquire a small firm and expand it into a more competitive force. Once a toehold acquisition is permitted, moreover, the merger must not be subject to retroactive attack simply because over time the toehold has been converted into a hammerlock.

Still further complications arise if the acquired firm itself was backed by enormous assets. One large conglomerate firm, for example, might acquire a division of another large conglomerate firm. The prospect of assaying different degrees of monster wealth and corresponding chilling effect is not alluring. So too, there may be other very large firms in the market—entry by yet one more may exacerbate the situation, and at the same time it may provide the first opportunity for thawing a chill that once prevented the acquired firm from competing vigorously with its larger rivals. Neither presumptions nor specific case litigation seem likely to provide good answers for these problems.

Special Complication

1. Weak Dominant Firm. One of the dangers of presumptions built on entrenchment theory is that they are apt to rely on artificial market-share definitions to identify the "dominant" firms that should be insulated from acquisition by a larger parent. The fact that a firm is the largest firm in its market cannot be equated with dominance. *U.S.* v. *Crowell Collier & Macmillan, Inc.,* illustrates the matter nicely.[53] Crowell Collier & Macmillan acquired G. C. Conn Ltd., the leading firm in the brasswind market. The court found that all competitors but Conn were healthy in terms of growth and profits. Conn was found barely able to attend to its own resurrection; the competitive enhancement of its position claimed to be imminent by the government was found to be impossible at present and highly doubtful for the future. The decision is a forceful reminder that close attention should be paid to the facts, as well as the theory. And if the acquired firm is not the largest firm in its market, the often speculative entrenchment theories may be strained beyond endurance. In the Arco/Anaconda acquisition, for example, Anaconda was third in copper ore and concentrate with about 8 percent of the market; and fourth in refined copper, with less than 10 percent. Entrenchment concerns were easily rejected; the district court added that Anaconda, although not a failing company, was not capable of effective and vigorous competition on its own.

2. Prior Relationships. Many of the entrenchment concerns spring from the advantages of relationships to a new and larger parent. Whether the matter is litigated on a specific case basis or is approached as a matter of presumptive rules, account must be taken of prior relationships in determining whether any new dangers have arisen. If an acquisition simply substitutes one large parent for another, structural showings alone are not likely to provide sufficient basis for predicting any entrenchment consequences. And if the acquisition substitutes ownership by a large firm for less formal ties that bound the acquired company to the same firm, it is again difficult to suppose that the formal change in the legal nature of the relationships is itself significant.

3. Triggering Effects. Another specific aspect of entrenchment theory that clearly cannot be captured in a presumption is the triggering effect. It is possible that a particular acquisition may, by a variety of mechanisms, cause other firms to undertake mergers they otherwise would have passed by. In *U.S.* v. *Wilson Sporting Goods Co.,* the court thought that the Wilson/Nissen merger might very well cause McGregor, Spaulding, and Rawlings to enter the gymnastic equipment market by merger rather than internal expansion.[54] A direct effect of this is to reduce the potential competition advantage of direct new entry. An indirect effect may well be that instead of a single firm becoming entrenched, a previously competitive market will be transformed into an oligopoly as a group of incumbent firms becomes collectively entrenched. Even in litigating individual cases, it has proved very difficult to make a plausible showing that such effects will occur, and this theory has generally been rejected summarily for failure to show any specific triggering mechanism.[55] No arguments whatever are available to justify a presumption cast in terms of triggering.

Tying Effect

Although the tying-effect theory has been approached as a matter apart from entrenchment effects, the underlying concerns are similar to entrenchment theory as well as to reciprocity concerns. Since the Merger Guidelines treat this matter as an aspect of entrenchment, it is best presented along with general entrenchment theory.

The basic concern of tying effect is that the acquiring firm may have such power over its customers that they shift to products of the acquired firm in order to gain favorable access to products of the acquiring firm, or vice versa. In some cases this concern may be borne out by actual postacquisition facts. After General Foods acquired SOS, for instance, it was found that it promoted SOS sales by offering discounts on pooled purchases of other General Foods products.

Most cases rely on more abstract possibilities. One of the major grounds for preliminarily enjoining Wilson's acquisition of Nissen was the fear that Wilson dealers, who received many kinds of assistance from Wilson, would probably treat Nissen's products more favorably than other products. Analogizing to reciprocity decisions, the court found no need to inquire into actual intent; it was enough that the opportunity for a tying effect had been created: dealers might curry Wilson's favor by pushing Nissen products even without any pressure at all from Wilson. Of itself, this approach seems to create a presumption that a new structure favorable to tying effects may be grounds for invalidating a merger. As questionable as this may be, at least it rests on case-specific findings as to the importance of Wilson's products.

Similar concerns may be found in the Clorox decision. The Court noted the danger that merchants might give Clorox better shelf space because of its affiliation with Procter & Gamble. If this phenomenon was thought to rest on the hope of favorable assistance from Procter in merchandising programs or the like, it would be a tying-effect concern. So in *U.S.* v. *Ingersoll-Rand Co.,* the court was concerned that a set of acquisitions would both create the broadest existing line of underground mining machinery and combine it with a financial subsidiary that made loans to customers.[56]

Other cases have rejected claims of tying effect on the ground that the products and markets involved simply did not warrant any concern. In *U.S.* v. *Wachovia Corporation,* the court found that acquisition of a commercial factoring business by a bank would not lead merchants to patronize the factoring business in hopes of getting favorable loan treatment, in large part on the ground that merchants who factor their paper are not likely to be strong candidates for ordinary commercial loans.[57] So in *ITT/Grinnell,* the court found that the prospect of package sales of Grinnell equipment with other ITT equipment was simply not realistic in light of industrial practices.

Taken together, these cases suggest that tying-effect theory is safe, if at all, only when grounded in specific marketing practices that follow a merger. To rely on the bare creation of a structure that raises a possibility of tying effect would be to threaten any product extension merger involving products marketed through common channels or to common users. Many such mergers do not involve any realistic possibility of tying effect, given the nature of the markets and products actually involved. Efforts to define presumptions would have to rely on strained assumptions about the leverage of one product and the susceptibility to leverage of buyers of the other product. More important, such mergers seem more likely than most conglomerate acquisitions to involve genuine efficiencies. Invalidation should not rest on mere slender possibilities.

Proposed Presumptions

The Merger Guidelines, avowedly tentative in all areas, are particularly tentative in the provisions that deal with entrenchment theory. They offer three examples of circumstances in which acquisition of a leading firm in a relatively concentrated or rapidly concentrating market may threaten anticompetitive consequences:

(i) a merger which produces a very large disparity in absolute size between the merged firm and the largest remaining firms in the relevant markets.

(ii) a merger of firms producing related products which may induce purchasers, concerned about the merged firm's possible use of leverage, to buy products of the merged firm rather than those of competitors, and

(iii) a merger which may enhance the ability of the merged firm to increase product differentiation in the relevant markets.

The first example, involving creation of a very large disparity in the absolute size of firms in the market, may respond to many of the entrenchment concerns listed above. As tentative as it is, it at least suggests a theory that adverse effects may be presumed to follow from such size disparities. Any such presumption is likely to be supported on two grounds. First, general theories of oligopoly behavior, market entry, and market expansion suggest that indeed absolute size disparities may have unfortunate effects. Second, it is virtually impossible to demonstrate such effects with any reasonable assurance in litigating specific acquisitions. The countering arguments are equally direct. The difficulty of demonstrating such effects may show that they are more theoretical than real. Theory, moreover, suggests that large firms may improve the conduct and performance of a previously stagnant oligopoly market rather than

stifle competition still further. The specific mechanisms of entrenchment, finally, are themselves phenomena that may involve
significant efficiencies. The case for a presumption cannot yet be
made either in theory or the clear lessons of experience.

The second example, built around tying effect, can be dismissed
either on the basis of the earlier discussion of tying effect or on the
ground that it is not meant to create a presumption at all. It is at
least consistent with this Guideline to conclude that attack will rest
on the specific facts of particular cases rather than any more
general assumptions.

The third example is akin to the second. It may mean no more
than that the Department is willing to proceed on the basis of
specific facts that show a risk of enhancing purely artificial product
differentiation. If it is intended to go further, however, it is suspect
on all of the grounds summarized above. It is simply not possible to
make clear judgments about the desirability of many of the efficiencies that may be involved in an enhanced ability to foster product
differentiation.

Professor Brodley's proposed presumption is much more precise
than the Guidelines suggestion. As outlined in his paper for this
symposium, it requires that the acquiring firm be in proximity to the
target market—but not as close as in the potential-competition
presumption; that the acquiring firm be among the 100 largest firms
and that it is a leading firm in the proximate market; that the structure of the target market is significantly oligopolistic; and that the
target firm be "the" leading firm with at least a 20 percent share of a
market that comprises total sales or assets of at least $100 million.
The only defenses permitted would be that the structure of the target
market has actually changed so as to justify a prediction that
eventually it will become nonoligopolistic, or that the acquiring firm
has voluntarily divested itself of assets comparable to those
acquired.

The argument in favor of this presumption avowedly rests
primarily on a social and political concern that any acquiring firm
that is a leading firm in some market and is among the 100 largest
firms already has substantial discretionary authority. Acquisition
of the leading firm in a significant oligopolistic market would
augment this discretionary authority in undesirable ways.

This presumption has only a loose connection with the abstract
theory of entrenchment. The primary elements are designed simply
to ensure that both firms have substantial elements of discretionary
authority. If there is any concern at all with the risk that the acquisition may entrench the market position of the acquired firm, it is

reflected in the requirement that the acquiring firm occupy a market that is proximate to the market of the acquired firm. Apparently this requirement rests on the assumption that the various mechanisms of entrenchment are more likely to operate as between firms in proximate markets. Although this assumption seems plausible as to many of the efficiency mechanisms of entrenchment, it seems strange to single out for special condemnation transactions that are more likely to generate new efficiencies. As to the mechanisms of pricing behavior, product differentiation, improved access to capital, or psychological reactions, it is difficult to trace any nexus between the proximity requirement and the prospect of entrenchment.

The elements of this presumption may not reduce the burden of litigation. Indeed, it would be possible to draw more prohibitive and less complicated rules from some of the cases described above. The requirement that the target market have a significantly oligopolistic structure may be as demanding as the showing required in the Procter/Clorox case, and perhaps more demanding. The opportunity to defeat the presumption by showing that the market structure has experienced such beneficial changes as substantial new entry or significantly increased competition may be more permissive and accordingly more complex.

Finally, the defense that comparable assets have been divested does not in any way reduce the prospect of entrenchment in the target market. It may not even reduce the expansion of discretionary authority that results from the acquisition, since the divestiture may occur in a more competitive market.

All in all, Professor Brodley's proposal is much more carefully drawn than the Merger Guidelines. Nonetheless, it does not promise any clear advance over present decisions.

RECIPROCITY PRESUMPTIONS

A. Reciprocity in General

The concern with reciprocity effects in mergers is illustrated by *FTC v. Consolidated Foods Corp.*[58] Consolidated Foods, an important distributor of food products, acquired Gentry, the second largest producer of dehydrated onion and garlic. As a result of the acquisition, it was possible that Gentry could increase its sales to food processors who desired to curry favor with Consolidated as a customer/distributor.

It is accepted by the Consolidated Foods opinion that reciprocity "is one of the congeries of anticompetitive practices at which the antitrust laws are aimed." Both Section 1 and Section 2 of the Sherman Act are regularly invoked in assaults on explicit reciprocity practices. The law has not yet much developed, however, because a staggering number of defendants have found it expedient to enter into consent decrees.

Because the law is little developed, and because it is possible that when it is developed further it will be developed poorly, it is important to note that reciprocity may at times be a good thing. Two firms may enter into reciprocal arrangements voluntarily, each seeking to share the variety of advantages that may be gained through bypassing reliance on market transactions of sale and supply. In other circumstances, use of buying power to increase sales may have the desirable effect of facilitating entry into a concentrated market: if Consolidated Foods had acquired a very small garlic company, and sought to expand it into effective competition with the two industry leaders that enjoyed more than 80 percent of the market, the results might have been highly attractive. Finally, a transaction that appears to involve an exercise of buying power may in fact involve price discrimination or disguised price competition in selling. Consolidated might agree to buy processed food items at inflated prices from its onion-garlic customers as a means of granting disguised discounts on its onion and garlic sales. Despite the bad name of price discrimination, this practice could prove highly beneficial in a concentrated onion-garlic market, and indeed might even be made available without any discrimination among customers as a disguised means of price competition.

These thoughts have suggested to many observers that it would be better to eliminate concern with reciprocity from conglomerate merger doctrine. Overt reciprocity efforts can be attacked when they occur. Some uses of reciprocity may be desirable. The recent antitrust siege on reciprocity has made it less likely that either desirable or undesirable reciprocity will occur in fact. Quite apart from legal rules, the workings of the market may in fact eliminate most possible problems with undesirable reciprocity. Many companies are organized on a profit-center basis that makes the possibility of reciprocity remote. Others have become convinced that reciprocity is simply bad business because it may lead to slackening sales efforts or reduced purchasing vigilance. In addition to these abstract limits on reciprocity theory, application in fact may be stymied by the difficulty frequently encountered in determining whether the bare fact that a firm makes substantial purchases translates into substantial buying power.

Notwithstanding these objections, reciprocity theory is enshrined in the cases and the Merger Guidelines. The cases are sufficiently thin and the Guidelines are so vulnerably detailed that it seems easiest simply to combine discussion of the general problems with the specific problems arising from the presumptions built into the Guidelines.

Reciprocity Variables

Given the simple setting suggested by Consolidated Foods, concern should focus on three markets. (1) Competing sellers of onion and garlic may be foreclosed from equal access to food processors. (2) Food processors may feel cabined by reciprocity pressure and purchase Gentry onion and garlic on unsatisfactory terms as to price, quality, delivery, or the like. (3) Food distributors competing with Consolidated may find that in times of short food supply, they suffer in competition with Consolidated because of the special relationships established by reciprocity between Consolidated and the food processors.

These concerns may be subject to relatively clear application if it can be shown that a particular merger was undertaken for the purpose of exerting reciprocity pressure or that reciprocity efforts have in fact followed the merger. Some cases have met that standard. Consolidated Foods was one of them. Another is *U.S.* v. *General Dynamics Corp.*[59]

If it is not possible to show a deliberate purpose or the actual practice of reciprocity, the question must be addressed whether it should be enough to show that a merger has created a structure that enhances the opportunity to exert reciprocity pressure. The opinion in the Consolidated Foods decision suggests that such a showing is enough. In *U.S.* v. *Ingersoll-Rand Co.*, the court quoted at length and approvingly from the district court's ruling that the creation of an enhanced opportunity for reciprocity was enough.[60] And in *Allis-Chalmers Mfg. Co.* v. *White Consolidated Inds.*, mere reciprocity potential was found controlling.[61] The Merger Guidelines clearly rely on opportunity alone. This tacit presumption that structure may produce effects remains alive, even in the face of a substantial number of other opinions that have found that reciprocity was unlikely after particular mergers because of product characteristics and individual practices of the merging firms.[62]

To whatever extent reliance is to be placed on the mere creation of a structure that enhances opportunities for reciprocity, it can make sense only if it is carefully tailored to the many difficulties that must be overcome. These difficulties may be grouped around the three separate markets involved.

Selling (Onion) Market

1. Competitive Structure. A preliminary inquiry that seems much more theoretical than real has often been suggested. If the onion market is competitively structured in a puristic sense, there is no need to be concerned about reciprocity. Any supplier can sell its total output and is indifferent as to the indentity of its customers. This qualification does not seem to be of any real importance. It may be more realistic to imagine that the market may be one of chronic shortage, with various sales-rationing devices, so that again there is no concern that any seller would benefit from adding buying power to its array of sales blandishments. Probably few markets are predictably of such long-run undercapacity that this qualification will obviate any concern. Even if such markets might appear, there is a corresponding risk that buyers might engage in reciprocal transactions by selling to the merged firm at low prices designed to disguise premium payments for scarce goods.

2. Merged Firm's Share. The Consolidated Foods opinion suggests concern with the fact that Gentry was second in the market, with a large share, and perhaps even with the fact that the market was apparently an effective duopoly. Nonetheless, the Merger Guidelines do not suggest any concern at all with the selling firm's market share, although they may leave the way open to avoid condemning acquisition of a very small seller by permitting an exception for cases of special circumstances that make reciprocal buying a remote possibility. Small market shares might well be taken into account, however, both because they reduce the danger of significantly foreclosing other onion-garlic sellers and because they suggest the possibility that desirable expansion may occur in a concentrated market.

3. Other Supplying Firms' Clout. If other onion-garlic sellers are also important customers of the food processors, Consolidated's acquisition of Gentry may have no impact, or may even offset reciprocity pressures that had previously favored Gentry's competitors. The Guidelines require that the merging firm, as buyer from the intermediate market, be a substantial buyer and a more substantial buyer than other firms selling onion and garlic. They do not specify whether concern should focus on the identity of the

338 / Antitrust and the Conglomerate Firm

products purchased from the food processors. If Consolidated purchases onion soup and other onion-garlic suppliers purchase garlic bread, there is at least room to inquire which set of purchases represents greater purchasing power over the processors. The complexity of such an inquiry hardly needs comment. At the same time, to ignore it is to disregard a potentially vital circumstance.

4. Intermediate Firm Purchases. The Guidelines require that the food processors purchase approximately 15 percent or more of the onion-garlic sales. The requirement corresponds to the notion that if their purchases are an insignificant portion of all onion-garlic sales, foreclosure of these sales opportunities is not apt to have a serious impact on other onion-garlic suppliers. At the same time, it ignores the real danger that there may be adverse impacts on the food processing market. It is quite conceivable that food processors will become so locked into reciprocity arrangements with onion-garlic suppliers that a firm that seeks to enter the food processing industry may find it difficult to obtain an adequate supply of onion and garlic. This possibility may warrant concern only if it can be shown that there are probable difficulties in access to onion and garlic supplies, but it cannot be dismissed out of hand.

5. Product Characteristics. Many products simply are not likely candidates for reciprocity effect. In *U.S.* v. *International Tel. & Tel. Corp.,* for instance, it was found that ITT's acquisition of Canteen would not threaten reciprocity effects in the market for food supply services, since adequate service is so important to employee morale that customers are not likely to be swayed by reciprocity.[63] Similar findings were made in the ITT/Grinnell opinion. Factors of this sort cannot be resolved by presumptions. At most, any presumptive rules would have to be conditioned on showing that the products involved are in fact plausible candidates for reciprocity effects.

Intermediate Market (Food Processing)

In theory, it is possible to identify several inquiries that might be addressed to the character of the intermediate market caught in the middle of the reciprocity effect. None of them seems of sufficient importance to be included in actual litigation or any presumptive rules.

If the intermediate market is fully competitive, firms in it will be indifferent to any particular sales opportunity and immune from reciprocity buying pressure.

If every firm in the intermediate market makes substantial purchases in the supplying market of the merged firms, there may be little danger that any firm in the intermediate market will be foreclosed from selling to the buying market of the merged firms. The opportunity to indulge such self-protection, however, may simply exacerbate the effects of reciprocity in the supply market.

The danger that the buying half of the merged firm may acquire an advantage over its own competitors is reduced if they, too, have substantial buying power over their common suppliers. Thus, if food distribution firms that compete with Consolidated have similar levels of buying power, there may be no special risk that suppliers will become locked into reciprocal patterns that favor Consolidated in times of short supply.

None of these qualifications seems of substantial importance. All may properly be ignored.

Buying Market (Wholesale Food Distribution)

1. Buying Power. Absent special circumstances, it seems fair to require at a minimum that the merging firms make substantial purchases in the intermediate market. The Guidelines adopt this measure, without adding any market share requirement. This test clearly rests on concern that competing sellers of onion and garlic can be foreclosed from sales to food processors by virtue of Consolidated's substantial purchases, without regard to the share of the processed food market represented by Consolidated's purchases. In *Allis-Chalmers/White Consolidated,* the court of appeals rested a preliminary injunction on the ground that the combined firm would purchase 0.25 percent of the country's steel sales, since this was a larger purchasing volume than any other seller of rolling-mill equipment. Although this small share suggests an exaggerated concern with ephemeral possibilities, it is not possible to declare flatly that reciprocity pressure was impossible. On the other hand, it is more important to recognize that either a dollar volume or a market share approach can disguise the fact that a substantial purchaser may be more dependent on its sellers than they are on it. Presumptions simply cannot bridge the gap between quantity of purchases and actual buying power.

2. Existing Relationships. The Guidelines do not ask what portion of onion-garlic sales goes to firms that actually deal with Consolidated, but only what portion goes to firms that sell in markets in which Consolidated is a substantial buyer. This approach reflects an astonishing reliance on the possibility of reciprocity effect unrequited—the notion that food processors will continue to shift substantial purchases to Gentry in hopes that Consolidated will start buying from them. This approach has been pushed by the government even to the point of arguing in *ITT/Grinnell* that ITT buys from industries that spend a great deal on plant expansion and that thus are likely customers for fire protection gear. The district court rejected this claim on the ground that ITT purchased from only a small percentage of the companies in those industries, and that its purchases were only an infinitesimal share of total sales in those industries. The underlying theory that any firm can have so much reciprocity power that many suppliers will curry its favor by self-induced purchases, over any sustained period of time, is too strained to be credited. This part of the presumptive approach clearly needs to be modified.

3. **Unused Power.** Logically, to be concerned that the merger will cause Consolidated to use such buying power as it has to foster reciprocal sales, it should be shown that its buying power was not fully used at the time of the merger or was used in ways that were likely to be less profitable than reciprocity. There is no apparent way to account for this problem in a presumption. For that matter, there is no apparent prospect of litigating this matter intelligently on a case-by-case basis. If reciprocity theory is to be used at all, it must disregard this qualification.

Skip Reciprocity

In the Ingersoll-Rand case, the district court was worried that Ingersoll-Rand would be able to increase sales of underground coal mining equipment to coal companies, because steel companies selling steel to Ingersoll-Rand would make it known that they preferred to purchase coal from Ingersoll customers. Clearly, presumptions cannot grapple with the prospect of adding yet another market to the structure and predicting at the time of merger that reciprocity effects may be extended this far. There is good cause to wonder whether any individual case will ever present facts so clear as to support this theory even on a very specific basis.

Summary

The conditions that may conduce to undesirable reciprocal dealing are complex. They also may be very rare. If reciprocity theory is not to be abandoned entirely in approaching conglomerate mergers, it should be limited to specific application in individual cases. The attempt of the Merger Guidelines to identify general market conditions that warrant intervention requires simplification or disregard of too many factors to be workable.

SIZE AND SIMILAR PRESUMPTIONS

Various theories may be found to attack conglomerate mergers on grounds that rest primarily on the sheer size of the firms involved. Some of these theories include elements of economic reasoning. The most direct theory goes to size alone. Presumptions might be supported by many of these theories. Some of the possibilities are set out below.

Multimarket Confrontation

An argument that has received considerable attention is that conglomerate mergers accelerate the process by which large firms come to confront each other in a wide variety of unrelated markets. It is then argued that such multimarket confrontation may induce an attitude of mutual forbearance, so that firms that otherwise would compete more vigorously in one market refrain from competition in hopes of forestalling competitive response in another market. As an abstract matter, this argument is subject to compelling objections. It depends initially on the existence of unexploited advantages and vulnerabilities in different oligopoly markets. In addition, it may assume a complex calculation that compares the effects of competitive moves not only in the market immediately concerned but also on individual rivals who may be able to retaliate in other markets by exploiting advantages or simply ruining oligopoly benefits for everyone.[64] Such objections may make too much of supposed rationality. The calculus of oligopoly behavior may rest more than anything else on fear of competition and the perception of competitiveness. The etiquette of oligopoly might cause multimarket firms to fear acquiring a competitive reputation that could cause misinterpretation of their noncompetitive moves in many markets. As more and more conglomerates come to face each other in an ever-expanding array of oligopoly markets, the working of many markets could indeed suffer.

To recognize the possible impact of multimarket confrontation is not to propose any specific rule. Presumptions cast simply on the number of oligopoly markets in which merging firms have substantial positions would invite unduly complex litigation or undue simplification. At the same time, the fear of such confrontation may lend support to alternative presumptions that rest simply on firm size.

Almost Horizontal Mergers

Professors Areeda and Turner have suggested that special rules might be adopted for mergers involving products that compete directly for some uses but cannot be found to comprise a single market.[65] The presumption they propose is essentially a substantial elevation of the market share and structure presumptions that are applied to horizontal mergers, recognizing that similar dangers exist but are considerably attenuated. They express doubt whether even this limited presumption is appropriate, in light of the risk that it would reach too far if economic evidence were excluded and would achieve little if economic evidence were admitted. The proposal is reasonable, and so are the doubts. As compared to present law, moreover, the effect of adopting the presumption is more likely to be permissive than restrictive. As matters now stand, there is a real possibility that such mergers will be treated as if they were straightforward horizontal transactions to be tested as such.

Cumulative Effects

Large conglomerate acquisitions may involve a variety of horizontal, vertical, product-extension, market-extension, and pure conglomerate effects. Although none of these effects seems of itself to present a probable threat to competition, it may be argued that collectively they add up to a significant probability that some one or more of the many possible dangers will materialize. It seems impossible to translate this argument into any plausible presumption that simply assigns an artificial probability figure to each possible effect and then assigns a cumulative probability that something bad will happen. Once again, this argument does little more than provide some additional support for presumptions resting on firm size.

Potential Entry Squared

An argument closely akin to the cumulative effects argument simply expands on potential-competition theory. Under this approach, it would not be required that any showing be made that a merger eliminates any present prospect of actual entry or edge effects. It is enough that at some time in the future one of the merging firms might come to generate a potential-competition benefit for any concentrated market now occupied by the other. This argument may provide some added support for presumptions resting on firm size alone, although that seems doubtful. It cannot do more than that.

Size Alone

Various statutory proposals have been advanced to adopt merger restrictions based on size alone, or on some drastically simplified combination of size and market concentration. The most important proposals have been reviewed by Professor Brodley.[66] There is no need to reiterate the proposals here, nor the supporting arguments advanced by their proponents. The essential arguments are reflected in much of the prior discussion. Present law has become so entangled with litigation of abstract economic theories that it is helpless. The difficulty of proving economic consequences in individual cases does not belie the reality that adverse economic consequences do ensue from large conglomerate mergers. Beyond these economic losses lie vital social and political concerns that require dispersion of economic power and dilution of private discretion to act free from market constraints. There is much—perhaps everything—to be gained by stemming a tide of conglomeration that is pulled by artificial forces of no economic value.

The arguments against such new statutory rules are equally general. As to matters of economics, they draw both on theory and on the difficulty of translating theory into measurable fact. In theory, conglomerate acquisitions may achieve important economic benefits. In fact, it is difficult either to show that substantial economic benefits are rare or that substantial competitive injuries are frequent. As to matters of social and political policy, these arguments draw from different postulates. There is less trust in the beneficence of government and less fear that we are approaching such vast concentrations of private wealth as to jeopardize individual liberty and freedom of choice.

Choice between these arguments calls for an act of judgment in an area that permits no clear demonstration of fact or theory. One judgment may be offered with some confidence. New presumptions cannot be justified solely in terms of economic theory or data. A second judgment is offered with more diffidence. Presumptions that are drawn in economic terms but justified in noneconomic terms seem likely to give the most confused and least satisfactory of all possible worlds. A third judgment is offered with great hesitation. The case has not yet been made for venturing beyond economic theory to condemn very large acquisitions solely on grounds of size. We should not hasten to adopt new legislation to protect against the fanciful prospect of a merger between Exxon and General Motors, even on the unlikely supposition that present law really could not discover adequate grounds to prevent it.

NOTES

1. See United States v. El Paso Natural Gas Co., 376 U.S. 651 (1964).
2. Compare Sterling Drug, Inc., 1972, FTC Dkt. 8797, CCH FTC ¶19, 961.
3. 378 U.S. 441 (1964).
4. Broadcast Music, Inc. v. Columbia Broadcasting System, Inc., 1979 99 S. Ct. 1551, 1556, 1557.
5. 415 U.S. 486 (1974).
6. United States v. E. I. du Pont de Nemours & Co., 353 U.S. 586, 597 (1957).
7. United States v. El Paso Natural Gas Co., 376 U.S. 651 (1964).
8. 378 U.S. 158 (1964).
9. 1979, FTC Dkt. 9028, CCH FTC ¶21,623.
10. 378 U.S. 158 (1964); 386 U.S. 568 (1967); 405 U.S. 562 (1972).
11. 410 U.S. 526, 537-38.
12. 418 U.S. 602 (1974).
13. See Budd Co., 1975 FTC Dkt. 8848, CCH FTC ¶20,998.
14. C.D. Cal. 1973, 367 F. Supp. 1226, *aff'd per curiam* 418 U.S. 906 (1974).
15. 1975, FTC Dkt. 8955, CCH FTC ¶21,063, vacated 2d Cir. 1977, 557 F.2d 24.
16. 2d Cir. 1974, 498 F.2d 851, *certiorari* denied 419 U.S. 883.
17. SKF Indus., Inc., 1979, FTC Dkt. 9046, CCH FTC ¶21,595.
18. 418 U.S. 602 (1974).
19. C.D. Cal. 1976, 415 F. Supp. 637.
20. D. Md. 1976, 430 F. Supp. 739.
21. E.D. Pa. 1978, 455 F. Supp. 108, 142.
22. 10th Cir. 1972, 467 F.2d 67, *certiorari* denied 416 U.S. 909.
23. General Mills, Inc., 1973, FTC Dkt. 8836, CCH FTC ¶20,457.
24. E.D. Va., 1976-2 Trade Cases ¶61,144, affirmed 4th Cir. 1977, 549 F.2d 289.
25. 1974, FTC Dkt. 8835, CCH FTC ¶20,611.
26. See the Fourth Circuit Decision in the Arco case, and the Black & Decker Opinion.
27. 1971, FTC Dkt. 8760, CCH FTC ¶19,646, enforced 2d Cir. 1972, 469 F.2d 498, *certiorari* denied 412 U.S. 928.
28. 1970, FTC Dkt. 8739, CCH FTC ¶19,288, vacated, 6th Cir. 1971, 450 F.2d 534.
29. See Allis-Chalmers Mfg. Co. v. White Consolidated Inds., D. Del. 1969, 294 F. Supp. 1263, reversed on other grounds 3d Cir. 1969, 414 F.2d 506, *certiorari* denied 396 U.S. 1009.
30. Corenco Corp. v. Schiavone & Sons, S.D. N.Y. 1973, 362 F. Supp. 939, affirmed on other grounds, 2d Cir. 1973, 488 F.2d 207.
31. See Harnishfeger Corp. v. Paccar, Inc., E.D. Wis., 1979-2 Trade Cases ¶62,786, affirmed on other grounds by unpublished opinion 7th Cir. 1979, 946 BNA ATRR A-15; Chemetron Corp. v. Crane Co., N.D. Ill., 1977-2 Trade Cases ¶61,717.

32. See Ford Motor Co. v. United States, 405 U.S. 562 (1972).
33. 418 U.S. 602 (1974).
34. See United States v. Hughes Tool Co., C.D. Cal. 1976, 415 F. Supp. 637; United States v. United Virginia Bankshares, Inc., E.D. Va. 1972, 347 F. Supp. 891.
35. 410 U.S. 526, 537–38.
36. *Id.,* n.13.
37. E.D. Pa. 1976, 455 F. Supp. 108, 142.
38. See Arco/Anaconda; United States v. Crowell Collier & Macmillan, Inc., S.D. N.Y. 1973, 361 F. Supp. 983.
39. 386 U.S. 568 (1967).
40. See FTC v. Exxon Corp., D. D.C., 1979-2 Trade Cases ¶62,972.
41. J. Brodley, "Potential Competition Mergers: A Structural Synthesis," 87 *Yale Law Journal* 1 (1977).
42. See Purex v. Procter & Gamble, 9th Cir. 1979, 596 F.2d 881.
43. 3d Cir. 1975, 523 F.2d 262, reversed on other grounds 1977, 429 U.S. 477.
44. 3d. Cir. 1967, 386 F.2d 936.
45. Emhart Corp. v. USM Corp., 1st Cir. 1975, 527 F.2d 177.
46. D.C. Cir. 1962, 309 F.2d 223.
47. C.D. Cal. 1976, 419 F. Supp. 931, reversed 9th Cir. 1979, 596 F.2d 881.
48. 1974, FTC Dkt. 8835, CCH FTC ¶20,611.
49. See *General Mills,* 1973, FTC Dkt. 8836, CCH FTC ¶20,457.
50. D. Conn. 1970, 324 F. Supp. 19.
51. 1972, FTC Dkt. 8814, CCH FTC ¶20,121.
52. 78 *Harvard Law Review* 1313 (1965).
53. S.D. N.Y. 1973, 361 F. Supp. 983.
54. N.D. Ill. 1968, 288 F. Supp. 543.
55. See the Crowell Collier and Macmillan Case and United States v. United Virginia Bankshares, Inc. E.D. Va. 1972, 347 F. Supp. 891.
56. 3d. Cir. 1963, 320 F.2d 509.
57. W.D. N.C. 1970, 313 F. Supp. 632.
58. 380 U.S. 592 (1965).
59. S.D. N.Y. 1966, 258 F. Supp. 36.
60. 3d Cir. 1963, 320 F.2d 509.
61. 3d Cir. 1969, 414 F.2d 506, *certiorari* denied 396 U.S. 1009.
62. The doubting cases are reflected in Carrier Corp. v. United Technologies Corp., N.D. N.Y. 1978-2 Trade Cases ¶62,393, affirmed 2d Cir., 1978-2 Trade Cases ¶62,405.
63. N.D. Ill. 1971 Trade Cases ¶73,619.
64. See Areeda and Turner, "Conglomerate Mergers: Extended Interdependence and Effects on Interindustry Competition as Grounds for Condemnation," 127 *University of Pennsylvania Law Review* 1082 (1979).
65. Note 64 *supra,* pp. 1082, 1091–1103.
66. J. Brodley, "Limiting Conglomerate Mergers: The Need for Legislation," 40 *Ohio State Law Journal* 867 (1979).

PART V

Summary and
Synthesis

Remarks

Betty Bock

Those who seek to influence or implement public policy on competition have, I think, better things to do than to focus on "conglomerate" corporations. It is, after all, difficult, if not impossible, to recognize a "conglomerate" in any categorical sense. The fact is that unlike Gaul, neither all corporations nor all acquisitions are divided up into three species: horizontal, vertical, and conglomerate. In real, as distinct from textbook or political life, the three classes overlap. And if one tries to capsulize a "conglomerate" concept into a size and/or degree of diversification formula, one finds that definitions that focus on size, as such, net in all corporations above whatever cut-off is selected and those that focus on degree of diversification net in virtually every large corporation. Nor do more complex definitions yield appreciably more significant results, although they can, of course, shift the number of perceivable conglomerates.[1] If, for example, Mobil Oil or Litton Industries is a "conglomerate," why not General Electric or the University of Florida?

This is not persiflage but, rather, an attempt to examine the foundations of one of the most popular images in today's industrial

The analysis presented here represents the work of the author; conclusions are not necessarily those of any organization with which she is associated.

organization vocabulary. For despite the antibigness or anticonglomerate syndromes of S. 600, S. 1246, and April 17, 1980, it is not clear whether those responsible for such current antibigness proposals are concerned with down-scaling real industrial mountains to "human" size or whether they are concerned with more pervasive measures for restructuring an unrealistically perceived industrial globe that includes the ground on which they stand.

To achieve modest clarity, we should, I think, restrict our view to real industrial mountains and acknowledge that all mountains merge with valleys. We should also acknowledge that mountains and low places alike have emerged and have been carved out over geologic time, and although we can speed up that time by anticonglomerate legislation and/or enforcement fiat, we can do this on a grand scale only at the risk of destroying our economic market system and our ways of life.

Let us begin by looking at a few numbers that suggest the shape of the terrain, then try to view the "conglomerate" environment apart from such numbers and, finally, attempt to integrate numerical and nonnumerical views in ways that suggest public policy alternatives.

SOME NUMBERS

Today's fear of corporate bigness rests on a series of assumptions that can be subsumed in the single theory that excessive size— and possibly excessive product and/or geographic spread—give a company, or set of companies, undue power to operate in ways that can do irreparable harm to public welfare. This is so, runs the theory, because excessively large and diversified corporations can avoid responsiveness to legitimate government and public requirements and at the same time exert undue pressures on political and nonpolitical institutions, at the expense of economic and social democracy.

It is not possible here to examine the full range of assumptions underlying this fear, but it is possible to consider two major numerical premises. (How true or how false the premises are depends on how the numbers are derived and how they are perceived.)

Changes among the Largest

First, fear that "conglomerates" will undermine, if not destroy, economic and social democracy depends in part on an assumption that today's largest corporations have been the largest over long periods of time and have been able to fortify their "dominance" at the expense of present and future smaller enterprises. The numbers do not seem to bear this out.

Numbers and Cut-offs. In 1947, the sales of the 50th, 100th, and 200th largest manufacturing corporations were $306.2 million, $188.7 million, and $89.3 million, respectively. By 1977, there were 517 manufacturing corporations with sales larger than the 50th largest of 1947; 687 with sales larger than the 100th largest of 1947; and approximately a thousand with sales larger than the 200th largest of 1947. If the 1947 figures are raised to eliminate the effects of inflation, there would still be in the range of 250 corporations in 1977 with sales greater than those of the 50th largest of 1947; in the range of 475 with sales greater than the 100th largest of 1947; and approximately 575 with sales greater than the 200th largest of 1947.[2]

Turnover of the Largest. Furthermore, the 50, 100, and 200 largest manufacturing corporations, however identified, are not identical in any two years—and the longer the time period, the greater the turnover. For example, by 1977, 19 of the 50 largest manufacturing corporations in sales in 1947 had been replaced by 19 others; 43 of the 100 largest had been replaced; and 85 of the 200 largest.

These figures produced turnover rates for the largest manufacturing corporations in terms of sales in 1977 of 38 percent for the 50 largest; 43 percent for the 100 largest; and 42 percent for the 200 largest.[3]

Differences among the Largest. Moreover, the 50, 100, and 200 largest manufacturing corporations have never been an undifferentiated set. Some of the entrants into the various size classes represent true increases in corporate size and rank and cause true displacement of other companies at the bottom of the sets; other entrants represent technical or merely semantic shifts. For example, some of the corporations among the 200 largest in assets in 1977 simply became members of this company because their product and service mix changed enough to move them from a nonmanufacturing to a manufacturing classification. Others moved from nonregistered to registered or from foreign to domestic ownership status. Such technical or semantic shifts do not denote real growth in corporate power at the top but are simply changes in the composition of the enterprises in the largest size classes.[4]

Growth and Acquisitions by Conglomerates

Second, fear that "conglomerates" will undermine, if not destroy, economic and social democracy also depends on published accounts of acquisitions that emphasize a new breed of corporation whose product lines are not substitutes or inputs or outputs for each other but are instead diversified in ways whose rationale is not clearly or simply apparent.

The fact is, however, that a "conglomerate" can be recognized only against a product, geographic, and time background. And what will be perceived depends upon how the background is composed and how it changes, as well as on the method of identifying the conditions under which a corporation will be considered a "conglomerate."

While any definition of a conglomerate is artificial, I propose the following, because it can be used in connection with data on the largest corporations available from standardized lists, such as the *Fortune* 500 largest list, and from standard compilations of large-scale acquisitions.[5] I propose for operational purposes to focus on what may be called "conglomerates based primarily in manufacturing." These will be corporations that were members of the 200 largest manufacturing corporations in total assets in 1977 and which, on the basis of published data, appeared to have been engaged in that year in five or more 2-digit major industry groups or ten or more 3-digit industry groups *and* appeared to have owed at least one-fifth of their 1977 assets to acquisitions of $10 million or more in assets over the 1968–1977 period.[6] Defined in this way, there were 45 "conglomerate" corporations and 155 other corporations among the 200 largest primarily manufacturing corporations in terms of total assets in 1977. (Other definitions would, of course, yield other numbers.) Using the above definition, we can ask how the 45 "conglomerates" compare with the 155 other large corporations in their over-all effects on changes in aggregate concentration and in the degree to which their major acquisitions affected changes in aggregate concentration in the 1947–1977 period.

Conglomerates and Changes in Aggregate Concentration. During the 1947–1954 period, the "conglomerates" of 1977 accounted for 13 percent of the average annual change in the share of total manufacturing assets attributable to all 200 largest manufacturing corporations; for 16 percent of such change in the 1954–1963 period; and for 60 percent in the 1963–1972 period; but they accounted for only 6 percent of such change in the 1972–1977 period.[7]

Major Acquisitions by "Conglomerates." Moreover, the assets involved in large acquisitions (of units of $10 million or more in assets) by "conglomerates" were small in relation to the annualized increase in assets of the 200 largest corporations engaged primarily in manufacturing in 1977: .27 of 1 percent in the 1947–1954 period; .42 of 1 percent in the 1954–1963 period; .73 of 1 percent in the 1963–1972 period; and .65 of 1 percent in the 1972–1977 period.[8]

These relatively simple results suggest that far from witnessing an agglomeration of corporate power at the top of any size scale through conglomeration, we have been going through a period of explosion of corporations above standard dollar cut-offs; substantial turnover among the largest corporations; and modest and declining growth by "conglomerates," whether through internal investment or large-scale acquisitions.

BEYOND NUMBERS

The preceding numbers suggest that in examining conglomerates, we have tended to focus on unduly short spans of time and have been unduly concerned with the difficulties of penetrating the meaning of the corporate logo. In the past, we believed we knew what Standard Oil of New Jersey, Otis Elevator, or Paramount Pictures did; but it is more difficult to comprehend the undertakings of an Exxon, a United Technologies, or a Gulf & Western. It is also more difficult to understand the operations of a modern university, a labor union, a federal executive or administrative agency, or a congressional committee.

Furthermore, while acquisitions can, of course, wipe out viable corporations whose managements are opposed to being taken over, they also are a way of infusing financial support and management know-how into weak firms and/or parts of firms, and, in the process, creating markets for companies that are not—or should not be—substantially different from markets for commodities, components, or finished products or services.

Markets for Companies

No major corporation can afford to be simplemindedly acquisition-minded for long. Indeed, large corporations have strong incentives to slough off what they perceive as low rate-of-return operations and to replace them with operations that appear likely to yield higher rates of return. Meanwhile, those who buy the divested assets perceive the potential returns for their own operations differently from the sellers. And this, of course, is what makes a market. (Consider, for example, Colgate-Palmolive's projected "house-cleaning" of previously acquired assets, as reported in the *New York Times* of April 12, 1980.)[9]

There is, I think, a clear need for a long-range view of markets for going companies—and parts of companies. While many small- and medium-sized firms will continue to contribute to private and public demand through their own independent management efforts, others will seek to be acquired. Meanwhile, still other corporations will want to restructure their operating investments through divestiture and acquisition. To permit such options, there must be a market for viable assets, not simply a plant, but a business; not simply a trademark, but a service organization. And such markets should be both broad and deep, in order to maximize the alternatives open to would-be sellers and buyers.

If markets for going concerns, or subunits of companies, are eliminated or circumscribed, the constraints will operate no differently from practices currently prohibited under the antitrust laws. Indeed, regardless of whether constraints on size or diversification are directly imposed by Congress or interpreted into the law by antitrust enforcement agencies, private plaintiffs, and the courts, they will amount to direct control of entry (and exit) and allocation of markets, as well as to indirect control of prices for companies. And this, of course, will be equivalent to monopolization or agreements to restrain trade.

Scale and Cost

It follows that there is a clear and present need to rethink the conditions under which we want to sanction freedom to restructure enterprises through open markets. The reasoning behind the emerging literature on the Experience Curve is highly suggestive on this question. The theorem behind the Experience Curve concept is not new, but the current formulation, as developed by The Boston Consulting Group (BCG), gives a more technical format to an older vocabulary.[10] The curve is designed to mirror the relation between volume of production and cost of producing given "products" and is based on what is said to be a wide range of experience that shows that for every doubling of output, a company can expect to lower its cost by 20–30 percent. A failure to reduce costs to this extent is, say the curve's proponents, a sign that the market has not been properly defined or that appropriate investment has not been made. (It could also be a sign of a market that cannot be expanded or of discontinuities in materials, machine operations, or distribution processes.)

It follows that in the early stage of development of an appropriately selected and defined market, there will be room for not more than three major producers and that the first, if it continues to invest and price to maximize its market share, will always have lower costs and larger sales volumes than its followers. The difference between the costs of different companies operating in the same market at the same time will be a function of the differences in their start-up times and in their investments mix. In the end, if the No. 1 company continues to invest and price in order to try to achieve successive doublings in volume, there can only be one company in any given market. And competition will be competition for different niches or submarkets within a more generalized market.

As time goes on, it will, of course, take longer and longer for a company to double its volume and eventually, instead of seeking such doubling, it will try to diversify by working its way into submarkets within its former market or into new markets. This constitutes a technical—rather than a power—oriented view of diversification or conglomeration.

POLICY IMPLICATIONS

The implications of this analysis cannot avoid disturbing those who adhere to hard-line structuralist principles. While, therefore, it cannot satisfy those who are seriously opposed to "conglomeration," however defined, it does imply three things for those who understand that complexity and change over time are distinctive characteristics of the modern world.

First, the individual "conglomerate," like the Cheshire cat's grin, will be a continuously vanishing phenomenon. "Conglomerates" will be seen as a shifting set of corporations with changing products and services, moving at different speeds along different and variously related Experience Curves. Competition then becomes competition in differentiated, rather than homogeneous products, selling at prices as low as volume permits. If prices are not so set, a market will in time attract new competitors.

Second, "conglomerate" acquisitions will no longer be feared, as such. Markets for going assets, whether entire firms or parts of firms, will be seen as being as necessary to a private/public enterprise system as markets for materials, components, and finished products and services.

Third, it will be more widely understood that economic as well as social change is marked by innovation, risk, and mistakes, as well as successes. And such innovation and risk, in turn, will generate short-run "monopolization" in narrowly defined market segments, sell-offs as well as purchases of going assets, and trade-offs among alternative forms of internal and external corporate investment.

Unsolved policy problems will, of course, remain in generous measure. Worth noting, for example, is the problem of the unwanted tender offer for a strong but small firm, perhaps a No. 1 firm that has created a market niche for itself and has moved so far along its own Experience Curve that it does not pay for potential competitors to enter the identical market. Also worth noting is the problem of whether there is danger in permitting individual firms to engage in unrestrained niching, or whether external limits should be imposed.

And so we come up against the question of whether we want to live primarily by specific rule or by case examination within broad-gauge criteria. Rules will, of course, force some error, while case study will force some uncertainty. Whatever mix of rule and case analysis we adopt, the most significant thing we can learn from the numbers and analysis presented here is that we can scare ourselves into economic rigidity if we continue to believe that conglomeration runs high, that it is increasing substantially through large-scale acquisitions, or that conglomerate acquisitions are never dissipated by competition and/or by divestiture.

If we want to maintain a flexible enterprise economy, we must recognize that both conceptual and factual considerations require that we focus less on "conglomeration," as such, and more on what we want from our major private institutions. Indeed, if we in the United States do not accept "conglomeration," or corporate growth and diversification, as progressive events at this stage in economic time, other countries will—and do.

We, therefore, have a choice concerning whether we want to view competition as an unendingly simplified series of transactions among nationally contained small firms, each of which is responsible for only a single output, *or* whether we want to renew our understanding of antitrust theory in ways appropriate to large, flexible, multicategory firms operating in a changing world order—or disorder.

NOTES

1. In 1972, this author wrote the following concerning identification of conglomerates and analysis of their effects. What was written then, in the early 1970s, is, in her view, as germane in 1980 as it was then.

   The literature on conglomerates is so large and diversified that it has become impossible to focus steadily on any one species, let alone to gaze on the genus whole. Indeed, although there are numerous verbal codes designed to make identification of conglomerates seem simple, corporate organization is not. Nor is published information concerning the internal operations of major business organizations sufficiently clear and specific to lend more than a semantic glaze to corporate classification games.

   The word "conglomerate" appears at least as early as 1941 in TNEC Monograph No. 27, where it denotes mergers that are neither horizontal nor vertical. This residual function was carried over into the 1948, 1955 and 1969 merger reports of the Federal Trade Commission, although the term itself was divided by three in the Commission's 1963 decision in *Procter & Gamble* to cover "product-extension," "market-extension," and "pure" conglomerate mergers.

   As the years have gone by the term has increasingly been used either in its single or multiple form to refer not only to the relations between an acquiring and an acquired company, but to any diversified form of business organization, as such. But there is a root difficulty in the use of the term because virtually all large enterprises are composed of multiple units which can collectively present horizontal, vertical and conglomerate aspects. Furthermore, a substantial number of the major acquisitions by major corporations can be classified in at least two—if not all three—categories.

   With its present broad residual meaning and with present problems of identification of conglomerates, it is not surprising that by the late 1960s there was sustained controversy as to whether the conglomerate form of organization menaced the future of competition or whether it represented a competitive adjustment to complex technologies and the rising needs of an expanding population. Indeed, differences in analysis have fed on disagreement based on lack of clear understanding of how and why conglomerates appear; how they grow, function, and perhaps die; and, therefore, how they are likely to affect the future of competition." (B. Bock, "The Conglomerate and the Hippogriff: An Inquiry into Some Contested Issues" *The Conference Board Record* (February 1972.))

2. See B. Bock, J. Farkas, and D. S. Weinberger, "Aggregate Concentration—How Big Are the Biggest Companies: Concepts, Numbers, and Perceptions," *Information Bulletin No. 57, The Conference Board* 11 (1979).
3. Note 2 *supra*, p. 7, Table 3a.
4. See B. Bock and J. Farkas "Statistical Games: 2, Relative Growth of the 'Largest' Manufacturing Corporations, 1947-1971—Subsets from an Unknown Set," *Conference Board Report No. 583, The Conference Board* 29-34 (1973).

5. There are no authoritative lists of the largest corporations, however defined. The most complete lists of the largest *manufacturing* corporations known to this author are the *Fortune* lists of the 500 and second 500 largest industrials in terms of sales, published since 1954. (See, for example, "The Fortune Directory of the 500 Largest U.S. Industrial Corporations," *Fortune* (May 8, 1978.)) A roughly equivalent list for 1947 can be put together by using a Federal Trade Commission list of the 1,000 largest manufacturing corporations in total assets in 1948—and backdating to 1947. See Federal Trade Commission, "A List of 1,000 Large Manufacturing Companies, Their Subsidiaries and Affiliates, 1948" (June 1951).

6. See J. F. Weston and S. K. Mansinghka, "Tests of the Efficiency Performance of Conglomerate Firms," 26 *The Journal of Finance* (1971). The Weston and Mansinghka definition of a conglomerate—and the one used here—does not depend on the identification of conglomerate acquisitions, but it is a definition of a diversified company, which has grown in significant part through acquisitions of assets of $10 million and over.

   As Professor Weston has indicated to this author, the definition is intuitively reasonable and seems to select the companies most people think of as conglomerates, but it is not the only possible definition. And it is evident that with different definitions, one would identify different corporations as conglomerates.

7. Bock, Farkas, and Weinberger, note 2 *supra*, p. 10, Table 5.

8. Bock, Farkas, and Weinberger, note 2 *supra*, p. 10, Table 6b.

9. The Colgate-Palmolive Co. announced in April 1980 that it planned to streamline its operations "by extricating itself from several lines of business. . . ." The company was said to be acknowledging that various unrelated categories of its business were weakening its overall effectiveness. It had put Helena Rubenstein on the block in 1979—with no takers—and was planning by April 1980 to discontinue its operations and divest itself of, among other things, Hebrew National Kosher Foods, Inc., acquired with Riviana Foods in 1978; Leach Industries, a racquetball racquets manufacturer, acquired in 1977; the Ram Golf Corporation; and a number of other businesses, including a $10 million olive and pepper company; eighty-eight Lum's and Ranch House restaurants in Georgia, Texas, and southern Florida; five sports equipment companies based in Britain; and various other holdings. (The *New York Times,* 12 April 1980, p. 31.)

10. See, for example, the following *Perspectives* by Bruce D. Henderson, President of The Boston Consulting Group: "The Experience Curve—Reviewed: I. The Concept," No. 124; "The Experience Curve—Reviewed: II. History," No. 125; "The Experience Curve—Reviewed: III. Why Does It Work?," No. 128; "The Experience Curve—Reviewed: IV. The Growth Share Matrix or The Product Portfolio," No. 135; "Cross Sectional Experience Curves," No. 208; and "The Experience Curve Revisited," No. 229. For a brief critique of the Experience Curve concept, see M. A. Adelman, "Comments on Antitrust Policy and the Experience Curve Model," in "Shifting Boundaries Between Regulation and Competition: Criteria for an Enterprise System," *Information Bulletin, The Conference Board* (1980).

Remarks

Theodore F. Craver

I am not here as an economist in the academic sense. I am here as an antitrust lawyer and as a lay economist. As a lay economist, I have had some difficulty in understanding the meaning of some of the terms of art of the academic economists I have heard here in the last day and a half, in the context in which they have been used. But I believe I have had no trouble understanding the concepts I have been hearing here, for as an antitrust lawyer I have dealt over the past 24 years with the economic-antitrust issues I have heard discussed here.

At the outset, I must note that I personally do not like the term "conglomerate." To me, it means nothing. It is like a glob. I prefer the term "diversified company," or "multi-product company," or "multiproduct, multinational company," if the company is diversified abroad.

In any event, we have not heard papers on the subject of highly-diversified or multiproduct companies, describing such companies and discussing the good and bad points of such companies. All of the papers I have heard have dealt with conglomerate acquisitions. Since this has been the case, I shall address myself to the issues presented by the papers.

Two issues concerning conglomerate acquisition have emerged here: (1) what are the reasons for conglomerate mergers? and (2) are conglomerate mergers good or bad? On both of these issues, my background may give me some basis for discussion. In the Antitrust Division I considered mergers from the government's viewpoint as an enforcer of the antitrust laws. In private practice and in corporate practice, I have considered mergers from the standpoint of the companies making them. The government experience was focused on arguments against mergers, and the private and corporate practice was focused on reasons for making mergers, as well as on ways of reconciling the legal arguments raised against mergers with the legitimate business reasons for making them.

The history of the growth of Litton may shed some light on the issues that have been raised in the last day and a half. For I perceive Litton as being very typical of corporations today. Litton, as I am sure you all know, is a highly diversified, multinational corporation. There are no large single-product, single-market companies left in our economy today. The only single-product, single-market companies today are, essentially, small businesses; and in the aggregate, these companies account for a relatively small part of our business economy and are too small to exert a leading influence. For various reasons, the large single product, single market companies have disappeared. Thus, today for all intents and purposes, our economy is made up of conglomerate companies, as the program labels them.

The clearest impression I carry away from this meeting is that the surface of conglomerates and conglomerate acquisitions has just been scratched. Much needs to be done in the way of further study. Most of the comments of the speakers I have heard go off on the wrong track. Those are the comments that discuss and advocate rules against conglomerate mergers. Those comments assume something is wrong with conglomerate mergers, but no one has come up with hard, documented evidence to prove this.

During the last day and a half, we have heard that conglomerate mergers are bad because they lead to greater concentration of assets in the hands of fewer entities, because they lead to undue concentration of political power, because they produce anticompetitive consequences in markets.

The study on political influence came up with nothing indicating that conglomerate acquisitions actually result in the conglomerate companies wielding undue political power. In any event, the whole study, I believe, has been superceded by Congress.

Congress studied the question of corporate political power at great length and concluded, in passing the bill allowing companies to set up political action committees, that corporations may make political contributions to candidates for Congress, subject to certain limitations and record keeping and reporting requirements. In passing the corporate Political Action Committee legislation, Congress clearly mandated that capital, represented by corporations, as well as labor, is now entitled to exercise political power. In fact, the Political Action Committee legislation was passed to help give capital a political influence more equal to the influence that labor, through its political action groups, had exercised for so many years before. So, I believe the entire discussion of political influence of conglomerate corporations has been resolved by Congress in deliberate action.

The study of concentration also has come up with nothing concrete. Some papers presented have suggested that certain statistics superficially indicate that there has been a small increase in concentration due to conglomerate acquisition, but other papers have shown that those statistics are flawed and that other statistics show there has been no increase in concentration due to conglomerate acquisitions. There, my colleague Betty Bock has achieved national recognition as an expert on the subject of conglomerate mergers as related to aggregate concentration in the economy.

On the question of anticompetitive effects of conglomerate acquisitions, this discussion has been very unconvincing. I have heard no study showing any general anticompetitive effects from conglomerate mergers. I have heard some speculation that a conglomerate merger that brings the resources of a larger firm into a smaller firm market could theoretically result in a diminution of competition, but I have heard no evidence that it would or does. On the other hand, the studies presented have shown some beneficial effects of conglomerate mergers, but I have found this discussion woefully weak.

We have heard that conglomerate mergers are made to displace inefficient management, to afford a better allocation of funds across markets, to diversify earnings so as to reduce the effects of cyclical markets, and to prevent bankruptcies, or to rescue companies on the verge of bankruptcy. These papers have focused on only a relatively few beneficial effects. In addition, they have focused mainly on incentives for conglomerate mergers, with benefits appearing to be secondary to the incentives as the reasons for making the acquisitions in the first place.

The discussion of the prevention of bankruptcies as a beneficial effect of conglomerate acquisitions seemed to me to be particularly unconvincing. Business bankruptcies are not a really significant phenomenon in the business economy. Of course, bankruptcies

occur, but they are almost solely limited to small businesses, and
they are highly cyclical, occurring mostly in periods of the business
cycle when money is tight and interest rates rise dramatically. This
is due to the fact that small businesses are especially vulnerable to
tight money and high interest rates. It is true that we have seen a
few examples of large companies facing bankruptcy, such as the
case of Douglas Aircraft a number of years ago and Chrysler
Corporation today. And we are seeing Ford Motor Company today
having serious problems in its North American operations, but its
foreign operations are still showing profits. But the instances of
large corporations facing bankruptcy are so rare that they do not
constitute a meaningful opportunity for a beneficial conglomerate
acquisition. Besides, companies that are facing bankruptcy do not
generally present an attractive candidate for acquisition. Thus, I do
not see preventing bankruptcies as an important beneficial effect of
conglomerate acquisitions.

In my opinion, the examples of beneficial effects of conglomerate
acquisitions we have heard here only scratch the surface. During
the 15 years I have been with Litton, I have had the opportunity to
study many acquisitions. Litton came into existence 26 years ago
when the company's founder and present Chairman of the Board,
Charles B. "Tex" Thornton, purchased for one million dollars a
small manufacturer of specialized vacuum tubes from an individual
named Charles Litton, and the company proceeded to grow from
that beginning by acquisition and internal growth—well over 50
percent internal growth compared to growth by acquisition—into a
diversified, multinational company with annual sales today of well
over 4 billion dollars. I have been with Litton during most of its
period of growth by acquisition. I have reviewed from an antitrust
standpoint most of the major acquisitions the Company has made,
and I have reviewed and recommended against many acquisitions
that the Company has not made. These reviews have necessarily
included economic as well as legal issues, for every acquisition
involves both. These are issues centering around the definition of
the product and geographic market and include actual as well as
potential competition, evolving technology, substitute products,
and elasticity of demand among products. One thing that cannot be
denied is that technology is expanding in quantum leaps, which
means that evolving technology, new products, and elasticity of
demand must be considered in conglomerate mergers. Another
thing that cannot be denied is that competition in our economy is
increasing in quantum leaps, from evolving technology both here
and abroad. My point is that all of these reviews of mergers,

proposed and effected, have shown me that there are many, many more legitimate business reasons for conglomerate acquisitions and beneficial effects than I have heard touched on or suggested here.

In light of the foregoing, I have found the discussion of presumptive rules for judging conglomerate mergers appalling. No firm case has been made against conglomerate acquisitions. The balance of the evidence presented—while only the tip of the iceberg—argues in favor of conglomerate acquisitions. Thus, any suggestion of presumptive rules against conglomerate acquisitions is woefully premature and unfounded.

One argument in favor of presumptive rules against conglomerate acquisitions attempts to draw support from Supreme Court decisions. I don't read the Supreme Court decisions as ever sanctioning rigid rules against acquisitions. The rule of *Brown Shoe* was not rigid in my opinion, for in the footnotes the Court explicitly left room for showing that an acquisition reaching the market shares held unlawful in that case could be shown to be pro-competitive and thus lawful. I don't view the Court's holding in *Von's* to be rigid because of the statement in *Brown Shoe,* which certainly was not overruled in *Von's.*

In the nonacquisition area, I don't view the Supreme Court as sanctioning rigid rules. I don't view the holding in *Schwinn* as being rigid in view of the final order in *White Motor,* and now we have *Continental TV,* which makes clear that *Schwinn* was not decisive. By the same token, the role of *International Salt* against the alleged pernicious effect of tying arrangements was not rigid, as found in the *A. O. Smith* case. Also, I never viewed the merger guidelines of the Antitrust Division as rigid, or even particularly helpful.

This leads, of course, to the conclusion that anything on the order of S. 600, which would put an absolute size limit on corporations, would be only the sheerest of folly and on a par with the imposition of Prohibition in the late 1920's.

I found even the discussion here against presumptive rules against conglomerates substantially unappealing because I heard what I thought was some wavering or uncertainty and what I thought was some sanctioning of rigid court-made rules for judging conglomerate mergers.

In conclusion, I believe much work and analysis needs to be done. I would welcome a more thorough analysis of conglomerate acquisitions because I am convinced the facts, when brought out in the open, will show that conglomerate acquisitions, made in accordance with the law as applied to the realities of the market, are beneficial to competition and the economy.

Remarks

Richard Schmalensee

This discussion of conglomerate mergers has touched on a great many theories. Those who are skeptical might refer to them as stories, but I shall call them theories. Some theories develop the idea that conglomerate mergers enhance efficiency; others, that they can lead to anticompetitive effects. Still other theories find neutral effects of conglomerate acquisitions on competition and efficiency but some other reason for their consummation. Dennis Mueller, for example, has stressed on a number of occasions the notion that managers have a disinclination to cannibalize their firm and will invest internally generated funds themselves even though it might be in the shareholder's interest to pay them as dividends. This sounds abstruse, but hard-headed financial observers have argued that Exxon and other oil companies, with few investment opportunities in their traditional areas and serious political constraints, are investing funds that should be returned to their shareholders, who can invest with fewer constraints. If you take this managerial investment incentive and add some of the tax considerations that we have talked about, you end up consummating mergers that have no great social efficiency implications.

Now the evidence that relates to all these theories or stories is very mixed. We have heard lots of facts: acquired firms tend to be above average in profitability, there tends to be premium over the preannouncement market value paid for the shares of acquired firms, and mergers occur in waves. We heard in the sixties that mergers occurred because stocks were overvalued, and overvalued stocks could be used to acquire other firms. Interestingly, we heard in the seventies that mergers occurred because stocks were undervalued and could be acquired cheaply. We have all these bits of evidence and stories. We have also learned at this symposium that it is very hard to measure the real social efficiency effects of mergers. This makes the evaluation problem very difficult.

Normally, we think of stock market data as very clean for purposes of drawing inferences. But there are a lot of difficulties in using stock market data to measure the effects of mergers. Specifically, there are problems due to changes in firm leverage, tax effects, and impacts on expectations. All these problems make it difficult to examine a typical merger or a collection of mergers and say that there has been a net gain that we can detect somehow. If you go to the data thinking that mergers on average have zero net social effect, you come away from the data with that same thought. It is very hard to reject that preconception on the basis of what we currently know. Similarly, if you go in thinking that the typical merger has a cost to society and that that cost is relatively small, you come away from the data retaining that. If you expect to find a slight gain, you come away from the data unable to reject that null hypothesis. This unsettling state of affairs seems to me to provide implications for both research and policy concerned with conglomerate mergers.

RESEARCH IMPLICATIONS

First, we need to think deeply about measuring the real effects of mergers. To advance knowledge, we simply must have some better measures than we apparently do have. Perhaps we need to give up on the purity of stock market data and go back to trying to purify accounting data. In any case, we need some way to measure the effects of mergers because without that we can only tell stories. Second, we need to rethink the research design of a lot of the papers that have been discussed here. They tend to focus on evaluating *all* mergers. Now, we know that mergers differ in a variety of ways, and we all know there are both good mergers and bad mergers. Of course, it would be nice if we could somehow relate the attributes of mergers or of the merger partners to the effects of mergers. To do that we would have to measure effects and ex ante merger attributes on a case-by-case basis, but there is some possibility that we might learn something.

The implications for economic policy as it relates to economic efficiency are a little bit difficult to draw, since what I have said is basically that we do not know very much. If you thus turn to the theory and the theoretical discussions we have had here, I think you will find it hard to make a case for any sort of overall restriction against mergers. The anticompetitive stories are not terribly strong. It is true that managers probably make some bad merger decisions. But if you prohibit the mergers, the managers may make bad internal investment decisions with the same money. If managers have general proinvestment biases, it is very hard to restrict them in any way likely to produce net social gain. If we knew more about how to sort out mergers, we could say more about the relation of particular types of mergers to economic efficiency, but we do not and cannot. There is no strong theoretical or empirical basis for restricting conglomerate mergers generally in the interests of efficiency. But, as Bill Comanor pointed out very clearly, that is not really the public policy problem. The problem is what we should do about conglomerate mergers not because of their impact on economic efficiency, but because of their potential impact on political democracy.

PUBLIC POLICY TOWARD CONGLOMERATE ACQUISITIONS

Let me now turn to the second thing we have talked about: public policy toward conglomerate acquisitions. This is discussed in the context of antitrust only because of a set of historical accidents including the naming of the policy areas. Somehow competition policy was endowed with a name that implies opposition toward conglomeration of enterprises. If "antitrust" had somehow been called "procompetition," it would be patently peculiar to talk about attacking large firms for their size when we admit that size is not a competitive problem. Just to remark on some of the material we discussed this morning, I think it is slightly bizarre to recognize the weak arguments of possible competitive harm but then to try to extend the law to touch conglomerate acquisitions by pushing those arguments as far as they can go. Given the discussion of how courts decide cases and given the difficulty and tenuous nature of the theoretical analysis, the impact of significantly tightening antitrust policy against conglomerates would be arbitrarily to single out some acquisitions for special treatment. This would prevent some mergers and not others. Such a policy really could not be described as anything other than arbitrary from a competitive or social point of view. One can certainly imagine other arbitrary rules that would have the same net effect on acquisitions but would be cheaper.

The appropriate first task in making intelligent policy in this area is to figure out what, if anything, is a legitimate problem. It seems to be the consensus here that competitive impact is not the problem. I think we need to go beyond invocations of Jefferson to a serious empirical discussion of what it is that people are actually concerned about. Is it size measured by assets, measured by employees, measured (as Bill Comanor suggested) by concentrations of discretionary funds, or something else? I would argue that until it is clear what the issue is, it is very hard to figure out what to do about it. It is, as George Hay reminded us, impossible even to tell whether a problem is getting more or less severe until you can define the problem precisely. I do not think we can define "the conglomerate problem" with any precision at all at this time. If we knew what the problem was, economists would have a role to play in determining a least-cost way of solving it.

After the public policy problem is precisely stated, we can begin to consider specific proposals. But until we articulate the problem, it is rather difficult to discuss any policy proposal in the absence of some notion of what goal it should serve.

Remarks

Peter O. Steiner

I have a sense of déjà vu. For some reason, we have failed to make much progress in evaluating conglomerates. At this symposium there has been a remarkably effective restatement of problems and ambiguities without a great deal of new insight. I will suggest why I think this is the case.

Initially, let me advance several propositions that we can probably all agree upon. If we can, the next conference ought to start there. First, mergers—be they horizontal, vertical, or conglomerate—can occur for a variety of reasons. All are presumably privately beneficial, but not all are socially beneficial. Among those reasons—and I am trying to stress here the heterogeneity of the merger phenomenon—is a search for market power. This search for market power may be in the market of the acquired firm or of the acquiring firm, or it may even be a search for market power in a more distant and subtle third market. Second, there is a possibility that real economies may exist: real economies of integration, real economies of management, real economies of capital formation, real economies of promotion, real economies of diversification, and so on. No doubt there are others, as I do not mean this to be an exhaustive list. Third, there may be pure tax incentives that motivate or add to the attractiveness of particular mergers. Fourth, there may be speculative motivations. Fifth, there may be managerial and other insider considerations or antimanagerial considerations in which the merger is an effective device in the fight for managerial control. And, finally, in this list, there may be a quest for political influence.

I do not think that these potential motives for merger require any proof. Much of what has been said at this symposium seems to be an attempt to prove the possibility of certain situations. But I do not think that we need to prove the possibility that there could be tax incentives for mergers. It seems to me that those possibility theorems are well established.

Having said that, it seems generally clear that the conglomerate merger is unique in some ways and like other mergers in other ways. Fundamentally, however, the problem is still the one of assessing whether a particular merger is motivated by reasons that we judge to be *socially* neutral, beneficial, or adverse. The problem with conglomerate mergers is that the *average* benefits and average costs tend toward equality. Thus, the larger the benefits the larger the costs of any particular merger. In any case, the point I want to make is that while the conglomerate merger is different in character from other mergers, it too is potentially desirable or undesirable. All of this is well established. I have heard it all before; indeed, I have said it all before.

What is my complaint? I have heard these interesting and important propositions rediscovered and rediscussed. It seems to me that what I truly miss is the distinction between the challenge of identifying the adverse benefits and the adverse costs of the average conglomerate merger and the challenge of formulating appropriate public policy that concerns distinguishing the individual from the average. The policy challenge is to recognize that mergers are heterogeneous: they are not all efficient, they are not all tax motivated, they are not all socially adverse, and so on. The problem is to recognize the phenomenon of heterogeneity. We should search for sensible partitions, either in terms of judicial roles, or legislative roles, or ways of thinking about the problem, that permit us to allow the particularly useful, to stop the particularly harmful, and to argue about the neutral and the uncertain.

There is an ideological partition that came out very clearly at this symposium, and I think that it is helpful to state it. Given the fact that there is uncertainty surrounding the effects of any particular merger, some of us (e.g., Joe Brodley and Dennis Mueller) would presume against the merger. In other words, there would be a presumption that the social costs would outweigh the social benefits. The merger would be prevented unless someone provided a persuasive argument to the contrary. In contrast, the other position, which is held by Bill Comanor and Ed Cooper, would reverse the burden of proof. Unless someone finds a convincing probability of some specific harm, the merger should be allowed. Although I subscribe to the latter view, I must admit that these two positions are simply different responses to uncertainty. There is no logical theoretical way of choosing between them.

Beyond these ideological positions, there is a real public policy issue. This concerns the location of the partitions or the equally important question of in what dimensions these partitions ought to be drawn. Since the partitions delineate the permitted and the not permitted, we must recognize their public policy significance. Now, the Kennedy Bill leaves me somewhat uncomfortable. It proceeds from the notion that a useful partition can be made in terms of the size of the acquired firm and the acquiring firm. The problem with that, it seems to me, is that size, whether it be size in assets or in sales or in anything else, is not very helpful. Firm size is positively related to the size of the potential benefits as well as to the size of the potential costs. If you say that this is a problem of identifying mergers of big benefits and little costs, versus little benefits and big costs, I would reply there is not much at stake in a tiny merger, and there is a great deal at stake in a big merger. Merely writing a bill that has to do with size is implicitly reflecting the belief that the costs are greater than the benefits. It is the device of those who are ideologically committed to the notion that when in doubt we ought to prohibit.

On the issue of restraining macro concentration, I really welcomed Comanor's coming out of the closet on this. It seems to me that he openly specified that this is a goal that is approved not on the ground that it makes sense but on the ground that it is popular. I am not appalled that Comanor holds this view, only that he feels justified in supporting it on the grounds that it is popular and gets popular support.

I suggest that this set of problems we are facing is difficult. Since when did popular wisdom give us solutions to hard problems? We may have to rename the Federal Trade Commission the "Bureau of Popularity Polling about the Nature of Democratic Institutions." Presumably, it would favor at this time price but not wage controls, public expenditure but no taxes, low gas prices but no allocation systems.

The debate on the law seemed to be more helpful, but I agree with Schmalensee that even though we had a nice debate over what the appropriate solution might be, we are still talking about solutions in search of a problem. I am not sure that we know precisely what problem merger guidelines and presumptions are supposed to solve.

About the Editors and Contributors

Roger D. Blair is Professor of Economics and Associate Director of the Public Policy Research Center at the University of Florida. He holds the Ph.D. in economics from Michigan State University.

Betty Bock is Director of Antitrust Research at The Conference Board. She holds the Ph.D. in economics from Bryn Mawr College.

Joseph F. Brodley is Professor of Law at Boston University. He holds the L.L.B. from Yale University and the L.L.M. from Harvard University.

William Comanor was formerly Director of the Bureau of Economics at the Federal Trade Commission. Now Professor of Economics at the University of California-Santa Barbara, Professor Comanor holds the Ph.D. in economics from Harvard University.

Edward H. Cooper is Professor of Law at the University of Michigan. A former private practitioner, Professor Cooper holds the L.L.B. from Harvard University.

Theodore F. Craver is Staff Vice President and Director of Trade Regulation for Litton Industries, Inc. Mr. Craver holds the L.L.B. from St. Mary's University.

George A. Hay is Professor of Law and Economics at Cornell University. A former Director of Economics in the Antitrust Division of the Department of Justice, Professor Hay holds the Ph.D. from Northwestern University.

Ira Horowitz is Graduate Research Professor of Management at the University of Florida. Professor Horowitz holds the Ph.D. in economics from the Massachusetts Institute of Technology.

Robert F. Lanzillotti is Dean of the College of Business Administration, Professor of Economics, and Director of the Public Policy Research Center at the University of Florida. A former Brookings Fellow, Dean Lanzillotti holds the Ph.D. in economics from the University of California-Berkeley.

Howard R. Lurie is Professor of Law at Villanova University. A former trial attorney at the Federal Trade Commission, Professor Lurie holds the J.D. from the University of Michigan.

Margaret A. Monroe is Assistant Professor of Finance at the University of Illinois-Chicago Circle. A Ph.D. Candidate in the Finance Department at the University of Florida, Ms. Monroe is a Canada Council Doctoral Fellow.

Dennis C. Mueller is Professor of Economics at the University of Maryland. A former Senior Research Fellow at the International Institute of Management of the Science Center Berlin, Professor Mueller holds the Ph.D. in economics from Princeton University.

Yoram C. Peles is Associate Professor in the School of Business Administration at the Hebrew University of Jerusalem. Professor Peles holds the Ph.D. in economics from the University of Chicago.

Stephen Rubin is Professor of Law at the University of Florida. A former Fulbright Scholar, Professor Rubin holds the J.D. from Columbia University.

John Siegfried is Professor of Economics at Vanderbilt University. A former Visiting Scholar at the Federal Trade Commission, Professor Siegfried holds the Ph.D. in economics from the University of Wisconsin.

Peter O. Steiner is Professor of Law and Economics at the University of Michigan. The author of *Mergers,* Professor Steiner holds the Ph.D. in economics from Harvard University.

Charles Untiet is an economist in the Antitrust Division of the Department of Justice.

Steven N. Wiggins is Assistant Professor of Economics at Texas A & M University. He holds the Ph.D. in economics from the Massachusetts Institute of Technology.